Into the Mainstream

Conversations with Latin-American Writers

Luis Harss
and
Barbara Dohmann

HARPER & ROW, PUBLISHERS

New York, Evanston, and London

FIRST EDITION

LIBRARY OF CONGRESS CATALOG CARD NUMBER: 66-20737

B-R

Into the Mainstream

Luis Harss was born in 1936 in Valparaiso, Chile, and was educated in Argentina and in the United States. He graduated from Stanford University in 1956 and spent several years in California and Guatemala. He is the author of two novels, *The Blind* (1962) and *The Little Men* (1963). He is at present living in Buenos Aires.

Barbara Dohmann was born in 1936 in Berlin and was educated at the Universities of Erlangen, Mainz and Paris. She has worked as an interpreter for the Council of Europe, UNESCO, and the Coal and Steel Community for the past several years, and is currently living in Paris.

Other books by Luis Harss

THE LITTLE MEN
THE BLIND

Contents

VI go w/ short stories
goes w/ theme

Into the Mainstream

Prologue,
with Musical Chairs

THERE used to be a tradition somewhere in Latin America—
was it Guatemala?—that poets, the favorites of the Muses, got
free bus rides. The privilege, apparently, did not extend to
novelists, who had either to pay their way or walk. If there was a
certain injustice in this state of affairs, it reflected an established
fact in our literature. Our poets were riding high when our
novelists were still eminently pedestrian.

Our first men of letters, naturally enough, given the aristocratic origins of our culture, were poets. They were the educated
few, gentlemen of refinement and sensibility, members of a
movable elite with headquarters in Europe, who dabbled in the
fine arts and worshiped abstract Beauty—in Latin, Castilian, and
academic Portuguese. Their art was an aside, a form of mental
acrobatics, or a social grace. No risk was involved. Nothing was at
stake. The notion of artistic vocation as a form of total commitment engaging the whole man was practically unknown. There
was nothing in the Spanish or Portuguese traditions to encourage
it. And perhaps the novel, in the modern sense of the word,
cannot exist without it. Which may explain why the form has
never flourished in Spain. The novel is a monomaniacal form
and can only live dangerously. In it a man pits himself against
the world in a confrontation that is vital, not merely aesthetic or
intellectual. He stands to gain or lose himself in the process. The

novel is egocentric. In this it differs from the epic, for instance, which lives outwardly, with its feet firmly planted in external reality. The novel is private, not public, art. And the land of the *Cantar del Mio Cid* and the mass productions of Lope de Vega never favored the vertigoes of introspection.

True, the anticipatory forms of the novel—if we consider the early chronicles and the ribald adventures of that famous medieval go-between, *La Celestina*—appeared in Spain as far back as the fifteenth century. *Amadis de Gaula,* one of the most famous romances of chivalry, dates from 1508. There was the pastoral novel, then the picaresque serial, exemplified in that roguish and rambunctiously cynical tableau de moeurs, *Lazarillo de Tormes.* And there was Cervantes, who in a way summed up, while transcending, the whole Spanish novel before him. He collected romances and pastorals in his *Novelas Ejemplares,* and fused the chivalrous and the picaresque in *Don Quijote* (1605–1615). But there the story of the Spanish novel practically ends. Cervantes was the first man in Spanish letters to venture inward, where the novel's true resources lie. He was also, very nearly, the last. The form was already moribund in Quevedo's *El Buscón* (1603). The seventeenth century—the late Góngora, Calderón—was a poet's age. The eighteenth—age of the boudoir—was a complete blank. In the nineteenth, again, poetry, such as it was, predominated. There was not enough traction for anything else. Spain had its Balzac in Benito Pérez Galdós (1845–1920). So did Portugal, in Eça de Queiroz (1845–1900). But they were flashes in the dark. The generation of 1898 in Spain, supposedly dedicated to renewal, filled the air with a lot of brooding but very little true introspection. In the twentieth century, in Spain as in Portugal, on those rare occasions when there have been signs of that "tragic sense of life" that has animated novelists elsewhere it has been the almost exclusive property of poets and philosophers.

Little wonder, then, that poets had a head start in our literature. One of our first figures of note was a feminist Mexican nun turned poetess called Sor Juana Inez de la Cruz (1651–1695). She was the wittiest writer in the Spanish language between the death of Calderón (1680) and the Romantic era. Poets held their lead resoundingly in the nineteenth century. It was poetry that gave our literature its great boost toward 1900, starting with the Nicaraguan bard, Rubén Darío, who imported the latest revolutionary forms from France, and continuing, as time went on, with Argentina's Leopoldo Lugones, Peru's César Vallejo, Chile's Vicente Huidobro, not to mention that illustrious son of a section crew foreman on a little frontier railway in southern Chile, Neftalí Ricardo Reyes y Basualto, better known today as Pablo Neruda. Poets—Octavio Paz in Mexico, for instance—still carry more than their weight in our literature. Typical is the case of Brazil, whose modern novel begins in the twenties, the heyday of aestheticism, under the tutelage of such renewers as Monteiro Lobato, Mario de Andrade, and a mystic folklorist called Jorge de Lima, all primarily poets. The most notable writer of the century in the Portuguese language is a poet-turned-novelist, João Guimarães Rosa.

The Latin-American novel is of humble birth. It dates from the second decade of the past century, when Mexico's Joaquín Fernández de Lizardi, an irrepressible vulgarian in the tradition of the anonymous author of *Lazarillo de Tormes,* serialized his picaresque feuilleton, *El Periquillo Sarniento* (1816). The feuilleton, a form of social satire wavering between scatology and preachy didacticism, was a healthy concession on the part of our literature to the realities of daily life, and eventually local idiom, therefore a fitting send-off for the lowly novel, whose strength— and handicap—was bound to be its often misguided but always well-meaning devotion to social causes. But that came later. Meantime, toward mid-century, the Romantic tide hit our shores, flooding our whole literature. Given our talent for hasty imitation, the result in the newborn novel was mostly forgettable. There was a positive side to it all, though, in the arrival of non-Spanish fashions that at least had the merit of diversity. There was a vogue of Chateaubriand and Lamartine, Sir Walter Scott, Fenimore Cooper, George Sand, Dumas, etc. Intercourse with these models left a dubious progeny. Werthers and Atalas appeared everywhere. A pure gem in the genre, Colombian in origin, was Jorge Isaacs' bucolic *Maria.* In Brazil, equally chaste and inconclusive, was Manuel de Macedo's ungainly *Moreninha,* enormously popular among the young ladies of the day.

The few works of lasting value in the Romantic era were predominantly historical. A rough list might include Ricardo Palma's colorful sketches, *Tradiciones Peruanas,* and, still, strictly speaking, in a nonfictional vein, the gripping essays of Argentina's great educator, Domingo Faustino Sarmiento, who drew a handsome portrait of provincial manners and mores in *Recuerdos de Provincia* and left a memorable gallery of character types, as well as a vivid study of a local warlord, in the classic *Facundo.* Sarmiento had style and elegance. So, to a lesser degree, did another Argentine writer, José Mármol, in his turbulent and exalted antidictatorship novel, *Amalia. Amalia* was part tract and often went overboard in its missionary zeal. The Indian epic, in its more inflated form, appeared at about this time. Here, once more, poets led the way. There seemed to be general consensus on the subject of the noble savage. In Brazil there was José de Alençar's *O Guarani,* in Argentina, Esteban Echeverría's *La Cautiva,* in Uruguay, José Zorrilla de San Martín's *Tabaré.* The novel took up the subject with diminishing splendor, a typical result, in Ecuador, being Juan León Mera's exotic *Cumandá.*

That the novel had not yet found itself can be seen from the fact that of all the prose works of the century only Sarmiento's essays can be said to be a cut above subliterature. We might add to the brief list of the salvageable an end product of the midcentury Gaucho epic. It was a genuine masterpiece of narrative poetry with a fictional sweep premonitory of the novel: José Hernández' *Martín Fierro.* It had drama, character, and moments of emotional plenitude that suggested new depths. In the eighties, however, this genre, by nature artificial and therefore incapable of organic growth, sank back into subliterature with the vapid novels of Uruguay's Eduardo Acevedo Díaz.

At the turn of the century many streams joined in our novel, which fluctuated from one to another, often disastrously. In times of moral crisis it turned polemic. With the rise of nationalism it devoted itself to political theory. In the midst of social turmoil it developed a guilty conscience and went to battle for the common man. Its concerns became increasingly local. Its various changes of focus were only partly spontaneous. The guidelines still came from abroad. The venerable tradition of Spanish regionalism, with its emphasis on the descriptive, produced its countless local variants: Indianismo, Indigenismo, Criollismo, etc. From other parts of Europe came Realism—descended from Flaubert, de Maupassant, Balzac—and eventually the Naturalism and positivistic scientism of Zola. A branch of our literature became socialized, as it discovered exploitation and class warfare. In Mexico, at the time languishing under the callous Porfirio Díaz dictatorship, there were such belligerent works as Mariano Azuela's *Mala Yerba;* in Venezuela, another storm center, the militant pamphlets of Rufino Blanco Fombona, who had no great literary distinction but voiced a general apocalyptic attitude toward the miseries of our emerging societies when he said: "Everywhere and at all times I've discovered the same common denominator of malice, pain, and stupidity."

More productive from the literary point of view was the strain of psychological realism that reached Brazil via Eça de Queiroz and produced its first great egoist, the humanist of despair, Machado de Assis, author of the tortured *Memorias Postumas de Braz Cubas* (1881) and *Historias Sem Data* (1884). There was nobody like Machado de Assis in the Spanish-speaking part of the continent, and even in Brazil, in view of what followed, he seems to have been a miraculous accident. The monstrously single-minded devotion he brought to his work was not seen again for decades. The age of involution had not yet dawned. There was comparatively little interest in Lima Barreto's amusingly satirical but superficial *Recordaçoes do Escrivao Isaias Caminha*. Of scarcely any more note was the Tolstoyan reformist vein cultivated in Argentina by Manuel Gálvez, the author of the evangelical *Nacha Regules*. On the other hand, the first decade of the century brought another remarkable essayist to the forefront: Brazil's scholarly explorer, Euclides da Cunha, who gave a glowing panoramic view of his country's interior in *Os Sertões* (1902).

Machado de Assis and da Cunha, were flukes—men bigger than their age. Their contemporaries, in search of relevance, tended either to give themselves entirely to immediate social concerns or, failing that, to escape into aestheticism. The latter tendency was accentuated by the arrival of French Symbolism, reincarnated in America in Rubén Darío's *Azul* (1888). Around 1900, possibly to fight its inferiority complex, part of our literature turned esoteric. There was Modernism with its Oriental breezes, its mixed metaphorical splendors, its shadows of old Spanish baroque. Typical was the poetic exuberance of Argentina's Leopoldo Lugones. In the novel a nostalgia for lost golden ages and medieval paradises produced a crop of curiosities in foreign clothing, snobbishly set in France or Spain. There was Carlos Reyles, a Uruguayan, with *El Embrujo de Sevilla,* and Enrique Larreta, an Argentine, with *La Gloria de Don Ramiro.* In Brazil, social militancy and aestheticism merged rather uncomfortably in Graça Aranha's *Canaan.* A variant of Modernism reached Brazil after World War I and settled in São Paulo with Mario de Andrade's *Macunaima.*

As of about 1920 we can still not speak of a Latin-American novel—our furnaces were not generating enough power yet—and the years that followed were richer in promise than achievement. 1919 was an important date in Brazilian literature with the publication of Monteiro Lobato's influential *Urupês* (Poisonous Mushrooms). Its portrait of village life, drawn through a poetic use of local dialect, raised a storm in Brazilian literary circles. Oddly, it was this child of aestheticism that gave a new impulse to the "slice of life" school. Regionalism, frugal in its means but prolific in its offspring, soon carried the day in what became known as the school of the northeast, which sought to vindicate the lot of the oppressed in sugar-cane fields and rubber plantations. It dominated the literary scene in the thirties. An early landmark, dated 1930, was Raquel de Queiroz' *O Quinze* (Year 1915), a meticulously detailed chronicle of one of the northeast's famous droughts. There was José Lins do Rego's candid story of the hardships of plantation childhood, *Menino de Engenho,* and the proletarian poetry of Jorge Amado in *Cacau, Jubiabá, Mar*

Morto, Terrás Do Sem Fin. A high point of this literature was Graciliano Ramos' *Angustia* and *Vidas Sêcas,* and its nadir was Amado's pamphleteering *Seara Vermelha* (Red Harvest), which marked a decline into hack work and sentimentality.

Meantime, in Mexico, it was the morning after the Revolution, a time of chroniclers: the Mariano Azuela of *Los de Abajo,* the Martín Luis Guzmán of *El Águila y la Serpiente.* The River Plate, still in the throes of the Modernist euphoria—these were the days of the early Borges and Leopoldo Marechal—was discovering syndicalism and labor wars. Yet the classic novel of the age was Ricardo Güiraldes' famous monument to the Gaucho mystique, the essentially decorative *Don Segundo Sombra.* Chile was in the hands of documentarists like Mariano Latorre, a dour landscape painter, and Edward Bello, who mythologized the Chilean spirit in a classic portrait of a local type known as *El Roto* (Ragamuffin). The Indian countries—Bolivia, Ecuador, Peru—were deep in the cause of social reform in mines and plantations. Bolivia's Alcides Arguedas led the way with his argumentative tract—a pamphlet and an exhortation—*Raza de Bronce.* There was a trend toward Indian mythology in the early work of Guatemala's Miguel Ángel Asturias, who later, as so many writers of his generation, turned toward social protest, a characteristic genre, very widespread, epitomized in the Ecuadorian Jorge Icaza's *Huasipungo* (Tenant Farm). And, finally, in tropical regions there was an environmental literature that reached its summit in José Eustacio Rivera's Colombian jungle saga, *La Vorágine* (The Vortex). All these works mark a stage in our novel, which rather innocently, and sometimes condescendingly, wore its heart on its sleeve. It tended to be righteous and complacent. It was a cultured, not a visceral, literature, intellectual rather than intuitive, conceived at once in epic terms and as a means of direct social action.

Typical of the climate of the twenties and thirties was the work of the Venezuelan Rómulo Gallegos. With Martín Luis Guzmán, Gallegos was one of the last of the distinguished old guard in the Latin-American novel still alive at the time of this writing. His panoramic view of his society—he was a consummate journalist, educator, and statesman, a frequent exile in times of dictatorship, and twice a candidate for the presidency, to which he was finally elected in 1948, only to be overthrown by the military shortly after his inauguration—is representative of a whole era in our literature. The platform of his party, Acción Democrática, which still dominates Venezuelan politics, was one of "national concord," and the same liberal and ecumenic spirit that animated his politics enlightened his work, which was always devoted to the cause of progress and civilization. He believed in the power of the word to move men to effective action. In the twenties and thirties Venezuela was in a period of transition. As all of Latin America, it was in search of a cultural identity. Gallegos wielded his art—which was of only moderate literary value—as a weapon in the common struggle. He saw his country as a battlefield between backwardness and progress, tradition and change, the foreign and the autochthonous, caste oligarchy and democracy, the past and the future. The options were those of a continent, and his attitudes those of a parliamentarian. Though city born and bred, he thought of Venezuela as a multiple whole capable of reconciling its differences, assimilating its various racial strains, integrating its teeming jungles, its open plains, its mines and rich coastal mudflats. His books were more the product of research than of first-hand knowledge. Before writing *Doña Bárbara*, for instance, he spent only a few days in the llano, the vast inner savanna that provides his setting. His portraits are mythical, his conflicts archetypal, the general tenor of his work abstract and symbolic. Yet he has a good eye for local colors and customs, a grasp of essential problems, and above all a sense of vastness, of widening horizons in what is still the land of the frontier, beckoning pioneers into its open spaces. Didactic and rhetorical as he is, he can catch the imagination. There is a certain magnificence in his oratory when he speaks of the "impressive silence and tragic solitude" of the plains, which are still living "the sixth day of Genesis . . . swept by the breath of creation."

A survey of Gallegos' career reads like a case history of Latin-American intellectual life, with all its creeds and crusades, in the early decades of the century. *Reinaldo Solar* introduces the theme of spiritual rootlessness and turn-of-the-century neurosis. It draws a picture of decadent Caracas society, its corrupt politics, frustrated artists, café reformers, derelict poets and bohemians, rabid revolutionaries with fanatic schemes, in an atmosphere of general moral bankruptcy representative of a generation torn between yearnings for the European womb and a passionate search for a local El Dorado. Reinaldo, the protagonist, an intellectual out of contact with his native soil, is a compendium of every malaise of the day. He fancies himself a superman, a high priest of a mystic cult in secret communion with telluric forces. In the background are the garbled voices of Nietzsche, Marx, Rousseau, Darwin, an undigested mishmash compounded with borrowings from Kempis' *Imitation of Christ* and Tolstoy's *Resurrection*. There is the standard pilgrimage to Europe, the spiritual metamorphosis that follows the return home, the crisis of conscience, the call of nature, and final holocaust as Reinaldo dies conducting an abortive revolution in the jungle.

La Trepadora, the work of a great matchmaker, is a tract in favor of interracialism. It portrays the ruin of old families and the rise of new classes through social change and racial mingling. The setting, this time, is the coffee plantation. An illegitimate son of the aristocratic Casals, Hilario Guanipa, a lovable rogue and roughneck, child of the land, happy drinker and shrewd businessman, sees his daughter, symbolically named Victoria, marry her first cousin, thus gaining legitimacy as she acquires the family name. Hilario, one of Gallegos' more vivid characters, is not only a force of nature but also a convincing psychological portrait of the phenomenon known as the mestizo, the man without specific ancestry who says: "I begin with myself." The headstrong, impetuous Victoria takes after her father. She is the climbing vine of the title that fuses with the trunk of the old tree.

Doña Bárbara, for some unaccountable reason usually rated Gallegos' best work—though his distance from his material is maximal here—is based on an actual case of a "man-eating" woman of the plains he read about in the papers, but never met.

It dramatizes the archetypal confrontation of the primitive and retrograde embodied in the eponymous matriarch who symbolizes local warlordism under the regime of dictator Juan Vicente Gómez—with the civilizing force of progress which has its paladin in Santos Luzardo, an intellectual who has abandoned the comforts of city life to develop a family property in the wilds. His prosopopoeial enemy is determined to break his will, but in the end his missionary spirit triumphs over "the brutalizing force of the desert."

Cantaclaro, incoherent in plot but often charming and elegant in manner, is "the Venezuelan version of the classic troubadour," a song to the plains, combining Naturalist touches with Modernist techniques and a free and easy use of poetic folklore. Cantaclaro (Chanticleer) is the nickname of the pseudonymous Florentino Quitapesares (Curer of Sorrows), wandering minstrel, errant spirit, the Venezuelan payador—traditional guitarist and raconteur—always on the move, galloping across the plains, free as a bird, blithe as a ballad, "his luck in his hand," spinning legends and fantasies as he goes. The plain, says Cantaclaro, is the place where "man is the measure of himself." In him Gallegos creates a bard and prophet of his land, attuned to the vatic poetry of nature.

Canaima, in the hallowed tradition of Rivera's *La Vorágine,* takes us to the rubber plantations in the jungles of the upper Orinoco, the haunts of savage Indians and ancestral forces that devour the civilized protagonist, Marcos Vargas, whose cause, according to the conventions of the genre, nevertheless triumphs later in his son. Canaima is an evil deity, a "frenetic god . . . somber divinity" of the local Indian tribes, personification of the demoniac, a sort of Ahriman, says Gallegos, come back to life in America. Vargas is an "adventurer of all adventures" along the road of life, on an edifying course into the heart of darkness, where the "jungle sickness" will absorb and obliterate him. But not before he enters into a rapturous embrace with Canaima. There is a histrionic encounter in which, awakening under concussion, he feels "free and alone as a man ought to be when the hour of his fate has struck"; for under his mortal skin he discovers "cosmic man, stripped of history," reunited with the original creative impulse. Meantime, he has had some instructive contacts with a local sage and tiger hunter, Juan Solito, who initiates him into primitive mysteries, and an Indian girl with the tribal denomination of Aymara, who helps him penetrate "the abysses of melancholy contained in the Indian soul." All of which is standard for the genre, which operates largely through nomenclature. The jungle is more mythological than real, a land of epiphanies, on the one hand, and colorful characters, on the other. Among the latter is another staple of this literature: the alcoholic Yank, not too unsympathetically treated by Gallegos, relatively charitable on this score compared to some of his colleagues. Here the type is represented by a Mr. Davenport, who provides comic relief with an intriguing theory he has developed that malaria is a disease of lazy people.

With *Canaima* Gallegos' creative period ends—his themes are exhausted, his scheme is complete—but his production continues unabated. In *Pobre Negro* he returns to the racial problem, this time centering on the Negro race, personified by the heroic Pedro Miguel Candelas, the leader of a nineteenth-century slave revolt, who loves and eventually elopes with his mistress, Luisana, the enlightened daughter of white landowners. Luisana, a woman of the future, bears a clear message, daring for its age. So do the protagonists of *El Forastero* (The Foreigner), also about revolution, in this case a student uprising in the thirties that affords Gallegos an opportunity to expand on his political theories. He envisions three stages in Venezuelan political life: military warlord tyranny, oligarchic despotism, and eventually, in the somewhat utopian future, constitutional democracy. The liberal revolution in *El Forastero* is doomed to failure—it is premature—but Gallegos, always uplifting, comforts himself with the hopeful thought that the next generation may do better, because "with every young man the world in some sense is born again." He carries his proselytism to the oil wells in the mudflats in *Sobre la Misma Terra* (Upon This Same Land), and, finally, to Cuba, at the time of the Machado dictatorship, in *La Brizna de Paja en el Viento* (A Wisp of Straw in the Wind).

Gallegos, with his epic scope, his idealism and messianic zeal, his talent for type-casting, his casual prolificness, his love of myth and folklore, his passionate attempt to come to terms with the realities of his country, exemplifies the achievements and short-comings of the main body of our literature in the first third of the century. It was artless, grim, or optimistic, as the case might be, but essentially innocent of eye. It was at once overambitious in its social aspirations and too modest in its private aims, which were secondary and often remained undiscovered. Its preoccupations were essentially extraliterary.

Novelists like Gallegos, in spite of their sometimes consider-able grasp of externals, because they lacked inner weight, some-how seemed only to skim surfaces. For all its polemic fire, their work lacked blood and muscle fiber, and therefore, ultimately, conviction. It believed in its message, its function within prevail-ing circumstances, but not in itself. It found its justification only in its purpose. The novelist felt he was relevant only in so far as he was topical. He was a recorder of events, a mediator and persuader who measured himself in battle. Art was incidental, it did not come from inner necessity. Therefore, when it was not directly committed to a cause, it was a luxury, and unconsciously regarded itself as such, tending toward aesthetics and dilet-tantism.

This was often the case in the River Plate, the most cosmopoli-tan area on the continent, therefore in a sense the most rootless, the most prone to vicariousness and evasion. Of course this was particularly true of the older generation, the contemporaries of Gallegos—Leopoldo Lugones, Ricardo Güiraldes, Carlos Reyles—whose assiduous pursuit of "spiritual values," a constant theme in the work of a Manuel Gálvez, for instance, often disguised a somewhat fatuous nostalgia for the effortless advan-tages of the Old World, combined with a constitutional incapac-ity or unwillingness to find a firm base in the New. For the unacclimated, the road back is the one of least resistance. The reverse of this aristocratic sickness—the "mal d'Europe," Gálvez called it—was a tendency to mythologize local realities instead of coming into direct contact with them. Perhaps that was a way of watering down what was too harsh to be taken straight. In any case, it created distances. There are strong remnants of this attitude in the Borges generation. Borges himself, especially in his early days, was a decided aesthete. The Buenos Aires that appears in his work, unlike the real one which had not yet been discovered mostly because it was assumed to be tedious and banal, is a glorified abstraction, a castle in the sky. The real city, went the argument, had no past or tradition, nothing of interest had happened there yet. In search of inspiration, the artist turned to folk legend, inventing it when there was none, poetizing slum life or the Gaucho myth. But this mythology remained purely formal, a gentlemanly game that in the end only accentuated the artist's marginality. A Borges, in time, through sheer talent, could transcend this predicament without ever quite overcoming it. Others were less fortunate. Some looked for a solution in social action. But it would be a mistake to think that artistically their choice was more satisfactory than that of the "formalists." Militancy, verism, were positions on certain specific issues, not vital attitudes. The "parti pris" is the diametrical opposite of a true art born of inner imperatives responsible only to itself. There is something as unreal about it as there is about preciousness. The skeptical, worldly spirit of Anatole France, very influential in Latin America in the twenties, might be taken as a symbol of the times. The art of the twenties, whether esoteric or socially committed, was agnostic. It lived on speculation and died in sophistry.

Yet all the time there were undercurrents that began to surface at the end of the decade, when a new type of artist appeared on the scene. The truth is that he had been around for a while, but in very reduced numbers, and had remained out of sight. There was no room for him in our art of surfaces. He represented not an aesthetic change but another human dimension, a deeper outlook. For him, life and art were one and indistinguishable. The first of the breed was Machado de Assis, a master of the contemplative who suggested for the first time in our literature that "there is a deeper way of seeing and feeling one's country that goes beyond the surface of external appearances."

What these deceptively simple words mean—and their implications are revolutionary for our literature—can be clearly seen in the work of Uruguay's highly individualistic Horacio Quiroga, who was born in 1878, six years before Gallegos, and therefore, as a member of the older generation, might reasonably be presumed to have suffered from all the ills of the time. There is, in fact, evidence that he did. As a young man he was something of an intellectual dandy. There was his Paris period, the usual spell spent in the City of Light, with its characteristic derangement of the senses, its fin de siècle mood, which were reflected in the jaded decadentism of his first published work, a volume of poetry that issued in the century—it dates from 1901—under the title of *Arrecifes de Coral* (Coral Reefs). So far he was indistinguishable from his contemporaries. But then something unexpected happened. What unwonted combination of factors produced it one can only guess at. No doubt the traumas of the age—immigration, urban growth, the rise of the middle class, the beginning of industrial alienation, eventually the delayed effects of the World War—had something to do with it. But basically, since everyone shared in these experiences, they explain nothing. Here we are dealing with the elusive, the imponderable. The first symptom of it was a book Quiroga published in 1917: *Cuentos de Amor, de Locura y de Muerte* (Tales of Love, Madness and Death). Quiroga was a great reader of Poe, and his early vague malaise had taken a strongly morbid turn. At this point one might be tempted to dismiss him as little more than a talented psychopath. There is something frail and sickly about his work, in which we recognize a pale image of the poète damné. But it has a subterranean force. We realize that the horror stories of 1917 are not just a form of fantasy evasion, they indicate a mind gone underground, and this state of mind in a way is more revealing of a society than an external portrait. Quiroga works in close contact with his material, which is therefore highly charged with personal meanings. It has inwardness. More than the times, which were dyspeptic enough and produced any number of literary hypochondriacs, it was probably Quiroga's tragic personal life that made him the man he was. He was accident-prone, and the years brought him one disaster after another. There was a long line of suicides in his family, beginning with his father, continuing with his first wife, a son, a daughter, and finally, in 1937, himself. He withdrew early from the world. For years he lived in northern Argentina, in the Misiones jungle, the setting for most of his later work. There, in a constant battle for sanity and survival, he developed a contemplative language attuned to the occult, the uncanny, the parapsychological, the abysmal, the subliminal, all those areas of experience bordering on the metaphysical, a word that can be applied for the first time in our literature. It describes his best work in the thirties: *El Salvaje* (The Savage), *Anaconda, Los Desterrados* (The Exiled), *El Desierto, Más Allá* (Beyond). The last title, which dates from 1935, is significant; it points the way. De Maupassant, Chekhov, are some of the obvious "influences" on his work, but not through direct and conscious adaptation, as was often the case with our Naturalists, when they attempted to emulate European models. In him it was a matter of deeper affinity. If he was not a great writer, because his creative means were limited, he was nevertheless a skillful welder of those raw materials of personal experience out of which true literature is made.

Almost inevitably, Quiroga was a short-story writer, not—except in a couple of weak moments—a novelist. The kind of tension, the concentration he needed for his work, was more than he could sustain for any length of time without getting winded. Our early "metaphysicians"—there was a touch of this in the "fantastic" side of Lugones, and also, within the same generation, in the witty conversationalist, Macedonio Fernández, an early Borges mentor—left only a sketchy record of what were essentially secret activities. Borges himself, who eventually rode the fantastic into the metaphysical—as did his Uruguayan counterpart, Felisberto Hernández, to whom the same principle applies—never invested his energies in a full-length work of fiction. Those who did were old-school writers, like Borges' compatriot and contemporary, Eduardo Mallea, whose elaborately discursive works, which flooded the thirties, under such titles as *Nocturno Europeo, Historia de Una Pasión Argentina,* rambled and dispersed their energies in a kind of abstract soul-searching that had no more dramatic consistency than Gallegos'.

The first novelist in the new vein, born in 1900, a year after Borges, was Roberto Arlt, an enigmatic figure, the son of German immigrants, by temperament and disposition obscurely marked for misfortune. Family difficulties, childhood misery, revolt against militaristic paternal discipline, early escape from home, years of penury and dereliction in the big city, were in good Freudian fashion, some of the factors that inclined him toward the twilight zone. He knew the life of the down-and-out, the city's lunatic fringe, its Dostoevskian underworld. What he found there he portrayed with brilliant gutter humor in a series of works—culminating with *Los Siete Locos* (The Seven Madmen), and *Los Lanzallamas* (The Flamethrowers)—that were at once a complete rogues' gallery of marginal characters and a map of a city's spiritual slum areas. Arlt was working at a time of disenchantment in Argentine history that coincided with the rise to political power of militarist groups, starting with the 1930 government of President Uriburu. But, just as his spotty culture—he was considered a hack writer in his day—was self-taught, his true sufferings were self-inflicted. He was an outcast by nature, one of the downtrodden of the world. His crackpot idealists, deluded theologians, emasculated pimps and pariahs were inner figments, imaginative projections of a private vision of things. For Arlt the human predicament was not essentially social but philosophic and astronomical. This realization, the fruit of an absolute disconformity, helped him to cut deeper into the soul of his society than any other writer of his day. He was not a literary man in the superficial sense of the word, and indeed in the realm of pure "literature" his work has great lacks. It is short-winded, full of misconceptions and malapropisms, and it falls apart for lack of structure. Yet Arlt has an instinct for buried treasure. He is ignorant, but never innocuous or insipid. He is a man who has come to grips with the world. He used to ask his intellectual friend, Ricardo Güiraldes, whose poetizations of reality, for all their finesse, he could never take much to heart, when he would start writing "seriously." Which underlines his attitude. Because his business as a writer was a matter of life and death to him. Working in obscurity, he discovered a city and the language that went with it. He took its pulse and introduced its sights, its sounds, its slang, sacred and profane, into literature.

Quirogan fantasy, the episodic Arlt, variously illustrate the difficulties of inner effort in an essentially outgoing culture. Cortázar, twenty-five years later, still had to travel the road of the fantastic story to reach the intermittent plenitude of *Rayuela*. Leopoldo Marechal, another distinguished member of the Martínfierrista generation, as Borges' contemporaries were called because of their association with a famous little magazine of the twenties named after the Gaucho epic, has spoken of "that lack of inner pressure" which exposes a man, "unarmed, to the invasion of outside images," a phrase that indicates a whole cultural syndrome. Marechal was one of those who suffered from it. He analyzed it in detail in his monumentally misanthropic *Adán Buenosayres*, a blockbuster that was published only in 1948, but was begun in 1930, at the height of the Martínfierrista era, of which it gives a complete picture involving all the contradictions—the effete sensibility, the strain of social militancy, the mythological bent, the opening into metaphysics—of the age. The fact that it took Marechal eighteen years to write his book is in itself significant. It is a rambunctious humoresque that drifts along through many loose episodes, with long arid stretches but moments of sporadic brilliance that reveal a first-class satirist on a Joycean romp through the purgatory and hellfire of Argentine society.

In *Adán Buenosayres*, which is built according to what we might call the Ptolemaic system, with man as the center of the universe, we have the first tentative approach to a complete novel in our literature. It is at once a Porteño (Buenos Aires) Odyssey and a Dantesque allegory, complete with a descent into Hell, here called Cacodelphia, "the tormented city . . . visible only to the eyes of the intellect," which is defined as a "counterfigure" or reverse image of "the visible Buenos Aires." Much of *Adán Buenosayres* is written in code—it is a roman à clé—full of private gags, "in" jokes, and the wraiths of absent people. But it lives in its swaggering, swashbuckling humor, a sort of inexhaustible slapstick and vaudeville that exploits language at all levels, from inflated poetic oratory to the boisterous boorishness and buffoonery of local slang. "Angelic humorism," the author calls it, explaining, tongue in cheek, that it is meant to reflect the indulgent attitude prevalent in celestial places toward human foibles. The characters, who correspond to signs of a private zodiac, are drawn on a large scale to give them "heroic stature" as symbols of their time. At stage center, listening to the music of the spheres, is Adán (naturally a projection of the author), a flamboyant poet and schoolteacher going through a spiritual crisis that takes him from aestheticism to a kind of Christian mysticism, all in the course of forty-eight hours of reckoning in which he exhausts the full repertory of the themes of the day. We begin with his "metaphysical awakening" in his room in the heart of Buenos Aires, a scene waggishly described as a "parody of Genesis" as he struggles to rise out of "primeval indifferentiation." Follows his daily mental rollcall: reveries of his past life; memories of his childhood on the farm, symbolic of a lost innocence; reminiscences of his ancestors, among whom were Calabrian adventurers and buccaneers who migrated to the River Plate, seduced by the glow of the New World; images of his true love, the unworthily pedestrian Solveig Amundsen, on whose "fragile essence" he has built his ideal. Adán is a dreamer, a man who from childhood has suffered from "cosmic terror" and has known that "sadness is born from multiplicity." He yearns for what he imagines was the simple heroism of his ancestors in their frugal life in contact with nature. Unlike them, he has always known doubt, longed for permanence while succumbing to "the devastation of time," fluctuating between a kind of divine exaltation and senseless depression. A notebook he keeps outlines his biography. He was a child in whom "the vocation for tears" preceded its cause. His soul early, "by virtue of its natural weight," placed itself "in the center of the wheel." His poetic impulse, born of a thirst for the absolute, took the form of amorous rapture. As a young man he became a "stranger and scholar in the big city." It was the beginning of a long game of

musical chairs in which he was always left standing. There was
the usual trip to Europe in search of spiritual ancestry, many
wanderings and "painful readings," and his impossible desire,
upon his return, to make his world "vibrate" according to the
"ambitious style" he had discovered in things abroad. The task
has proved endlessly frustrating in a city that, as the author puts it,
parodying a cliché of the day, is "dying of vulgarity because it lacks
a romantic tradition." *Adán Buenosayres* tries to fill the gap, to
build the city's fable and legend. Here we recognize the plight of
the rootless intellectual that Adán represents, caught between his
many phantasmagoric roles, "a cheater at every game, a weaver of
smoke rings." He is a Ulysses, with a vocation for grandeur but
an aching weakness for every siren song. At various times in his
life he has imagined himself a saintly ascetic, a healer and
miracle worker, a boxer fighting Dempsey in Madison Square
Garden, a gangster holding up a bank in Monte Carlo, a pioneer
in Patagonia, a Founder of Cities, Ruler of the Seven Seas,
creator of a Golden Age in his land, imposed by iron hand
through an inexorable application of "the political doctrines of
Aristotle." The mixture of the sublime and the banal is typical
of the three-ring circus he lives in. No better off than he is his
friend, Samuel Tesler, an "ecumenic" shirt-sleeve philosopher,
amateur Dionysus, born a Jew in Odessa, the son of a violin
maker, but nevertheless, in accordance with his own delusions of
grandeur, inclined to regard himself as a modern embodiment of
the mythical Gaucho, Santos Vega. And why not? As one descended from "the original Hermaphrodite," he claims variously,
in a gleeful spoof of Borges, to have been in his former lives "a
Fakir in Calcutta, a eunuch in Babylon, a shearer of dogs in
Tyre, a flutist in Carthage, a priest of the Temple of Isis in
Memphis, a whore in Corinth, a usurer in Rome and an alchemist in medieval Paris." His orgiastic past, like Adán's hectic
present, is a cover-up for inner emptiness. "In assuming a hundred invented forms," as Adán says to himself, "I've missed my
one true destiny."

So has everyone else in *Adán Buenosayres*. The stars of the
show, who provide something like a cross section of the local

intelligentsia, include Schultze, an astrologer with a theory about the Neo-Criollo, a new race of supermen, born of the conjunction of endemic forces, that will populate Argentina; Franky Amundsen, a globetrotting playboy, whose culture is derived entirely from pirate tales and detective stories; the pint-sized Bernini, an avant-garde sociologist, who believes in a mystical "spirit of the earth" that embodies the essence of Argentinism; Lucio Negri, "medical laureate," a stupid positivist who spouts the most advanced scientific theories; and, of course, Luis Pereda, armchair folklorist and grammarian in whose "phonographic criollismo" and "intellectual onanism"—an unkind dig—we recognize a fond caricature of Borges. Each of these personalities has his place in the mythical scheme of the book, which, in spite of mawkish passages that occur when it takes itself too seriously, is a joyous cavalcade through invective and profanity into the heart of that Argentina about which Borges once said that its only authentic passion was snobbery. There are the latest parlor games, i.e., hypnotism; hilarious soirées in literary salons; and juicy street scenes involving such unassimilated minorities as Greeks, Turks, Jewish and Italian storekeepers, and a Mr. Crisholm, who represents the "civilizing mission" of the British Empire, which, of course, owns the national railways and the Falkland Islands. There is a memorable visit to the slums, which turn out to be a hotbed of mythological fantasies. Indian hordes on the warpath blow by like a hurricane; in the dark, hoarsening with night, rumbles the River Plate, a symbol of that unshaped mud of the city that awaits a soul; and there is a nostalgic encounter with Santos Vega, the archetypal Gaucho, and his archenemy, Juan Sin Ropa, traditionally identified with the Devil of civilization, but here, in a gloatful gag on local demonology, also slyly equated with the Gringo (Italian immigrant), foreign capital personified by Uncle Sam, and finally the Wandering Jew. A tramp crouched over a bonfire turns out to be an "authentic magician," who vents his bile spitting out a rude curse, and a suburban wake acquires Olympian splendor as it becomes a veritable Parnassus of folk types. Around the corpse in his coffin gather mourners and scavengers: a gossipy circle of old

windbags, "priestesses of an inflexible liturgy," pickers of the
dead; an embittered tax collector; *taita* Flores, the last of a
vanished species, the "classic" hoodlum; a stray daughter of the
bereaved family, a barfly returning to the fold, whose story,
reviewed with delirious lyricism, could have been summed up
"in the words of a tango." There is a huge propitiatory barbecue
in gastronomic commemoration of the deceased, with roast
udder, genitals, and other vital parts, in the company of such
specimens of local flora as a beatific Blue Prince, who writes
poetry for the masses, an opera-singing waiter, and a citified and
incongruously Italianate payador named Tissone. A discussion of
aesthetics—done as a theatrical interlude—is followed by a visit
to a cornucopic whorehouse, where bliss mounts as a fight leads
to a general alarm and dispersal. Then, there is Adán's descent
into Hell under the guidance of Schultze, part practical joker,
part Vedic prophet and shaman, down spiral staircases, past
layers of burning pits. Here, in hot tars, are the sacred cows of
Argentine mythology, the Sins and Vices, and the author's pet
peeves—quacks, middlemen, swindlers, profiteers, hypocrites, sy-
cophants, advertisers, newspapermen, pedants—who are put on
the rack, drawn, and quartered. Soapbox invective alternates
with sheer flatus vocis. Among Marechal's favorite targets are
literary fops, and there is a cruel caricature of Victoria Ocampo,
the grande dame of Argentine salons—here called Titania—who
is portrayed trying to make the peons on her farm listen to the
music of Honegger. While he is at it, the author takes a side
swipe at Argentine literature, which he characterizes as so sopo-
rific that combined with a page of the phone book and a couple
of editorials from the lofty newspaper *La Prensa* it can bring
sleep even to the invincible dragon stationed at the gates of Hell.
A nice touch is a merry-go-round grinding out a bleary little
barrel-organ tune that turns out to be a Gregorian *Dies Irae*. By
now Adán is a terminal case of hardened arteries. And so, among
running gags and outlandish rodomontades, we come to the last
paragraph, a scatological masterpiece worthy of being anthologized for posterity.

Adán, with its obstreperous symbolism and disjointed virtuosity, is often out of control, but its gains—its inwardness, the freedom of its language, its philosophical resonance—are later consolidated in such works as Onetti's *La Vida Breve,* which continues the strain of Arltian subjectivity, and Cortázar's *Rayuela,* which makes a high art of semantics and epistemology and exploits the metaphysics of Buenos Aires humor to produce our first comic masterpiece. And so our novel grows—and not only in the River Plate. As the ten authors who form the subject of this book will hopefully demonstrate, progress has been on all fronts. The tendency, as in Marechal, has been toward the complete novel, which can be regarded in one of two ways. Either, in the traditional manner, it is a complete cataloguing of an outer reality—Gallegos attempted this, and so, in later years, has Carpentier in *El Siglo de las Luces,* Fuentes in *La Región Más Transparente,* Vargas Llosa in his recent *La Casa Verde*—or it is a complete run on an inner scale. *La Vida Breve* is a step in this direction. It attempts to exhaust the possibilities of a given emotional situation. So does *Rayuela,* which lives in extremities, pushing experiences to their ultimate limits. Our outward novelists, like Carpentier, are collectivists. In this they continue the naturalistic tradition. Our inward novelists are individualists, though here categories are very loose. Fuentes moves inward in *La Muerte de Artemio Cruz,* and Vargas Llosa, eminently subjective by temperament, is nevertheless, in his emphasis on externals, a throwback to Naturalism. What all these writers have in common is the increasing density of, and growing personal involvement in, their work. A metaphysical Borges is not always so far from a collective Carpentier, who enters the philosophical dimension in *La Guerra del Tiempo.* On the other hand, though in different ways, both are strongly "literary"—aesthetes rather than vitalists. Carpentier's *El Siglo de las Luces,* in spite of its historical base, is as pictorial as Gallegos and as abstract as Borges. And *Rayuela,* powerful and vital as it is, is not entirely free from a kind of aristocratic aestheticism. It also pulls toward abstraction. Perhaps in this sense the metaphysical ultimately joins the collective. Both Carpentier and Cortázar work with mental figures. Their contexts and frames of reference differ.

Carpentier is a historian who deals with movements; Cortázar is an astrologer who deals with character charts. But they both try to go beyond, into the cosmic and archetypal. Carpentier takes the highway, Cortázar the short cut. Like Onetti, Cortázar tends toward marginalism. But the marginal, paradoxically, is perhaps the fastest way to hit dead center. In Cortázar, as in Carpentier, a strong influence is Surrealism, whose resources are subliminal. And perhaps here is where all our good novelists meet. The complete novel might be that which reconciles all experiences—the inward and the outward—at the base. Asturias, another Surrealist—in *Hombres de Maíz*—looks for this reconciliation in a poetic assimilation of Indian mythology. Our fiction as a whole, over the past years, has tried to find the point of confluence of the mythical and the personal, the social and the subjective, the historical and the metaphysical. Guimarães Rosa—in *Corpo de Baile, Grande Sertão: Veredas*—shows that the task has not been in vain.

One thing we can say about our fiction today is that it has grown considerably from some years back in professionalism and sophistication. Of course it is really our writer who has grown. There is more of him in his work because he has learned to live better with himself. As he shortens the distance to his material, many of the old problems and distinctions that bothered generations past are beginning to vanish. For instance, it is increasingly meaningless to distinguish between the regional and the urban. Before, the two words denoted differences of mentality; the regional was parochial: it dealt with local human types and topical problems. The urban was more complex, worldly, and therefore universal. Now the difference is becoming merely a matter of setting. After all, Quiroga was a regionalist in a sense. In the thirties and forties, in Peru, there was a new resonance, and an unfulfilled promise, in the work of José María Arguedas. In Mexico, in the forties, Agustín Yáñez, another regionalist, was trying to give his art new breadth and relevance by adapting modern techniques from such unlikely sources as Dos Passos' *Manhattan Transfer,* a book of tremendous influence in our literature, especially in Mexico and Central America where its effect can be traced all the way down to Carlos Fuentes. The influences on regionalism today run the gamut from Joyce to *The Plumed Serpent*. Surrealism opened new dimensions to Miguel Ángel Asturias. Scandinavian literature lit the way for Rulfo. There is a region, but hardly regionalism any more, in Colombia's García Márquez, in whom we detect the influx of Faulkner, Hemingway, and Camus. Shadows of Faulkner again inhabit the regions of Vargas Llosa. In fact, Faulkner has been the single greatest influence on our literature in the past twenty years or so. This is as true of regional as of urban literature. Sometimes the influence has been beneficial, as on Vargas Llosa, at other times damaging, as on Onetti or Argentina's voluble Ernesto Sábato. In any case—whatever its effects—it marks an attitude. Faulkner was the paragon of the dedicated artist, visionary, and weaver of absolutes. And, as our narrative art comes of age, it inherits this eternal vocation. Whether it reflects existential Angst in Sábato, Sartrean phenomenology in Vargas Llosa, or estrangement in Onetti and Rulfo, the novel lives in its sense of responsibility, not only to a time and place but to a universal human need. In fertile soil the harvest is bound to be plentiful; the seeds already planted are many. Borges and Cortázar, in part, rescue the Anglo-Saxon tradition of fantastic literature, tinging it with Orientalism; Carpentier turns toward Spanish baroque; Fuentes identifies with the anarchic trend in U.S. literature. The possible combinations open to us are infinite. It would be dangerous to underestimate the Spanish tradition, which is still strong; our novel remains predominantly external and descriptive. Nor can one ignore certain atavistic subcultural hangovers in our writers, a lingering imitativeness in style and technique, for instance. But the sui generis, the original, are already emerging. Enough to think of *Rayuela,* not to mention *Grande Sertão: Veredas,* that late descendant of great European tragic art, which puts the "regional" novel squarely in the twentieth century.

That is where our literature belongs, because, more so every day, whether in our cities or our backlands, that is where we live. The old notion that caused so many bitter and fruitless contro-

versies in our literary world, about the "autochthonous" or
"authentic" having to be local or regional, seems outdated today.
With the perspective of time we can see it for what it was: an
argument over false alternatives, based on mistaken premises.
Naturalism, which claimed somewhat extravagantly to have been
born of spontaneous generation on our continent, was as much
an import as Modernism. Neither aestheticism nor social commitment had a monopoly on truth, in both there was an element
of the specious and the gratuitous. Our literature, chronically in
search of itself, has always been made of overlapping lines, and
in the given context of his generation an aesthete like Borges was
no more or less "authentic" than a regional chronicler like
Martín Luis Guzmán. The determining factors that might allow
us to decide on their relative merits would have to be—as they
always really were—talent and achievement. Today Rulfo is no
more or no less "autochthonous" than Cortázar or Onetti. Our
old writer, whether his name was Borges or Carpentier, was in
doubt of his identity, therefore self-conscious about it. Today he
can work more freely. Our world has become universalized and
he is more at home in it, more worldly not in the sense of the
spurious cosmopolitanism of before but in the positive sense of
the man who no longer wonders where he belongs because he
feels himself to be a part of the universe. The complexities of the
modern state, cultural internationalization, world politics are
such that his environment no longer isolates him. Our continent
is a microcosmic crucible and melting pot. Wherever we stand
today we are at the center of the world, the point of fusion where
all trends meet. In reality we always have been there without
knowing it. But now, as Borges says, our awareness of the
breadth and range of our tradition means that we can no longer
limit ourselves to any one part of it. The polemics that raged
around the "autochthonous" a generation ago were a cacopho-
nous mixture of cultural nationalism, false pride, and a sort of
pseudo-patriotic exaltation that did little to throw light on the
real problem. Was fantastic literature, for instance, less "authentic" than the Gaucho epic, *Don Segundo Sombra?* Both were
artificial genres, built entirely on literary conventions. That

made them no less valuable or real, or, in the deeper sense, "authentic" for the author who found in one or the other an adequate means of expression for an inner vision. When the vision was lacking, both were apocryphal. A lot of the confusion on the subject rests on the notion that authenticity is synonymous with the physical presence of a place. This produces the highly geographic literature of Carpentier. But Carpentier, a scholar and intellectual twice removed from the reality he is depicting, often captures the spirit of a place a lot less effectively than a highly subjective Onetti, or a Cortázar, who is Argentine to the bone in every word he writes, though he lives and often sets his work in Paris. And what are we to say of Asturias, who came to Indian mythology through Surrealism? He still has a fine sensibility to environmental forces. So do Rulfo and García Márquez, those two poets of rancor and melancholy, who are much more interested in atmosphere than geography. The truth is that the roads to self are many, and once you are there it is safe to say that everything will be authentic that comes naturally. Our writer is beginning to realize that fiction is an illusion that must be convincing simply on its own terms, something it can never fail to be so long as it springs from intuition and vital experience.

If, on the whole, our writer is not yet introspective—this is an area we are just entering, with great difficulty—he is now quite capable of the sustained effort, concentration, and sacrifice required for his work to be valid as personal insight. He has, as has García Márquez, started to go beyond statement and testimony to revelation and discovery. He not only records what is already there, but adds something new. If he takes what he finds in reality, it is, he realizes, because he finds what he brings there. Certainly not all our writers fit into this picture. Our literature still distrusts the inward, which, being impalpable, may perhaps seem negligible. We are great materialists who tend to measure things by their weight and size. Thus, characterization is not one of our fortes. Novelists as different as Capentier and Vargas Llosa, for instance, not only avoid it almost completely but actually deny its value. They inherit an old Naturalist fetish, according to which individual psychologies are incompatible with good sociology, which must presumably remain anonymous. An old belief of this literature is that people are all the same within a given situation, which defines them entirely, leaving no room for, or at least canceling out all interest in, what might be called inner life, which is declared irrelevant or unimportant. In fact, it is a faceless literature, a literature without people. Its obvious problem is that it remains impersonal. The Naturalist claims objectivity, but if there is such a thing as objectivity in fiction, it would come from multiplying perspectives and points of view, not eliminating them. Therefore, in a sense, the more characters a novelist is "inside" the more objective he will be. This is the Tolstoyan principle, which we have not yet mastered. The reason seems to be our old enemy: inner poverty. At best we create atmosphere, not character. Subjective novelists like Onetti and García Márquez, who have learned to capture intangibles, mirror a single self many times in their work. But there are signs, in Cortázar, in Fuentes, in Guimarães Rosa, that as we discover what is human in ourselves we will begin to touch bottom in others.

There have been considerable developments in other areas. The novelist's attitude toward his society, for instance, is a lot more ambiguous and complicated than it was some years ago. Most of our young novelists now are as committed politically as their predecessors, but they make a clear distinction, as they should, between activism and literature. The first has to do with immediate issues, the second with invariables. This elementary notion is new in our literature. And little wonder. Starving societies have little energy for long-term spiritual concerns. Their literature is one of sermons and crusades. Only now, with relative prosperity and cultural maturity, can our novelists feel free to work at their true depth. For most of our young novelists, the Cuban Revolution, for instance, has had spiritual repercussions not unlike those of the Spanish Civil War thirty years ago. But, of course, the experience has struck closer to home and has therefore been lived in a more complex way. For those who support the main principles of the revolution—the leveling of social classes, racial equality, universal literacy, national self-determination—it has not been an innocently political experience. Revolution, in 1965, is not a doctrine or an ideology but an ethos. It is the sense of a deep social and cultural transformation going on at the heart of a continent finally coming to terms with itself. The novelists' contribution to the cause is to tap and shape the new forces it has released, not by persuasion but by reflection.

Conditions have been particularly favorable for the novelist in the past ten years or so. For one thing, with education filtering down to the bottom layers of the middle class, there is the beginning of an audience for our literature, which no longer operates either in a small restricted circle, where the clique spirit rules, or a complete vacuum. Twenty years ago, our reading audience, such as it was, read almost nothing but imported literature, scorning the local product, which often, to say the truth, deserved no better treatment. But since then writers and audience have grown together. They have begun, literally, to meet socially. Both, with some lingering exceptions, are residents of the middle class and have something to say to each other, because they speak the same language. Though we probably have no writers of strictly proletarian origin yet, modest birth, with a bit of luck and hard work, no longer automatically leads to oblivion. If personal friendships and connections in high places still help, so does the lottery of literary contests and scholarships. Magazines, newspapers, cultural organizations are more important every day as means of support. But, above all, printings of books are increasing. Publishers are more willing than before to speculate on local talent. Coteries are breaking up and cultural inbreeding is vanishing with them. Some countries, like Argentina, still have strong literary "establishments" whose ceremonious members spend their time lionizing each other. But back-slapping homage is no longer a guarantee of literary recognition. Few of our good writers today belong to mutual admiration societies. Talent can stand on its merits, assured of being respected for its true worth. The situation has its dangers. The writer can no longer rest on his laurels. Repeat performances are not enough. He must develop. A few years ago early achievement was often followed by a lifetime of stagnation. There were, to use the Fitzgerald phrase, no second chapters. After a good first book, the new idol became institutionalized. Today the writer, because he sets his own standards by which he will be judged, either grows with them or is found wanting if the standards remain stationary. A radiant example of this is Cortázar. Unlike a Borges, who hit his stride in the forties and has kept pace unchangingly ever since, Cortázar has come far since his early work. True, we have some apparently dead-end writers like Rulfo and Onetti, but their difficulties reflect very personal problems. Writers like García Márquez, who found an early mold and settled into it, are now having second thoughts, and are trying to find new alternatives. Success has not spoiled them. Some, because of financial impediments—almost all our writers hold more or less demanding and time-consuming outside jobs— are slow workers. But their aim is high and their forward movement constant. A recent boon has been the markets that are opening up to them abroad as their works are translated. Another old problem, communication across national borders within Latin America, once almost nonexistent because of lack of means of distribution, is slowly being overcome. Our two cultural poles are still Mexico and Buenos Aires, but whatever their origin, our writers are increasingly in contact with each other. It used to be said that the capital of Latin America was Paris, because that was the only place our writers ever met, usually in exile. Those who could afford to travel joined the league. But today, thanks to such international editorial ventures as the Fondo de Cultura Económica in Mexico, which has a state subsidy—as does the Casa de las Américas in Cuba—their works move up and down the continent even when the authors stay at home. With this new stimulant, intramural competition has given way to a sense of common achievement and solidarity. The exception, alas, because of old cultural and linguistic barriers, which—though more apparent than real—are still high, is Brazil. But here, too, no doubt, the breakthrough will come soon. Our two literatures, as this book may, hopefully, help to show, are not so far apart as we may think.

Among the points they share nowadays is a growing concern for language, traditionally one of our weaknesses. The United States had its Mark Twain, its Gertrude Stein, its Hemingway and Sherwood Anderson, who formed a sort of continuum in the task of shaping a distinct fictional idiom for the novel. They taught the novel to talk, to find its voice and become expressive. The novel's mode of speech reflected a rhythm of living and a way of being. Its early craftsmen realized that words, which always mean more than they say, are powerful in relation not to what they say but to how they say it. They give a novel its pulse, its deeper self. For us, this basic truth dawned rather late. We have no real tradition in the kind of linguistic work one finds in other literatures where the fictional medium is a faithful mental reproduction of the social milieu. Our early novelists wrote randomly, sometimes well, sometimes badly, in accordance with their individual talents, but always with a sense of estrangement within a language of somewhat foreign structures, ill-adapted to local patterns of thought and speech, and therefore tended either to the carelessly journalistic or to the academic and rhetorical. They did what they could with the makeshift means available to them. Attempts to modify the instrument met with strong resistance in conservative literary circles. Among the first to try to inject new life and flexibility into it were the Modernists, who broadened its metaphorical framework. But in their hands language remained rarefied. It was left to the regionalists to bring it down to earth, but they tended to have a utilitarian attitude toward language. They turned it into a consumer product, simply filling it with colorful localisms, and often going overboard into pure dialect. More sophisticated writers resorted to "custom" art. Many early rebels against academicism, like Borges, ended up inventing their own language, a sort of abstraction halfway between the real and the literary. A variation on this theme is the landless, and still strongly rhetorical, language of Carpentier. Perhaps the first important attempt to do something radically new was the vibrant folk poetry of Asturias, which has the subliminal exuberance of automatic writing. It incorporates popular rhythms of speech while avoiding the worst

pitfalls of regionalism. All these writers, like Guimarães Rosa in
Brazil, were working practically from scratch. The vast geographic spread of our continent, with its infinite inflections,
makes the task of creating a language one of phenomenal proportions. Today a Rulfo still works from very different premises
than a Vargas Llosa. Yet the fact that our fiction is being written
and read as it never was before means that its language is being
nourished constantly at all levels and is becoming more natural
and instinctive. In Rulfo, as in García Márquez, without losing
any of its immediacy, it has acquired a true "style" of almost
classic purity. In Fuentes it has gone baroque, as it has in Vargas
Llosa, our most elaborate technician in the field, while retaining
some rhetoric. Onetti has manufactured his own special rhetoric.
For each of these writers, without exception, language is a
primary concern at all times. One of the elements of language
they are using with increasing mastery is humor, which as we
know not only rings familiar bells in the mind but can also
deliver coded signals that lead to hidden meanings. It is also a
sign that as we grow up we are taking ourselves a bit less
seriously than we used to. We can talk best about the things we
can laugh about. Here the great renewer is Cortázar, who has
carried the principle to a revolutionary extreme, as the basis for a
critique of knowledge and a disruption of mental categories.

And perhaps that is what our art of fiction is all about today.
Its job is to give an image, an inkling, a gauge, of a deep social
transformation. Because fiction, being an impure art, rooted at
once in social reality and inner life, can offer perhaps the best, or
at least the most vivid, index of a people's mental quotient, in a
language that is at once intimate and universal.

There is a general impression that we have reached the final
stage of a process. The mid-sixties are beginning to look like a
turning point. Our novel—and its subsidiary form, the short
story—is still on probation. It is too soon to say whether the few
figures of real distinction that are emerging from underdevelop-
ment are a freak or a promise. But if the difference between an
accident and a tradition is sustained effort, then there are some
favorable signs. Our novelists today, for the first time, can learn

from each other. Each is highly personal in his work, yet part of a cultural unit. His contribution is not lost. There is accumulation, and the beginning of continuity. In this sense we can speak of the true birth of a Latin-American novel.

It was with this idea, which occurred to us in mid-1964 after reading Cortázar's *Rayuela,* that we set out to do this book. We took a long trip that started in Paris, with *Rayuela,* which in itself is a kind of mental safari, and though we set out more or less as tourists, sampling the sights at random, it soon became a voyage of discovery. The first thing we discovered is that Latin-American literature is a mystery to most people, including most Latin Americans. Standards of scholarship in our part of the world are low, the general lack of information, and the absence of reliable sources make serious work difficult. Latin-American literature has no real critical tradition. A resulting handicap is the blurring of the borderline between the serious, the well-meaning, and the purely entertaining or commercial. Granted that these categories are not always mutually exclusive. But we found that some well-known names in our literature, which we have omitted at our risk and peril, were more noteworthy for their popularity than for their artistic merit. Others, of establishmentarian fame, were products of promotional campaigns. Here we have tried to be particularly discriminating. We have avoided literary strategists. Our criterion, we hope, has been not reputation but quality. That said, we might note that we are not authorities, experts, or specialists in the subject, but simply interested aficionados who followed their private judgment, thinking things out as they went along, and ultimately relying on their taste as readers. Our purpose was not so much critical analysis as the kind of open-minded confrontation that comes from entering into the works of others in a free and easy inquiring spirit, with a minimum of slants and preconceptions. Though of course we are not foolhardy enough to claim complete objectivity, nor do we think that if such an absolute were possible it would be particularly desirable. It would be neutral, for one thing, and we have tried to be active partici-

pants in our work. All we can say is that, if we have our angles
and our bias—in favor of "inwardness" in the novel, for instance
—they, and it, are our own. Whatever our mistakes, we take
comfort in the belief that we have been arbitrary enough to be
honest.

This is not a study in depth of our fiction, but an outline, a
first approach, a general picture. We intended it as a sort of
introductory reference book, done in a scholarly way, solidly
researched, based on exhaustive readings, but, hopefully, conversational enough in tone and spirit to be readable itself. Our
emphasis was more diagnostic than definitive. We tried to detect
symptoms, trace certain main lines, catch glimpses of possible
directions, suggest some tentative evaluations, weigh results and
alternatives.

As for our method: each of the ten essays in this book is a
separate unit, implicitly related to the others but conceived to
stand independently. It was chance as much as necessity that
dictated this particular format. The insurmountable difficulty of
obtaining accurate information regarding our authors' lives and
works on the basis of research alone kept leading us to the only
reliable source: the authors themselves. It was around our personal encounters with them that our work grew, more or less
naturally acquiring the shape it has. The proportions within
each essay vary, but the elements are always the same. The
nucleus is a conversation. The author speaks, moves, reflects
on himself and his work, and we try to catch him at a moment in
time, to fix a gesture, an attitude that will reveal the man and
illuminate the artist. The idea is to find a focal point that will
radiate beyond, drawing surrounding areas into its circle of light.
Thus, in each case there is a portrait, a profile, a presence on
stage. We try to make it live, then extend its sphere of influence,
rounding it out with background material and critical commen-
tary. We wanted to provide a kind of forum for our authors, so
they could be seen and heard from all sides, in relation to
themselves, their work, their society, their times. The psychobio-
graphic, as opposed to the more comprehensive historical, approach, while sacrificing some cohesion, seems to us to have the

advantage of vividness. A figure of speech, a turn of phrase, can be more eloquent than volumes of explanations. We did our best to shorten distances, and make them as painless as possible. The authors, on the whole, were most helpful and cooperative. They "sat" for us willingly, putting up with note pads and tape recorders. With some we had long sessions full of our laborious questions and their patient answers. Others we met more fleetingly. There were the loquacious, and the laconic. To "place" them better, when possible we looked them up at home. Tracking them down was sometimes strenuous. Our trip took us from France and Italy to Mexico and all the way down the American continent to Buenos Aires. We realized, in time, that we were being passed along a sort of circuit. Most of our writers are in contact with each other, and each opened the door to others. We are particularly grateful to Cortázar, for his contacts in Argentina, and to Asturias and Fuentes, for the weight they put behind us in Mexico. Also to Fuentes, Vargas Llosa, García Márquez and, again, Cortázar and Asturias for going to the trouble to read, correct, and occasionally rewrite parts of their statements in the essays on them. Works that were out of print were lent to us by the authors themselves, for which we thank them. Vargas Llosa and García Márquez were kind enough to show us manuscript copies of forthcoming works.

Our selection of authors lays no claim to infallibility or exclusiveness. There is a bad habit everywhere nowadays of glorifying certain figures at the expense of others. Our book tries neither to magnify nor to belittle. Of course there is judgment implicit in every choice. But we insist that ours is personal, and has no wish to be final. We simply wanted to touch on what seemed to us certain high points of our literature, emphasizing what we understood to be of particular value or significance today. We took into account such factors as variety and geographic distribution, but only secondarily, subordinating them to simple preference. In general we could say that, without attempting to establish hierarchies, we picked those authors who seemed to us either to fulfill a tendency or to transcend it. Thus Asturias, for instance, has done something a bit different within regionalism, which is equivalent, in our view, to saying that he has gone beyond it. The same applies to Rulfo, García Márquez, and Guimarães Rosa. There are writers in this selection—Borges, Cortázar—who depart widely from the norm. Some may be an aside, others a point of departure. We have tried to measure them by their own standards. Ideally we would have liked to strike a balance between such not-necessarily-incompatibles as urban and regional, naturalistic and "metaphysical." But we have always stressed the outstanding rather than the representative or typical, on the ground that the latter is more often typical of what is wrong than of what is right in our literature. Thus certain noticeable omissions, such as old-line regionalism, a literature that is slowly on the wane as our novel graduates from the tract, the topical, and the truculent.

Ten, we hope, is a quorum. The session opens in September, 1964, and closes in August, 1966, dates between which we carried on our various debates, not necessarily in the order in which they appear. Grouping our authors was a problem. The exceptional, by definition, does not fit into a neat category. For the sake of convenience, we finally decided on the simple expedient of dividing them roughly into generations. The arrangement has the advantage of providing a chronology of sorts. Thus we have those born around 1900: Borges, Asturias, Carpentier; those born around 1915: Cortázar, Rulfo; those born around 1930: Fuentes, García Márquez, Vargas Llosa. Some—Guimarães Rosa, Onetti—straddle two generations and are placed between. Needless to say, mental generations do not always correspond to those of the calendar, and often contradict them. Thus Cortázar is our "avant-garde," and Vargas Llosa, the youngest and technically one of the most proficient of our novelists, is at bottom one of the most traditional.

Our language throughout our work was, of course, Spanish. The exception was Guimarães Rosa. We did what we could with our bad Portuguese, and helped ourselves along with German and French translations of his books (there are none in Spanish). The rest of the time we read originals. The snatches of conversation that appear are all translations. We also did our own translating whenever we quoted from the authors' work. Official translations are available in many cases, but we avoided them. Their notorious inaccuracy has often been misleading to students of our literature. We tried to be faithful to the spirit of the works we were dealing with. In the same way we tried to give a fair account of our authors, to see things through their eyes and represent their views fully, even when we could not identify with them. To those who may recognize themselves here, we dedicate this book, where, if we have done our homework well, their voices will speak for themselves.

I

Alejo Carpentier,
or the Eternal Return

"LATIN AMERICA, novel without novelists" was the unhappy verdict, a generation ago, of the peripatetic Peruvian critic L. A. Sánchez, one of the first men on the continent to digest and evaluate our literary production. In our part of the world, he said, reality, the unknown, surpassed fiction; its voluptuous vastness defied formal classification. Unlike the poet, who, as a Neruda, or even as unregenerate an aesthete as Rubén Darío, had already proved, could transport his subjectivity with him wherever he went, the most lucid novelist, for want to a focal point, was reduced to portraying the chaos of primeval matter. His senses and faculties were overwhelmed by the incoherence of his surroundings. A pessimistic view shared by many of Sánchez' contemporaries, whose love affair with their continent was doomed to remain unrequited. "Twenty years ago, I would have agreed," says our Cuban master, Carpentier, a man with a lifetime's experience behind him as a commanding figure in our literary scene. But no longer. The novelist today has enough experience in his art to transform the luxuriance of nature into a manageable force that will enrich his work rather than suffocate it.

Carpentier can speak with authority on the subject. His work, in fact and spirit, spans two full generations. He has been a forerunner of our new novel and today is still one of its most distinguished proponents. Years ago, when our writers were still passing a hat around for ideas, he helped set its goals. He brought to his work an ordered resonance and sense of proportion that were a clear challenge to the atonal and the aphonic. His pronouncements, which were not meant for Cuba alone, carried well beyond its borders. He was perhaps the first of our novelists to make a conscious and concerted attempt to encompass the Latin-American experience as a whole, without undue concern for the superficial differences created by regional or national boundaries.

In word and deed, Carpentier is something of a prototype of the Latin-American intellectual: home-grown but culturally crossbred, an appropriate formula in a society that, as he says, is the product of racial symbiosis and spiritual miscegenation. He was born in Havana in 1904 of parents who had moved to Cuba only two years before: a French architect father and a Russian mother who had studied medicine in Switzerland. He seems to owe more to them than to his environment. His course was defined early and followed what could be described as a classic itinerary. The skeptic atmosphere at home reflected the more or less beatific liberalism of an era that, as he remembers, placed itself under the guiding star of Anatole France. The fading glories of old Havana provided the theatrical scenery for the drama of his early life. His first love, probably under paternal influence, seemed to be architecture. But circumstances forced him to switch to journalism. It was, as always in Latin America, not only the road of least resistance for the aspiring writer, but in his case the most immediate form of political involvement available. Strife was in the air, and he went to battle. By 1924 he had become editor in chief of the magazine *Carteles*. There he took to the political lectern and was promptly rapped on the knuckles for it. In 1927 he landed in prison—for seven months— for having signed a manifesto against the dictator-of-the-moment, Machado. Today he speaks with pride of this manifesto as having been premonitory of the principles of the Cuban Revolution. In 1928, out of prison but restricted to home territory, he began thinking of exile. He was on the eve of a long pilgrimage. Helped along by the friendship of the French poet Robert Desnos, at the time on a visit to Cuba, he escaped to France— borrowing Desnos' identity papers—where he was met with the pomp and circumstance of what he fondly recalls as a "diplomatic reception." He planned to stay in Paris for a couple of years, until the storm blew over at home. Instead, he was there for eleven years.

Paris, as usual, was many things, with something for everyone. Carpentier, a man of catholic interests ranging from magic to musicology, developed a wide repertory of activities. He was a close friend of the Surrealists, who had a decisive influence, he believes, in discovering the Latin-American continent for Western culture. Their taste for the primitive and the unconscious led many of them on semiarchaeological expeditions into the continent's tribal past. Carpentier contributed for a time to their magazine, *Révolution Surréaliste*. He soon realized he did not belong in the movement itself, but the dictate of Breton, that "nothing but the marvelous is beautiful," a statement that became a synthetic creed with the minor Surrealists who exploited it mechanically, entrenched in what Carpentier calls the "bureaucracy of the marvelous," nevertheless opened his eyes to the authentic wonders of his homeland. On the American continent, the "marvelous," he realized with the dazzlement of the overcivilized man, was a daily element of nature and reality. Since then he has made a cult of that "magic realism" that in his view expresses the continent. Incongruity and paradox, he says, are at the heart of Latin-Amercan life. In Latin America everything is outsized and disproportionate: towering mountains and waterfalls, endless plains, impenetrable jungles. An anarchic urban spread overlies breathless virgin expanses. The ancient rubs elbows with the new, the archaic with the futuristic, the technological with the feudal, the prehistoric with the utopic. In our cities skyscrapers stand side by side with Indian markets that sell totemic amulets. How to make sense of this profusion—of a world whose crushing presence dwarfs man, confuses his senses, staggers his understanding and imagination?

For Carpentier, as perhaps for all people caught in an oscillating motion between different time zones, the answer has been a sort of compromise in time and space. He has lived in two worlds. In one the clocks stopped long ago. In the other they are running faster every day. He has known the fatigues of trying to keep up while remaining behind. In this, as one of our eternal straddlers, he speaks for a continent that throughout the centuries has always needed distance and detachment to gain an adequate perspective on itself. Europe was the vantage point. The road to insight—Enlightenment, as he might say in his somewhat grandiose phraseology—led through displacement and uprootedness.

In a sense, the years in Paris were nothing but a preparation for the eventual Return. Carpentier lived them looking over his shoulder. He realized that life abroad, even when profitably employed, was one of those Unending Days that could lead nowhere, for the spiritual outcast, but into the night. He ached for the American continent. His age-old craving was to "express the world of America," to make its lost rivulets become tributaries to the mainstream. For this realization he thanks the Surrealists; they sent him plunging into his true self. Those who had traveled to America, Mexico in particular, had returned with dazzling accounts of old civilizations. Perhaps their interest in things ancient and primitive soon became an affectation with them; but in him it took on a kind of atavic force. America was his vocation. His problem was to feed that vocation. "At the time I had no feeling at all for the essence of the American world," he says. So he mounted a sort of campaign around it. "For years I devoted myself to reading everything I could find on America, from the letters of Columbus on down through the texts of the 'Inca' Garcilaso de la Vega, all the way to the eighteenth-century writers. For eight years I think I did nothing but read American texts. I saw the American continent as an enormous haze which I tried to grasp because I felt vaguely that it was going to be central to my work." Getting organized, he soon found out, was

only the first halting step in a difficult process. America was
something of a forbidden fruit for him. As his work shows, it was
a long time before his bibliophilia could find a solid base in vital
experience.

Our novel was in its infancy when Carpentier started to write.
It was little more than scenography, regional in scope, Mani-
chean in outlook. It was pompous and verbose. But, worst of all,
it had no real backbone. It often sidestepped and overlooked the
very issues it was trying to face. Whether it was called *La
Vorágine* or *Don Segundo Sombra,* as a rule it was written by
urban intellectuals who had journeyed into the back country,
much as Zola not too long before them, to observe and record
local life in its various manifestations, which were as likely as not
to slip through their fingers. The result of this almost philatelic
precision was usually mere romance or picturesqueness, with a
dab of "social consciousness" thrown in to assuage the author's
civilized guilt feelings. Carpentier himself indulged this pro-
pensity in his first novel, *Ecue-yamba-o* (dialect meaning,
roughly, Praised Be the Lord, 1933), where he rather guilelessly
attempted to depict Afro-Cuban culture from the "inside"
though, as he admits today, his acquaintance with that culture
was so far from being intimate that he missed its key element:
animism. His subject had literally not come to life for him. A
studious smattering of folk mythology, he discovered, was no
substitute for intuition. A more thorough grounding was needed
in the ways of a place to reveal its spirit. Documents were not
enough. They could be not only misleading but an actual
stumbling block. After all, native cosmogonies were not so much
a system of thought as a way of feeling. "Rationals," the Indians
used to call their white brothers, who were always trying to
reason out the things they could not understand. The word was
well applied. Because the white man was a great streamliner. He
could distort reality even as he documented it. An example of
this is the *Popol Vuh,* the sacred book of the Mayas, which
records genuine oral traditions, but was distorted in its original
translation by a Spanish priest. It was also compiled—and perhaps censored—at the time of the Spanish Conquest by a Chris-

tianized Indian under the influence of Catholic missionary schools. Which shows some of the difficulties a scholarly novelist like Carpentier may have had in trying to gain access to a world he could only murder to dissect. He froze gestures where he should have captured movements and postured where he meant to catch basic attitudes. In this he was a man of his age. Trying to find its image in the more or less hermetic remnants of cultures of the past, with which it had no direct connection, was one of the first great temptations of our novel. It thought it could discover a collective unconscious in itself. It dug and delved for it. But the results were rarely more than subcutaneous. No one knows this better than Carpentier. Books like *La Vorágine, Don Segundo Sombra,* and *Ecue-yamba-o* were important stepping-stones in our cultural advance because in their time they helped awaken Latin America to an awareness of its surroundings and heritage. But the fictional matter they were made of was mostly illegitimate. They were mental conceptions, sometimes rich in intellectual substance but poor in human vibrations. There was something intrinsically fraudulent and absurd about the picture they drew of a Latin America that was all fable, on the one hand, and bleak naturalistic monotony, on the other. The Latin-American experience was something else. It proceeded at other levels, in other dimensions. What these were we are perhaps only beginning to realize today. But Carpentier was one of the first to ask himself the question. He went exploring the length and breadth of our world, trying to assimilate everything he found there until it became ingrained. Perhaps his efforts were too self-conscious, therefore doomed to failure. He never seems to have quite outgrown the Latin American's obsessive, almost pathological fear of being twice removed from reality. But battling this fear has been a fruitful process. He has worked harder than almost anyone else at following footprints in the sand, deciphering inscriptions on old monuments, and reading the signs on the trees. The result is a body of work of unusual scope and vigor.

Carpentier thinks of Latin America in terms of certain constants—or, to use the Sartrean term he favors, "contexts": its overall determining composites, social, geographic, political, eco-

nomic, historical. In *Tiento y Diferencias* (Prelude and Variations), a book of essays he published recently in Mexico, he
divides the continent into several main "blocks": the mountain,
the river, the plain. Each of these, he told us, talking over the
subject, is "a section that has its own characteristics. For instance,
the Andean zone with its predominantly Indian culture; the
Caribbean area, where there is a common Afro-American denominator." In the sum of their essential features he finds the
continent's profile. Ever-present, overshadowing man, is the telluric background, at once redundant and multiple. The crux of
the matter is the age-old struggle for survival and renewal. We
are at once young and old. The eternal conflict that Gallegos
portrayed somewhat schematically as civilization versus barbarism, in Carpentier acquires historical and social complexity, as
well as a sort of categorical immutability. Carpentier performs in
the grand mode. His themes are all drawn directly—with a
minimum of literary transposition—from the surrounding "contexts." His aim is to register what is specific, and at the same time
archetypal, in the Latin-American experience. Every possible
factor must be taken into account, he says. The Latin-American
artist, if he is to measure up to his task, must be at once a
miniaturist and a muralist, a moralist and a minstrel, a sociologist and a poet. Carpentier places special emphasis on the
linguistic context. A phenomenon peculiar to Latin America, as
he points out, is the fact that a single language will carry us
across twenty different frontiers. The least nomadic of us is
inhabited by a sort of migratory second nature that keeps us in
mental flight, alert to invisible spaces and altitudes. Our historical context is no less remarkable. Enough to think of the parallelism of different ages existing simultaneously, superimposed; as
Carpentier might put it in his biblical terminology: Genesis,
Babel, and the Apocalypse. The Latin-American continent is the
only one, he says, somewhat hyperbolically, "where a twentieth-
century man can shake hands with a man from an age before
railroads and newspapers, coexist with the Middle Ages, or be
the contemporary of some other man in an isolated province who
is living the Romanticism of 1850." Add to that the ethnic

context: the mixture of classes and races; the political and economic context: the boom-and-bust atmosphere of an agricultural society in the throes of rapid industrialization, whose sources of production are so thoroughly at the mercy of world markets directly or indirectly controlled by foreign interests that it can be swept overnight from wealth into bankruptcy. Atmospheric influences—what Carpentier calls "the luminous contexts, the lights that envelop man"—are also an important part of the picture. Not only historical currents and geographic contours but also climatic conditions shape the character of a place. In this area Latin America presents a wide spectrum ranging from the transparency of mountain air through desert glares and quick tropical twilights to the fireworks of the aurora borealis. Carpentier has tried to develop a sixth sense to detect them all.

Carpentier says: "I think the view the Latin-American intellectual has over the world is one of the vastest, most complete and universal man has ever had. For me the American continent is the most extraordinary world of the century, because of its all-embracing cultural scope. Our view of it must be ecumenic." In our revolutionary age, he believes, Latin America has at last acquired an identity of its own that will allow it to make its voice heard and weight felt in the world. Its indigenous realities are quickly becoming a part of the universal experience. We are not only on the threshold of a new age, says Carpentier, but have already entered it. Our maturity is reflected in the work of our novelists, who bear the imprint of their continent's distinct personality. Our derivative phase is over. Carpentier feels highly optimistic about our literary future. He says our novelist today has already reached a level of achievement comparable to that of novelists anywhere.

As for himself, in spite of his undoubted literary merits, perhaps his main importance is as a self-appointed spokesman for the New World, as well as something of a continental institution. It was in this double capacity that we met him briefly in Paris, in the midst of a backbreaking round of conferences. His tight schedule had exhausted him and he was anxious to be left alone. Nevertheless, he gave us our "sitting." He seemed a bit out of his element alone with us. He is accustomed to speaking before an audience. He dislikes direct questions, preferring simply to be handed a topic on which he can expand at will, in the process displaying his considerable gifts as a conversationalist. But he has never refused to give an account of himself. He works full time. He received us in an empty hotel room overlooking a wintry street corner. He seemed absent, and there was something curiously inaccessible about him. "Overwork," he said, heaving himself into a chair. He had the air of a much-traveled man, at first glance tanned and fit, obviously in his time a man of action, but on closer inspection a tall, stooped figure heavily weighted by age. His handsome but weather-beaten face was deeply furrowed. He had been having some heart trouble. He spoke slowly, occasionally articulating with some difficulty—he would rather speak French than his peculiarly throaty, strongly French-accented brand of Cuban Spanish with its clipped word endings —and at moments his mind seemed to wander. Our presence in the room then became almost superfluous. He spoke in a professorial tone, with vague gestures, often referring us to his work for further instruction and, more often than not, sounding like it. We remembered seeing his name inscribed—among those of other notables—on a huge memorial plaque in a movie on Montparnasse. A matter of particular satisfaction to him, he told us, was the fact that his books are on the current curriculum of the Institute of Hispanic Studies in Paris. For a Latin American —Paris being the Hall of Fame—this is a sort of final consecration.

It culminates a long and varied career. The years Carpentier spent as a young man in Paris served him well. He kept busy— and usually in good company. The Surrealists were not the only ones who had a lasting effect on him. He branched out into many fields, stocking up on a wealth of erudition he later drew on to nourish his work. He was the director of Foniric, a publishing house whose specialty was issuing recordings of literary texts that ran the gamut from Whitman to Aragon. He was editor in chief of the magazine *Iman,* which, though published in Spanish, was devoted mostly to French writers (but discovered the works of a then-unknown poet, Pablo Neruda). He helped produce a film on Voodoo. Perhaps most notably—every artist should practice a second art besides his own, he says—he was a student of musicology and wrote scores and librettos for cantatas and comic operas based on American themes. Between bull sessions with Alberti and García Lorca he studied the problems of musical synchronization and wrote an opera with the "father" of electronic music, Edgar Varèse.

His association with musicians proved fertile. There are signs in his work that he has a special understanding for their problems. He also owes music a formal debt. Musical principles figure prominently as structural elements in his work. *El Siglo de las Luces* (Explosion in a Cathedral), as he says himself, is a kind of symphonic construction in which the three main characters embody male, female, and neutral themes. In *Los Pasos Perdidos* (The Lost Steps) the somewhat overbearing protagonist—a figure on a pedestal—is a musician. But probably the outstanding example of Carpentier's "musical" thinking is his novelette *El Acoso* (Manhunt), where the whole plot unfolds in a dramatic sequence timed to coincide with the duration of a performance of Beethoven's *Eroica*. The artificial structure—the rhythmic beats, the measured silences—tends to collapse the piece, but at moments also contributes to its impact.

Typically, *El Acoso* proceeds on several levels. On one it aspires to be a social document, to give a sampling of contrasting elements in the Cuban population—a classy prostitute, a poor clerk, a Negro wetnurse, a disenchanted revolutionary—which are brought into conflict in a specific dramatic situation. Formally—or "musically"—the author says, it "has the structure of a sonata with an introductory section, an exposition, three themes, seventeen variations, and a conclusion or coda." The sophisticated use of such plastic devices as leitmotifs reminds us that as far back as 1945—*El Acoso* was published in 1956—simultaneous with a trip to Venezuela, where he had been invited to found a radio station, Carpentier had been commissioned by the Fondo de Cultura Económica in Mexico to write a history of Cuban music. The book—*La Música en Cuba*—appeared in 1946.

Europe was behind him then. But the Return had
easy to accomplish. Nostalgic childhood memories of
Havana—which he has recently commemorated in
graphic essay issued by the Cuban state press—had dr
briefly to Cuba in 1936 in the hope of finding some way
there. But, unable to make a living at home, he had so
forced to leave again. In 1937—after a hurricane at sea—
in Spain, then in the throes of the Civil War, attending a w
congress in the company of, among others, his countryman,
mulatto poet Nicolás Guillén, the Peruvian poet César Vallejo,
and André Malraux. In the midst of exploding bombs and
bloody street fights, he recalls, he found himself sharing a hotel
room with George Lukacs, the Hungarian Marxist critic.

There followed three more years in Paris, until finally, in 1939,
tired of sitting in halfway house, he packed up and set off, this
time for good, for Latin America. He was staking a lot on his
trip. Cuba, chronically unstable, was only moderately hospitable
to him. He scraped by for several years on the proceeds of radio
programs, which he wrote and directed, an all-absorbing enterprise that he hated. He must have been having second thoughts
about his return when at last, in 1943—ten years after the
publication of his first novel—came his big break. Louis Jouvet,
the French actor, stopped off in Havana on his way to fulfill an
engagement for a series of performances in Haiti. Carpentier,
never a man to turn down a chance to be on the move, accepted
an invitation to join the bandwagon. The conjunction of circumstances was providential.

In Haiti—which, with his usual inquiring energy, he toured
from top to bottom—Carpentier, a great frequenter of museums
and old church archives, discovered the extraordinary career of
the early nineteenth-century Haitian Negro monarch, Henri
Christophe, a despotic but forward-looking empire builder who
harked back for inspiration, on the one hand, to the French
court and, on the other, to his legendary African ancestors, the
mythical King Dâ, incarnation of the Serpent, and Kankan
Musa, founder of the western African empire of the Mandingos.
Henri Christophe, until then practically unresearched—though

he had already seduced more than one writer, including Eugene
O'Neill in *Emperor Jones*—was an ideal fictional character and
supplied the basis for Carpentier's second novel—dated 1949—*El
Reino de Este Mundo* (The Kingdom of This World). In true
Carpentier fashion, Christophe is treated more as a symbol—a
historical presence, one might say—than a person. His figure
appears on stage only toward the end of the book. Meantime a
whole age is telescoped. Carpentier is above all a chronicler. His
shifting sights focus at moments on individual figures, but only
to cast them against their historical background. Mentalities are
portrayed in terms of general traits drawn with sweeping brush
strokes. Thus the book opens on the humble figure of the Negro
slave Ti-Nöel, who, like the rest of the simple and ever-hopeful
local population, changes hands continually in the cataclysmic
course of events: the eighteenth-century Dominican slave revolt,
the exile of the colonists to Santiago de Cuba, the Haitian
government of General Leclerc, brother-in-law of Napoleon,
finally the highminded tyranny of Henri Christophe. Now we are
fast on the heels of Mackandal, an armless sorcerer and terrorist
with mystic revolutionary ideals, now in the superstitious animist
mind of Ti-Nöel, now in the splashy quarters of Pauline Bona-
parte, a sumptuous beauty having her precious nude body mas-
saged in the tropical sun by her Negro footman Soliman, now in
the streets, spectators of anonymous mass movements. A sense of
the recurrence of events pervades the book; individual acts
become the components of set patterns. The style is sober, almost
impersonal. The architecture comprises a number of disparate
elements that are not always well integrated, but key scenes—
among them, the colorful "Shakespearean" death of Henri Christophe in the lonely splendor of empty palace halls, in the center
of his vast Citadel—are engrossing and well sculptured.

Of special note in *El Reino de Este Mundo* is the ambiguity
with which Carpentier treats the revolutionary theme. A lot of
his readers have wondered where exactly he stands in relation to
the subject. And the truth is that he seems to have mixed feelings
on it. Revolutions, in Carpentier's books, are always short-term
failures but, as he goes to great pains to assure us, harbingers of

greater things to come. Thus here as elsewhere—for instance, in *El Siglo de las Luces*—the odds are stacked against individual lives, which go down to be trampled by events, more or less blindly invested in the forward march of history. Marxist determinism? Fatalism? There is probably no final answer to the question. Carpentier is not a propagandist. He deals with the problematics, not the ultimate utilitarian validity, of revolution. His personal progressive philosophy—which at times borders on professional optimism—is well known. But as a novelist he properly subjects ideology to temperament. Which may explain why in *El Reino de Este Mundo* we have the impression he is giving in to a kind of grim stoicism when, in a somewhat ponderous aside he allows himself toward the end of the book, he proclaims: "He [Ti-Nöel] understood now that man never knows for whom he hopes or suffers. He suffers, and he hopes, and he labors for people he will never know, who in turn will suffer, hope, and labor for others who will not he happy either, because man always pursues a happiness beyond the part allotted him. But the greatness of man consists precisely in wanting to better the world, to impose Tasks on himself. In the Kingdom of Heaven there is no greatness to be conquered, because everything there is established hierarchy, limitless existence, impossibility of sacrifice —rest, delight. That is why it is only crushed by pain and Labor, but gallant in his misery, capable of love in the midst of misfortune, that man can find his greatness, his full measure in the Kingdom of This World."

Undoubtedly there is a duality in Carpentier: the political militant alternates, at unexpected moments, with the ecumenic scholar for whom the essence of history—which can be annoyingly reactionary—is that it repeats itself. So it is, for instance, that revolutions become establishments, which eventually, rounding out the cycle, succumb to new revolutions. Progress is relative, a chronological concept that can be measured only within a given historical context, in a more or less finite period of time. On an absolute scale, outside time, there is no forward—or backward—movement, only the endless swing of a pendulum from a point suspended in space to its antipode. At the center of

gravity is the archetype. What in human lives—which are lived
in time—are complexities and contradictions, in the broader
scheme of things, frozen, abstracted from the flow, become generic attitudes. In a sense this is the notion that underlies Carpentier's startling collection of stories, *La Guerra del Tiempo* (The
War of Time, published in 1958), where it is variously illus-
trated. In the story "Semejante a la Noche" (Like the Passing of
the Night) we have the stylized portrait of a soldier on his way to
battle. It is the eve of his departure. He is any soldier anywhere.
He does the things any soldier would do under similar circumstances: packs his bag, takes leave of friends and family. What
gives the story its flavor is its peculiar narrative "twist." In the
first scene evidence points to the fact that the soldier is a Greek
embarking for Troy; in the second, though otherwise unaltered,
he has become an eighteenth-century Frenchman off to fight in
the American War of Independence. In successive scenes the
historical backdrop keeps changing; yet the soldier, in his archetypal situation, is always the same. As in *El Siglo de las Luces*—
which is very specifically located in time, and yet so generic in
concept that for the first eighty pages or so (a sweeping overture),
the author has so contrived the elements of his drama that we
could as easily be in the twentieth century as in the eighteenth—
the experience has been simplified, purified, stripped down to its
essential elements. The soldier is the shadow of a reflection of an
almost Platonic image. Even the language is landless, abstract.
Similarly, in what is perhaps Carpentier's most accomplished
creation, the story "El Camino de Santiago" (The Road to
Santiago), which takes place at the time of the Conquest, we have
the timeless prototype of the Indiano (or first-generation American) only half transplanted from Europe, rootless in his new
land, inwardly divided, eternally torn between the old and the
new continent. A realistic opening soon leads into the realm
of parable. The theme of exile and return is treated symbolically as a recurrent coming and going of different people who
are always the same Indiano, fugitive reproductions born from
the same archetypal mold, homeless wanderers destined to perpetuate themselves through time. In a continent spanning all

the ages of man, the past and the future are epitomes of each other. The world is a palindrome. Such, in unusually vivid understatement that contrasts strongly with the oracular tone that often mars the author's novels, might be the theme dramatized in the story "Viaje a la Semilla" (Journey Back to the Seed), where a man achieves a sort of immortality on his deathbed by relapsing in memory to his origins and appears re-entering the womb as he dies.

The presence of the timeless in the temporal—and the universal in the particular—as a crucial element of the Latin-American context is elaborately exemplified in Carpentier's third novel, *Los Pasos Perdidos* (1953—translated as *The Lost Steps*). Here the chronicle, artfully transposed—through the medium of a first-person narrator-protagonist who keeps a journal—becomes a lengthy and sometimes laborious meditation on life, time, and history. The vaporous characters are avatars of different aspects of the common stock of experiences. On a moral plane—and that is what counts—we can identify the protagonist with the author. The theme of the book is the Return from abroad of the wanderer, who has become a foreigner and a stranger to himself —"lost the key to his authentic existence"—and is back to pick up his scattered pieces. The experience is conceived in terms of an elementary symbolism: a trip up a vast jungle river, back through time, up the stream to the source. Somehow neither the staleness of the symbol nor the verbal grandiloquence surrounding it completely detracts from its effect. At his best Carpentier can make symbols ring with meaning. If he spends too much time clearing his throat, he can also sing true. Here he gives us some fresh insights into an old subject. In *Los Pasos Perdidos,* possibly his most personal, therefore most fully realized, novel, while his mind—which remains academic—formulates, there are moments when his eye is almost innocent, as if it were seeing things for the first time. He redeems his pledge to his continent. Certain descriptive passages have a selfless quality that raises spiritual autobiography to the level of collective myth.

The book was written in exile in Venezuela—a land, he says, which "in a sense is a synthesis of the whole continent: its enormous rivers, its immense mountains, its virgin forest"—and, in fact, describes a trip the author took up the Orinoco River to the great savannas, the old terrestrial paradise of the Conquistadors, "one of the most unexplored areas of the American continent." A postscript identifies the setting. But the specific spot on the map is not important. In the course of the narrative the river is nameless. It could be any river in America. The narrator could be any man mounting the stream in search of the past of mankind and his own childhood.

Unlike his regionalist predecessors, Carpentier, while obviously in search of a sort of basic communion with nature, does not pretend to be an integral part of the spirit of the place. On the contrary. As an intellectual—an outsider—he frankly maintains a certain distance. The dramatic substance of the book, such as it is, derives from his efforts to shorten this distance. The experience is more cerebral than visceral. Esoteric elements add to the exoticism of the setting. The protagonist of *Los Pasos Perdidos* is a musician with a theory on the mimetic and magic origins of music who has been commissioned by a museum connected with a North American university to sail up the river in search of certain tribal instruments to add to the museum's collection. He undertakes the trip reluctantly, oppressed by a vague malaise occasioned by nebulous events in his background that have plunged him into a sort of general worldweariness and defeatism. Essentially—the premise, unfounded, therefore, inevitably unlikely, is taken for granted—he is a displaced person foundering in the apocalyptic world of the Twentieth Century. We accept this at face value. As in a reverie, we read: "I had been uprooted during my adolescence, blinded by false notions, seduced into the study of an art whose sole purpose was to feed the merchants of Tin Pan Alley, then had wandered around a world in ruins, for months, as a military interpreter, before being cast back on to the asphalt of a city where misery was harder to face than anywhere else." The city, though never named, we gather from allusions is New York; in any case, it symbolizes Modern Civilization. "Having lived it," notes the protagonist, "I knew the terrible fate of those who wash their only shirt at night, cross the snow with holes in their soles, smoke the stubs of stubs and cook in closets, finally becoming so obsessed by hunger that their whole intelligence is concentrated on the single thought of eating." Though materially improved in recent times, his big city life has become increasingly meaningless. He is saddled with a temperamental wife, Ruth, an actress who is caught up in an uninterrupted circuit of performances that have reduced their conjugal relations to a sad ritual coupling on Sundays; and a mannered French mistress, Mouche, who subscribes to fortunetelling, astrology, and a sort of vague Existentialism. The moment has come for a complete Break. All this is more or less impressionistically—and dispassionately—recorded in the protagonist's journal, a device that Carpentier uses freely, to think out loud, daydream and analyze, with greater concern for tonal unity than for a day-to-day recording of events. The stage machinery is rather heavy. But, once it has been set up, the theme emerges clearly. We are on a ceremonial "voyage of Discovery" into the heart of darkness. There are unmistakable echoes of Conrad, not only in the lushness of Carpentier's style but also in his Gothic-symbolic treatment of character and drama. Though at least on one main point the two authors are poles apart. Conrad's heart of darkness is a world of primitive savagery. Carpentier's vision is Edenic.

Our drop back in time takes us first to an unspecified Latin-American capital in the throes of a revolution, then through backland villages where we encounter vestiges of nineteenth- or eighteenth-century life, through feudal areas, finally to the tribal world of the Stone Age, deep in the jungle, in an area approachable only through an almost hidden opening in the thicket on a bank of the river which, significantly, overflows in the rainy season, wiping out all traces of human passage, engulfing the signs that mark the way, which vanish under the waterline—beyond memory. We have come to the parting of the waters, to the land of Genesis.

The characters that populate the scene, though often, as the author has pointed out, based on real people, are personifications rather than persons: the gold prospector, led by fabulous visions of El Dorado; the Greek adventurer answering the call of some lost ancestor with a volume of the *Odyssey* under his arm; the pioneering priest carrying the Church into the wilds; the Adelantado—provincial governor in the old colonial hierarchy—representative of the secular arm, a Builder who has founded a city in the jungle. Of particular importance to the protagonist is the figure of Rosario, the embodiment of the female principle, symbol of the original matrix, of lifegiving Mother Earth, source and fountain, under whose mythological sign he places himself in his quest for regeneration and rebirth. For she is "all woman" and yet "nothing more than a woman": an elementary, uncomplicated creature who carries life deep in her vitals and for whom "the center of the world was wherever the perpendicular midday sun shone." With his love for her—a lifetime experience though, measured in calendar time, the Return has taken little more than six weeks—his broken existence comes full circle. He has unlived the ages of man; the End has become the Beginning. On the instinctual level—unfortunately the one least convincingly described—he has found happiness, harmony, fulfillment. He has no desire to return to civilization. He has discovered that "here you can ignore the year in which you live. It is an error to say that man cannot escape his times." But on another level he is vulnerable: a man of the twentieth century, after all, a prisoner of another age with all its baggage and ballast of entanglements and commitments, inhabited by his retroactive "memories of the future." Being an artist, his plight is particularly painful; art, he says, belongs not in Genesis but in Revelation. As an intellectual, gifted—or damned—with awareness, he is the end product of the cumulative weight of history he carries in him. He must be in contact with his century; he cannot disconnect himself. "The march up exceptional roads," he says, "is undertaken unconsciously. One is unaware of the extraordinary nature of the experience at the moment of living it. . . . New worlds must be lived, rather than explained. Those who live here do not do so out of intellectual conviction; they simply think this, and not the other, is the good life. They prefer this present to the present of the builders of the Apocalypse." A choice that is not open to the protagonist, because "he who tries to understand too much, who goes through the pangs of a conversion, who is capable of harboring qualms when embracing the customs of those forging their destinies in this primitive clay . . . is a vulnerable man in that certain worldly powers that he has left behind continue to exert their influence on him." Therefore, "none of this was meant for me, because the only human race that cannot live outside time is the race of those who make art," whose job it is "to anticipate the shape and expression of things to come . . . in full awareness of everything that went before them." But the personal failure of the protagonist—which fulfills the book's dramatic requirements, and was also, according to the author, designed to "avoid the taint of a happy ending"—suggests a possible triumph open to the man for whom the sense and substance of the American experience are inborn, a matter not of reflection but of heartbeat. For him, jungle rivers would be inner bloodstreams. Is Carpentier such a man? Perhaps more than one would suspect. He laughed when we asked him this question and said: "All I can tell you is that Rosario is my wife."

In *Los Pasos Perdidos,* as in most of Carpentier's subsequent work, a lot, perhaps too much, is done through language. Tightly packed sentences loaded with meticulous detail and precious ornament pile on each other to form endless, monolithic paragraphs that can be hauntingly evocative in their polyphonic richness but are all too often static and exasperatingly rhetorical. There is what amounts to a morbid fascination with words in Carpentier, a kind of gluttony—resulting in a sickly obesity—that can be deeply disturbing to the reader. He excels in set pieces, particularly descriptive passages; he can sum up an age in its objects. But the landscape gardening is obtrusive. Increasingly, in his later work, the dynamics of plot and action tend to succumb under a clutter of archaism and filigree strewn about as liberally—if not as randomly—as quaint crockery in an old curio shop. The syntax is stiff-jointed. There is almost no dialogue— and when there is, it rings false. It punctuates, never reveals. There are few concrete scenes on which the reader can focus his attention. The eye wanders in search of landmarks. At worst,

Conrad becomes Poe—of whose prose Carpentier says expansively
that it is "one of the greatest of all times." A judgment that is a
sort of verdict on the man who utters it. Because, whatever one
thinks of Poe, Carpentier, at least so far as we can make out, has
nothing in common with him but words. And therein lies the
danger. Where breadth substitutes for depth—the horizontal for
the vertical—one has the feeling that words act as a sort of
process of sublimation. There is a fear, or inability, to tap below
the surface of things. This is one of the unfortunate traits of an
unintuitive literature. In Carpentier it can be highly destructive.
It blots and blurs. There seems to be something lacking in the
scene. The author has either fallen short or overreached. The
view is incomplete because there is no inner eye to register it.
The poverty of private means somehow produces an elaborate
public-address system. But at a price. The inner man claims his
due. Shallowness finds its compensation in more or less neurotic
defense mechanisms. In Carpentier the result is a deliberate
verbal excess that he rationalizes claiming it is perfectly consistent with his intentions and general outlook. Which it is, of
course. In fact, Carpentier is more interested in his context than
his people. He focuses less on acts than on tides and trends. In
this he believes himself to be in step with the march of Latin-
American fiction today. There is that character in a Carlos
Fuentes novel who says that in our part of the world there are no
people, no individualities, only impersonal conflicts of natural
forces and social movements. The Fuentes character speaks with
the voice of Indian tradition, which regards the human person as
an embodiment of the collective spirit. But in Carpentier the
notion is applied to modern mass society in general. The task he
has set himself of shaping its amorphous clay has determined his
aesthetic. In view of which we can better understand his predilection for prototypes, on the one hand, faceless crowds dissolved in street scenes, on the other. He calls his style "baroque"
—a term he uses to describe not so much a form as a temperament or disposition. "Latin-American art is baroque or isn't at
all," he says categorically, calling attention to the exuberant
"foliage" in his own work. Baroque, in his concept, means such

otherwise unrelated things as the sugar-frosting colonial architecture in Mexico, the music of a Villalobos, and the fantasy of a Borges. But the term applies most specifically to that vein in our literature which runs toward the panel. Not that the panel is always baroque. But it is, to varying degrees, in a Carlos Fuentes, a Miguel Ángel Asturias, a Carpentier, who in one way or another try to infuse life into their work with verbal flourishes. The success of the effort seems to depend to a large extent on the source of the language they use. In the best of Asturias and Fuentes language is instinctive and spontaneous. The flourish lives because the gesture is natural. In Carpentier we sense stacks of dictionaries in the background. We can speak of his language as a sort of transference. One thinks of the old Arab artist who was not allowed to represent living forms. He expressed his awe of the divinity in arabesques.

Carpentier states the case differently. The Latin-American artist, by definition, he says, not only works on a broad canvas but wants to "cover every inch of the surface," to "leave no dead spots." The Old World artist can mention his objects in passing; they are well known to his audience and easily recognized. "Everyone knows Heine's pine tree." But in the New World, we—like Adam in the garden of Eden—are still in the stage of "naming things." We must contribute a complete and detailed inventory of our undiscovered streets, houses, forests, lakes, mountains, to incorporate them into the experience of Western man, to make them a part of the universal sensibility.

Carpentier has a highly visual imagination. He literally paints his scenes. When he is having difficulty with a particular passage, he says, he tries to imagine how a painter would see it, then proceeds to tackle it à la Bruegel, à la Hieronymus Bosch, à la Goya. Like a Flemish master with rococo tendencies, he rounds out every volume, breaking the whole down into its component parts. Nothing is left for the reader to fill in. Therefore, he gains no perspective on the scene, which remains a flat surface.

In Carpentier characters pose, usually with their backs to the reader, blocking the view—they remain opaque—or are simply spun around the stage as walking symbols of ideas or attitudes.

They bow in and out, puppets on a string. Lacking an inner dimension, or even any believable psychological complexity, they exemplify, rather than dramatize, the issues. A lot of heads knock, but there are no real confrontations. Carpentier despises what he calls "the little psychological novel," a pejorative term he seems to apply to any book involving situations—especially when subjective or emotional—that are not of direct public relevance. If his view seems a bit drastic, we must remember that what interests him is not individual experience but the "epic substance." "I like big themes," he says. "They are the ones that confer the greatest richness to the characters and plot of the novel." Though he admits at the same time that "the great settings are those that most easily betray the novelist."

A forceful, if only partially successful, attempt to reconcile abstract concept with concrete fact is his major novel, as it is generally considered, *El Siglo de las Luces* (literally: The Age of Enlightenment; published in 1962, translated in 1963 under the title *Explosion in a Cathedral*), where he goes further than ever before in his determination to produce a vast synthesis of the American experience. His love for historical personages inspired his choice of his central character: Victor Hugues, a footnote figure in the French Revolution, one of indubitable historical relevance yet sufficiently unknown and unrecorded for the author to have been able to improvise his fictional existence entirely "on the basis of his actions."

Born of a forced stopover—result of a plane crash—of the author's on the island of Guadeloupe some years ago on his way to Europe, *El Siglo de las Luces,* with its luminous moments, its bursts of eloquence, is woven of many themes, in many keys and registers. In spite of its flaws—its mannerisms, its hystrionic attitudes, its weak dynamics, its overload of static sequences—it is certainly an imposing architecture, unbelievably intricate, breath-taking in its sweep, staggering in its erudition, which testifies to the author's encyclopedic command of subjects ranging from philosophy and plastic arts to occultism, medicine, and archaeology.

El Siglo de las Luces traces the immediate repercussions of the

French Revolution in the New World, particularly in the Spanish and French Caribbean. As in his other revolutionary stories, *El Reino de Este Mundo* and *El Acoso,* Carpentier walks a tightrope between the specific and the archetypal. In broad outline the story is invariable. A first phase of feverish idealism, high-mindedness, illusion, fanaticism soon bogs down in bureaucratic bumbling, which leads first to corruption, then to blind violence, and finally degenerates in disillusionment and stoic resignation. The revolution eats its own children. Not all is negative, however, seen in relation to the long-term march of history. The remarkable career of Victor Hugues—who is described as a sort of "hypostasis" of Robespierre in the New World—documents the author's thesis. In the early days of the revolution Victor Hugues is an obscure merchant from Marseilles who has piloted commercial ships in the Mediterranean and whose adventurous spirit has led him to set up shop in the Caribbean. His entrance into history dates from the night his store in Haiti was burned down during a slave revolt that shakes his vaguely liberal conscience into an awareness of the imperatives of the moment. The whole Caribbean is in a ferment and Hugues, blowing with the winds—a fluctuating weathervane with connections in all the right quarters—begins his meteoric rise to power. A Mason one day, a Jacobin the next, ruthless with his enemies, Spartan in his personal life, cynically opportunistic in his service to his changing masters, he is the epitome of the man of action, intellectually vigorous but unquestioning, whose role it is to reduce abstract ideas to the level of practical realities. His rising star takes him to mainland France, where he places himself under the wing of Fouché and Robespierre, then back to the New World as a representative of the French government to displace the British in Guadeloupe, finally to rule as governor of Cayenne (French Guiana), where, history tells us, he administered justice with an iron hand until his death around 1822 on his plantation.

On these bare facts Carpentier builds his epic against a colorful background that embraces the whole of the Caribbean basin —and straddles the Atlantic to France and Spain—to compose a

picture teeming with natural and historical catastrophes so prolific and overlapping that it is difficult sometimes to distinguish
whether one is being shipwrecked on the high seas, buried in an
epidemic, or slaughtered in a Jacobin bloodbath. The efficient
pragmatic machinery of Victor Hugues survives earthquake and
landslide. Banners and slogans come and go, eclipsing each other.
Jacobin Hugues is for freedom and equality and the abolition of
slavery. But political considerations lead him to tolerate the slave
trade conducted by pirate boats flying under the French flag
when their cargo is captured from British boats and unloaded in
ports in the Dutch West Indies. The Napoleonic period brings
the restoration of slavery in his domains. The flagrant inner
contradictions of the revolution are summed up in the image of
Victor Hugues arriving in the New World on his first assignment,
under the auspices of the National Consulate, at the height of
the revolution's "allegorical" splendor, with the symbol of his
power: the guillotine.

Like *Los Pasos Perdidos*, *El Siglo de las Luces* is more notable
for its dialectics than for its drama. Yet the author has applied
himself to hinging his plot on live characters. Victor Hugues
gives the book its strictly historical dimension. But *El Siglo de las
Luces* is also a chronicle of family fortunes. The family in
question is Cuban; it is composed of Carlos, his sister Sofía, and
their sickly cousin Esteban, who are spectators of, then partici-
pants in, the Big Events of the New Era, which overtakes them in
mourning over the recent death of their father in their patri-
archal mansion in old Havana. The death of the paterfamilias,
and, with him, a whole form of life, leaves them destitute in their
decadent surroundings, which are suddenly thrown open to the
winds of change. Their middle-class props quickly cave in under
them as news of the revolutionary turmoil brewing in the Old
World begins to filter through to them in their cloistered Spanish
colony. While Carlos in his down-to-earth functions as elder
brother—he appears on stage only as a link in the narrative—
tends to the family business, attention centers on Sofía and
Esteban, excitable young people who nourish vague dreams of a
revolution conceived according to the enlightened principles of

the eighteenth-century French philosophers, whose works—
banned in the Spanish colonies—they have been reading in
secret. Their imaginations are aflame; there is no outlet for their
discontent, which becomes open frustration. They have been
leading a curiously topsy-turvy life that—timeless in its contours:
their situation faithfully reproduces that of a real family the
author knows in modern Havana—reflects their general derangement and the disruption of the era. In a setting a bit à la
Cocteau—one thinks of *Les Enfants Terribles*—with echoes of
Paul et Virginie, among cobwebbed furnishings and dusty pic-
tures, notably the symbolic oil by a Neapolitan master that gives
the book its English title, they while their time away wandering
aimlessly from attic to basement, roaming the streets at night,
sleeping in the daytime. An aura of shared childhood mysteries
hovers over their relationship, which, in its culpable innocence,
could almost be described as incestuous. Esteban is practically a
cripple; periodic attacks of chronic asthma keep reducing him to
a bedridden shambles. Sofía—a name carefully picked, says Carpentier, for its etymological meaning: understanding, gay savoir
—is sister, nurse, and mother to him (she is one of Carpentier's
characteristic Woman Figures). Their ingrown world is definitely
shattered when fate knocks on their door in the person of Victor
Hugues, whose arrival—fresh from the Haiti holocaust—coincides with their bereavement. At first regarded with suspicion
and resentment, in spite of his letters of recommendation to their
father, Hugues soon becomes a frequent visitor in the house,
whose young hotheads come under his disturbing influence. The
New Era makes quick inroads in the family. Esteban is miraculously cured of his asthma by the half-magic, half-scientific
mumbo jumbo of a Negro witch doctor—and certified physi-
cian—Ogé, a friend of Victor Hugues and symbol of the age's
paradoxes when he chants unintelligible voodoo formulas while
at the same time—with great ceremony—proceeding on the very
reasonable task of uprooting a growth of allergenic plants in a
courtyard behind the patient's sickbed. Meantime Sofía, the
romantic crusading spirit aroused in her, has become Victor
Hugues's mistress. Esteban, on his part, worships Hugues's pro-

phetic image. His awakening to historical awareness is made to coincide with his passage, through sexual craving, from restless adolescence into manhood.

The lives of the two cousins are now inextricably entangled in that of Victor Hugues. Each of the young people has a symbolic role to perform in the book. Esteban is somewhat incongruously portrayed at once as a sort of hot-eyed Candide and the prototype of the wavering intellectual who cannot face up to reality. "He is the person who would like a change in the prevailing structures," says the author, "but only on the condition that the change occur on his own terms. If things don't happen the way he wants them to, he lets go. . . ." Fired with revolutionary fervor, he follows Victor Hugues to France, where he is promptly assigned a minor bureaucratic job in the south, close to the Spanish border: a great letdown for him. He had gullibly considered himself entitled to more considerate treatment than that. But he has no sense of proportion. As are all the righteous, he is easily scandalized. The mechanisms set into motion to spread the revolution to Spain break down. There is treachery in the ranks as firebrands quickly become turncoats. Between purges, governments rise and fall in Paris, where successive waves of terror lead from the Directorate into the Consulate. Esteban, horrified by the cutthroat tactics of the world's saviors, realizes, too late, that his high ideals have gone up in smoke. Victims have become executioners. "I dreamed of a very different revolution," he tells Victor Hugues wearily during one of their ever-rarer meetings; to which the old cynic, dismissing his recriminations, answers with the timeworn phrase: "Who asked you to believe in something that didn't exist? One doesn't discuss a revolution, one makes it."

Esteban's is a classic case history of misguided well-meaningness; he learns his lessons the "hard" way. When Victor Hugues is sent to Guadeloupe with the gospel of freedom in one hand and the guillotine in the other, Esteban is through. As heads roll, he returns home to Havana in defeat, loftily declaring that "the Promised Land is within."

But for Sofía the revolution has just started. During his

absence, for utilitarian reasons, she has married a businessman who at this time, after a brief partnership with brother Carlos, conveniently enters his deathbed; whereupon Sofía, flouting convention, takes flight to join her old lover, Victor Hugues, at present established in autocratic comfort in his mansion in Cayenne.

She is given a dour reception. Time has taken its toll on Victor Hugues. Their affair has gone as stale as the revolution itself. Sofía, though unshaken in her messianic faith, is realistic. Rather than be made a senseless casualty, she withdraws. Where to go now? Impossible to return to Havana, where Esteban meantime has been picked up by the colonial authorities for his revolutionary and "Masonic" activities and shipped off to prison in Spain (a final irony). Sofía decides her place is at her cousin's side. In Madrid she somewhat mysteriously obtains Esteban's release and sets up a ménage with him in a quiet suburb. His hardships have broken him. His sole source of joy is his beloved Sofía, in whom he recognizes the bastion and haven he has always yearned for. His empty campaigning, he realizes, has never been anything but a search for her, the Original Woman and root of his existence. Thus, for him, the revolutionary experience has ended in a sort of return to the womb.

Follow years of monastic retirement for the two cousins. Again we confront the author's ambivalence in regard to revolution. Esteban in his futility—the ultimate futility of all human endeavor—provides the book with its philosophical context, which could be described as one of Christian fatalism. But the true sense of the book, says Carpentier, is to be found in the person of Sofía, whose coolheaded appraisal of events is more in the spirit of Marxist humanism. Sofía understands that "men may fail, but ideas continue to make headway until the time comes for them to be fully realized." The notion is reflected in the book's epigraph, an ominous quote from Zohar: "Words are not uttered in vain." As the author states explicitly toward the end of the book: "The presence of Victor [Hugues] had been the beginning of something that would take the form of vast cavalry charges in the plains, journeys up legendary rivers, military expeditions across immense mountain ranges. An epic was about to be born that would accomplish in the lands of America what had failed in old Europe." He is referring, of course, to the wars of independence, which were placed under the sign of the ideals of the French Revolution.

Because of its dense fabric, *El Siglo de las Luces* is hard reading. In spite of the hectic pace of the events it describes, its wealth of embellishment and overuse of pictorial effects clutter the scene, which—perhaps deliberately, as the metaphorical picture, Explosion in a Cathedral, in whose "apocalyptic immutability" and "silent tumult" there is a plastic equilibrium, "a note of peace"—seems to hang in suspended animation. The result is a vast still life that appeals more to the mind than to the emotions. The reader's involvement is minimal. Above all, we miss the sense of inner predetermination that subordinates action to character.

Yet the book's ecumenic spirit, in particular its allegorical relevance to modern times, is not lost on the reader. The essential features of the American world Carpentier describes—its lights, its landscapes—are as much in "context" today as they were yesterday. America, for Carpentier, is not just a place, but a state of mind that enforces a set of values which in turn shape a way of life. The basic myths man lives by are changeless. Thus, the Revolutionary Experience that did itself to death in the eighteenth and nineteenth centuries has returned to be relived in the twentieth. Carpentier stresses this when he says *El Siglo de las Luces* was originally composed between the years 1956 and 1958, then, significantly, revised after the author's return to Cuba in 1959 to join the forces of the Castro revolution (which is why it was not published until 1962). The things Carpentier has been "naming" in his work have come to pass. Yet in a sense they always existed. Social events in Latin America have something of the same permanence as the mountain ranges and seascapes that make up America's timeless profile. A description the author gives us of an island archipelago off the Venezuelan coast—which he sailed through in the fifties and paints as he saw it then—has a retrospective validity that makes it seem perfectly in place in *El*

Siglo de las Luces (chapter 26), a century and a half earlier. It is
one of those instances in Carpentier's work of an acute combination of foresight and retrospect. "I wrote that chapter on the
deck of the boat," he says, adding: "I'm like an animal. I don't
analyze certain things. I write them as I feel them, under the
effect of blinding illuminations." But that is only half the story.
Actually, Carpentier is the most calculating of all authors. He
willingly confesses to the painstaking efforts he expends in laying
out his books. He keeps a strict schedule, working mostly in the
late afternoon because, he says, he does not believe in "early
morning flashes of inspiration." Whatever makes the sparks fly,
"before I sit down to write a novel, I make a sort of general plan
that includes layout, a sketch of events—horribly badly done—a
map of the place of action. I choose the names of my characters
carefully, always in terms of a symbolic chart that helps me to
visualize them. . . . I'd be absolutely incapable of writing a chapter without knowing beforehand exactly what was to go into it."

The import of Carpentier's work must be seen in relation to
his personal role as apostle and apologist for the Cuban Revolution, whose contemporary realities, in his view, embody ancestral
truths of premonitory significance for all of Latin America. The
novelist's duty, as he sees it, is to help define these truths, then
place himself at their service. Not as an agitator—our "literature
of violence," as someone called it, belongs to the past—but as a
moralist. What was once the novel of "social protest"—which, as
Carpentier says, was unreal to the extent that it dealt with
something that had not happened; the social protest framework,
whatever its statistical validity, being a sort of controlled situation more or less arbitrarily assembled to prove a point—has
given way to a genre more independent from immediate concerns, therefore better qualified to assess and evaluate. Carpentier is not a starry-eyed fanatic but a man aware of the complexities of the revolutionary task and the toll it takes on man. He
offers a cool appraisal of the facts. Every revolutionary age has its
martyrs. Yesterday's guillotine is today's firing squad. Perhaps the
Massacre of the Innocents is one of the constants of history. The
ending of *El Siglo de las Luces* is instructive. Esteban and Sofía,

suddenly one day emerging from retirement in Madrid, join a street riot—senselessly—and are trampled to death by the mob. A fitting climax in an "enlightened" century which was also, as the author points out, a century of almost medieval obscurantism, of secret societies, slavery, witchcraft, and Black Masses. But Esteban and Sofía, or their nameless doubles—or descendants—are alive in Cuba today, once more arraigned before the tribunal of history, perhaps waiting to be sacrificed again. Whether for a good purpose or in vain, time will decide. Meantime they will continue to fulfill their roles as accusers and accused, advocates and prosecutors, tirelessly pursuing an eternal argument, without ever being able to rest their case.

Carpentier believes in the power of ideas as few men do. In his latest book, *El Año 59* (year 1959), the first volume of a trilogy—a "cycle"—on the Cuban Revolution, he tries to show their effects directly at work on mass movements. On the basis of a few fragments that have appeared in the Cuban magazine published by Casa de las Americas, it would seem that in *El Año 59* Carpentier has set himself an impossible task. There are no protagonists at all in *El Año 59*. In fact, there are no individual characters, only groups that grow to become human waves. They are identified from the grandstand by their shapes and colors. As planes take off from the Havana airport, carrying hordes of refugees, wandering crowds on obscure errands fill the streets downtown. They carry a dim message, blind actors extrapolated from unknown variables. There is no real plot, only a sort of general computation of events, which soon overflow. The effect is disconcerting. There is no room in this literature for dissent or maladjustment, no real possibility of dialogue. Carpentier has become a mighty teletype that reproduces everything that is fed into it. The air crackles as chattering switchboards pass the information along buzzing lines. As the maze becomes increasingly tangled, we wonder whether we are being mauled in a picket line or murdered in a football rally. We are in a world of flags and balloons, leaflets and loudspeakers. The intention, says Carpentier, is to give a picture of a "collectivity" moving as in "a planetary system." The question is whether such a scheme—a plastic nightmare—can be validly realized in a novel. Can external conflict substitute for characterization? Is it possible to breathe life into a literature that dispenses with the human person? Is the rally really a step forward from the tract? The tentative answer seems to be negative. At least in this case nothing works out as it should. The mind soon tires of acrobatics and goes on strike. *El Año 59* is nothing but a stunt.

Besides his literary work—which includes a recent play, *El Aprendiz de Brujo* (The Sorcerer's Apprentice), on a colonial theme, centering on the person of Cortes—he occupies a position of great responsibility in Cuba as head of the National Press, a government enterprise that is one of the products of the revolution. In the deficiencies of Carpentier's work we recognize the old dilemma of the man torn between the needs of his art and the immediate demands of his society. He has been active in Cuba's literacy campaign. Books are his gospel. In our conversation he pointed proudly to the fact that his Press had published the unprecedented number of twenty million volumes in 1964 and was planning twenty-seven million more for 1965. Whatever his over-all outlook on the human condition, we had the distinct impression that he was a man with a historic role clearly cut out for him. He made no bones about where he stood. "Cuba is not an isolated phenomenon," he said. The revolution is a jealous mistress. If her immortal cycle exacts a mortal tribute from him, it will not be the first time our literature has lost a good man to history.

II

Miguel Ángel Asturias, or the Land Where the Flowers Bloom

THOSE who live their times suffer them and sometimes learn to speak for them. There is something of the court of appeals in our literature. It has been a place for airing grievances, the house of plaints and petitions. The poor have slept on its doorstep, waiting to be heard. "A lot of money in a single hand always looks a little dishonest," says the proverbial Asturias, a big-hearted man who has championed their cause in the temple and the marketplace.

We are in Genoa, a town of smokestacks, winding alleys, stockyards, warehouses, fisheries, and laundry lines. It is a sunny afternoon in the spring of 1965. A figure of Churchillian portliness and formidable aquiline profile receives us in a modest penthouse apartment on the top floor of the Doria Palace overlooking a back courtyard near the Piazza San Matteo. The room is casually and scantily furnished. Asturias has few possessions: scattered books and papers, a few random decorations, a patch of newspaper clippings—reviews—on an otherwise bare wall. He seems hardly to notice his surroundings. A package of groceries sags on a shelf, about to fall off. There are noisy guests in the hallway. In his house, a crossroads for all sorts of company, people come and go. He is kind and monosyllabic. He watches them quietly, smiling at them with his deep shadowy eyes.

As we come in, drafts sweep through the house like ocean breezes, blowing doors open. A small electric heater spreads its frugal glow in the middle of the floor. This is the workroom, which bad weather can make inhospitable. Our host is apologetic. "It's been such a cold winter, we haven't been in here for months," he says, rising slowly to greet us. In this country there is no winter. But that is of little comfort to him. The mildness of Guatemala's mountain air is far away. Asturias has spent half his life in exile.

He reminisces over cups of coffee, with his sprightly Argentine wife, Blanca, hovering nearby, occasionally interrupting to add some anecdote of her own. He talks as he writes, with warm humor and a sort of neglect that seems almost indolent, though it probably betrays nervousness. For emphasis he raises his voice, drumming his fingers on the table—hard enough to make the cups jump—then lapses into a sudden silence. He has little flair for conversation; he likes to tell a good story, spin out a joke or epigram, then let it settle, while he ponders something else. He lives in his own world. Blanca tells us he often wanders around the house with his hands deep in his pockets, talking to himself. He has the curious reserve of the Guatemalan, the distant look of a mountain people dwarfed by huge expanses full of specters and mirages that incline the mind to reverie. Perhaps nobody in our literature has come so close to penetrating the latent and irrational in our culture. Asturias is less a speaker than a listener. What he hears is the voice of a landscape of misty forest lakes peopled by ancient sprites and goblins that wear human masks and perform playful human acts in order to reveal old truths. Though touched by Naturalism—of the tropical variety, the kind that has been known to produce the worst results—his work is closer in tenor to the morality tale and the medieval fable. It is part pantomime, part ventriloquism. Many threads meet in it: the myth and magic of Indian lore, the Spanish dream-world tradition stemming from Quevedo, the pamphlet and the picaresque, the phantasmagoric demonology of Goyaism, the enchantment and conjury of Surrealism. Whether in the realm of pure legend or that of social protest, he creates an atmosphere of otherworldliness sometimes uncomfortably close to soap opera or the cartoon, but at best inhabited by a gentle whimsy and a tenderness for the creatures of this earth that can enliven the crudest caricature. Asturias is a puppeteer whose fairy tales are a sort of divine comedy made of hellish visions and nightmarish realities.

Life, from the beginning, poked cruel fun at Miguel Ángel Asturias. His earliest memories date back to the bloody dictatorship of Estrada Cabrera, under whose reign of terror Guatemala entered the twentieth century. Asturias was born in 1899, a year after Estrada Cabrera came to power.

"My mother," he says in a voice full of resonant quavers, "was a schoolteacher. My father was a judge. He occupied an important position on the bench. . . . Estrada Cabrera was a lawyer from Quetzaltenango. He first came to power as Secretary of the Interior under President José María Reina Barrios. In this position he started maneuvering backstage to take over the government. The President was found dead in the street one day, murdered. Many people think Estrada Cabrera was responsible for his death. With Reina Barrios out of the way, he was second in succession to the throne. The first in line being absent at the time, he had himself named provisional president. Soon he put himself up for re-election, supported by the army and also the U.S. companies that took over the construction of the national railways. Guatemala had already finished building its own railway from the capital to the Pacific port of San José; the line extended about three fourths of the way to the Atlantic port of Puerto Barrios. Estrada Cabrera handed the whole thing over to the American railroad company. This was the birth of imperialism in Guatemala. The treaty of 1904 gave everything away for free. That was how Estrada Cabrera began to gain American support." The juicy concession, says Asturias, attracted other U.S. interests. Capital investments brought huge profits in those days. Soon the famous United Fruit Company had a foothold in the country. "The company's boats used to stop over in Guatemala to load bananas, in exchange for which it had agreed to carry mail south to Panama and north to New Orleans. Gradually the company began to realize the commercial possibilities of the arrangement. That was when they started acquiring their huge landholdings."

Meantime, toward 1902 or 1903, there had been some student uprisings against the dictator.

"Estrada Cabrera," Asturias recalls, "expected my father to take legal steps against the students. He refused, so he lost his job. My mother also had her courses taken from her. They had to leave the capital and move inland to the town of Salamá, capital of the province of Baja Verapaz." There Asturias spent his early childhood, in close contact, he says, with his land and people. Though not far from Guatemala City in actual distance, Salamá was worlds from it in every other way. "In those days it was a four-day trip to get there. You traveled on muleback and slept out on the road at night." On the whole it was quite an adventure for Asturias. One of his grandfathers had properties in Salamá. He was a man of the land, experienced in its ways. The child and the old man soon became inseparable. "I followed him wherever he went," says Asturias, who has vivid memories of the days they spent horseback riding together. The sights they saw he took back with him to Guatemala City when his family returned there in 1907.

It was no homecoming. The city was a tomb under the iron boot of the Caudillo, who was to have himself re-elected a total of three times by his rubber-stamp Congress. A strange sense of unreality prevailed, a mixture of the outlandish and the sinister. A long wake had begun. People lived behind closed doors, speaking in whispers. There was little overt resistance to the dictatorship, since an attempted coup organized by a group of professionals, doctors and lawyers, had been ruthlessly crushed and was followed by a general purge. Those who were not shot had committed suicide, their families had been exterminated. A subsequent student uprising—conducted by polytechnicians and cadets of the military school—had been an equally dismal failure. The rebels were wiped out, and a whole generation was gutted. The country was on its knees. The jails were full.

There was something magic, almost uncanny, about Estrada Cabrera, who played on popular superstitions to keep the country in a sort of holy dread of him. "It was an invisible dictatorship. Nobody ever saw the President. There was only hearsay, rumors." Guatemala was completely cut off from the world. "We had no radio, no airplanes. Two or three times a month boats touched at our ports, that was all. No newspapers came in without the government's consent. All we ever saw were the two official newspapers. Our isolation was complete."

In time the President became a myth. Asturias tells us he got to know the man quite well after his fall.

"I was secretary of the court where he was prosecuted. I saw him almost daily in jail. And I realized that undoubtedly such men enjoy special powers of some sort. To the point that when he was behind bars people said: 'No, that couldn't be Estrada Cabrera. The real Estrada Cabrera got away. This is some poor old man they've dumped in there.' In other words, the myth couldn't be in prison." The grotesque humor of the situation was accentuated by the fact that toward the end of his rule Estrada Cabrera had surrounded himself with witch doctors, faith healers, and Indian fortunetellers who held orgiastic dances on the grounds of the Presidential Palace. He had become a part of his own mythology. And, in a sense, he had been his own victim. The dreads he had set off in his people had eventually worked against him.

The crucial date that marked the beginning of the end for Estrada Cabrera, says Asturias, was December 26, 1917. At ten o'clock on the memorable night of December 25, Guatemala City was leveled by a terrible earthquake. "The whole capital collapsed. That's why Guatemala City is an ugly place now. It had a very different character before, baroque in architecture, ceremonious in its ways. I remember a Guatemala where people dressed in tails and top hat; they wore gloves and carried canes. . . . But now suddenly the earth shook and everyone was left out in the street. And it's curious but undoubtedly the earthquake not only shook the earth but also jolted consciences." In fact, it had historical repercussions. The whole country was turned upside down. It was an occasion for national solidarity. "People from all walks of life suddenly found themselves thrown together in the streets in nightshirts and pajamas. We had to live in tents. So what was the result? Those who had lived withdrawn, out of touch with the rest of the population, joined the crowd. No doubt this was one of the factors that contributed to Estrada Cabrera's downfall. From 1917 until 1920, the year he was overthrown, the situation quickly deteriorated. In 1917 my generation, no longer intimidated by memories of previous reprisals, entered the political arena." That same year a statue of the dictator was stoned in the main courtyard of the university. Estrada Cabrera raged at this unprecedented affront. Then there were meetings and demonstrations, one of which became a rally. Students were imprisoned by the police and then, surprisingly, released. "The situation was very tense. Since direct student action was almost unknown in those days, Estrada Cabrera didn't know how to handle things. This was the state of affairs when we came to 1920."

The dawn of the New Year was full of foreboding. "That morning leaflets appeared under every door in Guatemala City inviting the population to join a new Unionist party in order to celebrate the hundredth anniversary of our independence, which was due in 1921, with demonstrations for a united Central America. Here, too, Estrada Cabrera didn't quite know how to react. We students immediately gave our support to the motion." By then things had gone a step farther, and people were calling for an end to the dictatorship. There were persecutions. But we continued to demonstrate—peacefully. We were unarmed. Until in April the National Assembly unseated Estrada Cabrera, declaring him unfit to govern."

There were elements of gallows humor even in Estrada

Cabrera's final days. "Carlos Herrera had been named provisional president. Estrada Cabrera had promised to leave the country. He was on the point of bailing out, it seems, when one night in April shots were fired from his house, which was on a knoll in the outskirts of Guatemala City. Then we realized he hadn't gone. There was an eight-day battle to reach him. His residence was surrounded, but on the night when it was going to be taken by assault, the British and American ambassadors intervened in his favor. So he was spared. He handed himself over and was put under house arrest. He was brought to trial and imprisoned until his death three or four years later."

After the long twilight of the Estrada Cabrera years, the country had to be put back on its feet. The year 1920 was an active one for Asturias. "We founded the Association of Unionist Students, an affiliate of the Unionist party. We put out a newspaper called El Estudiante, which was very violent politically. But, with Estrada Cabrera out of the way, we started to realize that Guatemala's problems were not only political and if we continued to play politics, as we'd been doing so far, we'd end up defeating our purposes and our influence would go to waste. So we founded what was known as the Popular University. We realized that so long as our people could neither read nor write and knew nothing about the duties and responsibilities of citizenship we'd commit the same mistakes indefinitely and there'd be no progress. The Popular University was founded in 1922. We'd counted on an enrollment of perhaps two or three hundred people, but it soon reached over two thousand. So naturally we lacked space and facilities. Fortunately the rector of the National University came to our rescue with classrooms. Classes were in the evening, after seven o'clock: workers, ordinary people off the streets, men and women. The government helped out. We were backed by the new President, General Orellana. Our purpose was to demand a sacrifice of our citizens. Because the trouble in Guatemala, as in many of our countries, is that people are accustomed to contributing nothing to the general welfare. We wanted to change that. We had to go out of our way a bit to give our evening classes, which were free. It required an effort.

Sometimes it was raining. . . . The project grew. Soon there was a branch of the Popular University in every province. It started to play an enormous role in the country's life. We had our representatives in the National Assembly. They proposed that the University be officially subsidized. . . ."

Meantime the fortunes of the Asturias family had improved. Asturias' father had become an importer of sugar and flour, which he sold to the people who inhabited the surrounding countryside. He held a constant open house to accommodate his clients, and the gatherings that took place in the courtyard at nightfall, under the trees, were an endless source of wonder and information for the young Asturias. "It was a huge courtyard with an enormous carriage entrance. The buyers came in on their carts, or driving their mule teams. They arrived in the morning or the afternoon, did their marketing, then packed their loads to be ready to leave the next morning. They spent the night in the courtyard. There they built their bonfires and slept in arbors, under canopies. I had many friends among them, and I heard them talking every night, telling their stories. For me it was a second contact with the people of the back country."

Asturias, a law student, was working on his thesis at the time. His subject: the perennial "social problem" of the Indian. His research, if by definition somewhat theoretical, nevertheless often sent him on expeditions to farms and ranches. In those optimistic days devoted to public service, the young felt themselves to be an intimate part of the course of events. The future seemed full of high promise. But things soon began to go wrong. Shortly after graduating from law school Asturias and another lawyer were appointed to defend an officer accused of the murder of President Orellana's chief of staff. There were complicated legalities involved. The defense lost the case; the accused was sentenced to death and shot. The army's attitude during the affair had been less than dignified. The military were becoming increasingly influential in the government. When Asturias and a couple of friends, Epaminondas Quintana and Clemente Marroquín Rojas, published a set of belligerently antimilitaristic articles in an issue of a weekly newspaper they had founded, *Tiempos*

Nuevos, Epaminondas Quintana was cornered and clubbed one evening in an alleyway called Jesus' Lane. The beating nearly cost him his sight and hearing. Asturias heeded the warning; his family shipped him off to London in 1923.

One of the first things he did in London, Asturias recalls—he was there to study economics—was visit the Mayan collection in the British Museum. The objects he saw were like scarecrows out of his own past. They were a mute reminder that although time and distance had effaced the tattered splendors of the old Indian civilization, its vision of the world and its modes of thought were not entirely gone. He had caught glimpses of them at home, dormant, fossilized in an inscrutable population reduced to misery and despair. But their signs could still be read. Perhaps he had begun to find traces of them in his own conscience. The fourteenth of July—Bastille Day—of 1923 he was holidaying in Paris, when wandering through the Sorbonne he came on an announcement for a course taught by Professor George Raynaud, a specialist in Mayan rites and religions. It was a moment of truth. For five years Asturias studied under Professor Raynaud, who had spent a lifetime translating the sacred book of the Mayan Quichés, the *Popol Vuh,* into French. The old Spanish version, dating back to the sixteenth century, showed the accommodating hand of its author, Padre Ximénez, a Jesuit priest who lived in fear of the Inquisition and gave a somewhat biblical rendering of the text. A new version had to be worked out, minus the ballast. Asturias and a Mexican colleague, González de Mendoza, undertook the job, using the French translation as a starting point. It was hard, scholarly work and, as usual in such cases, only meagerly remunerative. To support himself Asturias worked as a journalist. He contributed articles to newspapers in Mexico and Guatemala. He finished work on the *Popol Vuh* in 1925–26.

It was at about this time that, partly as an outlet, he began to write a lot of poetry. In 1925 he published his first volume of poems—in a private edition in Paris—called *Rayito De Estrella* (Little Starbeam). It was occasional verse, written mainly for the ear, full of extravagant sound effects and metaphorical fireworks.

"Phantomime" is the term he coined to describe these poems which attempt to make the phantoms of Indian legend live in wordplay and surrealistic pantomime. (They show a melodic Asturias whose sonorous refrains reflect the verbal preoccupations of the era of Joyce, Fargue, and Gertrude Stein.)

This was a highly productive period for Asturias, one of our most prolific writers. Taking time off from his studies under Professor Raynaud, he had started plotting some sketches based on the tales and legends he remembered from his childhood. The spirit of the old Indian masterpieces he had been reading—the *Popol Vuh*, the *Chilam-Balam*, the *Rabinal-Achi*—came to inhabit them, at times somewhat erratically, and the result was a strange hybrid that the esoteric French poet, Paul Valéry, called "dream poems." His work on them was interrupted in 1928 by a trip to Cuba and Guatemala, where he gave a series of conferences that were later collected under the title *La Arquitectura de la Vida Nueva* (The Building of a New Life). *Leyendas de Guatemala* was finally published in Spain in 1930.

But the most important product of those years—though, for political reasons, it was published only much later, in 1946—was Asturias' first novel, an eloquent and bitter indictment of life under the terroristic Estrada Cabrera regime called *El Señor Presidente*. He had started the book back home in Guatemala, as early as 1922. It began as a story called "Los Mendigos Políticos" (Political Beggars), which the author had prepared for a literary contest. The story accompanied him to Paris, where it increased and multiplied. "A group of friends—César Vallejo and Arturo Uslar Pietri, the Venezuelan novelist—and I used to get together and exchange stories and anecdotes on dictatorships we knew about. I must have kept everything I'd heard under Estrada Cabrera in the back of my mind, and I started to remember things. I used to tell them out loud. It occurred to me then that 'Los Mendigos Políticos' could turn into something much larger, That was how I started to write *El Señor Presidente*. The story was spoken before it was written." Which is why the sound of the human voice can be heard on every page, he explains. The narration has the directness and occasionally the startling unexpected-ness of oral speech. "While I wrote I told myself the story and I wasn't satisfied until it sounded right to me. I could recite whole chapters by memory." It was a book that was in his blood. It rolled straight off the tip of his tongue with what the Chilean poetess Gabriela Mistral called "the ease of a breath of air." It throbbed with the rhythms of thought and feeling, the pulsations and associations of popular speech often captured on the very rim of consciousness. Yet, contrary to appearances—many pages give an effect of disorderliness and slapdash methods—it was not an easy book to write. Before being put away in about 1930, it had been corrected over and over, shelved more than once and recopied from first page to last a total of nineteen times. That its freshness and spontaneity were not entirely lost in the process is a tribute to the author's sure instincts as a storyteller.

Today a lot of the material of *El Señor Presidente*—its rather crude satire, the clumsiness and sentimentality of the love scenes woven into the plot, its loose-jointedness, the lurid extravagance of many episodes, its ghoulish, faceless heroes, and the contrived mechanisms of coincidence that bring them together—seem dated. The book has lost much of its shock value. The worthy General Canales who dies of a heart attack over the betrayal of his frivolous daughter, Camila, when she flouts family pride and prejudice by marrying the President's favorite and right-hand man in a state wedding, no longer seems very believable. The favorite himself, the exotic Cara de Ángel (Angel Face) who is described as "beautiful and evil as Satan," cuts a less convincing figure today than he may have some years ago. What is still fascinating is the Gothic horror of a vision that sets off deep inborn fears as the mind drifts rudderless through a gallery of grotesques that recall the *Caprichos* of Goya and the *Dreams* of Quevedo. The opening pages, rich in surrealistic wordplay, plunge us into the hazy minds of low-life characters—monstrous cripples, beggars, discards, derelicts—squatting on the steps of the Portal del Señor in the shadow of the capital's cathedral. We are in a hallucinatory mental underworld, between sleep and wakefulness, among hair-raising whispers, bloodcurdling tortures and intrigues, all flamboyantly magnified and deformed, as if

they were being sighted through what the Spanish novelist Valle
Inclán, who provided an early model for the genre in *El Tirano
Banderas* (Tyrant Banderas), called his "trick mirror." Basically
what gives the book its power is the sense that its prismatic
reflections only slightly distort a sordid reality well known to
anyone who has walked the slums of Latin-American cities. In
spite of the melodrama, the broken lives that fill the pages of *El
Señor Presidente* seem as gruesomely "timely" today as they did
forty years ago. Guatemala is never mentioned in the book.
Asturias' hooded hangmen inhabit the haunts of the imagination. There, buried alive with all their tantrums, they continue
to dance in their graves. Like the stories of *Leyendas de Guatemala, El Señor Presidente* combats—or eludes—hard fact with
daydream. Its effect is purgative. One thinks of the cruel humor
of Buñuel. In fact, the cinematic quality of *El Señor Presidente*
contributes to making it the grueling ordeal it is. Its bright
images splash eerily across the screen, yet like cinematic images,
they give a curiously paradoxical impression of shallow depth,
diffusing a kind of underwater bleariness. An oppressive clarity—
the effect of overexposure—soon becomes a dark glare.

Asturias stresses the influence of Indian literature on his work.
"The Indian narrative unfolds on two levels: the dream level
and the level of reality. Indian texts portray the everyday reality
of the senses, but at the same time they convey an oneiric,
fabulous, imaginary reality which is seen in as much detail as the
other one."

It is this second reality which prevails in the scenes centering
on the somewhat remote figure of the President, who takes an
ominous bow every now and then, but remains abstract and
symbolic: a totem presiding over a court of miracles, a disembodied voice blaring over a loudspeaker. In spite of his close
acquaintance with the man of flesh and blood, Asturias did not
attempt to draw Estrada Cabrera as a person. The fallen idol he
knew was of no use to him. He was interested in the myth.
Dictators of the Estrada Cabrera type, he says, appear only in
mythological-minded countries: Mexico, Guatemala, Ecuador,
Bolivia, Peru, Venezuela, Cuba, Haiti (the Afro-Indian belt). *El*

Señor Presidente was an attempt to show under what sorts of conditions such a myth could flourish.

The years that followed the writing of *Leyendas de Guatemala* and *El Señor Presidente* were painful for Miguel Ángel Asturias. On his return to Guatemala in 1933, after a trip that took him through Europe and the Middle East, he found himself again fighting dictatorship. This time it was the puritanical regime of Jorge Ubico, which coincided with the worldwide rise of Fascism. One of Ubico's first acts when he took over the government was to abolish the Popular University. Once more the country was reduced to silent resistance. For a decade, apart from some newspaper work—and broadcasts for *El Diario del Aire* (The Newspaper of the Air)—Asturias wrote nothing but poetry. He coined cryptic titles for it: *Émulo Lipolidón* (1935), *Sonetos* (1937), *Alclasán* (1938), *Anoche 10 de Marzo de 1543* (Last Night, 10th of March of 1543, published in 1943). Each volume was a stoic shrug and a grim chuckle. Countries apprenticed in hopelessness learn to thumb their noses at misfortune. Finally in 1944, with Ubico deposed and after a brief transitional period when the country was ruled by a triumvirate, Guatemala's first free elections brought a reformist government to power in the person of the "spiritual socialist," Dr. Arévalo, who had been living in exile in Argentina. A heroic effort was needed to undo the damage of the previous years. The "decade of the revolution" had begun. It issued in a period of travels for Asturias, when he became one of the revolution's most active representatives abroad. In 1945 and 1946 he was in Mexico. There at last he felt he could publish *El Señor Presidente*. From 1947 on, for several years, Asturias represented his country as Minister-Counselor to the Embassy in Buenos Aires. During the whole of 1948 he worked on his second novel, *Hombres de Maíz* (Men of Corn).

If *El Señor Presidente* continues to be an interesting relic, it is probably for *Hombres de Maíz* that Asturias will be remembered. The book had been incubating for ages. In it we are frankly in the timeless realm of magic and mythology. The book represents an enormous creative effort, and was written, says Asturias, with a sort of rhapsodic intensity. The incantatory, trance-like quality of the prose registers the author's determination to tap below consciousness, to achieve modes of thought and forms of speech capable of evoking the ghosts of ancestral memories. This is no mere semantic game. Asturias was in search of what he calls "an American idiom." He realized that flowery rhetoric, ornament, and academic elegance had been the curse of our novel. Our writers, with their nostalgia for Castilian purism, had been too civilized. Their imitations of Spanish "carpentry," as Miguel de Unamuno called it, had alienated them from their language, whose resources had hardly been tapped. A housecleaning was in order, and Asturias took it upon himself to wield the broom. He deliberately broke with the mental structures of the Spanish tradition. He wanted to revitalize the language, not simply, as might have been the danger, by making it absorb regional terms but by restructuring it from the inside. He is one of our first writers—they are only a handful, even today—to realize the huge potential of the spoken tongue. In his work language is thematic; it becomes a form of research, of inner plumbing that disrupts set patterns of syntax to draw its rhythms from thought and feeling. The whole sense of Asturias' work has been in his unremitting effort to find a voice to fit his vision. "In *Hombres de Maíz*," he says, "the Spanish we speak approaches an outer limit beyond which it becomes something else. There are moments when the language is not just a language but acquires what we might call a biological dimension." For Asturias, language lives a borrowed life. Words are echoes or shadows of living beings. The faith in the power of words, as Octavio Paz has pointed out in one of his essays, is reminiscent of an ancient belief that words are doubles of objects in the external world and are therefore an animated part of it. The rhythms of speech are instinctual and subliminal. And the subliminal is close to the mythical. "Rhythm," says Paz, "is a return to original time." It is at the source of myth and ritual, which lie latent in it, waiting to be tapped. And myth and ritual are archetypal forms of a people's ethos, inklings of its image of the world. Prelogical associations form a sort of code in which an author like Asturias, apprenticed to their sorcery, deciphers secret messages, hidden or forgotten realities. In Asturias, metaphor is magic; it conjures up the unconscious.

Says Asturias: "In *Hombres de Maíz* the spoken word has a religious significance. The characters of the book are never alone, but always surrounded by the great voices of nature, the voices of the rivers, of the mountains. The background is no longer mere theatrical scenery as it was, for instance, in the Romantic novel. The landscape has become dynamic; it has a life of its own." A life that strikes a deep chord in a novelist like Asturias. For him, landscapes are as eloquent as people. Nature's signs are a system of correspondences in which sounds and sights are organically related to scents and colors. His contacts with his land are passional. "That's why I have to keep going back to Guatemala. Because when I'm away I stop hearing its voice. Not so much the voice of the people as that of the landscape. I start losing my feel for it, and then I can't handle it so well any more."

To recapture lost voices he resorts to the familiar method of automatic writing. With the exception of *El Señor Presidente*, which was written with deliberation, chapter by chapter, all his books, starting with *El Alhajadito* (Little Boy Blue), a prose poem that was begun in the twenties, abandoned, then finished in 1961, have to some extent or other benefited from this method. Asturias prepares his books carefully before he sits down to write. But then, having recited them inwardly until he knows them by heart, he lets himself go.

"When the book is ripe and ready I get down to work. In the first version I let out everything that crosses my mind. I type, because if I wrote by hand I wouldn't be able to read my writing afterwards. I work steadily, usually from five till nine in the morning. The first version is completely automatic. I go straight through it, without ever turning back to see what I've left behind. When it's done I put it aside for a month; then I take it out and look it over. I start rewriting, cutting, changing. With what I have left I work out the second version. What I obtain from automatic writing is the mating or juxtaposition of words which, as the Indians say, have never met before. Because that's

how the Indian defines poetry. He says Poetry is where words
meet for the first time."

The Indian, says Asturias, uses words sparingly—and cau-
tiously. Like hoary Gaspar Ilóm, the legendary hero of *Hombres
de Maíz,* he says what needs to be said, nothing more. "The
Indian is very laconic. For him words are sacred. They have an
entirely different dimension from the one they have in the
Spanish language." In the *Popol Vuh* and the old Indian texts
words not only have a ritual value but are actually elements of
worship. They are the nourishment of the gods who feed on
nothing else. The Mayan gods created man expressly for that
purpose: to receive his praise. His words were their sustenance.
"That's why, before they created the warriors, the priests, or the
wise men, the gods created the artists: the flutists, the singers and
dancers, and the painters. Because the only thing that amuses the
gods, the only thing that can relieve them of their boredom and
tedium is art. Therefore, for the Indians, words are fundamental,
magic elements endowed not only with powers of witchcraft and
enchantment but also with miraculous healing powers." Here is
where the euphonious discursiveness of the Spanish language and
the ceremonious starkness of Indian speech part company. "The
Indians' primitive script was a form of ideographic writing—like
that of the Chinese, the Spaniards used to say, when they saw the
first hieroglyphics. For the Indians writing and painting are one
and the same. They say so themselves in their old manuscripts:
'Because it has been painted it is no longer seen. Because it has
been painted it is no longer read. Because it has been painted it
is no longer sung.' In other words, because it has been written."
For the Indian, even today, words capture the essence of things.
To be able to put an exact name on something, says Asturias,
means to reveal it, to bare it, to strip it of its mystery. "That's
why in the villages of Guatemala all the men answer to the name
of Juan, all the women to the name of María. Nobody knows
their real names. If a person knew the name of a man's wife, he
could possess her, in other words, snatch her from her husband."

Asturias has learned to use words for this purpose: to grasp the fundamentals of things, to penetrate the shadow world and expose underlying meanings. Words are landmarks and signposts. They can be fetishes. Not, says Asturias, that he uses words with any conscious strategy. "I think if I had it would have come out mannered and contrived. But words at certain moments are like needles on a compass. Language sometimes is a way one has of approaching landscapes, people, and situations. For instance, in *El Señor Presidente* there are many instances where words have an important role to play, especially in setting the pace for the narrative. There are alliterations, refrains, and another fundamental element: onomatopoeia. Onomatopoeias are an important ingredient of all Indian languages; they were a way the Indians had of reproducing many natural phenomena. The Indian also used something else: what we call parallelism. Parallelism is the reiteration of the same thought uttered with different words within a single paragraph. Of course this device occurs not only in Indian literature, but also in primitive Spanish literature. You find it in the medieval romances, which date from a time when the Spanish language wasn't yet fully stabilized. Parallelism has been very important for paleographers, because often in the exegesis of old Indian texts, when a line was obscure, the repetitions that supported it helped us decipher it. The Indians were also very much given to something you find in my work: the multiplication of syllables within a word to give a particular sensation or impression." Asturias gives the example of *árbol* (tree), which the Spanish augmentative raises to *arbolón,* the Indian superlative to *arbolonón.*

"Language," says Asturias, "presents many problems for the Latin-American writer. We have the eternal problem of *criollismo* [regionalism]. There were times, and it's still true in some cases today, when our authors incorporated a lot of local words into their writing, thereby, of course, practically slamming the door shut in the reader's face. I've gradually tried to broaden the base of my language to put it within reach of as many people as possible. The wordplays in books like *El Señor Presidente, El Alhajadito,* and *Leyendas de Guatemala* were first tries, preparations for the task I was to set myself in *Hombres de Maíz.* In

Hombres de Maíz the novel form acquires something of the character of a popular epic. Words play a deeper role. *Hombres de Maíz* explores the hidden dimensions of words: their resonance, their shadings, their fragrance. Because our problem is to create a literature which speaks neither of asphalt, nor glass, nor concrete. It must speak of the freshness of the earth, the seed, the tree. Our literature has to give a new scent, a new color and vibration." Its cadences must fit its myths. "And when we speak of myths we speak of a living thing. I have a feeling myths are a little bit like malaria. Malaria appears as a headache, a stomachache; it festers and spreads. Which is more or less what myths do. They die hard." Asturias stresses, however, that he is not a mythmaker. "We must avoid letting our continent be judged solely for its myths." Myths exist everywhere. Asturias is interested primarily in their dynamics. They are a living aspect of the popular imagination, therefore vuluable passwords or master keys into the understanding of certain social realities.

Hombres de Maíz is a complete Indian cosmography. The tribal community of Gaspar Ilóm, proud chieftain descended from the old blowpipe hunters, is in the throes of disintegration. The cause is the conflict between the traditional way of life of a people who grow sacred corn for ceremony and sustenance and the gangrene of mercenary outsiders who want to exploit the land for profit. Gaspar Ilóm, symbolic embodiment of ancestral forces—he speaks "for all those who have spoken, who speak and who will speak"—has been poisoned during a banquet by the men of Chalo Godoy, a sergeant in the service of the forces of "progress," and, according to the lore of the land, has entered a timeless existence from where he hovers over his people, clamoring for revenge. The cyclic recurrence of human life condemns his descendants to re-enact his tragedy. In a world of fluid identities, they are his reflected images. Those who transgress by succumbing to the temptations of the new way of life have a terrible retribution visited on them. Thus, Tomás Machojón, who has strayed from the fold by marrying a white woman, the Vaca Manuela Machojón, has his son taken from him; he meets a violent death as he goes up in flames wandering after the image of the lost youth, a great horseman who rides his horse to death in a burning cornfield. Children die; crops fail; wells and rivers dry up. Wives—cursed with "ambulatory sickness," also known as the "spiderweb walk"—become errant. Their siren shapes appear to travelers on a high cliff where "the heart tires and the bones ache from the cold that reigns there at midday and at all other times," to lure them into the abyss. Such is the lot of Goyo Yic, the protagonist of one of the three or four parallel tales that make up the book. He is a blind man who has been abandoned by his sinful wife, María Tecún. His search for her takes him first to a witch doctor, who removes his cataracts, then to the cliff where he narrowly avoids being drawn into the precipice that opens at his feet. Goyo Yic, personally blameless, suffers from the cumulative guilt of the community. A fault comparable to original sin has opened his eyes. He is man after the fall, stripped of his innocence. His problem is how to recognize his vanished wife now that he has eyes to see; he only remembers her voice. And that is his loss. Because "the man who truly loves does not see his beloved. She is the flower of the *amate*, which only the blind see." The *amate* is a type of fig tree that provided the Indians with a milky resin and bark out of which they manufactured their scrolls. It has no flower. "The popular belief," says Asturias, "is that the flower is hidden inside the fruit. It blooms only in the eyes of the blind." It is, of course, a symbol of love, but also, perhaps, of occult truths: the truths from which Goyo Yic has now been banished. His heartbroken pilgrimage through the mountains—drinking himself into oblivion from a huge gourd of illegally distilled firewater—leads him into disgrace and decay. He becomes a wandering peddler, a walking ruin, and finally, in a touching scene into which Asturias has poured all his tenderness for the wounded humanity of his people, confesses to a friend, as they shamble along the dusty road, with the wind in their faces, that he has given up all hope of ever recovering his woman—or his roots—again: "Before I was looking for her in order to find her; now, in order not to find her." The memory of love, for him, has become a vague qualm. What is lost is gone forever.

Hombres de Maíz is a turbulent, disarticulated, free-flowing book, full of laughing skulls and dancing skeletons. Says Asturias: "In *Hombres de Maíz* there are no concessions. There is no story line. Whether things are clear or not doesn't matter. They are simply given."

We are in the realm of portents and miraculous cures. Time is circular. The past and present, the actual and the imaginary, coexist in the minds of the protagonists. Ritual gestures, expressions, and events recur at irregular and unpredictable intervals. The "telluric" element—the voice of the landscape—is ever-present. As in all of Asturias' books, some of the best scenes are humorous, often lovingly malicious, portrayals of village life: feasts, holidays, weddings, drinking bouts, dancing sprees, religious festivals, market days, wakes and funerals. The book would be incomplete without the usual amusing caricatures of eccentric foreigners drifting through the backlands: Padre Valentín Urdáñez, a Spanish cleric reminiscent of the colonial priests that came to the New World with the Conquistadors, who keeps a journal in the style of the old chronicles of Bernal Díaz; Don Casualidón, another priest, a greedy schemer blinded by a lust for gold that affords the author an opportunity to insert a little moral tale on the vanity of worldly goods; the mythomaniac German expatriate Deféric, with his theory on how the Indians "sacrifice" themselves to feed their legend; the famous Northern visitor, O'Neill (Eugene?) and his fabled love for a local maiden, whose shrine has become a much-celebrated tourist attraction.

At the root of the Indian's ambiguous outlook on reality, says Asturias, lies his concept of the duality of all things: fact and fiction, being and becoming. For the Indian, man is a transient being, a bird of passage, momentarily embodied in his individual self, from which he aspires to be released in order to join the whole again. His separateness and isolation are an anguish to him. Therefore his constant nostalgia for a lost paradise somewhere in his dim past, a land "beyond"—symbolized by the figure of Woman, the eternal wellspring and Earth Mother, "name clamored by all"—that the Nahuatl poets called "the land where the flowers bloom." Man on earth is a mere puppet, a

shadow of his true self. The Indian, because of his fear of isolation, is an eminently communal being. "There are no loners
among the Indians," says Asturias. The lone Indian suffers from
a sort of "metaphysical" sadness, a paralysis of the will that he
calls Zahorí and describes as "the moment when a man is alone
with himself under the sun." His solitude, says Asturias, is not
introspective; oneness, for him, is depersonalization. His concept
of himself is such that he easily migrates—or transmigrates—in
his thoughts to enter other beings or regress through time to his
legendary origins.

"The Indian lives backward, not forward. The Mayans had
computed time three hundred thousand years back into the past.
But when they looked ahead they thought in terms of periods
that spanned no more than twenty years. Every twenty years they
thought the end of the world was due. They held the belief that
man had lived through different solar cycles. We are now living
the fifth solar cycle, which they represented as the sun in motion.
They called the sun 'the one that moves' and equated it with the
heart in the body. Therefore the great hecatombs in the times of
the Aztecs. The heart was sacrificed to feed the sun. They were
increasingly afraid that the sun would come to a stop one day;
then everything would collapse. Historically speaking, their fears
were probably inspired by memories of the great natural disasters
of the neolithic era."

The Indian's yearning for his immemorial past finds concrete
expression in the myth of the Nahual, which appears again and
again in the pages of *Hombres de Maíz*. The Nahual is a man's
protective spirit, a sort of guardian angel; it takes the form of
whatever animal the man has been identified with at birth. His
animal-soul, one might call it. Every man longs to be joined in
intimate and transcendent union with his Nahual. Such is the
case of Nicho Aquino, the village mailman, whose Nahual is the
coyote. Nicho Aquino is lost in the mountains on a rainy day. He
is rescued by one of the Brujos de las Luciérnagas—ancients or
sages with visionary powers (as the "glowworm" in their name
indicates), descendants of the ancient seers who made fire out of
flintstone and dwelt in tents made of the skins of virgin does.

The mailman, who has become worthy of reincarnation and dis-
embodiment, is initiated to secret rites that will strip him of the
weight of individuality and propel him into the generic flow. It
is an awesome experience for him. Batting blinded eyes, he enters
a deep cave and is led on a vertiginous descent into the underworld of Xibalba, land of his ancestors, where he will "dream of
sights he never saw, of trips he never took, paradises he never
knew." The drop down into the bowels of the earth is at once a
return to instinct—the Nahual—and a passage into immortality.
Nicho Aquino gradually discards his outer skin: "the shell, the
puppet." He is told that "life beyond the hills is as real as any
other life" and that in the depths of the earth he will find "the
secret way." He is put through a ceremonial re-enactment of the
steps of man's creation as recorded in the old traditions. First
man is made of crumbling mud, then of breakable wood, finally
of fruitful corn. Nicho Aquino has borne holy witness to the
unfathomable. He has confronted his past, assumed the history of
his race, and henceforth will be invulnerable in war, invincible
in love, destined for riches on earth and stardom in heaven.

To what extent Asturias has been successful in rendering
Indian modes of thought and feeling in *Hombres de Maíz* is hard
to say. He speaks no Indian language and admits that his incursions into Indian psychology are intuitive and speculative at best.
But that, in spite of the many factual errors that a pedantic
anthropologist could point out in his work, does not invalidate
them. Intuition is a surer road than scientific analysis in these
matters. "I heard a lot, assumed a bit more, and invented the
rest," he says. But his invention was not arbitrary. After all, in
establishing the climate for his inventions, he was projecting
shadows from the back of his own mind. From the point of view
of language, the results are mixed, not always entirely free of
literary echoes. But almost every page is full of the kind of otherworldly intimations that indicate that the author was listening
closely to his inner voices. There are exalted and limpid moments in the book, which often shines with a spiritual glow rare
in our literature.

"Stories are like rivers. They roll on, sweeping everything they can along with them," says Asturias, who had barely published *Hombres de Maíz* (1949) when he was already hard at work on something else. In 1950 he published *Viento Fuerte* (Strong Wind), the first volume of a tumultuous trilogy dealing with the exploitation of Guatemala's banana plantations by the United Fruit Company. There is much of the treatise, and more of the pamphlet, in *Viento Fuerte,* which—oddly—focuses on the efforts of two idealistic Americans, Lester Stone and Leland Foster, to humanize the exploitation of the banana lands by turning it into a cooperative venture of benefit to the local population. The fact that Asturias chose two Americans as his protagonists—a perilous undertaking that lays the work open to questions of verisimilitude—throws a curious light on his intentions. One suspects he is doing his best to shy away from the tendentiousness that characterizes this literature, bending backward to be fair, as it were. But in vain. (In spite of their folkloric ways, which endear them to the reader, Lester Stone and Leland Foster are outsize silhouettes that never quite come to life.)

"The idea for the book came in 1949. I was in Guatemala on a visit, and I realized then that I had been out of contact with certain aspects of Guatemalan life. I'd lived in the mountains, I'd lived with the Indians, I'd lived in the city; but now some friends invited me to stay with them in Tiquisate and Bananera to have a look at the banana plantations. I was in both places, and both of them provided me with the setting for *Viento Fuerte.* At the same time I read a report that appears in a book called *El Imperio del Banano* (The Banana Empire). It was done by a couple of American newspapermen who were sent to Central America to study the policies of the United Fruit Company. The report of these American newspapermen is almost identical to the one presented by Lester Stone at a meeting of the company's board of directors in *Viento Fuerte.* Of course in *Viento Fuerte* there are also a series of portraits and episodes taken straight from Guatemalan life."

These "popular scenes," as usual full of humor and tenderness, are probably the best in the book. But they are secondary, often sketchy, rather carelessly thrown in simply as décor.

Taken as a whole, *Viento Fuerte*, its sequel *El Papa Verde* (The Green Pope, 1954), and the volume that rounds out the trilogy, *Los Ojos de los Enterrados* (The Eyes of the Buried, 1960), have the plaintive—and sometimes abrasive—belligerence of protest literature. The frankly polemic intent produces the usual aberrations—among others, a sort of panic atmosphere that attempts to extort sympathy from the reader by loading issues that trigger automatic reflexes. To expose and denounce is to simplify, which means falling into artistic disgrace. There is an artificial setup, a sort of counterfeit reality, that never quite rings true. The author himself is divided between art and argument and the result is a hybrid product which has neither integrity nor authenticity. One might add that the writer who takes sides always manages to be in the right. This is one of the many ways one has of playing it safe. The position taken absolves the writer of any real attempt at depth, and in fact, of course, it disengages him from his material. He is no longer involved in it. He uses it as a prop to support an a priori argument. When the components of an equation are all known in advance, the results are bound to be tautological.

Asturias admits there may be some validity in these objections to *Viento Fuerte*. "But I think the term 'protest literature' simplifies things too much. Let's turn the problem around to see it as I do. I think all great Latin-American literature has been a literature of social protest." He uses the term broadly. Protest, as he sees it, is not a way out of things, but into the thick of them. "For me," he has said more than once, "the novel is the only means I have of making the needs and aspirations of my people known to the world."

Asturias sees a fundamental difference between the aesthetics of the Latin-American novelist and those of his European counterpart. The European novelist, he says, has to a certain extent overcome the pull of nature. Therefore he can devote himself to exploring the complex problems of individual psychology. On the other hand, the domain of the Latin-American novelist is still to a considerable extent the "green hell" populated by the "human plants" of the Naturalist school. Our fiction is therefore largely a social and economic geography of the continent. Its mission is to digest, evaluate, and criticize.

"Latin-American literature is never gratuitous. It is a literature of combat. It has always been that. I'm referring to our great literature. If we go back to the period of the Conquest, we find what I'd call the first great Latin-American novel, the *Crónica de la Conquista de Nueva España* by Bernal Díaz del Castillo. Why does Bernal Díaz write this book? To complain to the King that after all his years of service to the Crown he has been forgotten. Perhaps here protest is not very effective because it is too explicit." But then came colonial literature, which was relatively highly developed in Guatemala, the General Captaincy of the Viceroyalty of Central America, consequently the site of culturally active monasteries and the first Central American university. "Around 1770 a Guatemalan poet, Rafael Landívar, published a work in Modena, in Latin, called *Rusticatio Mexicana*. In this work Landívar, a Jesuit who was expelled from Guatemala in the times of King Charles III, protests the building of great European fortunes at the expense of the riches of the American continent. In other words, our literature was born under the sign of protest. Born from a conflict that I think is real, not invented; because Landívar, like the rest of us, was aware of the exploitation of the Indian. Continuing along this road to Romantic or pre-Romantic times, we find the same struggle going on at the time of Independence." A case in point is the Argentine historical novel, *Amalia,* by José Mármol, one of several written toward the middle of the nineteenth century to protest despotism and dictatorship. "Then we have Sarmiento's *Facundo* which," says Asturias, perhaps stretching a point, "is another of the great Latin-American novels. And we could go on this way listing any number of books whose purpose has been social protest."

Says Asturias, whose words acquire a special pathos and relevance at a time when most of his literary countrymen live in exile, withdrawn into poetry: "I think the function of our literature up until now has been to expose the suffering of our people. I think it's difficult for this type of literature to be purely literary, to be concerned merely with what is beautiful or pleasing to the eyes or ears."

Not that Asturias neglects this aspect of his craft. Even his United Fruit trilogy contains numerous passages of magic and mythology, including a mythical portrait of the Green Pope—the big boss of the concern, headquartered in a New York skyscraper—whose ominous remoteness has sinister overtones distinctly reminiscent of those of the figure of the President in *El Señor Presidente*. But the Asturias of 1950, whose militancy is not very different from that of the proletarian novelists in the United States in the twenties and thirties, is no longer just the skillful literary craftsman he used to be. If some feel his talent has partly gone to waste with the years, it is because he has had more pressing concerns than literature. In 1951, a time of national emergency, he played an active role in the history of his country.

1951 was the year Jacobo Árbenz, Arévalo's successor, came to power in Guatemala. Árbenz, a retired colonel who had been immersed in the fight against dictator Ubico, inherited Arévalo's reform programs. His job was to implement them. "Arévalo's presidency had been the time of revolutionary laws, as they were called, although there was nothing revolutionary about them, because in England, for instance, these same laws date back to about 1880. They were social security laws, labor laws, there was the beginning of a land distribution, under the agrarian reform law." In spite of strong resistance to these laws, "Arévalo managed to complete his term, although he had to put down some twenty or thirty attempted uprisings. Then came Jacobo Árbenz. I think certain circles in the country let out a big sigh of relief when Árbenz was elected, because they said: 'A colonel. . . . All army men can be bought.' But it was the other way around."

In 1952, while Asturias was engaged in a diplomatic mission in Paris, the agrarian reform law was stirring up trouble in Guatemala. "Árbenz expropriated some lands that belonged to the United Fruit Company. The company wanted to be compensated for the full amount at which they estimated the value of the land, whereas the government decided it would pay the amount at which the land had been declared for purposes of taxation.

The dispute was taken to court. The government won the case. Soon embassies and chancelleries were involved. And one thing led to another. The United Fruit Company started to spread the word that the Árbenz government was Communist. There followed the Conference of American States in Caracas, at which Foster Dulles introduced his famous resolution condemning international Communism. Guatemala voted against it; Mexico and Argentina abstained. Undoubtedly the invasion of Guatemala was already planned. Árbenz cabled me in Paris asking me to return and sent me as ambassador to El Salvador (1953). It was a difficult post, because it was across the Salvadorean border that the American-backed Castillo Armas invasion was expected to arrive. I was able to arrange things so Castillo Armas couldn't come in through there. He had to cross in from Honduras, through an inhospitable, mountainous region. He arrived with eight hundred men, rented and borrowed, some from Honduras, others from Santo Domingo, a few Spaniards, Panamanians and Venezuelans, and some Guatemalans. Guatemala immediately put ten thousand men under arms. This was where things stood when the bombings of the capital and other towns started, in an attempt to panic the population. In fact, Castillo Armas had already been defeated and, according to report, ordered to withdraw with his men. An inter-American conference was being prepared in Brazil to apply economic sanctions on Guatemala. But they weren't needed, because U.S. Ambassador Purefoy had been pulling strings and he'd done a good job of it: the army had turned against the government."

This is the situation described in Asturias' collection of stories, *Weekend En Guatemala* (1956), a book written in pain and outrage, practically in the heat of battle. He realizes it stands up poorly as a work of fiction; but then, at the time, the burning issues it deals with afforded him little distance and perspective. The government had collapsed. Árbenz, a victim of bribed betrayal, had taken refuge in an embassy. Castillo Armas had won the day. In 1954, a bitter date for Miguel Ángel Asturias, he was stripped of citizenship, and began eight years of exile in Buenos Aires.

Since then, until very recently, when there was a favorable change of government, Asturias had been home only on short visits, on tourist visas. He made a living in Buenos Aires as a correspondent for *El Nacional,* a Caracas paper, and as an adviser to the Editorial Losada, an Argentine publisher. In 1962, after the fall of the liberal Frondizi government in Argentina, political pressures forced Asturias to move to Genoa. There he contributed his services to a cultural exchange organization called Columbianum. He traveled a lot, ran for the presidency of the Pen Club in 1965—he lost the place to Arthur Miller—and was frequently seen at writers' conferences and symposia. In 1965 there were rumors—later confirmed—that he was a candidate for the Nobel Prize. Not winning it must have come as a great disappointment to him, not so much for its prestige value as for the mobility it would have given him. Blanca, who could not predict the next turn of the diplomatic wheel (now, in August, 1966, Asturias has just been named Ambassador in France), told us the prize would have conferred a seal of immunity on him at home. "They wouldn't dare bother us then," she said wistfully, with a distant glance out across the bay, toward the land where the flowers bloom.

Over the years, alongside his novels, Asturias has kept up a constant production of poetry, which has appeared under such titles as *Ejercicios Poéticos Sobre Temas de Horacio* (1951), *Bolívar* (1955), and, more recently, *Clarivigilia Primaveral* (Springtime Moonlight Watch), inspired by those Indian themes that he has always handled with such authority and affection (he has edited an anthology of pre-Columbian verse). His verse is still occasional. It is worth mentioning mainly because, as he says, it has been a sort of language workshop for him.

"I started out writing poetry, not prose. In 1918 I was already writing poems. But I didn't publish anything then. I didn't consider myself one of the best poets of my generation, which was an outstanding one in that respect in Guatemala, though many of its best representatives got lost along the way, died or stopped writing. . . . So I turned to prose. I went on writing poetry, but I kept it to myself; it was something more personal and intimate.

In 1948, when I was in Buenos Aires, Rafael Alberti and Toñio Salazar, who were there at the time, were enthusiastic about some of my poems, so they arranged to have an anthology published by the Editorial Argos. It was called *Sien de Alondra* (Lark's Brow). Then, later in my career, I had the idea of trying to write poetry with Indian themes. It would be something very simple and direct. In *Clarivigilia Primaveral,* which started out as prose, something in the vein of *Leyendas de Guatemala,* then became free verse, I think I've mastered this discipline. I'd been practicing it for a long time, but mostly as an exercise. But a very important exercise for me. Poetry has been my laboratory. And there's something else. I think Latin-American poets have a big role to play in our novel, when they're able to handle it. Because our novels exhale poetry. They have a lyric quality that raises them above themselves."

A word might be said about Asturias' theater, which, though scanty and limited in scope, has also been a release for him. He mentions *Soluna* (1955), a sort of Indian miracle play that exploits the wonders and prodigies of the popular imagination. *Chantage* and *Dique Seco* (Dry Dock) are polemic. He is particularly fond of *La Audiencia de los Confines* (name of the high court of justice in colonial times), which centers on the benign historical figure of Fray Bartolomé de las Casas, an enlightened Jesuit priest who fought bravely in his day for the abolition of Indian slavery in the New World. Though *Audiencia* (1957) is in many ways a period piece, the curious thing is that when it was first staged in Guatamala by a student group in 1961 it caused a local scandal. "The public, the press, said it was against the Church, against the rich, that it was frankly leftist. Yet it was nothing but Fray Bartolomé's words, slightly transcribed to modernize the language. It was precisely the speech he delivered before the high court several centuries ago."

Asturias does not presume to be able to judge whether his theatrical work is stageworthy. Though he allowed a volume of his *Collected Theater* to appear in 1964, he feels ill at ease in the medium. "The theater," he says, "is from the mouth outward. The novel is from the lips inward."

Nowhere is this more evident than in his latest novel, *Mulata de Tal* (roughly: A Certain Mulata, 1963), where he takes up the thread of mythological adventure he began unraveling in *Hombres de Maíz*. As in *El Alhajadito,* the early prose poem he finished in 1961 (which contains several children's stories), we are in the realm of pure fancy. The frenzied metaphorical language that transfigured *Hombres de Maíz* has given way to something lean, graceful, and straightforward, animistic as a fable, mysterious as a fairy tale with jungle beanstalks. The book rambles and occasionally, especially toward the somewhat muddled end, things seem out of focus and the reader gets lost in the maze. But perhaps we are meant to be ogling the world through a broken looking glass. The story unfolds with the deceptive simplicity of nonsense verse. The author, in full song, gives free flight to his imagination. He hands himself over to his voices, which take command and improvise at will. If the characters seem to get out of control, it is because they live autonomously, roaming at random among the intricate webs they have woven for themselves.

Says Asturias: "I think my language in *Mulata de Tal* has a new dimension. In *Hombres de Maíz* it was still overloaded with religious and mythical terminology. *Mulata,* on the other hand, is done in popular language, as a sort of verbal picaresque, with that wit and whimsy simple people have for spinning out phrases and playing with concepts. I think the first thing we have to notice in *Mulata de Tal,* rather than the plot of story line, is its invisible elements, its purely enigmatic content. Basically *Mulata* is a retelling of the myth of the sun and the moon. We say the sun and the moon cannot share the same bed because if they did the sun as a male and the moon as a female would breed monstrous children. That's why when the Mulata marries the protagonist, Yumí, she never shows him her face when they make love. She always gives him her back. We don't know why, whether because she has abnormal tastes or for some other reason. The Indian texts say the gods dealt out severe punishments to those who made love 'facing the wrong way.' We don't know whether the reference is to homosexuality or simply to abnormal posture. Besides being a popular picaresque, *Mulata* has that astral dimension, you might call it. You have those two astral bodies orbiting without ever joining. The Mulata is the lunar principle. The starting point of the story is a legend popular in Guatemala: the poor man who comes into riches by selling his wife to the devil. It's a very widespread legend in Guatemala. As to what the devil does with the woman, there are different versions. In one, he makes off with her, then he returns disguised as a woman to punish the man who sold him his wife. The man falls in love with the devil and the devil makes life impossible for him. Then the man yearns for the good little woman he used to have. . . .

"The Mulata herself is a figment I invented. I called her Mulata in order not to use the word Mestiza, because it didn't seem to me the mixture of bloods was enough in Mestiza. I avoided Zamba, which would have given a combination of Indian and Negro bloods, because I didn't think the term would suggest that special grace of movement you find in the Mulata. . . ."

As for the dwarfs in the book—Yumí's wife turns into one— they are also common figures of the popular imagination in Guatemala. The old Indian chieftains used to surround themselves with dwarfs who performed the role of buffoons or court jesters. Other popular figures in *Mulata* are a group of hectic dancers who have taken on the appearance of wild boars.

Asturias adds embellishments to each legend, but respects its basic terms, careful not to step out of bounds and break the illusion of verisimilitude he attempts to maintain throughout. Thus, when Yumí's pact with the devil backfires and the whole world blows up in his face, we are in the presence of an event that has its correspondence in reality. "There are many cases in our countries of people who have been cleaned out overnight by an earthquake or an erupting volcano." The text contains oblique allusions to this natural calamity.

Soon we are in Tierra Paulita, a sort of fabulous Never-Never Land where Yumí and his elfin wife have gone to become healers.

"The parts of the book having to do with the Catholic Church are interesting, and typical. Because these are the Catholic churches in our countries. It's a type of Catholicism very much mixed with local beliefs, where the Indian officiators often wield more authority than the priest in his own church. In *Mulata* we have a priest surrounded by the forces of evil. Basically, that's what the novel is all about. The Indian forces of evil: Cabracán, the god of earthquakes, and Huracán, the god of hurricanes, want to wipe man off the face of the earth. For them man is an intruder in the universe. They want to destroy him. That's what we might call the Indian viewpoint. But Catholicism has a different concept of evil. Satan does not want man destroyed. On the contrary, he wants man to multiply in order to increase the population of hell, if we can put it that way. So naturally the two conceptions clash."

An example of the interweaving of conflicting mythologies can be found in the Dance of the Giants, in which Gargantuas the Brobdingnags behead one of their brethren, who turns out to be a representation of St. John the Baptist. The climax of the novel is an apocalyptic holocaust that devastates the land, leveling man and beast. There is a vision of a "white fire" that could be flaming brimstone or an atomic blaze.

In *Mulata*, alas, an old Asturias weakness is more evident than it is in some of his previous work. Asturias relies too heavily on his senses. He is not a thinker, and his work tends to be conceptually weak. There are times when he seems not to know too well what he is doing or where he is going. He lets the irrational get out of hand, and then meanings are lost. In *Mulata* he lumbers and strays. But his impish humor carries many good pages. He himself feels the net result is positive. He says he thinks he has come close to fulfilling his lifelong ambition of achieving a satisfying synthesis of the material and mythical worlds of his people. Even so, he has a staggering amount of works planned for the next few years.

"I've started a series of stories like those of *Weekend in Guatemala*," he tells us, "except that these will be called *Los Juanes*. I have Juan Girador (John the Spinner), Juan Hormiguero (John the Anteater), Juan el Encadenado (John in Chains). They're popular stories people tell which I haven't been able to fit into a novel. At the same time I want to publish a series of five new novels on Guatemala, also made up of stories I remember, like those in *Leyendas*." Then there is a novel, provisionally entitled *El Bastardo,* that belongs partly to the United Fruit cycle. "*El Bastardo* is going to be the novel of my generation, of the twenties, of my student years. I have to reconstruct that whole era and the life we led in those days. It belongs in the United Fruit cycle in the sense that it will attempt to show how the Guatemalan petite bourgeoisie defeated its own purposes in contributing to the failure of the revolution."

Asturias, like Carpentier, feels optimistic, not only about his own work but about the future of Latin-American literature in general. Our literature is young, but healthy, vigorous, and prodigal in its manifestations. The Latin-American artist is one of the few who can still feel he is tapping ancient sources of inspiration that may yet yield new forms of expression. "We can contribute an earthiness, a natural, animal force, a violence of new blood," says Asturias, "that will enrich Western culture and broaden man's understanding of himself."

If much of his own work is topical and therefore, perhaps, perishable, he finds nothing in that to discourage him. It corresponds, he says with unaffected simplicity, to a certain stage in the development of our culture. With the quiet wisdom of an old Mayan Buddha he assures us: "the future will bring something else. There will be more mature or able novelists who will present issues more broadly or dramatically. I see my work as an experience I undertook without any explicit or exclusive literary intention, but rather as what you might call a mandate of fate. I didn't want to be a writer. I didn't decide it. I've tried to find a way to express the things I've felt. I think my experience will be of use to others who want to work with the primitive Indian elements of our world, with aspects of popular life, using them in measured doses, as I have, without falling into the excesses of *criollismo* or, on the other hand, settling for cosmopolitanism. During the years I spent in Paris I saw many cosmopolitan writers who wrote about Paris, about Versailles. Ever since those days I felt it was my calling and my duty to write about America,

which would someday be of interest to the world. I think in the
future other novelists and poets will find more forceful, effective,
or eloquent ways of doing what I have done. I think for all of us
writing is a matter of going through a certain type of experience. . . . Among the Indians there's a belief in the Gran
Lengua [Big Tongue]. The Gran Lengua is the spokesman for
the tribe. And in a way that's what I've been: the spokesman for
my tribe."

III

Jorge Luis Borges, or the Consolation by Philosophy

OF a tribe all his own is this artisan and antiquarian who has become an almost legendary figure—a missing person—in our literature. His existence has sometimes been questioned, if never really doubted, for he seems to have evaporated through the years. He is a wisp of a man, almost blind, frail as a shadow at nightfall; a man of strong and often arbitrary convictions, in life as well as literature, but so mild of manner, so gentle and shy, that one could almost walk through him in the street. Even in his set habits, he seems unpredictable. Strangers who find him tapping his cane on the edge of the curb in heavy traffic will sometimes help him across at a corner, only to have his translucent features suddenly vanish as he blows away in the wind like a page torn out of some old book. Which he may well be. "Life and death have been lacking in my life," he says, with the slight affectation of dilettantism he has always cultivated, perhaps a remnant of the intellectual dandyism of his early days in the aristocratic Barrio

Norte. This "indigence" he offers as an explanation for his "laborious love" for minutiae. "Few things have happened to me, and many have I read," he says; and: "I am infested with literature." There is some doubt as to whether he wrote his books or they wrote him. Perhaps he is a figment in the mind of the reader as Shakespeare was said to be in the mind of Francis Bacon. He would be the last to contradict such a thought. As others wonder about him, he willingly admits he does not know to what genre he belongs, "whether to Realism or fantastic literature."

His name is Jorge Luis Borges. His home is Buenos Aires. But that is only part of the story. There is "another" Borges, as he calls him, who lives in a world apart, a timeless planet lost in space, lit by the light of some fallen star, among echoes of distant voices and leather-bound editions of old manuscripts. He has a scholar's quiet tastes. He praises simple things: bread and salt, the seasons, the art of friendship, the taste of coffee, sleep, habit, forgetfulness and diversity. These are the things with which he has been on speaking terms. For the rest, who knows but that a basic reticence and timidity may have put it beyond his reach forever. Admiring women surround him, but he has never married. There is a lost love somewhere in his youth. The girl in question appears as a pale image, to whom he says in an early poem written in English: "I offer you the bitterness of a man who has looked long and long at the lonely moon." There was a "trivial parting" in the streets of Buenos Aires that began an "endless separation." Since then, he confesses sadly in an elegy, in spite of his travels to far countries, a phantom of regret has screened him from his experiences, and at bottom he has seen "nothing or almost nothing but the face of a girl from Buenos Aires." No doubt a part of him that is dedicated to the memory has worn away with it. His passions have been of the mind. Like Kant, whom he once tried to read without success, he has found solace and outlet in thought and fantasy. He has loved maps, etymologies, chess, the classics, algebra, eighteenth-century type, hourglasses, Dante, Swedenborg, Verlaine, Walt Whitman, St. Francis of Assisi, Schopenhauer "who may have deciphered the

universe," the music of Brahms, "mysterious form of time," and
the past made of "the secret and immemorial rivers" that con-
verge in him.

his character Of Borges one can say, as he said of Valéry, that in a century of
spiritual mercenaries who worship the idols of blood and chaos
"he always preferred the lucid pleasures of thought and the
secret adventures of order." His work has been a long consolation
by philosophy. Of W. H. Hudson he has written revealingly that
"more than once he undertook the study of metaphysics," but
"he was always interrupted by happiness," words in which there
may be a tactful admission—and a hidden yearning. Out of
reserve, and shunning the exhibitionism of self-pity, he turned to
investigations of time and eternity. His intellectual abstractions
are a form of discretion. Behind them one senses the deep
unhappiness of a solitary soul only too well aware of its insuffi-
ciencies. He has been called cold and cerebral. It would be more
accurate to say refined and civilized. His feelings are carefully
disguised in his work; there are only tacit references to daily life,
few direct social concerns, no easy sentiments. The psychologies
of his characters, as the anecdotes they live, are schematic; plots
and persons are archetypal. All these might be serious shortcomings, but he has made virtues of them. Beneath the cool surface is
a gentle humor and whimsy, a warm intelligence and humanity.
He has been much misunderstood or misrepresented by the
ignorant or malicious. His impish sense of humor often an-
tagonizes people. He delights in seeming naïve and contrary, and
when cornered, at a loss for words, he will improvise a speech or
a principle. Four or five years ago he refused to attend a local
writers' conference because it was costing the bankrupt government too much money. Not long ago he enrolled in the Conservative party, out of "skepticism," he explained (he has defined
politics as "one of the forms of tedium"). Lately he has been
signing every anti-Castro manifesto that comes his way. He
has declared himself at various times anti-Nazi, anti-Communist,
and anti-Christian. He is a great joker who loves to pull legs and
puncture balloons. In Venezuela recently, addressing a literary
establishment that expected a paean in praise of local color, he

spoke on Walt Whitman. He is unimpressed by the partisans of
"indigenous" literature. In the River Plate there are no Indians,
he says. In constant demand on the lecture circuit—he is rushed
back and forth in cabs by officious attendants—he is likely to
leave his subject in midsentence to pursue the drift of his
thoughts into an examination of some obscure etymology, or to
shock his patriotic audience by claiming (always accurately) that
Gaucho poetry is an artificial invention of literati, that football
was imported from England, or that Carlos Gardel, the tango idol,
immortal in Argentine hearts, was a Frenchman.

Recognition, except in the most exclusive intellectual circles,
has come slowly at home. He was first discovered, translated, and
read in France, and it is only now, when his books circulate the
world over, that he is becoming well known to his countrymen.
Even so, his reputation is much in dispute. Some dubious admirers have paid him the backhanded compliment of saying he
will be remembered for his poetry, which is relatively negligible.
Nationalists have accused him of empty exoticism, a Communist
critic anathemized him for hating the working class, another
enemy reviled him for contributing to the nation's juvenile delin-
quency by editing detective stories. The truth is that he has found
unworldly enjoyment in just about every literary genre except the
novel and the theater. He has written suspense thrillers, film
scripts, articles, essays, prefaces, prologues; edited collections of
books and anthologies; annotated classical texts; and produced
excellent translations of a dozen writers ranging from Faulkner
to Gide. Everywhere he has established his own canons. The esoteric element in his work that disturbs so many of his readers is a
source of somewhat wistful satisfaction to him. About the position
of the writer in Argentina he says: "Here there was a circumstance that seems unfavorable, but actually, when you consider it,
is a blessing. I mean the indifference most Argentines have toward
literature. It can be an inconvenience, because the writer feels
isolated. But it's also an advantage, because no one writes for the
public. In other countries you hear people say that the writer
prostitutes himself. Here he couldn't prostitute himself even if he
wanted to." He recalls when he started writing that even editions

of Lugones, the best Argentine poet of his day, were of no more than five hundred copies. Two or three years might go by before an edition sold out. "And I remember the surprise, the disbelief, with which I received the news that a book of mine, ambitiously and paradoxically entitled *Historia de la Eternidad,* had sold I think it was thirty-seven copies in a single year. I felt like looking up those thirty-seven people, thanking them, asking them to forgive me for having written such a bad book." The reason was not only modesty. In a way, far from objecting to having only thirty-seven readers, he was pleased, because "one can more or less imagine thirty-seven people. It isn't too many yet." Perhaps, deep down, nowadays that he has thousands of faceless readers, he longs for the old days when he could be sure he was writing only for himself and his friends. That is part of his outlook. His class and generation were brought up in a broad humanistic tradition, which was the privilege and prerogative of a small intellectual elite. Borges has always been accused of Europeanism, a meaningless charge that does not bother him in the least. For one thing, his type of "Europeanism" is as Argentine as the pampa, for, after all, Europe is our past. Cultural eclecticism combined with a nostalgia for his undiscovered land have been constants of the Argentine character ever since the nation was founded. Says Borges: "I think our tradition is the whole of Western culture, and I also think we have a right to that tradition."

Few men have lived that tradition more intensely than Borges, who has always imagined Paradise in the form of a universal library containing the written and unwritten scripts of the ages. Its atmosphere is the air he breathes, a unanimous presence that accompanies him wherever he goes. At home in his small genteel apartment in downtown Buenos Aires, near the historic Plaza San Martín, after the tight schedule of a day that includes public appearances and private lessons—of Anglo-Saxon—he relaxes between the walls of rare editions that have been his constant companions from what seems like the beginning of time. There are teas with his mother, a delicate little woman with brittle features, who looks his age, travels with him and scolds him for not keeping warm, calling him Georgie; and quiet evening gatherings with his spirited collaborator, Adolfo Bioy Casares and Bioy's wife, Silvina Ocampo, old friends in the pursuit of learning. Borges lounges in an easy chair in his favorite position, with a leg up over the armrest, reaching for books out of the shelves. He can hardly distinguish titles any more—he has to be read to, and he works by heart, memorizing the short texts he will later dictate—but he goes straight to the book he wants with sure touch and instinct. He knows where everything is. And little wonder. The books come to him almost before he goes to them. They are constantly on file in his mind. Not by chance is he head librarian of the National Library, his den and sanctum. It is a huge pseudo-Renaissance building of fanciful ornamental splendor, with a vast dome over an abyss many floors deep bordered all the way by rows of stacks brimming along circular corridors rimmed by high banisters. From the central axis rooms fan out in all directions like entries in an endless card catalogue.

Here one afternoon, at an appointed time, we come in under airy high ceilings shadowed by clusters of heavy moldings, to the edge of a tangle of tiled corridors that lead out of sight past innumerable glass doorways. We are within "the serene contours of order," surrounded by "time desiccated and magically preserved." As we round the bend of a wooden staircase, a mounting curve begins for us. The "gravitational pull" of books that Borges so often evokes in his writings exerts an almost physical influence on us. Punctual as ever, he receives us on the first floor, in a decorous conference hall, where he sits in a light tailored suit and waistcoat, on the tip of a chair, at the end of a long table, looking tiny and remote. He can barely make us out and, like a deaf man who raises his voice so others can hear him, seems withdrawn, as if our indistinctness were a reflection of his own invisibility. His tone is diffident. He is patient, accustomed to being exploited and imposed on at all times. He sits with his hands turned in, as if he wanted to hide them up his sleeves, talking in a voice that sounds like a loud whisper. As in his books, which address each reader so personally, one has the rare feeling right away that one is being taken into his confidence. He handles an impeccable English and French and manages a reasonable German, and will go out of his way to accommodate his allusions to his caller's language and nationality. Speaking for him is thinking out loud. He is so shy that at first he hesitates, falters, and swallows hard to cover an embarrassing silence. He clears his throat in anguish. But once he gets started he is hard to stop. With a radiant smile, his hazy eyes sometimes out of focus, the left one blinking under a bushy brow, he begins to weave webs of thoughts in the air like smoke rings. The truth is that he loves to talk and soon gets carried away in conversation and when interrupted hates to break off. There is something permanent and invariable about his voice and gestures, which spread like ripples on a still pool. It seems he would prolong every situation indefinitely, eternally if he could, so that one can imagine his life as an interminable series of wrenches and forced partings. "A flight," he has called it, complaining with a sort of innocent guile that it is not to him but to the "other" Borges that things have happened. He has wanted it that way. The "other" Borges was an obstacle that had to be got rid of. He was allowed to live only in order to be annulled: a substance whose function was to be gradually eliminated and replaced by its shadow. For years Borges has been struggling to deliver himself of the "other." Metaphysics and mythology, he says, have been his means of whittling him down. In a famous meditation on Shakespeare, which is really a self-examination, he may well be pointing a finger at himself when he portrays the bard as a sort of actor or posturer upon the stage of the world, a man bent on shirking the weight of self, adept in the habit of "pretending he is somebody, in order to disguise the fact that he is nobody," all in a futile lifelong effort to "exhaust the shapes of being."

Borges was born with the century—on August 24, 1899. His was a comfortable and cultivated household. There was an English governess called Miss Tink and an English grandmother in whose library in a residential outskirt of Buenos Aires Borges did his first readings. He recalls a garden "behind a grate of iron lances" and an unlimited selection of English books. His Anglophilia dates from then; he learned to read English before Spanish, and English is still the language in which he reads by

preference. The enfant terrible in him has even gone so far as to
say that there is no need to know any other language because
English literature contains all things. He remembers his grandmother sitting him on her lap to read him British children's
magazines. His favorite stories were about animals, especially
tigers—perhaps the forerunners of those "dream tigers" that
populate his work. A dear friend and mentor was his father,
Jorge Borges, a man of many skills: lawyer, linguist, psychology
teacher, translator, and author of a forgotten novel. Some of his
brilliant amateur spirit must have been inherited by his talented
children. Back from a visit to the zoo, Borges and his sister, Nora,
today a well-known painter, used to sit in fascination listening to
their father's melodious recitations of Yeats and Swinburne. For
years the children were educated at home because of Jorge
Borges' fear of contagious diseases in school, and it is perhaps
because of his sheltered upbringing that Borges was an introverted, frightened child. His special dreads were masks and
mirrors. There was a tall mirror at the foot of his bed in whose
multiple images—his duplicates—he saw the specters of fabulous
prehistoric beasts. At least one of his poems records this fear of
ephemera. He found refuge in his books. He remembers the
amazement he felt when he discovered that the letters of a closed
volume did not get jumbled and lost during the night. His
literary exercises began early, and were duly erudite. At the
impressionable age of six, he wrote a story in old Spanish called
"La visera fatal" (The Fatal Eyeshade). He had already completed an English text on Greek mythology. By the time he
entered school in fourth grade, at the age of nine, besides the
Argentine staples: the *Cid,* Cervantes and Gaucho literature, he
had already consumed and digested Dickens, Kipling, Mark
Twain, Poe, H. G. Wells, *The Arabian Nights,* and William
Morris' translation of the Nordic *Volsunga Saga.* Soon he was
deep in Johnson, Conrad, Henry James, De Quincey, Chesterton,
Stevenson, and Bernard Shaw. From 1914 on he did his high
school studies in Geneva, where his family had retreated after
war erupted during a trip to Europe. In Geneva he taught
himself German, reading Heine with a dictionary, whereupon he

became engrossed in German translations of Chinese literature. After the war he perfected his English at Cambridge. By then he had communed with Carlyle and Walt Whitman and his greatest philosophic admiration, Schopenhauer. Deep in *Die Welt als Wille und Vorstellung,* he was writing a friend in Geneva letters in a French that was considered good enough for samples to appear on the literary page of a newspaper.

From 1919 to 1921—years of literary experimentation—Borges was in Spain. First in Seville and later in Madrid, he fell in with a group of young writers, the avant-garde of the day, who, because they gathered around the magazine *Ultra,* became known as the Ultraístas. Dada was all the rage in France, and its offshoots were spreading. The Ultraístas, violent conscientious objectors to the excesses of Ruben Darian Modernism, were renewers of Spanish verse, which was bogged down in traditional rhyme, on the one hand, exotic symbolism, on the other. They were imagists. Their freewheeling metaphors anticipated Surrealism, and the work of some of the best contemporary Latin-American poets, especially Vicente Huidobro (1893–1948), in his early days their major exponent in Chile, and, later, Neruda. But the movement itself soon died out. When Borges brought it back to Buenos Aires in 1921, in spite of a hectic manifesto he issued that same year, it was already moribund. "The Ultraist mistake," he later called this period. He has always enjoyed controversy, but never set much store by sectarianism. Soon after his return, rediscovering his city in the person of a mythical young girl with pigtails, he wrote: "The years spent in Europe are an illusion. I have always been, and always will be, in Buenos Aires." Perhaps the declaration rings a bit false. The truth is that it took him some time to become acclimated. Meantime he launched a literary magazine called *Prisma,* where he flirted with various mildly scandalous opinions that were of shock value in his day. Perhaps the deepest influence on him at this time was the brilliantly eccentric philosopher of the absurd whose friendship he had inherited from his father: Macedonio Fernández, an "oral genius," as he calls him, comparing him, typically, to an incongruous list of persons such as Pythagoras, Socrates, Christ,

Buddha, and Oscar Wilde. Macedonio Fernández, though somewhat wayward in his writings, was a great "metaphysical" wit and humorist, famous for his epigrams and bon mots. They founded the magazine *Proa* (1922), and together they explored the devastating paradoxes of the Idealist philosophy of Hume and Berkeley, which Borges seems to have found providential. Borges reveres the memory of the genial conversationalist whose voice he can still hear in the back of his mind "repeating that the soul is immortal." Together they walked tightropes across many broken boundaries.

The twenties, with their proliferation of literary magazines— "secret magazines," Borges calls them, referring to their limited readership, which usually began and ended with their contributors—was a period of great intellectual ferment in Argentina. Contemporary Argentine literature begins with the so-called generation of 1922, made up of writers all born around 1900, who were associated with such pioneering editorial ventures as the magazine *Martín Fierro*. The older generation—the gentlemanly Ricardo Güiraldes, the witty regionalist Roberto Payró, the folkloric Benito Lynch, the Tolstoyan moralist Manuel Gálvez, the king of Modernists Leopoldo Lugones—was passing away. A new aesthetic was being born which thrived on diversity. The Martinfierrista tendency was actually a vague compound formed under pressure of the most varied trends and currents: German philosophy, the Russian novel, Marxism and radicalism in general. After a series of shifts in position, two main literary "schools" were established, opposed, in a friendly way, says Borges, to each other. They were named after their locations: Boedo, a proletarian neighborhood, where the emphasis was on social content—these were the "committed" writers; and Florida, a residential quarter, where the outlook was more purely literary and disengaged. As usual in such divisions, a good deal of demagoguery was involved.

Seen from the vantage point of the years, the polemics between the Boedo and Florida groups seem slightly unreal to Borges. Some of the more outstanding figures of the time—Roberto Arlt, Leopoldo Marechal, Ezequiel Martínez Estrada, Borges himself—

were independents, only marginally connected with one or the other group. There were writers who sat on the fence, or belonged to both sides.

Says Borges with a wicked glint in his eye: "I would have liked to belong to the Boedo group, because I wrote poems about the suburbs. But I was told I was already included in the Florida group. And since it was all make-believe . . . We were all friends. Our differences were exaggerated. There was even a certain violence. But that violence was part of a game."

Not everyone would agree with him, but he insists that underlying the disputes of the period there was something akin to a deep community of spirit. The rest was a "publicity trick." Because, as he explains caustically, Argentine literary life has always had a tendency to take its cue from its French counterpart, and Paris, he says, is less interested in art than in the politics of art. The French literary scene he describes as a sort of gang war fought by cliques and committees that trade in terms borrowed from the jargon of politics and military strategy. As for himself, distrusting easy definitions—left and right—he subscribes to the habits of English literature, which on the whole, in spite of certain groups like the Pre-Raphaelites, has been "an individual literature. As Novalis said: 'Every Englishman is an island.'" His view may be prejudiced. He certainly frequented French models in his time. But the fact remains that whatever poses he struck during the twenties, at bottom he held counsel with himself.

In 1923, abandoning the field, he was off on a second trip to Europe with his family. In his absence, that same year, his friends greeted the publication of his first book of poetry, *Fervor de Buenos Aires*. He followed it up, back from his trip in 1925, with *Luna de Enfrente* (Moon Across the Street). Then came his first volume of essays, *Inquisiciones* (Inquiries), and in 1926 the second, *El Tamaño de Mi Esperanza* (The Size of My Hope).

Borges' early work, especially his poetry, which tends to be pompous and rhetorical, is full of a nostalgia for neighborhood sounds and the Argentine countryside—the "barrio" and the pampa—as well as a preoccupation with national characteristics typical of a soul-searching generation that produced our most penetrating spiritual analyst, Martínez Estrada, and the passionately didactic essay-novels—*La Argentina Profunda, Historia de Una Pasión Argentina*—of Eduardo Mallea. In Borges the somewhat self-conscious preoccupation with Argentinism—a sign of cultural rootlessness—often takes the form of inflated patriotic declamations and prideful evocations of martyred ancestors, such as his great-grandfather, Isidoro Suárez, a cavalry officer to whose command he attributes an important victory in the War of Independence, and his grandfather, Colonel Francisco Borges, whose honorable life came to a sorrowful end in "solitude and useless courage" in a frontier war with the Indians. Borges has later had second thoughts about these flamboyant "exercises in apocryphal local color" that abound in anthologies of his work, but he says: "The best way to be free of an error is to have professed it."

And it was not in vain that he did. Though his verse seems tired and dated, it is candid. There is a confessional strain in Borges' poetry that provides clues to an understanding of his other work.

"A man who talks, not one who sings," he has said of himself, quoting Stevenson, who was fond of comparing the pages of his books to letters he might have written his friends. And so it is in the best of those early poems, where confidences alternate with passages of a personal correspondence that might be chapters out of a spiritual diary. There are moving passages of quiet celebration of private occasions and places. "End of the Year," "A Stroll," "Suburbs," "Return," "Dawn," "Dusk," "Saturdays," "Farewells" are typical titles. There is some highly reserved love poetry. The verse, for the most part, is free. At the time, in his ignorance, Borges says he thought free verse was easier to handle than rhyme and meter. Bucolic descriptions occasionally give way to melancholy reflections on the sense of the passing of time, always very acute in Borges, who keeps reminding himself that "time is living me." There is a statement of poetic intention where he calls his poems "psalms" of a man who in his "idle wanderings" bears witness to the wonders of the world.

The essays of this period, in which there is hardly a hint of the later stylist, deal mostly with literary subjects and linguistic problems approached through discussions of Joyce—whom he admits he does not understand—and other foreign and local writers. Borges notes his readings, pays his respects to his admirations, with a special nod for Idealist philosophy, and shows varying degrees of acquaintance or familiarity with German Expressionism and other literary fashions of the day. The style is insufferably pompous and overwrought, full of waggish puns and wordplays. Among metaphorical flourishes is the lament, much in vogue, that "nothing has happened yet" in the city of Buenos Aires, which lacks a symbol, fable, or figure large enough to be worthy of comparison with the grandiose backgrounds that inspired the Gaucho epic, *Martín Fierro.*

El Tamaño de Mi Esperanza, which Borges has withdrawn from his complete works, is the most embarrassing example of this early vein. It is mannered, sententious, and grandiloquent. Artifices of expression are accompanied by coquetries of spelling that imitate—or affect—Argentine pronunciation. The idea is to find a way out of the strictures of classic Castilian into a more digestible local idiom, but the author simply commutes between the false and the synthetic, falling into cuteness and caricature. Insisting that "the city awaits its poem," he limits his range needlessly in acordance with the principle he decreed in *Inquisiciones,* that "melancholy, static mockery and subtle irony" are the only notes a local art can strike without falling into alienation. But these are mere tentative fumblings, cockily contrived—as he admits in a postscript—to disguise a basic lack of assurance. More attractive is an interesting "profession of literary faith" where we begin to recognize the real Borges, who expresses his conviction that "all literature is autobiographical" and proposes as an aesthetic norm that "language is an efficient ordering" of the "enigmatic abundance of the world."

Rounding out this period, besides another volume of poetry, are *El Idioma de los Argentinos* (The Argentine Language), an essay that won a literary prize in 1929—he spent the money buying the Encyclopaedia Britannica—and a study of a poet of the Buenos Aires slums, whose merits he overrates: *Evaristo Carriego. El Idioma de los Argentinos* testifies to the progress he was making in his thinking on linguistic matters. In a note that is a challenge to such perpetrators of Spanish purism as Rodríguez Larreta, he declares war on academic dictatorship and "the scholarly boredom of professional linguists." "Language is action, life; its time is the present," he says. Yet he wisely warns against the danger of confusing the timely with the topical. Between an imported rhetoric and a home-grown dialect, he advocates an intermediate position, which he has stuck to ever since.

He has always had particularly harsh words to say against the sclerosis of Spanish literature. The tyranny of the Academy, with its outworn rules of diction—its mental blocks—has had a paralyzing effect on the Spanish imagination. He tells us: "I think Spanish literature, outside of five or six great books, is rather poor. It can't be compared to other great literatures. There's a fine beginning in the old ballads and romances. I don't think Spanish folk poetry is inferior to any other. Then we have Fray Luis de León, *Don Quijote,* and a few sonnets of Lope de Vega. But right after that Spanish literature begins to decline. There were great writers like Góngora and Quevedo, but obviously they belong to a decadent period. Their concept of literature was already too self-conscious. Then we have the eighteenth and nineteenth centuries, which are wastelands. When at last there's a renewal," he adds, referring to Modernism, "it comes from America, and of course under the influx of French literature, which was better known and understood in America than in Spain."

When Borges started to write, the Spanish tradition in America, provincial and ingrown by any standard, had fallen into a sort of planned obsolescence. It was bound to seem a straitjacket to the man who wrote with true inner urgency. And Borges had already discovered that "there is no other fate for me."

In 1931 Victoria Ocampo launched *Sur,* the most important and long-lived of all "little magazines" in Argentina, which has kept afloat through the years thanks to constant transfusions from the personal fortune of its philanthropic founder. Borges was a frequent early contributor, active in everything from editorial work to film reviewing. Meantime, in 1935, he published *Historia Universal de la Infamia*, which was followed in 1936 by *Historia de la Eternidad*, both milestones in his literary development.

The first is a sort of curio shop: an assortment of odd stories of rogues and blackguards gleaned from various historical sources. The author is still learning his craft; he overdoes certain effects such as long lists full of inner contrasts, abrupt breaks in continuity, deliberate incongruities. But here, for the first time, we have techniques and procedures that can be recognized as Borgean innovations. One of them is the habit of condensing lives into two or three key scenes. Cataloguing eccentricities, we realize, is his way of creating mental portraits that, as he says, "are not, and do not try to be, psychological." The style, as he qualifies it today, is baroque, a fact that has led him to dismiss these works as freakish, vain, and frivolous. "An irresponsible game," he has called *Historia Universal de la Infamia*, claiming, somewhat ruefully, that there is nothing under its sound and fury, that it is all "a surface of images." No doubt to an extent he is right. He committed a kind of fraud, faking and forging others' stories instead of inventing his own.

"I think that's generally the case among young writers," he tells us. "They're painfully aware of the fact that their ideas are not very interesting, so they disguise them as best they can, using, as the case may be, neologisms, archaisms, syntactic extravagances, strange constructions. Out of timidity and insecurity."

Historia Universal de la Infamia is a tour de force. We have resplendent accounts of the careers of such infamous miscreants as Billy the Kid; Lazarus Morell, an unscrupulous Mississippi slave trader; Monk Eastman, a gangster in the pre-Capone era; Tom Castro, an impersonator; Kotsuké No Suké, a cowardly master of ceremonies for the Emperor in feudal Japan; and Hákim de Merv, a masked dyer turned seer, better known as the leprous Veiled Prophet of a mystic Oriental sect. The predominance of blood and gore, even in their abstract Borgean forms, betrays the secret predilections of a bookish soul bent on working off garish fantasies. Included in the collection is Borges' first attempt at straight narrative fiction, a synthetically slangy story of a challenge, duel, and vengeance in the suburbs. The latest edition of the book—most of Borges' slim works have been updated and augmented since publication—contains such rare tidbits as an Arab fable on human vanity and the tale of the magic death of a Sudanese despot.

All of which belongs in the category of what one might call a literature of compensation, a term that can also be applied to *Historia de la Eternidad,* where Borges, become a sort of disembodied intelligence mounting a stream through mental landscapes, traces the different conceptions Western society has had of eternity from antiquity to modern times. He migrates from Platonic archetypes, through Idealism, to Nominalism, struggling toward that "lucid perplexity" which he says is "the sole honor of metaphysics." He is a man "torn to the point of scandal by a sequence of contradictory loyalties," whose compulsive play with time is born out of a feeling that "succession is an intolerable misery" because human desire "naturally tends toward eternity." "Life is too poor not to be immortal," he says. To arrest its flow, turn it backward, find divergent and asymmetrical possibilities in it, is his desperate yearning.

In an accompanying article on Kenningars—primitive, often outlandish, Scandinavian metaphors—he confesses himself still in part "inhabited by the ghost of the dead Ultraist" in him, who "enjoys these games." In fact, he seems doomed to them. They are not so much games as performances.

There are essays in the same volume on cyclic and circular time and the Nietzschean idea of the Eternal Return. "The present is the form of all life," Borges quotes Schopenhauer, perhaps rationalizing a fervent hope.

The various doctrines are dealt with only insofar as they satisfy his own personal needs. He does not necessarily subscribe to any of them. His purpose, he says, is "to explore the literary possibilities of certain philosophical systems. In other words, accepting

Berkeley, or Schopenhauer, or Bradley, or the dogmas of Christianity, or Platonic philosophy, or ideas on reversible time, or whatever, to see where one can go from there, literarily speaking." He has never written as a missionary, but simply as a poet. "So that if certain people have thought they detected a metaphysical system in my stories, the system may well be there, but deep underneath, because I certainly haven't intended to write fables to illustate one system or another. Besides, in all my stories there's an element of humor, a bit of a joke. Even when I deal with the most serious subjects, such as the notion that life and dreams are synonymous, it's all there with a grain of salt." What matters to Borges are the affinities and insights he has found in certain systems that, like Solipsism, or Hinduism, with its denial of the physical universe, or Mahayana Buddhism, which explodes the conventions of self and identity, have been useful to him as starting points for his mental adventures.

Historia de la Eternidad is a sort of master key to the Borgian mansions. From this point on, though in constant metamorphosis, Borges' themes, more limited in number than in scope, have varied little with time.

The year 1938 was crucial. His father died, and for the first time in his life Borges held a job—as assistant at a municipal library. Then, though he had always had bad eyesight and suffered from insomnia, a serious accident aggravated his ills. Mounting a staircase at home, he banged his head on a window casement and was in the hospital for three weeks, feverish and delirious. Convalescing from an operation, he wrote his first fantastic story: "Tlön, Uqbar, Orbis Tertius." It was his way of putting his house in order. But it was also his inaugural address. Something had come into focus.

The next years were full of activity. He had already helped edit an anthology of Argentine literature (1937), and now, with Bioy Casares, whom he had met in 1930, he put together an anthology of fantastic literature (1940) and another of Argentine poetry (1941). In 1941 he published his first masterpiece, *El Jardin de Senderos que se Bifurcan* (The Garden of Forked Paths), and, again with Bioy Casares, under the joint pseudonym of

Bustos Domecq, the amusing *Seis Problemas Para Don Isidro Parodi*, a brain twister that combines light social satire—of pretentious literati, featherheaded society women, intellectual dandyism—with a spoof of detective stories. The meticulous Don Isidro Parodi, in the tradition of armchair detectives, reasons his cases from a prison cell, where he has landed as the result of a frame-up. He has his Dr. Watson in Aquiles Molinari, a double-crossing newspaperman who takes credit for the cases solved by his mentor. 1944 was the year of a key work: *Ficciones.* In 1946, again with Bioy Casares, this time under the pseudonym of Suárez Lynch, he produced a curious criminological specimen, *Dos Fantasias Memorables,* written in a sort of intellectual's slang, a calculated reductio ad absurdum, not devoid of self-parody, of cultured attempts to create a pseudo-Argentine language out of underworld talk. The Borges-Bioy Casares team's admiration for crime fiction was consolidated that same year in the first volume of an anthology of detective stories.

The war years seem to have been years of withdrawal for Borges. In the midst of the general tumult and commotion, we hear his unfanatic voice like an insidious whisper deploring the fact that almost all of his contemporaries, whether or not they knew it or admitted it, were Nazis or unconscious racists. In a wistful article written at the time he proposes Argentine individualism and anarchy as possible antidotes against worldwide creeping statism.

Perhaps these were a poor man's comforts. In 1946, after having signed a manifesto against dictator Perón, who was being canonized, he lost his job as a librarian; even worse, he was appointed poultry inspector in the Buenos Aires markets. He resigned as a civil servant to take up teaching at an English cultural organization. While he lectured for a living, he went on publishing: the essay *Nueva Refutación del Tiempo* (New Refutation of Time, 1947), the stories of *El Aleph* (1949), a study of Gaucho literature (1950). In 1950 he was elected to the presidency of the Argentine Writers' Association (SADE), a dangerous position in those days of political crisis; gaping policemen sat in on his conferences on Oriental philosophy. He kept the post until 1953, by which time

he had published two more masterpieces: *La Muerte y la Brújula*
Death and the Compass, 1951) and *Otras Inquisiciones* (Other
Inquiries, 1952). In 1955 he helped compile a memorial to
Leopoldo Lugones, and joined Bioy Casares in a selection of
Cuentos Breves y Extraordinarios (Brief and Extraordinary
Stories) and two film scripts dealing somewhat unsuccessfully with
the Buenos Aires gangster milieu at the turn of the century.

It was after the fall of Perón that, with the bulk of his work
behind him, his fame began to grow. He received honorary
degrees and a chair in English and American literature at the
University of Buenos Aires, where he was prone to hold forth
with his usual good-natured absentmindedness, rashness, and
effrontery, refusing permission for his lectures to be taped. That
same year he was selected to the Argentine Academy of Letters
and named director of the National Library. In 1956 he was
granted the National Literary Award. In 1957 he collected some
loose ends in *Discusión* and joined Bioy Casares again in an
entertaining catalogue of mythological monsters, with descriptions of their customs and habitats, the *Manual de Zoología
Fantástica*. The year 1960 brought his Summa, a tidy little
volume that gives a final distillation of his essential themes:
El Hacedor (The Maker—or Poet). Finally, in 1961, the year
when he shared the International Editors' Prize with Samuel
Beckett, he put together a methodical, if arbitrary, *Antología
Personal*. That same year, ever on the road of learning, he gave a
course at the University of Texas, where he must have caused
some amazement and alarm when he doubled as a student of Old
English. A conference tour of the United States was followed, in
1963, by another of Europe, where he was much celebrated,
especially in Paris (where he stopped traffic by reciting Verlaine
in the street). Most recently he stirred up trouble during his visits
to Venezuela and Colombia, but he is traveling less and less.
Each day spent at home is a new page turned in the book of the
world.

Books are his context, his setting, his frame of reference. In
their echoes, allusions, and cross references he has found as much
drama as another man finds in a life of action. He can sum up a

fate in a footnote. A good part of the excitement of a Borges text
derives from the force and felicity with which he threads his
elusive bibliographical figments into a suggestion of a meaning
that is never fully revealed. "The solution of the mystery is
always inferior to the mystery," he says; a principle he has
worked into an impressive literary method. To give himself freedom of movement, he has invented his own genre, halfway
between the essay and the story. The proportions of the ingredients vary, but his tendency is always, as he says, to appropriate
religious or philosophic ideas for aesthetic ends. A sort of acro-
batism is involved; his postulates are short cuts to intuition.
Behind them is a concern for ultimates that remain forever
hypothetical. He says every educated man is a theologian, without necessarily being a believer. He himself is a sort of priest
without a church, maneuvering among different articles of faith
that he invests with sacramental value at one moment, only to
declare them heretical the next. His achievement—according to
his own notion that "art is not Platonic" but concrete—has been
to give his airy abstractions flesh and blood. They are his
dramatis personae. He adopts them in preference to real people
and events because they embody eternal themes, whereas the
reality of the senses "is always anachronistic." In Borges thought
becomes anecdote. Giving it stage presence serves his intention
always to tap deep at the root of experience, to encompass what is
universal and essential in man. Like Walt Whitman, with whom
he often identifies, he assumes a generic position where personal
experience takes on "an infinite and plastic ambiguity" in which
—as in sacrifice or redemption—there is something for everybody. "To be everything to all men, like the Apostle," says
Borges, is the secret aspiration of all lasting art. Therefore the
artist can only allude to things, never name them. He conveys
not immediate meanings but a sense of what lies beyond them.
Borges says that art—like the Idealist universe of Tlön—is "not a
mirror of the world but an element added to the world." It
means a new perspective. Entering it is like being in a state of
expectation. Like music, happiness, "faces whittled by time,
certain twilights and certain places" that seem to hold out a

visionary promise, it hints at something just beyond our grasp. And "this imminence of a revelation that eludes us is, perhaps, the aesthetic event."

To put us on the brink of this "aesthetic event," Borges resorts to many ingenious devices. He will invent an author and exalt him through a list of imaginary works, some of them incomplete, therefore open to interpretive emendations, that amount to a complete mental diagram of their creator. He will speculate on the Emperor who built the Chinese Wall and also had all the books burned in his empire, presumably to start history with himself, and offer us several contradictory explanations of the facts, without deciding in favor of any of them, simply counterpointing them, opposing thesis and antithesis to obtain a cathartic synthesis. He will chronicle the history of an idea, as in *Historia de la Eternidad,* or track a legend in its transformations through time. The method may be adapted to literary criticism, as in his essays on the various translations of Homer and *The Arabian Nights.*

"Perhaps the history of the world is the history of a few metaphors," he says in "La Esfera de Pascal" (The Sphere of Pascal), where the metaphor in question is that of the circle, which was taken as a symbol of perfection in Plato, of being in Parmenides, of God in the Middle Ages, of the universe in the Renaissance, and finally of existential despair in Pascal. He has traced literature back to the cult of oral tradition, and the novel form back to its origins in allegory. Typical is "El Acercamiento de Almotásim" (The Approach to Almotasim), an early story, embryonic in form, where he summarizes the plot of an imaginary book, detailing the adventures of the hero, whose hypnotic search for the mythical figure of Almotasim, read between the lines, where it is undermined, is a humorous allegory, twice removed, on the paths followed by the human soul in its mystic ascent toward the divinity. Then we have those two magnificent structures. "Tlön, Uqbar, Orbis Tertius" and "El Inmortal," which are outlines of utopian communities that, like phases of the moon, act as catalysts of mental processes.

Though heir to the undercurrents of fantastic literature that have been gathering force in the River Plate from the days of Quiroga and Lugones, and in spite of obvious debts to the English tradition, a Borges story is something very special. Each is an original. Borges' vein is less the mood piece than the theorem. There are last-minute switches and surprise endings in the manner of detective fiction; mixtures of slapstick and metaphysics, of the plausible and the outlandish, of facts and apocrypha. There are stories within stories, and—as in his tale of an Arab philosopher's search for the meaning of the Aristotelian terms "comedy" and "tragedy," which precipitates a meditation on historical consciousness—vanishing narrators. Borges is a murderous satirist, as he shows in moments of mockery, when he lampoons literary enemies, following the rules laid down in his own "Arte de Injuriar" (Art of Injuring), which recommends such deadly verbal weapons as parody, false charity, flattery, and "patient contempt." The sense of a story might be in the exegesis it gives of some previous text. In this category are his various "glosses" of *Martín Fierro,* plus "El Muerto" (The Dead Man), his story of a neighborhood tough from Buenos Aires who joins the ranks of a bandit in Rio Grande do Sul, whose kindness kills as he turns out to be "a maverick mulatto version of Chesterton's incomparable Billy Sunday." Such mutations testify to Borges' belief in the power of suggestion that acts and objects have when transformed in the mind of man. So it is that in a tale that Borges somewhat coyly admits "is not entirely free of symbolism," the description of a Babylonian lottery becomes a parable on the inscrutable will of God, in whose world life is an infinite drawing of lots. Ingredients in every Borges story are hermetic allusions to obscure facts of history incorporated for no other reason than their enigmatic value, which contributes to the general atmosphere. Some stories are illustrations of theories explored in his essays. "El Milagro Secreto" (The Secret Miracle) can be traced to various sources, among them Borges' own *Nueva Refutación del Tiempo,* one of his lengthiest incursions into the Idealist world of Berkeley and Schopenhauer, with a detour into the Sensationalism of Hume, to whose considerations on the nonexistence of the material world outside the perceiving mind (which is also shown to be of questionable existence) Borges contributes an argument against time. The general tenor of the argument—granted the author's warning that he disbelieves in it himself—is that if there is no continuity of being, no underlying substance to harbor consciousness, there is no flow, no cause and effect, no serial development, therefore no time. We are left with nothing but flashes of perception in the void. And so, in "El milagro secreto," which operates by a kind of suspension of disbelief, a characteristic basis for Borges' ontological arguments, we have a condemned Jew in Nazi Germany—who, like Borges, has written forgettable poetry that he regrets; searched for God in the pages of his books and gone blind in the process; and written texts arguing that "the number of man's possible experiences is not infinite," so that "a single 'repetition' is enough to demonstrate that time is a fallacy"—miraculously favored by God, who grants him a year outside time to finish mentally composing a play while he is standing in front of the firing squad. The story is a perfect example of the skill with which Borges integrates his themes into the fabric and psychology of the narrative.

The fitting of form to fancy is so diabolically clever in Borges that dismounting the component parts of a story in no way reduces the mysterious fascination exerted by its secret mechanisms. In his best work, wherever we look, everything seems to "click." In "El Enigma de Edward Fitzgerald," for instance, it is perfectly in harmony with the general scheme of the story that Omar Khayyám and his English translator should be doubles because of the ideas professed by the former—a believer in transmigration—on the basis of which, as Borges says, one might speculate pantheistically that the Englishman was able to re-create the Persian because deep down they were identical. The theme recurs in "Los Teólogos," a high point of Borges' craft, where it emerges from an account of a rivalry between two theologians, one of whom combats a heresy with arguments that are later themselves deemed heretical, a deviation for which he is burned at the stake, having been denounced by his rival, who in turn dies a fiery death, only to discover in the other world that accused and accuser are one and the same person in the mind of

God. The heresy in question, by no coincidence, is a variant of the Platonic notion of cyclic time and the recurrence of all things and all acts, claiming variously that every man is two men, that all human acts entail their opposites, or that the world is made up of a number of limited possibilities which, when exhausted, must begin to repeat themselves.

Another example of Borgean synchronization is in *La Muerte y la Brújula,* where an intricate web is woven around a bookish detective who is attracted to his death through a reading of Hebraic texts left behind by a dead Talmudic scholar. In the same pattern is "El Jardín de Senderos que se Bifurcan" which is a spy story on one level: a Chinese informer for the Nazi kills a man named Albert (who lives in a house in a labyrinthine garden) in order to let his masters know the name of the city they must bomb, a name that coincides with that of the victim. But, as by prearrangement, Albert turns out to be a Sinologist who before dying interprets a book written by his executioner's ancestor, Ts'ui Pên, to illustrate its author's belief in infinite divergent, convergent, and parallel series of time, one of which, branching off into what appears as a chance act—actually only one possible end result of innumerable contradictory possibilities unfolding simultaneously—led the murderer to his victim.

"Tlön, Uqbar, Orbis Tertius" is perhaps the epitome of how Borges' material goes to make a story. The characteristics of the brave new world called Tlön are perfectly consistent with the intentions and sense of the story. References to Tlön are said to be found only in the most recondite sources: a forgotten treatise, a freak edition of *The Anglo-American Cyclopedia.* Tlön is the brainchild of a coterie of scientists, technicians, moralists, artists, and philosophers who have compiled its astronomic and planetary features, thereby giving it mental—and, by extension, real, if not physical—existence under the direction of some unknown man of genius. Indispensable for the story's verisimilitude is the fact that Tlön is an idealist world whose inhabitants have no concept of space; for them reality is a galaxy of unrelated, independent acts or perceptions that one of their languages renders as "poetic objects." Cause and effect in Tlön have no validity; they are considered associations of ideas. There is no truth, only surprise. Science, under the circumstances, is difficult or spurious, except for psychology, which deals with states of mind. The twist that turns all this speculative material into a story is the account Borges gives of the gradual infiltration of Tlön into the real world. As with the clique in "La Secta del Fénix" (The Sect of the Phoenix), whose secret rite—coitus—has become a common act, the occult society that created Tlön—where metaphysics is a branch of fantastic literature—has dispersed its dynasties of solitary men through the world, to transform it into the image of their creation.

Perhaps one of the top envoys from Tlön is Borges himself. As he says in *El Hacedor,* that bewildering silva of varia lectio as he calls it: "A man sets out to draw the world," but "shortly before his death he discovers that the patient labyrinth of lines he has drawn composes the image of his own face." But, of course, that face is the face of all men. Art is an acrostic, he proposes in another of his obiter dicta: "a mirror held up to the reader, and also a map of the world." Its visible features reproduce the invisible traits of the eternal Face beyond all faces. In Borges, personal identity is a momentary aspect of generic Being. He speaks of a universal memory, without which each man would take an incalculable portion of reality into the grave with him. And he comforts himself in the destitution of his individuality by postulating the eternity of literature, where "the dream of one man becomes the memory of all men." He often stresses the "ecumenic," "impersonal sense" of art, so strongly felt by him that in *Otras Inquisiciones* he declares: "For many years I thought the near-infinity of literature was in a single man" who appeared under different names and guises, to fulfill inter-changeable roles, as in Angelus Silesius, where God and man alternate as dream and dreamer. "The plurality of authors is illusory," he says elsewhere.

A development of this theme, which produces some of Borges' finest pages, is the essay on Coleridge's *Kubla Khan,* where Borges expounds a theory of archetypes—a sort of Jungian collective unconscious that might be a proof of supernatural life—based on the fact that Coleridge's poem was visited on the poet in a dream, as the palace the poem evokes had been on the Mogul Emperor who built it in the thirteenth century. In "El Enigma de Edward Fitzgerald," we have again two avatars separate in time and place inhabited by a single identity. In the fictional realm, one of the neatest realizations of this theme is "Las Ruinas Circulares," where a man dreams another into existence, only to discover—as he escapes death by fire, which cannot consume him—that he is being dreamed by a third. Borges can extend the notion, with minor adjustments, to literary criticism, as in an article on an early Gaucho poet, Hidalgo, whose poetry was not particularly noteworthy but whose memory was nevertheless bound to survive in the doubles destined to be his literary descendants. Or he can apply it to help clinch a point in a story, as in "Tlön," where the concept of plagiary does not exist, because "it has been established that all works are the work of a single author, who is timeless and anonymous." It is effectively invested in a note on *Don Quijote*, where Borges concentrates on the ambiguity that exists between author, reader, and fictional creations. In the second part of Cervantes' masterpiece, he points out, the hero has read the first part of his adventures, an inversion in which he finds the suggestion that "if fictional characters can be readers and spectators, we, their readers or spectators, may well be fictions." In this vein, perhaps the nicest touch is in "Everything and Nothing," where a Borgean Shakespeare is imagined in Heaven telling God: "I, who have been so many men in vain, want to be one and myself," to which the voice of God answers: "I am not myself either; I dreamed my world as you dreamed yours, my Shakespeare, and among the shapes of my dream were you, who, like I, are many people and no one."

For Borges—as for the Pascal of *Deus Infinis*, who spoke of every molecule as a solar system, every sun as a satellite—the universe is a pattern of intimations and correspondences in which the least part implies the whole. He finds evidence for this view wherever he can, in a single page calling on such varied authorities as Schopenhauer, Leibnitz, and Bertrand Russell. He finds further confirmation in certain objects that he invests with mystic significance. They may be anything from the common grain of sand in an hourglass, in whose trickling it seems to him he senses "cosmic time," to the obsessive coin in "El Zahir." Zahir, in Islamic belief, Borges explains—it means "notorious" or "visible"—is a term applicable to "the beings of things that have the awful virtue of being unforgettable and whose image finally drives people to madness." The coin so endowed in the story leads the protagonist, a young man in the throes of artistic creation, to discover that there is no fact or event, however humble, that does not entail the whole of history. Likewise, in "El Aleph," we have a Wellsian crystal ball—another Zahir—that is "one of the points of space that contain all other points." It may well be a reminiscence of Alanus of Insulis' famous sphere whose center was everywhere and whose circumference was nowhere. The Zahir, with its spellbinding properties, was one of the ninety-nine names of God. And Aleph, says Borges, is related to the letter En-Soph of the Cabalists, which symbolizes "limitless and pure divinity."

"All knowledge is but remembrance," said Plato in a phrase quoted by Borges, for whom, as he says it was for Carlyle, universal history is "an infinite sacred book" where all men read and write, and are in turn read and written. The world as a book in which man, author and protagonist, tries to make out the meaning of his life, is a key notion in Borges. It appears in "El Culto de los Libros," where he quotes Léon Bloy, a frequent reference, who claimed that "we are verses or words or letters in a magic book" whose ceaseless existence he equated with the world. Elsewhere Borges recalls the Cabalist idea that the external world is a language of cryptograms and crossed words that man once understood but has forgotten and can no longer decipher. And in "La Biblioteca de Babel" (The Library of Babel) we have Borges, the blind librarian, reasoning that if the library exists ab aeterno, it must also be total, and there must be no two identical books in it. On the other hand, there might be a single "cyclic" book that would be "the perfect sum and cipher of all the others." It would have been written by the Author of authors, whose vision is absolute.

There seem to have been moments when Borges has approached this absolute vision. He is on the verge of it in "Poema Conjetural," one of his favorites, where he speaks of having found "the missing letter, the perfect form known to God from the beginning." But the hope is soon lost. The secret word or formula needed to unlock the code will forever remain unknown. That is his plaint in his poem "El Otro Tigre" (The Other Tiger). Tigers—perhaps a reminiscence of Blake?—are chronic symbols of the unattainable in Borges. He speaks of his search "on a late afternoon" for the tiger that is "absent from the poem." An echo of Mallarmé's *"fleur hors de tout bouquet"*? It was Mallarmés who said the world exists to be put in a book, and like him, Borges is out to find a chimeric "system of words." A dramatization of this theme is the story "La Escritura del Dios" (The God's Script), where a Mayan high priest of the Pyramids, confined to prison by conqueror Alvarado, shares a partitioned cell in a dungeon with a jaguar, in whose spots, which are runes or glyphs—the jaguar, in Mayan cosmogony, was one of the attributes of God—he attempts to catch a glimpse of a divine revelation promised in Indian tradition for the end of time. The revelation—when it comes, in the form of a fiery wheel—recalls Schopenhauer's kaleidoscope, where the figures of history keep changing masks and costumes, though the chips of glass—the actors in the repertory—are always the same.

Borges—a mystic Montaigne—proposes the possibility of considering eternity a sort of immanent dimension, similar to that state theologians have defined as "the lucid and simultaneous possession of all instants of time." It would be a form of sharpened awareness in which total recall would become premonitory foresight. The fullest exposition of this scheme is the complex story "El Inmortal," which he calls "a sketch of an ethic for immortals." With Swiftian inventiveness, it explores the possible effects immortality would have on men. Marco Flaminio Rufo, ex-military tribune in the legions of Imperial Rome, a wanderer on a spiritual pilgrimage, where ordinary categories are in suspense, comes upon the fabulous uninhabited Citadel of the Immortals in the middle of the desert. The city is made up of

senseless ancient splendors: upside-down staircases, empty pal-
aces, corridors leading nowhere. The only inhabitants of the
desolate region are cavemen who dwell outside the city walls.
They turn out to be Immortals who, living in the realm of pure
thought, detached from the vicissitudes of temporal life, have
neglected and abandoned their city, secure in the knowledge that
"in an infinite lapse of time every man is put through all things."
Personal destiny is therefore of no interest to them. Their trance
is catching and gradually infects the narrator-protagonist, who,
we notice, begins using the "we" form to tell his story, indicating
that he is slipping into the role of an Immortal himself. This is
one of the achievements of the story. Being everyone, Marco
Flaminio Rufo soon finds himself becoming different people, his
alternates, in history. He is in Stamford in 1066 with the armies
of Harold, then he is a scribe in Bulaq in the seventh century of
the Hegira, then a chess player in Samarkand, an astrologer in
Bikaner, and so on through the centuries. But a basic presence
inhabits him throughout his long odyssey. He has read Pope's
Iliad and lived the adventures of Sindbad the Sailor. He is at
once Ulysses and Homer.

If literature is inexhaustible, it is "for the simple and sufficient
reason that a single book is," says Borges. A corollary of the
axiom is the notion that forerunners in literature not only
prefigure their successors but are retrospectively regenerated by
them. Thus, Hawthorne's story "Wakefield" "foreshadows Kafka,
but Kafka modifies and sharpens the reading of 'Wakefield.' The
debt is mutual; a great writer creates his forerunners." He revives
antecedents that would, in fact, not exist without him.

A clear case of the retroactive effect of posterity is the witty
"Pierre Menard, Autor del Quijote." Here—if we accept things at
face value, the story is also a take-off on academic criticism—a text
is enhanced by a subsequent interpretation. Pierre Menard, perhaps stimulated by Novalis' idea of complete identification with a
given writer, has devoted his life to the subterranean and thank-
less task of rewriting two fragments of *Don Quijote* word by word.
He has read the book only once, years before, and the vague
memory he has of it is like "a hazy preview of a book not yet

written." What Cervantes, centuries earlier, did naturally and
spontaneously, in harmony with his age and mentality, Menard
has to do consciously. Cervantes' assumptions become his interpretations. The end product is identical with the original, but immensely richer because of all the research and scholarship that
have gone into it. Historical imagination has added subtle layers
of meaning to the old imprints on the palimpsest.

The roads boring through Borges' book of the world form an
endless labyrinth. This is precisely the image Borges resorts to in
"El Jardín de Senderos que se Bifurcan," where the two—the
book and the labyrinth—are equated. There are manifold labyrinths in Borges. Some, like the labyrinthian trap in *La Muerte y
la Brújula,* are mere metaphors for the vagaries of thought or
time or the tortuousness of human action; others, like the house
of the Minotaur in "La Casa de Asterión" with its fourteen—or,
in hermetic language, infinite, since fourteen is infinitely sub-
divisible—doors, courtyards, and fountains, are explicit symbols
of the world. There are forced itineraries, contorted, disconcerting, and complicated but inevitably leading somewhere, as in the
underground maze in "El Inmortal," which surfaces in the
Citadel, and therefore marks the passage from one dimension
into another; and multiple choice patterns, where progress is
erratic and every turn a crossroads, as in the Citadel itself. The
garden in "El Jardín de Senderos que se Bifurcan" is a compound of the predetermined and the unpredictable. Then there is
the most magnificent labyrinth of all, the world of Tlön, a fiction
—a larger library of Babel—thankfully embraced by suffering humanity as a symbol of order in chaos.

To nourish and sustain this fiction is perhaps the sense of all
of Borges' work. There is an "essential monotony" in Borges that
is, paradoxically, one of his most luminous qualities. He has
always cast his net in the same waters. But in it he has caught
hints of higher meanings. At the same time he has found shelter
in its antiseptic radiance. Like one of Hemingway's bars, or big-
hearted rivers, in wartime, it has been his clean, well-lighted
place—his safety zone. No doubt there is something of him in his
Arab hero, Abencaján, who hides at the center of an elaborate

maze of winding corridors, claiming he wants to escape an
enemy, when in reality he wants to attract the enemy into the
labyrinth to kill him. Meantime, he assumes the enemy's name.
Which is all part of the pattern. There is a strong element of
bluff in it all. Abencajan may well be like the narrator of "La
Forma de la Espada" (The Shape of the Sword) who, under an
assumed identity, tells the tale of an informer in the Irish War of
Independence, attributing his crimes to someone who turns out
to be himself.

Switches of identity, always pitfalls for the unwary, are given
different interpretations in Borges. There is the case of a man in
the province of Buenos Aires in the twentieth century who is
murdered by his godson as Caesar was by Brutus, without
suspecting—it is just a fait divers—that he is dying "so that a
scene can repeat itself." Then there are the curious parallel fates
of Droctulft, a barbarian who switched allegiance and died
defending Rome against his own people, and an Englishwoman
assimilated into an Indian tribe in Argentina in the days of
Borges' grandmother. The two stories seem like contraries; actually, sub specie aeternitatis, they are complementary. In "El Sur"
(The South), where Borges conjures up nightmarish memories of
his hospital days, a man in a coma in a hospital ward dreams his
atavistic death in a knife fight in the beloved countryside inhabited by his ancestors. Along the same lines is "La Otra
Muerte" (The Other Death), where two alternate versions of a
man's life intercept and tend to obliterate each other, finally
revealing themselves to be projections of an ancient theologian's
speculations on the problem of personal identity.

A complication—or resolution—of this theme is the pithy
"Deutsches Requiem," Borges' contribution to an understanding
of the spiritual roots of Nazism. Otto Dietrich zur Linde, born a
partial cripple in Marienburg in 1908, lost his faith reading
Schopenhauer, and came to consider Germany "the universal
mirror of humanity, the conscience of the world." Appointed to
rule over a concentration camp during the war, he happens on a
remarkable inmate, a renowned Jewish poet, whom he tortures
and executes, less as a Jew than as "the symbol of a hated part of

my soul." Says Otto Dietrich: "I agonized with him, I died with him, I was somehow lost with him." He is like David who judges and condemns himself in a stranger. Because what one man does all men have done. Victim and executioner—like the Yin and Yang implicit in the Tao—are indivisible.

In search of a concrete assignment, man finds himself sentenced to an inner multiplicity that is a source of acute anxiety to him. Perhaps that explains the eagerness with which Borges' characters aspire to play their predestined part in the pattern. "There are few possible themes," Borges wrote long ago. "One of them is the meeting of man and his fate." Out of this word Borges has made a law. In *Historia Universal de la Infamia* we already had the case of Bogle, Tom Castro's mastermind, who was run down in the street one day by a carriage that had been pursuing him "from the bottom of time." But fate or dharma goes deeper than that in Borges. It has to do with man defining himself. Thus, we have Otto Dietrich comforting himself with the "clever" thought that he has chosen his own misfortunes, as he hurtles down a preset course where "every casual encounter is an appointment, every humiliation a penance, every failure a mysterious victory, every death a suicide." In every life, however long or complicated, says Borges, there is a crucial moment when a man knows forever who he is. So it is with Emma Zunz, Borges' only female protagonist, a psychotic spinster, pathologically afraid of men, who is out to avenge the death of her father, a conclusive event in her life, which in fact stopped with it, frozen in the icy glare of "the only thing that had ever happened in the world, which would continue to happen forever." Emma goes about her plan with clockwork precision. She acts as an automaton, one of those pawns Borges describes in his poem on chess, moved by an invisible hand whose workings are inscrutable. She is not unlike Tadeo Isidoro Cruz, who, once an outlaw, now a soldier in the service of government forces, out hunting for the renegade Martín Fierro, meets his man and his moment of truth in "a lucid and fundamental night" when "at last he saw his face" and "heard his name."

On the threshold of such a night, fiddling with the "curiosities of literature," as he calls them in a "hostile" poem addressed to a Spanish Baroque poet who is one of his pseudonyms, a man who was denied the "essential passions" has achieved that higher mathematics of language which, as he says, "can simulate wisdom."

"To know how a character talks," Borges has written, perhaps less about his fictional creations than about their author, "is to know who he is. To discover a tone, a voice, a particular syntax, is to discover a fate."

Over the years he has refined his instrument till it has become one of the most flexible, concise, and efficient in our literature. At the same time, in accordance with his belief that "every scrupulous style contaminates its readers with a considerable part of the worry with which it was worked," he has contrived to keep its workings inconspicuous. He aims at ease and grace, intimacy and informality. He has freed himself of his early luxuriance of metaphor, his exaggerated incursions into slang, to obtain a precise balance of elegance and idiom. Above all, he has concentrated on universality, contracting certain habits that favor it, such as using words in their etymological sense. "The perfect page in which not a word can be altered without damage," he says, explaining his avoidance of a language of immediate connotations, "is the most precarious of all. The changes in a language erase secondary meanings and shadings; the 'perfect' page that contains these subtle values is the one most affected by these changes." The language of pure idiom is the most vulnerable of all. For one thing, there is no such language. As a literary norm—in Gaucho poetry, for instance—it was made up for the most part by men of letters who invented their own conventions for it. Even if it had a separate and independent existence, which it does not, it would be no more representative of the language spoken by the average man in the street than the Spanish of the Academy. In any case, attitudes go deeper than words. Either to be an Argentine is a fatality—a vocation—says Borges, in which case it cannot be avoided; or else it is a pose. Shakespeare was inescapably English even when his plays were set in Denmark or Italy. Borges cites his own *La Muerte y la Brújula* as an example of a story that is felt to be deeply Argentine in tone and temperament—as his patriotic poetry is not—although the names of the streets mentioned are French and the settings and scenery are echoes of the Paris of Poe. He has always been democratic in his borrowings, with a predilection for English style and syntax, which have had a strong influence on the structures of his writing: his adverbial forms, his punctuation, his exceptionally brief, compact paragraphs. He is a master of understatement, of dispassionate irony and conversational humor.

At sixty-six, in delicate health and severely handicapped by his failing eyesight, he is still as active, but no longer as inventive, as before. He seems to have settled his accounts with the world and completed his business with himself. Perhaps, in a sense, he has outlived himself in his own figments.

Looking back on his career, he sees nothing in it he could have improved or prevented. "When you reach my age," he says, as he shows us to the door, where he lingers, prolonging our departure with an endless handshake, "you realize you couldn't have done things very much better or much worse than you did them in the first place."

The few bits of poetry he has published recently have been increasingly introspective, classic in form and conventional in thought. He says nowadays he is more interested in truth than originality. Each poem is a summing up. As far back as 1953 he had written: "You have spent the years, and they have spent you." Now we find him gently reproaching God, who with "magnificent irony" gave him—as He had his predecessor, Paul Groussac, who also lost his sight in his old age—at once the books to read and the darkness of his "mortal eyes." With wonder and curiosity he looks forward to the risks that may still await him in the vast and populous realm beyond the night. Somewhere, a bibliomancer to the end, he identifies with the legendary Hector, gradually abandoned by the fading universe, until finally "a stubborn mist erased the lines of his hand, the night emptied of stars, the ground slid under his feet." In his latest poem, "Emerson," as usual putting his words on another's lips, Borges strikes a wistful note. He has read the essential books, he says, and

composed others for which he will be remembered. He has
learned what it is possible for humans to know, and shared
it with others. But, "I haven't lived. I would like to be someone
else." He may be remembering his own words written long ago,
that "you can only lose what you have never had." But it is too
late to do anything about that now. "Space and time and Borges
are leaving me." It has all gone or passed into the possession of
the "other" Borges, so that, in the end, "I don't know which of
the two of us wrote this page." Which is only justice. For as
Borges, effaced by fame, knows, "glory is one of the forms of
oblivion."

IV

João Guimarães Rosa,
or the Third Bank of the River

VENEZUELA has its llano, Argentina its pampa, Peru, Bolivia, and Ecuador their puna, and Brazil its sertão. In each of these geographical areas there is an image of a land and its people. To name the sertão is to evoke a vast highland expanse that stretches across a third of a country and several geological eras. At the heart of it is the state of Goias, an immense open plateau extending west toward the Mato Grosso, south to include a chunk of Minas Gerais, east to Bahía, and north toward Maranhão and Pará, where heath becomes tropical rain forest, then jungle, as it declines into the Amazon basin.

The sertão is many things: mountain range and valley, moor and marsh, glade and gorge, windy peak and chasm. There are tertiary rock formations gutted by deep caves, tortuous underground rivers surfacing in hidden springs, patches of desert where nothing sprouts but crabgrass and cactus shrubbery. The sertão is changeable: an oceanic spread with shifting contours that tease the mind and deceive the eye. Its center is everywhere, its perimeter forever expanding out of sight. Its inhabitants are a rugged race of seminomadic herdsmen who move with the seasons like migratory birds guided by an inner compass, taking their bearings from a few elementary landmarks: the arraial, or village, a small oasis in the plain; an occasional tract of farm-land, the fazenda; the dimpled slope that may lead to a watering hole; the vereda, a fertile grove between high ledges, dominated by the enormous shadow of the local palm, the buriti. This is the land of the limitless Guimarães Rosa, who has read his life in its lines, which are written on the palm of his hand.

A big land has produced a big man. Guimarães Rosa is a Mineiro, and Minas Gerais, with its proximity to big urban centers—São Paulo, Rio de Janeiro—and a back door on the hinterlands, the Campos Gerais, which are already part of the sertão, is an area at once ingrown and outgoing, a fruitful combination that has been known to nourish rich temperaments. Brazil's first great novelist, Machado de Assis, was a Mineiro. He was a Swiftian pessimist with a long memory of a bitter life lived inward and occasionally drained, a drop at a time, in bleak but burning works written "with the pen of mockery and the ink of melancholy." Mineiros are great sufferers. The cloistered strain in Mineiro literature has predominated in latter years with the growth of city life, which has produced the lonely dreamworlds of a Cornelio Pena, the moody reveries of a Carlos Drummond de Andrade. But there is another kind of Mineiro still deeply rooted in homestead soil. He is slow-thinking, sober of gesture, measured in his ways, silent and introverted, but a great lover of life. His close-mouthed shyness is a wary front for an ample soul accus-tomed to roaming across open spaces. He is the man who never bathes twice in the same river, who gallops bareback in the wind and sleeps under the stars, with an ear to the ground, where he hears the drumming of centuries.

Such a man is Guimarães Rosa. He was born on the edge of the sertão, in 1908, in the German-sounding town of Cordisburgo, to a patrician family of remote Swabian descent, cattlemen for generations. Guimarães, originally spelled Wimaranes, was the name of the capital of a Swabian kingdom that held sway for about a hundred years in northern Portugal before the invasion of the Visigoths. Northern Portugal provided many of Brazil's early settlers. They were a hardy lot that left a sturdy offspring. The

Wimaranians, and their various mutants, were legion. One of
Brazil's first regional novelists—Bernardo Guimarães in the mid-
nineteenth century—bore their seal. Another carrier was a renowned mystic poet called Alphonsus de Guimaraens, an early
translator of Heine. Among them were pioneering frontiersmen
who moved inland to stake their claims in far pastures that
sometimes were green and flourished to become prosperous
fazendas. To cast anchor in that weather-beaten land was always
a sort of compromise with an opposing urge to drift. Life was
never entirely sedentary. Under the builder was the wanderer.
Guimarães Rosa embodies this duality. He was always something
of a maverick, he says, and has strayed far enough to prove it, yet
wherever he has gone he has carried the throb of the sertão like a
pounding in his skull. He remembers an unbridled childhood on
the farm, where herds of brooding oxen ran wild and the night
was full of clattering hoofs. The mind sped across measureless
distances that remained immaterial, because there were no fixed
points in space to capture the eye, which, instead of projecting an
image, absorbed it. In the prelapsarian sertão the past is hazy,
traditions are diffuse, contacts are immediate. It is not in an
aimless chase after lost origins but in a direct and vital confrontation with the forces around him that a man forges his individual conscience. There is mediumry in every gesture, a tapping
of latent energies, even a sort of midwivery, as he is born and
reborn out of himself every day, replenished at the source. "I'm a
strange bird," says Guimarães Rosa, who can sit in a chair for
hours, concentrating, without a twitch, lost in the kind of
divination that precedes the poetic impulse in him. He rides the
line down into the still waters at the root of being known to
those who have learned to "transform the power of the sertão in
their minds and hearts."

Other writers have been in the sertão before Guimarães Rosa.
There was Alfonso Arinos, who took a celebrated spiritual
journey *Pelo Sertão* (Through the Sertão) in 1898. More notable
was the Bahian explorer and journalist, Euclides da Cunha, who
gathered material for a momentous evocation of *Os Sertões*
(1902) on an epoch-making expedition with government troops

that had mounted a major campaign against one of the most
famous badmen of the time, Antonio Conselheiro. Da Cunha, a
reformer on the stump, combined documentary zeal and fine
scholarship with poetic flair. He gave a dramatic account of the
campaign, and also drew an authentic portrait of social crisis, in
a vigorous, flexible, baroque style of enormous influence in
Brazilian literature. Guimarães Rosa in some sense takes up
where he left off, but on another level, far beyond anything da
Cunha probably ever dreamed of. He not only fulfills a vision
but culminates a whole literature. He is at the confluence of
many streams, a humanist, like da Cunha, but also, and perhaps
more important, a badman, like Conselheiro. Where da Cunha
scratched the surface, he draws blood. The fires that feed his
work are abysmal. So is his language, often invented, always
hammered out in a deep inner forge. In this he is in the tradition
of a long line of renewers who in various ways fought a more or
less losing battle against the petty tyranny of the flat style pre-
dominant in Brazilian fiction, which, in spite of enormous mineral resources, has always been allergic to new forms of expression.
There was Oswald de Andrade of the revolutionary São Paulo
trilogy, *Os Condenados* (The Condemned, 1922), and, close at his
heels, the versatile Mario de Andrade—a part-time poet, novelist,
teacher, critic, musician, and full-time aethete—of *Macunaima*
(1928), an imagistic prose poem featuring a prodigal "hero without a character" explored through a euphoric use of folklore.
Macunaima was an intellectual contraption that finally foundered
in artifice. But it was a steppingstone. Guimarães Rosa goes all the
way down the road, and out the far end. He stands squarely in the
mainstream of modern literature, with its complex Proustian wiring, its Joycean undertow. At his shoulder is the Goethian alchemist, only a shade removed from the Dostoevskian mystic. Not
that he echoes anybody. He is the original mesmeiro, to use one of
his own terms: the man who is always himself, perfectly sui generis.
What distinguishes him from other writers on the continent is not
a literary tendency, which he transcends, but a frame of reference.
He is a philosophic novelist in command of both vital forces and
the powers of introspection. His work has stature because it gives

the full measure of the man behind it. He is our only all-around
novelist.

With Guimarães Rosa, Brazilian literature turns a new leaf. It
has come a long way from its somewhat rarefied beginnings in
the seventeenth century, when academic inbreeding produced a
satiric poet often considered Brazil's first literary figure, Gregório
de Matos, whose choicest work was an unpublished *Erotica*. The
hothouse strain, a form of cultural parthenogenesis in Brazil, as
elsewhere, can be traced down the centuries through the Romantic era, to the Parnassians and Symbolists and their descendants today.

A stronger current, often in violent reaction to the first, is the
one that carries from the early chroniclers down through the epic
of the Romantic era and the feuilleton, an activist form wielded
with a vengeance in Brazil, where local idiom was first exploited
in invective, through the many Realists and Naturalists who
flourished at the turn of the century, to their heirs apparent, the
regionalists, who took over the literary scene in the twenties and
thirties and have practically monopolized it ever since. Unlike
the urban novel, a relatively minor form concentrated in two or
three big cities, today Brazilian regionalism comes from all parts
of the country—for instance, Rio Grande do Sul in the work of
the popular Erico Verissimo. But its headquarters is still the
impoverished northeast of *Vidas Sêcas* (Barren Lives), the site of
the famous "sugar-cane cycle," which has absorbed the efforts of
fine poets like Jorge de Lima, powerful novelists like Graciliano
Ramos, and propagandists like the prolific Jorge Amado. The
historic and sociological aspects of manorial life in northeastern
plantations were explored by Brazil's sharpest essayist, Gilberto
Freyre, whose scrupulously documented and always fair-minded
work gave considerable impulse to a cause that soon became
fiercely proletarian and often declined into partisan politics.
Certainly there is much to be said for the northeastern novel, the
first to reveal some of the more desolate aspects of Brazilian
reality in their true color, but its conventions, suspiciously
homogenous, have worn, and it has begun to seem a bit prehistoric. There is grace and facility in Amado, for instance, but in

spite of an occasional poetic gust, his work is in a tired vein, too often narrowly ideological, with the seal of the committee and the sentiment of the potboiler. The genre has all the familiar inconveniences. Its emphasis has been, predictably, on the collective, on occasion carried to extravagant lengths; there is the amusingly ludicrous case of a novel written in cooperation by five different people. A far cry from this is Guimarães Rosa, to whom the word "regional" no longer applies as a synonym for limitation. He can cover broad spaces because there is plenty of room inside him. In him outer scope is inner range. His sertão is the soul of his country, as the Chekhovian steppes were the soul of Russia.

He is a mystic, part Catholic, part Taoist and Buddhist, with a religious sense of life, a fervent respect for all living things, and an unquenchable thirst for ultimate knowledge and enlightenment. As an artist, who annexes things on contact, his approach to reality is above all intuitive, but that does not preclude the sterner disciplines that reinforce insight with intellectual grasp, and the encyclopedic knowledge of his land that enriches his work at every level is as much a product of exhaustive research as it is of direct observation. He is a bit of an archaeologist, anthropologist, entomologist, ornithologist, and general sage and wizard, who can recite a magic litany as easily as he can decline Latin terminologies or decipher a chemical formula. He is at once a surveyor and a prospector, for whom the talismanic is a form of the contemplative.

It was by a roundabout course that he came to literature. In 1930 the child of the sertão, then twenty-two, was an eager young man on the move with years of apprenticeship ahead of him. The first stop was Belo Horizonte, the nearest thing to a big town in his neighborhood, where he cultivated an old taste for the natural sciences and, eventually took up medicine at the university. There, like Dr. Faustus, among vials and philacteries, pursuing spectral glows, he must have caught a glimpse of the philosophers' stone. It had many facets. Not all of his time was spent in the laboratory. He was still a medical student when a revolution broke out in the area, under the banner of liberalism,

and he abandoned the microscope for the scalpel. Those were the
early Getulio Vargas days, when everyone bore arms in Minas
Gerais, often at random, inspired one day, disaffected the next.
He enlisted with the revolutionary forces, volunteering as army
doctor, and rode with them until 1932, when he switched allegiance, to join the legalists. Perhaps a secret budgeting was at
work in all this and he was on both sides of the fence, or neither.
In any case, by the time the war was over, in 1933, whatever his
principles finally were, he seemed to have carried the day. He
came out with the rank of captain. Meantime he had been
practicing off and on in a village in western Minas, an outpost in
the days of dirt roads and no railways. He got plenty of field
work done. He was the sole village doctor, a local mainstay, with
a wide radius of activities, mostly on horseback. He was often
gone for days at a time, covering huge distances to reach his
patients in outlying areas. As herbist, geneticist, veterinarian,
healer of organic ills, he learned to see life in its full biological
dimension. Since then he has been a general practitioner in
many fields. Restless at home, he set out to see the world. An old
wanderlust had been stirring in him, and it grew daily so acute
that finally, in 1934, after a series of competitive tests, which he
passed with flying colors, he abandoned medicine and moved to
Rio de Janeiro to enter the diplomatic service.

   It was the beginning of a long career that soon took him
halfway around the globe. During the early war years, from 1938
to 1942, he was consul in Hamburg. His next post, between 1942
and 1944, was in Colombia. He was in Paris in 1946, back in
Colombia in 1948, and Paris again later that same year, until
1951, as First Secretary and Embassy Counselor, and eventually
delegate to UNESCO. From there, rounding a last corner, he
returned home to occupy one of the top rungs of the diplomatic
ladder as Cabinet Chief in the Foreign Ministry, a post he held
until 1953. Since then, as Minister Plenipotentiary, First Class,
with ambassadorial rank, as he points out in an amusingly
pompous curriculum vitae, and headquarters in the resplendent
Palace of Itamarati in Rio, he has not moved from Brazil. He is
in charge of the Department of Frontier Demarcation, an ideal

job for him because of its traveling requirements, which include occasional cross-country jaunts that keep him in close touch with his sources. He has been pretty much a citizen of the world, but since his early days in the service, when he started to write, he says, out of nostalgia for the good earth, he has been able to get mentally organized only at home.

In his palatial office in the Ministry, where he receives us, he reigns in sober splendor behind solid oak doors that swing open as he advances, straight as a rail, with twinkling eyes and solemn stride, a Brazilian sage of Weimar, the universal man, at large in the world and at ease with himself.

A weighty pause, a statesmanly nod, a sly, slightly ironic smile, kindly if a bit patronizing, and he takes charge of us. He wears a suit befitting a lofty public functionary of somewhat stocky girth, a dashing bow tie with yellow dots, impeccable attire in harmony with the general airiness of a man playing a role he enjoys and at the same time feels a little below him. He squints at us curiously, wondering who we are. He is very nearsighted, but perhaps a touch of vanity, which seems entirely in order, prevents him from resorting at first to his horn-rimmed glasses. With quiet assurance he leads us into the sanctuary, which contains a large desk and closet, both austere, and, with his nose now humorously pinched between his spectacles, he lowers himself into a deep leather chair, with his back to the window, where streaks of powdery sunshine come filtering in to settle in his light-gray hair.

A puzzling man, this Guimarães Rosa, who seems to take himself seriously only to chuckle at himself; at bottom perhaps a bit of a self-doubter after all, it occurs to us as we leaf through fat folders with him: albums of newspaper clippings, letters from editors praising his work, sheaves of glowing reviews in half a dozen languages, batches of notes, all out of the cluttered shelves of the closet across the room, which seems to contain his life's work. The "strange bird" is a hermit who loves nature and animals, shuns literary life, holds counsel with nobody. He has everything he needs in his office: his manuscripts, the innumerable geographical publications he subscribes to, his reference books. Apart from his occasional assignments for the Ministry, he spends his time in seclusion.

Physically and temperamentally he carries his German ancestry clearly written on him. He is a ponderer. He shows us his Teutonic features: his flat occipital, his green eyes. German, with its infinite subtleties, is the foreign language he seems to speak best, from natural preference.

We mix it with English, French, his battered Spanish, our broken Portuguese. He is a great linguist, philologist, etymologist, semanticist, who, besides Portuguese and, of course, the basics —German, French, English—reads Italian, Swedish, Serbo-Croatian, and Russian, and has studied or dabbled in the grammars and syntaxes of most of the other main languages of the world, including such tongue twisters as Hungarian, Malayan, Persian, Chinese, Japanese, and Hindi. Understanding the structures of other languages, he says, with undeniable logic, helps you use your own; it reveals hidden possibilities, suggests new forms. It also sharpens your ear to people. A Pygmalion who likes to shape characters from their speech, he can tell a man, his region, his occupation, from his accent.

A Guimarães Rosa book is born from long meditation. At some point, when he is ready for it, it gathers momentum, and then he piles up paper at his desk and writes furiously, in longhand, pouring out everything that crosses his mind. The first version is always profuse, and slapdash. Its purpose is to "occupy the territory," which will later be mapped out in precise detail. He sees the general movement of the work, the over-all plan, but most important, he has a certain feel, he tries to catch and capture something at the heart of it, a "metaphysical germ," he calls it, a vibration, a deeper resonance to which he will accommodate his plot, setting, and the psychology of his characters. The central germ is what determines the rest, its proportions, its orbit. He moves freely around it, often overreaching, sidestepping, at the mercy of backwash and overflow. There is always an element of chance in his work, he says; he tries to make even his mistakes and oversights work to his advantage. The first version done, the groping begins. He types out a clean copy with two fingers, deleting excesses, trying to trick himself into accepting necessary cuts, always painful to him, to the point that waste material is never thrown out, but collected in a notebook called "Rejecta," where it may be of use later or remain buried forever. "If I had another hundred years to live," he says, "I wouldn't have time enough to write down all the stories I have in my head." In fact, stories proliferate in his mind; practically everything he touches turns into one. He is a storyteller in the old sense, seeing life and meaning everywhere, in faces, gestures, objects, incidents. Yet he is in no hurry. He has all the time in the world to do what he has to do. He reworks his material endlessly, even after publication, often in each subsequent edition. He is touchy about the results. It has taken him many long and sometimes bitter years to get where he is now.

Probably no one disputes his position today. But his literary career has been rocky. This in spite of the fact that his very first work, a volume of poems called *Magma,* which was entered in a contest held by the Brazilian Academy of Letters in 1936, not only won first prize but even moved the jury to declare the second prize vacant becase *Magma* was considered to be in a category by itself, beyond compare. Yet it was never published as a whole. In fact, he withdrew it. The war intervened, and by the time it was over he had lost interest in those early poems. The few scattered samples that appeared in magazines are collectors' items. It was ten years before his next book, *Sagarana,* written in 1938, saw print. Again there was the war between. He was abroad. *Sagarana* had to fend for itself. It had a curious career. It was presented to another contest, anonymously, in a lacquered envelope, and caused such a stir in literary circles that the prominent publisher José Olympio floated an article in a newspaper wondering about the identity of the mystery author, who maintained a lofty reserve on the matter. When the book finally came off the presses in 1946, it sold out in a week. Brazil's great man of letters had been born. Yet the verdict was by no means unanimous. As an outsider to the literary milieu, Guimarães Rosa found vested interests agitating against him. He was called

abstruse and esoteric. The truth is that he is so far above the
standards of Brazilian literature that he was systematically ignored or berated for years. Though on his way to being widely
recognized in Europe, in the Spanish-speaking part of the continent that surrounds him he is not only almost unknown, but his
work, except for one or two stories, has not even been translated.
He can take some comfort in the thought that he is an overwhelming presence in the Brazilian firmament, towering head
and shoulders above poets and novelists alike, who all have
complexes about him. *Sagarana* is by now a classic. In 1956 he
published two masterpieces almost simultaneously: *Corpo de
Baile* (Corps de Ballet) and the much-acclaimed *Grande Sertão:
Veredas* (which appeared in the United States in 1963 under the
inane title of *The Devil to Pay in the Backlands*). In 1962 he
upset the literary establishment by taking a sudden turn that
seemed to promise a complete renewal in his significantly entitled *Primeiras Estórias* (First Stories).

From the beginning, whatever he did, he was a master of the
inner landscape, where breadth is depth and the light touch is a
sign of the grand manner. He wears his erudition gracefully. He
is an instinctive writer with a natural sweep, a kind of psychosomatic force, weighted at the base but open all around to cosmic
breezes. "Learn, from the rolling of the rivers" were the words of
the Buddha, which he quotes somewhere, to good purpose. He
has made the rivers run deep, and often touched bottom in them.

To inhale the sertão, trace its spiritual coordinates, find its
inner correlatives, has been the sense of his work. He has been
everywhere in the vast plain, in jeeps, on horseback, on cattle
trains. He has waded rivers, scaled cliffs, herded animals, hunted
wildcats, slept in open fields with the cowhands, as the night
closed in and the trees swayed, full of dark chatter, and the
ground opened at his feet. What he saw, and assimilated, he
recorded, but always on the steep edge of it, with an eye beyond
it. He captured appearances, but his true interest was in proportions. In the perishable he touched the permanent. "I don't read
the newspapers," he tells us, perhaps stretching a point which,
nevertheless, remains essentially valid. Day-to-day events he pays

hardly any attention to. "I'm against time and in favor of eternity," he says. So in his work, in the simplest anecdote, there is always a hinge that opens a door into the wide blue yonder. Here, as he says, we detect the Faustian, the man who has sat at every table, tasted all the fruits of the earth, been an anvil for every hammer, gone to every length, even, when the need called for it, to the point of making a pact with the Devil, in an effort to gain ultimate wisdom and serenity.

For Guimarães Rosa, who always finds the whole in the part, discovery and invention are one and constant, because the resources he mines in himself yield a metal that is basic and common to all men. Everything and everybody he comes in contact with leaves its mark on him, he says. "I take my luck where I find it." He does not disdain, and indeed sets great store by, the reportorial (which is not at all the same thing as the journalistic) which provides the backbone for the rest. In this sense, in the honorable tradition of Euclides da Cunha, he wants to contribute something good, something positive and constructive to the understanding of the physical and spiritual physiognomy of his land. When he was preparing *Grande Sertão,* for instance, he conducted extensive surveys and investigations, consulted files and archives, spoke with German and French travelers and explorers, then went everywhere himself to chart his course, gathering tons of notes, enough, he says, to compile a complete monograph of the country. He works like a scientist turned poet. *Grande Sertão* contains so much factual information, all of it so accurate in the minutest detail, that it could have been written as a scientific treatise. It could have been ten times bigger and better than it is if he had stuck to a cold enumeration of the facts, he says. He knows everything about "the real, the authentic, the inside Brazil." Why go to so much trouble? Partly, no doubt, to guard against snipers: the critics, who accuse him tirelessly of deforming reality. He defies them to prove it. He is always a step ahead of them. But, essentially, his concern for factual precision is a matter of architecture. He knows that it is the unimportant things in fiction, the strategic details, that often betray you and therefore require the most attention. They provide the groundwork, the furniture, on which, and with which, the rest is built. At the same time they camouflage and disguise. He uses them as a handy pretext, he says, a mask that at once hides and reveals his true intention, which is to get down to fundamentals: people, and what moves them. Acts and events, in this scheme, are inner tubing, the pipelines the sap flows through. They seem to be a surface network, but actually run underground, into the mysterious, the subconscious, the diabolic and unfathomable. Gestures, attitudes, are a system of equivalences under which the real story is told. At its core, like an exploding nebula, is the "metaphysical germ," the spark that sets the combustion going.

The novelist's job, says Guimarães Rosa, is to reveal and unfold, not simply portray. The novelist works with the things that pass unobserved for others, captures them in motion, brings them out into the open. He is, in Stalin's words, which Guimarães Rosa subscribes to, an engineer of souls, not in the narrowly ideological sense of the word, as a propagandist for a particular creed, a shaper of public opinion, but in the sense of affecting man deeply. Most people, perpetually caught unawares, live without noticing their surroundings. Not Guimarães Rosa. He remembers that on his nights on the plains with the herdsmen he often called their attention to things they had lived with all their lives but had somehow missed, taken for granted without stopping to register them. He opened their eyes, refreshed their view—which really meant reminding them of what they already knew, perhaps, but had forgotten. To awaken what lies dormant in man, to revive his wonder for the world, is the eternal task of a novelist like Guimarães Rosa, who magnifies nature to humanize it.

A sort of Virgilian breath blows through the sertão, where naming things is creating them. Every experience is full of intimations, every object, infused with a life of its own, bears its message for the man who can read it. The mineral, vegetable, and animal worlds are made of interlocking forces that lead back and forth into each other, waiting to be released. The man who interprets them expresses them, as if they were an extension of himself. From then on they inhabit him, transfiguring him.

In Guimarães Rosa the close up does not preclude but enhances peripheral vision. The contemplation of the smallest and most commonplace object can split the world at the seams, opening up into the abyss. Therefore, in his work every gesture is significant. It engages the whole man, who commits himself in a fundamental posture that always reflects a deeper way of being. External reality is no more than a point of departure, a swirl around the true center of gravity, where man finds and loses himself. Thus the sertão, with its supernatural overtones, its pantheistic animism, becomes a symbol for the mystery and vastness contained in all things. But it is also a thing in itself.

No one has penetrated so deeply into the psychology of the inhabitant of the sertão, the sertanejo, as has Guimarães Rosa. He draws from life, but also from song and legend, from the obvious and the occult, the real and the imaginary. His characters are ordinary people, wayfarers through life, in search of their elusive selves. The sertão is a place of extremes, where you touch "the depths of misery and human suffering," but also the heights of love and joy. Tumultuous wars, violent friendship and enmity, dread and daring, a kind of pagan dance of life and death among totemic splendors are the constants on the sertão. The sertanejo is exalted and abject, a happy hunter always on the verge of being hunted. Life is dangerous; it can get out of hand at any time. What he builds today may be blown away tomorrow. What he is he may suddenly cease to be. Every step is a possible pitfall. In action and passion alike lurks sudden oblivion. Behind the familiar, forever threatening, hovers the strange and the unknown.

To evoke this primeval experience in all its phases, Guimarães Rosa rescues the storytelling habits of the ancients, using an oral prose where the aside or detour can be as important as the main current of the story, where aphorism alternates with adage, thought wanders, wayward, following rhythms of speech, on a natural devious course into sidetrack and roundabout, picking

up anecdotes and reflections that are always rendered spontaneously, without any elaborate "techniques," simply as they come
and flow. The effect is baroque, minus the dead weight, a
turbulence constantly tolling off the tip of the tongue. Romances
and, sometimes, poems Guimarães Rosa calls his novels, which
occasionally suffer from lack of processing, but have life in every
verse. The language is densely emotive, mixing erudite terms
with dialect, turning phrases always unexpectedly, inverting,
somersaulting, full of interjections, proverbs, sound plays, rhetorical questions, consonances, pleonasms, expletives, alliterations, archaisms, Latinisms, Indianisms, coined terms, word
games—conundrums, pnus, riddles—flashes of repartee, an almost hypertrophy of all the elements of popular talk, even
internal rhyme. Typical is the way he invented his title, Sagarana, from the Icelandic saga, joined in wedlock with the Indian
suffix "rana," meaning "like" or "pseudo." He often uses phonetic spellings, augmentatives, diminutives, or stands words on
their heads to give them a hidden charge, to exploit their latent
potential for allusion and connotation. It is precisely in his
linguistic craftsmanship, which is one of the glories of the
Portuguese language, that he has most often been taken to task.
Because he uses idioms endemic to certain regions, amalgamating
them as he sees fit, he has been accused of travestying the
language. But he knows better. As everywhere, the countryside in
Brazil has preserved certain old forms of speech gone out of use
in more civilized areas, and he notes every inflection. Parts of
Grande Sertão, for instance, he says, are so loaded with elements
of regional talk that they are more accessible to the man of the
backlands than to the critic, who has to go digging in old
dictionaries to get at the source of them, which often dates back
as far as the fifteenth century. None of which bothers Guimarães
Rosa. However scabrous his surfaces, the theme and substance of
the story always shine through with a quiet radiance that is
communicated even to the physical shape of sentences and paragraphs. For instance, he likes to start sentences with an S, a letter
that gives "fluidity." An S launches Sagarana.

Sagarana is made up of nine stories, some in a light vein, all slightly fanciful, told leisurely, with a sort of playful irony very much in character with the author, who resoundingly demonstrates the truth of the old saying that the style is the man, not the manner. If Guimarães Rosa has not yet reached full maturity in these stories, which often remain anecdotal, the whole man is already there, at the heart of things, with a full repertory. He is the omniscient author whose indulgence for human foibles comes from a deep respect for human grief. He strikes only telling blows. He knows there are no small moments in life, detached from the rest, that every gesture is total, implying all others, that there can be bliss in anguish, and that the divine is never far from the infernal. So it happens that hate may save, love may kill, and a smile on the lips may mean death in the heart. All this we learn from the gleeful trill of a bird on a branch, the buzz of an insect, the song of a pebble rolling in a brook. The effects are achieved always with the simplest of means, a language subtle but direct that lights sparks in things while hardly touching them. Guimarães Rosa does wonders even with animals. There is the gallant little spotted donkey Sete-de-Ouros—the Seven of Golds in Spanish playing cards—"mute and resigned" in his old age, "all calm, renunciation, unused force," in his last breath as a loveless, sexless hybrid—drowsily sinking into "deep reservoirs," echo chambers, we soon realize, in which he hears the humming of spheres. Sete-de-Ouros has seen better days, and changed hands and names many times since then, including once when he was stolen and had a heart branded on his rump, for all the good it did him, now that he has outlived his usefulness and the vultures are circling overhead. But he has not yet come to the end of the line. There is the wisdom of age under his knotted brow, and he had his chance to prove it. A bustling day dawns on the farm. The cattle are being herded to market, and because the weather is bad and there are currents to wade through and there is nothing like experience in these matters, he is called on to lead the march. And, lo and behold, he becomes the hero of the day, braving the rapids. An insignificant tale, as the author comments, yet somehow important, perhaps because of the gravitational pull provided by that unknown force that suddenly "decides fate and

sends men and donkeys alike tripping on the road to greatness."
If Sete-de-Ouros, rising to the occasion, mysteriously outdoes
himself, he is not the only one. The spark of life, spinning in the
void, can take up residence even in the dreamy eyes of a pair of
battered oxen. We see them in their daily labor, pendulous,
emasculate. Here they come, plodding along under the yoke,
their minds lost in shapeless reveries, wandering toward lost
pastures. In an open meadow, with sudden yearning, they
encounter a herd of their wild brethren, who awaken atavistic
impulses in them. On they trudge, sluggish as ever, still mooning,
but almost inadvertently there is a break in the dreamworld, a
run in the fabric, and the driver, who is dozing on his seat, is
jerked off the cart, whicr rolls over him, crushing his skull under
its huge wooden wheels.

A kind of primitive and innocent savagery, paradisiacal at
times, abysmal at others, rules in the sertão, where men roam like
nomadic spirits, swallowed up in their shadows. There are no
safety zones. Each man tries to cast roots, to find shelter, to build
himself a clearing in the wilds, but at the edge of every experience, however humdrum, are shady areas where curtains part to
reveal some hidden chasm. Wherever a man is, the ground may
cave in under him, starting him down on a bottomless fall.
Hardened unbelievers may succumb to superstitious fears. There
is the case of a somewhat smug young man who deprecates local
Mumbo Jumbo, only to be struck blind one day wandering in
the brush. He is lost, in more ways than one. The tangle of
shrubbery in which he thrashes about is really an inner maze.
Down he topples, head over heels, along the beanstalk, drained
of himself. To break the spell, he must drink many drugs. The
sertão is a vast pharmacopoeia where there is poison in each
potion, which can be lethal or lucky, according to the brew. The
wise man who would ward off disaster learns to respect the magic
potential in things, to possess what will otherwise possess him.
This being the eternal lesson in Guimarães Rosa, that reality is
not one and stable, but a momentary suspension that, at the tap
of an amulet, can blast wide open to let in the pandemic forces of
destruction.

In the sertão people meet occasionally, and sometimes part forever. A man has a house and wife, a small capital, a foothold in space and time, a backlog of personal experiences to support him, but cohesion and continuity are a mirage, a sheer coincidence in the economy of an expanding universe, where bubbles explode almost before they form. A flash of lightning can split an old tree. So it happens with Turíbio Todo, who for years staves off evil and keeps the devil at bay. But one day his wife runs off, and his life collapses. He lived in a house of glass that a sudden feud shatters. He goes after Cassiano Gomes, the man who seduced his wife, to shoot him, but, out of luck, misfires, putting a bullet through Cassiano's twin brother instead. Now Cassiano is after him. For both, life suddenly becomes an endless plunge down the "road of bitterness," where a man loses everything, even what he never had. For weeks and months they ride across the sertão, waylaying each other, at times traveling parallel without knowing it, nearly meeting at crossroads, at others challenging each other from afar, until finally Cassiano dies of heart failure. Turíbio, relieved, heads for home. But the road done cannot be undone. The duel continues, with Turíbio as the sole remaining target. Along the way he meets a stranger, a sort of avenging angel, who summarily closes the vicious circle, fulfilling a promise Cassiano extracted from him on his deathbed. He is a will-less executioner, who, with many apologies—and Guimarães Rosa's usual mixture of humor and tenderness, laced with irony—lets fate force his hand.

Happier, but no less unpredictable, is the lot of Lalino Salãthiel in "A Volta do Marido Prodigo" (The Return of the Prodigal Husband), a "biographical sketch" in a picaresque vein, a Guimarães Rosa specialty. Lalino is a mysteriously heliotropic creature, born to shine undimmed in daytime and moonlight. He works on a road-building gang and dreams of the fancy women in the distant and fabulous capital Rio de Janeiro, for where he sets off one day, abandoning wife and family. Nothing works out too well, but he always manages to land on his feet. He is a lighthearted rogue, with a song in his heart, riding the high tide of life like the foam on a wave. On his return to the village after living it up for several months in town, he finds his wife has taken up with a Spanish settler. That triggers the clown in him. He keeps visiting her, fanning the old flame, just for the fun of it, to raise a stir. Because he has other coals in the fire. He starts dabbling in local politics on the mayor's payroll, courting votes for the forthcoming elections. Nothing can beat Lalino. He goes from joker to court jester. The wheel of the world turns and those who are on top of it whistle along with it.

One of the loveliest stories in *Sagarana*, in which the author seems to project personal experiences less highly transposed than usual, is "Minha Gente" (My People), a mood piece that could have come out of the early Mann or Hesse. A young doctor is on his way to visit his uncle in the country, and the trip is full of nostalgic overtones for him. There is the manic local school-teacher, Santana, a chess addict, who meets him at the station, on horseback, with the chessboard, to continue a Ruy Lopez or Queen's Gambit they had interrupted months or years before, a symbol of old realms of the mind they once scanned together and now scan again. Woven in with this theme, as they trot along and night falls, is the doctor's rapturous re-encounter with his natural surroundings. He stops to savor colors, scents, tastes, sounds, to examine a twig, leaf, or flower, finding beauty and meaning everywhere, in the shapes of things, their fragrance, even the harsh scientific terms that describe them. The story moves quietly, with a sort of tranquil ecstasy, into dusk and dark. On the farm there is Uncle Emilio, busy politicking nowadays, and his bounteous daughter, Maria Irma, a prairie flower whom the doctor, with blossoming senses, soon falls in love with. That she rejects him, while leading him on, is of little importance. He flirts with his own feelings. His passion for her is part of a more general elation, which suddenly crumbles when he goes fishing with a wistful friend, Bento Porfirio, who is having an affair with a married woman. They are casting out and drawing in their lines, happy as hummingbirds, when the wronged husband comes charging out of a bush. The next moment the body of Bento Porfirio is floating in the pond, which is deep, with shifting hues, like the eyes of Maria Irma.

Eyes open everywhere in *Sagarana*. Visible events are always
signs of hidden developments, seasonal reflections of the ages and
moods of men. A ruined village, apparently racked by malarial
fevers, has really been deserted because the spirit went out of it.
The same can happen to a man. It does, in the fascinating "A
Hora e Vez de Augusto Matraga" (The Time and Turn of
Augusto Matraga). Augusto is another case of a slaphappy man
who has known prosperity and then fallen on hard times. He is a
sort of Job of the sertão, who has sinned against faith, played the
losing side in politics, and been left destitute, with debts and
mortgages, an adulterous wife, and a daughter who warms every
bed in the neighborhood. It would seem a blind fate has turned
against him. But when the ax falls, it is not the outer bloodshed
that counts but the internal hemorrhaging. In his punishment
Augusto finds a godsend. It is a call from on high that leads him
on to a life of holiness. He roams the country like a tramp to
settle in a far village, where a priest tells him to work and pray,
for life moves on and better days may come again. "Everyone has
his time and turn," says the priest. "You will have yours." And so
it comes to pass. Augusto prospers again. But he does not regain
happiness. Something is still wrong. He does penitence. He fasts,
denies himself drink, women, tobacco. But all in vain. The
lighted way is hard to find, and his hour has not yet come. Yet,
sure as day follows night, it will. He has almost given up when
one day the village is raided by bandits, the notorious jagunços,
led by the famous badman, Joãozinho Bem-Bem. Augusto be-
friends Joãozinho, sensing his fate is tied to him in some way. He
is invited to ride with the band—the devil calling him from the
deep—and is tempted to accept. But something holds him back.
He soon finds out what it is. When the bandits leave, he sets out
on a new pilgrimage, heading south, under the stars, after a flight
of birds, who show him the way. In a far village, where God takes
him by the hand, he meets Joãozinho again. The bandits are
about to wreak reprisals on the village. Then Augusto, illuminated, realizes he is a marked man. He rises to the height of his
calling as he dies killing his friend, Joãozinho, to save the village,
which proclaims him a saint.

Turíbio, Lalino, Augusto, are instinctive beings whose experiences are on an elementary level and yet carry far beyond that. The reason is that the author endows them not only with a rich sensory apparatus but also a lively intelligence and a full emotional range. They are psychic creatures. To be able to transform raw energy into psychodynamics is Guimarães Rosa's peculiar triumph and glory. He shows what can be done with simple people, who are not necessarily simpler than anyone else, when they are given the proper legs to stand on and the right lungs to breathe with, and exposes the fallacy of those advocates of corporate effort who argue that the inner man is of no use to the novelist whose interest is primarily social psychology. In Guimarães Rosa it is by being distinctly individual that each character becomes universal. He is given a face and gestures, a personal outlook, even an implicit metaphysic, without for that being made any less representative of his time, place, class, and position. In being irreducibly himself he speaks for others.

Eloquent proof of this is the masterful *Corpo de Baile,* an immense book composed of seven novellas of varying lengths, some long enough to stand as independent novels, others briefer and more concentrated, but all drawn from the same life-giving spring. There is a sublime gift in Guimarães Rosa that puts a blessing on everything he touches. The setting, as usual, is the sertão and the surrounding areas which open into it at every turn, like rivers into an ocean. The angles and perspectives are many, as the vision is shifting and manifold. "The center of the circle is naturally fixed, but if the circumference were, too, it would be nothing but a huge center," Guimarães Rosa quotes Plotinus in the epigraph. And that sets the tone, and the scope. Again, the protagonists are the simple local denizens, mostly herdsmen, small landowners, and assorted colorful characters: hermits, seers, wise paupers, wandering bums and minstrels, in passage through this life to the next, one and multiple in the brief span allotted them, where nothing much happens in many cases, and yet everything does, because the sertão, an outsize miniature of the world, is a huge cup brimming over into which each man is emptied as he drinks his fill from it.

"Big is the world," Guimarães Rosa says again and again in *Corpo de Baile*, a refrain that becomes a leitmotif, as the whole universe chimes in on it. It rolls over hill and valley, like a trumpet call that can become "a threat or a hymn" as it goes thundering down waterfalls, or suddenly parts to reveal the ominous figure of the giant buriti palm rising like a totem with its magnificent cascading panache to overshadow the landscape, "immense and silent . . . like a church" that "makes you think of Heaven," recalling a time of "common joy . . . when all things spoke on the high plains." In the land of the buriti, where "even sleep is dangerous, an abyss," every flutter in the dark is a portent of imminent loss, a new brink. For "everything that transforms life happens quietly, in the shade, without warning."

For Soropita, once a champion herdsman, now retired into cozy domesticity on his ranch with the love of his life, the wondrous and gay Doralda, the blow strikes from behind, a flash of doubt in certainty. Soropita has reached home base. He has built his harbor in the high seas. His story opens with his ride home from Andrequicé, a township a day or so away, where he has gone shopping. He is on his trusty horse, enjoying the beautiful scenery. He is loaded with gifts: the latest installment of a weekly radio drama—a ritual performance—he has memorized to transmit to the people of the area, who will broadcast it over the countryside; presents for his wife: scented soap, medicines, a length of cloth for curtains. He never fails her with his trinkets and baubles. Doralda deserves the best. In her he has found serenity and contentment. In times past he was a fast man with a gun who lived a wild life on the plains, brawling, whoring, reveling with the best. But no more. Nowadays he makes a modest living from a little store he has in the nearby village, Āo, where he sells household goods. No great enterprise, perhaps, but he makes ends meet, and on the whole he can say that life has been lavish to him. He is satisfied. But also a bit nostalgic. As he trots along he lingers on memories of his past life, which flit through him like "wandering streams." He even takes a certain somewhat morbid pleasure in finding a worm in the apple: a family secret. Doralda has a shady past. He met her in a whorehouse. The thought is a torment, and at the same time tantalizing. The stage is set for the drama. The trouble with Soropita, as he says to himself, is that he is a man who feels both joy and suffering more than others. He shows it when he runs into Dalberto, an ex-bandit and old companion in debauchery. A pang shoots through him. The rules of hospitality compel him to invite his friend, whom he has not seen for five years and who has strayed far off the beaten track, foraging with his men, home to dinner, but he is afraid Dalberto may have run into Doralda somewhere in the course of his wanderings and will recognize her. The inner battle he fights, as jealousy begins to gnaw at him, soon reduces his life to a complete shambles. Reminiscing as they go, Soropita and Dalberto start kicking closed doors open. At first they skip along, fancy-free. But soon they are goaded into sensual memories, which touch on raw nerves. Among Dalberto's men there is a tall Negro whom Soropita fears as a symbol of all his dreads. Doralda must have taken more than one Negro to bed with her in her day. She was famous in the trade, and open to all mail. In his vagaries Soropita sees her being brutally violated by the black man. The image fuses with a story Dalberto is telling him of a girl he has come upon in a whorehouse whom he is thinking of marrying. He wants Soropita's advice on the subject. An insinuation? "A shadow of sadness" invades Soropita, "numbing him, a premonition that something unpleasant was going to happen." At home he is listless, uneasy, on edge. To torture himself, he forces Dalberto to stay overnight. He watches his every move, with a sharp eye for Doralda. In every glance she exchanges with Dalberto he seems to detect a suspicious intimacy. He makes them drink, hoping to loosen their tongues. When nothing happens, he is almost disappointed. He frets and fumes, until Dalberto finally retires. Then he subjects Doralda to a harrowing inquisition, relishing her humiliation as he makes her strip before him. They spend half the night going over her soiled past. He is on the verge of violence at every moment. At the same time he is racked by a sudden longing for purity, a chaste love for her, the source of life and happiness, mother of illusion. He sees Dalberto's departure with satisfaction the next morning. But not

before he has it out with the helpless Negro, who finds himself
rolling in the dust. And so, with a transport, another day dawns.
Soropita takes a deep breath. He lives intensely. After his burst
of conflicting emotions he gradually regains his balance with a
return of the old sense of peace and plenitude, as the broken
pieces of his life start to come together again.

Less fortunate, it seems, will be the hell-bent Pedro Orosio in
"O Recado do Morro" (Message from the Mountain). Pedro is
another reckless giant with cosmic lungs, on a vertiginous course
to victory or downfall. He is a great lady-killer whose philander-
ings have earned him many enemies. Obscure antagonisms pursue him wherever he goes. But he plays with fire. Nowadays he
works as a guide and scout in the plains. On this particular
occasion he is conducting several men of learning on a tour of
the high plateau leading to his native land, the Campos Gerais.
There is Mr. Alquiste, a foreign naturalist who collects mineral
specimens and samples of the local flora and fauna; a blond
priest, brother Sinfrão, who acts as interpreter; Jujuca do Açude,
a landowner from thereabouts, and Jujuca's farmhand, Ivo, who
nurses a grudge against Pedro because of a woman he lost to him.
On these simple elements hangs a broad tale. They are on a long
trek, a nostalgic voyage for Pedro, back to childhood haunts, his
old stamping ground. He is proud to be the host. He feels king of
the place, of the surrounding forests, the green slopes, the great
cliffs, high bluffs and ledges, deep gullies, gorges and rivers. But
danger is near. Always in sight as they advance, immutable at a
distance, is the monolithic Heron Peak, a bleak omen rising in
the rocky landscape, "solitary, dark, triangular, like a pyramid."
An oracular voice from the peak, interpreted by Gorgulho, an
addled hermit who lives in a bat cave and looks like a dragonfly,
bears a message in which there is a secret warning for Pedro. It
comes through garbled and there is nothing to be made of it, but
the trip begins to take on a hidden meaning. Pedro shudders, his
face smarting in the wind. Ghostly relics come creeping out of
crypts and grottoes. There is Catraz, Gorgulho's brother, a mad
inventor, followed by another local crank, a goitrous prophet of
doom. Back safe and sound in the village they started out from,

Pedro takes off to celebrate. He is in fine form. It is Saturday and
he has a little girl friend in town, a real fine young lady, a
perfect jewel, the daughter of a respectable muleteer. He has
marriage in mind for one of these days. Meantime his eye
wanders. Life is a lark. There is gayness and ferment in the air.
As the party starts in the streets, festive songs are born on guitars.
They will take root in people's hearts, spread far and wide, on
the lips of travelers, the tongues of the blind, who will recite
them on roadsides. Pedro is bursting out of his buttons with life
and energy. But beware. Just across the street, lost in dark
reveries, is the Collector, another oddball, a hoary old-timer who
imagines himself immensely wealthy and spends his time blithely
counting his blessings, chalking huge sums on a wall. Pedro is
walking the plank. There is Ivo, full of good-fellowship, inviting
him with a comradely thump on the back to come have a drink
with him, by way of reconciliation. Off they go to a cabin on the
outskirts, where suddenly the trap is sprung. Pedro, with a few
drinks under his belt, blearied and softened, has been ambushed.
Ivo's men are there to kill him. They close in. For a split second
Pedro is on the thin line between life and death. But then, with
a toss of his mighty shoulders, at a single seven-league stride, he is
off, loping, scaling mountains, jumping from star to star, toward
his native land, already wrapped in primeval mist as he plunges
into "that voiceless whisper in which one remembers what one
has never known and awakens in a dream, beyond pain and
peril."

So a hero finds his legend, as the whole of nature rejoices for
him. A variation on the theme is the merry "Uma Estoria de
Amor" (A Love Story), where Manuelzão, "big Manuel," another
Brobdingnagian who administers a fazenda for an absent landlord throws a huge party to baptize a small local chapel he has
built on a hillock, over his mother's grave, an occasion that
becomes a moment of happiness and fulfillment in the lives of all
the people in the surrounding countryside. Manuelzão, as manager and overseer for the potent Federico Freyre, is respected as a
big boss in the area, a title he has earned through courage and
hard work. There was blood and sweat in his early life as a

cowhand. What he has he has made from scratch, and he bows to
no man. The chapel is his crowning achievement, the high point
of his career. In his gleeful mood, the sky is the limit. He will
throw a big bash, break all the windows to celebrate. Perhaps
because deep down he knows he has aged and the end of the road
is near. He has been having presentiments of his coming death.
As a safeguard, he has brought an illegitimate son, Adelço, and
Adelço's wife, Leonisia, the apple of his eye, to live with him.
They will take over for him. He is looking forward to a ripe old
age surrounded by his grandchildren. The trouble is that Adelço
is a shiftless do-nothing. But so much the worse. The party is in
full swing. The crowds are arriving. There is brother Petroaldo,
a ruddy priest; a happy troglodyte called João Urugem; the usual
cross section of local humanity, including a couple of vagabonds
taken in for charity on the fazenda: old Camilo, and his girl
friend, a fleabitten old windbag who once shared a hut with him,
Joana Xaviel. Joana is a famous storyteller, who is soon transfigured by inspiration as she bursts into song. The party is a big
success. It lasts all night, through the next morning, and into the
following evening. In the course of it Manuel has his ups and
downs. The small miseries of life are present in every joy. There
is the bitter thought of Adelço, the loafer, who has no love for his
father. Suddenly Manuel is fatigued, thoroughly depleted. The
currents of death run deep in life, a clinging vine spreading
mortal coils in dark arteries. Melancholy follows euphoria.
Manuel feels out of his depth. It is all beyond him. "When the
sun sets, the day darkens and I see nothing any more." But then
old Camilo, whom nobody ever suspected of any talent, sits down
to tell a tale in rhymed prose that lifts every heart to new
heights. Shadows part, and we are in the realm of myth, "at the
beginning of the world," in that age when "man had to battle
the other animals in order to be the first to receive a soul." It is a
"simple poetry" composed by "the birds, the trees, the earth, the
rivers," life itself.

A drink of the same heady draught is "Buriti," a loving
portrait of a farm on the sertão, Buriti-Bom, and its inhabitants:
stern and stalwart iô Liodoro, a gentleman of the old school;

Maria Behu, his pious spinster daughter; the beautiful Gloria, his youngest child, just coming into bloom, anxious to love; Isio, his other son, who lives across the river with Dijina whom the family does not accept because of her doubtful antecedents; and Lalinha, his daughter-in-law, a city girl he has taken under his forceful wing after she was abandoned by his other son, the derelict Irvino.

"Buriti" is a story of family life on the farm, the passing seasons and the passions that go with them. The setting is the high plain, near a marsh, under the shadow of the magnificent Big Buriti, a totemic effigy towering overhead like a steeple. Its swaying image is in the heart and mind.

Life is hard on the plain, sometimes a long chore and travail, but it has its compensations. Buriti-Bom is one of those clearings in the wilds, a still pond in the rapids, where in spite of surrounding tremors everything is ultimately safe, fine, and noble. Or so it seems at first. But under the surface, as usual, runs a fault that at any moment can split open to become a gaping pit. Lalinha is the first to lose foot, out of sheer inertia. She is on a long rest cure, but not entirely by choice. It was iô Liodoro, the patriarch of the dynasty, who moved her to the farm, to put her in cold storage until Irvino returns for her. But as the wait for Irvino prolongs itself indefinitely, it becomes senseless. She no longer loves him, or cares whether she will ever see him again. The exorcisms and sorceries of various itinerant fortunetellers are of no avail. She is in a false role. Yet she dares not leave. Iô Liodoro, a widower for many years—he has women all over the countryside—has a strange hold over her. She cannot live without a man forever. There is a heavy atmosphere in the house. Lalinha and iô Liodoro find themselves meeting evenings in the sitting room, after the rest of the house has retired, holding their breaths, in sustained passages of lyric beauty, to talk of a love that can never be consummated. Then there is Gloria, waiting for Manuel, a young doctor traveling cross country on a jeep, vaccinating cattle as he goes. He dreams of her. In his mind Buriti-Bom is the center of the world, the wayfarer's haven. He has left his love there, and his image lingers with it for a while, then wanes. He is gone for a long time. Meantime Gloria has struck up a blazing affair with a neighboring landowner, a "friend of the family," the libidinous Gualberto Gaspar, whose wife has gone insane. Gloria seems headed for a strong dose of the same medicine. A symbol of the shifting quicksands that threaten to engulf the family is the enigmatic Chief Zequiel, who lives in terror in an abandoned mill on the edge of the property, where night begins. He is a squatter, like old Camilo, cast out by the tide, which keeps sweeping in after him. For years he has been sleeping with an eye open, in paranoic fear of some unknown enemy, listening to the nightmarish sounds of the sertão, whose spirit haunts him. He sleepwalks among hidden meanings, a sort of headless oracle, an avatar of all the dreads that the shadows hide. A croaking voice, the twitch of a branch, a batting wing, a stirring in the marsh, the chirp of an insect, the rustling of a prowler, all are an awesome part of that immense night that he defines as "everything the day cannot hold." A statement that adequately describes the whole of *Corpo de Baile,* where still scenes are bottomless ponds that open like inner eyes. The strange images floating there are not of this world. They belong in another order, where a burbling brook that suddenly runs dry in the middle of the night, leaving an uncommon silence in the air, becomes a metaphysical event that alerts new senses, awakening sleepers to the vacuum of space. Dogs howl, horses stamp, and the heart misses a beat, as it leaps ahead of itself.

It often does in *Grande Sertão: Veredas,* Guimarães Rosa's most ambitious work to date, a monumental epic of the sertão and at the same time a spiritual "testament," as he calls it, of an imposing richness and grandeur.

Here, at last, is that rare thing fulfilled: the outer whirl that becomes inner spin. *Grande Sertão* is not just a world, but a whole cosmos. It is a terminal book, a Summa. It touches on all the points of the compass to become a total experience that engages the reader at every level. It did the author, too. He put everything he had into it. The situations, psychic, emotional, imaginative, are exhaustive. For those who want social significance, it is there, too, in its proper subordinate place, in subtle synthesis with the rest. Nor does intensity sacrifice breadth. *Grande Sertão* spreads over almost boundless landscapes. It even tends to sprawl and ramble. But it has a strong central hinge: its protagonist, Riobaldo, also known as Tatarana, or Firefly—a euphemism for sharpshooter—an ex-jagunço, now, like Soropita and so many other characters in Guimarães Rosa, a settled fazendeiro, who recalls for the benefit of a faceless listener, who provides the sounding board, his early adventures around the turn of the century with his armed band, under various commands. Riobaldo's life was both of the flesh and of the spirit. With his memories he regurgitates a lifetime's wisdom and experience.

The method is characteristically Guimarães Rosan. *Grande Sertão* may have been born from one of those casual encounters in the street the author likes, which sometimes lead to unusual discoveries. There was the time he rode a cab in Rio and recognized an ex-cowhand in the driver, who turned out to be from his region. Soon they were fast friends. "I took the man to have a drink with me," Guimarães Rosa tells us, "and we sat and talked all evening." They not only got along famously but went on something of a binge together. He had the man tell him his life, while he sat with a glint in his eye, taking piles of notes. Similarly inclined, presumably, is the listener in *Grande Sertão*. The Conrad-like convention somewhat hobbles the story, which is perhaps overly discursive, but also shapes it. A single initial impulse that gathers momentum as it goes—there are no chapters—becomes a mighty outpour somewhere between a confessional monologue and a happy-go-lucky picaresque, comic, parodic, effusive, extravagant, recalling both the medieval romance and Cervantes. But the self-torturing, inner-questioning strand that runs through the book like a dark thread is in the great tradition of the Russian and German novels. The structure is circular. The voyage through space and time ends where it begins, in the psychic present, a constantly evolving mental substance out of which conscience is gradually formed.

The jagunços were a mixed lot, refugees from justice, most of them, at times soldiers turned mercenaries, at others simply homeless peasants on a stipend, idealists some, occasionally proud professionals comparable to Japan's samurai or Italy's condottieri. They were mavericks, fiercely independent, diehard individualists, loyal friends, deadly enemies, who fought under different political chieftains and local warlords and lived from pillage, rape, and destruction. They often engaged in bloody wars among themselves, sacking the land as they went. Once in a while they were a civilizing force, when led by a man of vision. There is a kind of duality in their lives that Riobaldo embodies: an aspiration to great things, to feats and glorious deeds, combined with an irresistible bent for abjection, crime, and savagery. In them clash the elementary contradictions of a primitive land in the making. The great semilegendary figures of wise and brave leaders pass through *Grande Sertão:* honorable veterans like Zé Bebelo, Joca Ramiro, Medeiro Vaz, and also archetypal traitors like the Machiavellian Hermogenes.

The jagunço's home is the plain: he is on the move day and night, sleeping, loving, and dying where he can. Such is the story of Riobaldo, who was lured into the profession by his love and admiration for the mysterious Diadorim, who is less a person than a symbol of all that is elusive in man's fate. Diadorim, unknown to Riobaldo, whose passionate attachment to his beloved seems to have disturbingly homosexual overtones, is a woman in disguise. She is like the girl in the old Spanish legend who wore mail and set forth to battle the Moors to avenge her father's death. In fact, this is precisely Diadorim's situation. She is after the errant Hermogenes, her father's murderer. There is purity and constancy in her single-minded dedication to her end, which is long in being fulfilled. In Riobaldo's mind she stands for exalted will devoted to high purpose. But she is more than that. The fact that he spends years at her side, under her tenebrous sway, without ever suspecting the true reason for his fascination, until her death reveals it, is a sign of the eternally unfathomable that lies beyond immediate appearances. If the androgynous Diadorim seems something of an anomaly in the order of things, she is only a manifestation of the epicene in life, the ambivalence at the root of all human experience. She and her archenemy, the evil Hermogenes, apparently poles apart, are probably one at the source.

It is according to some such scheme that *Grande Sertão* is built. Riobaldo, from the vantage point of sedentary middle age—modest affluence, conjugal stability—is taking stock. The time has come to try to figure things out, to make a clean breast of everything. The corpse lies in state, waiting for the autopsy.

There is a lot in Riobaldo's life that remains impenetrable and disconcerting to him. He seems to have dealt with mysterious forces that sometimes favored, sometimes defeated, him, but always somehow managed to slip through his fingers. Life is strange. It takes away with one hand what it gives with the other. A man never knows where he stands. Thus Riobaldo was always a brave jagunço with worthy feats of valor to his name. He stood his own and feared no man. Often he teetered on the brink of oblivion. But, one way or another, he pulled through. Not only out of good luck, it seems to him. There must have been some other obscure factor working for him. A thorny problem. But he thinks he has hit on the solution. He must have a secret pact with the Devil. He remembers the countless times he saw the Evil One whirling in the dusty plain. At one point they came to an understanding, which led to partnership. There is a mystic encounter on a starless night in which we see Riobaldo in Satan's combustible embrace. After which, inhabited by the forces of survival of the sertão, Riobaldo is invincible. He rides in triumph, a living conflagration, torch in hand, rising through the ranks, until he is one of the top leaders in his region. Yet one day, for no comprehensible reason, he folds his banner and withdraws. Ever since he has been struggling to make sense of it all.

The world is crazy, says Riobaldo, nothing adds up and man will never know the true reasons for his actions, no matter how hard he digs for them. You can rack your brains until the cows come home, it leads nowhere. Things happen too fast. You can never keep up. Try to catch the Devil by the tail, all you do is pull the rug out from under yourself. Looking back, it all seems

almost unreal to him now. "You dream, and it's over." Perhaps
man is a creature out of Hell, who therefore has no choice but to
join Satan's hordes. Yet he seems to act of his own free will. How
to reconcile the two notions? There is a missing link somewhere.
The outer dialectic that keeps man swinging between good and
evil, he senses, is really an inner pendulum. He who feels trapped
by circumstances is actually a prisoner of his own nature. His
pact with the Devil, Riobaldo realizes, has been his attempt to
come to terms with the unknown forces in himself.

Thus the sertão, the plain of life—the land of the soul, the
home of the brave—enters the realm of allegory. Those who cross
it in search of meanings, following the lines of their fate, are on
the road to self. First and foremost among them is Riobaldo. He
has been a happy hunter, shooting at every target, hoping sooner
or later to hit the right one. Even when he seemed to be playing
a role cut out for him, he realized indistinctly that he was on his
own secret pathway through life. The stops along the road—the
veredas, those palm groves in mountain hollows—were inner
signposts. In each, like a promise renewed, he found his image,
his identity. Even as he chose he was chosen. That much he
knows now. "Everyone has his own strictly private road to follow,
except that usually one doesn't know how to find it. . . . but it's
there all the same. . . . It must be. Otherwise life would just be
the stupid mess it is. Every day, at each moment, there's only one
act for us that's right and proper. It's hidden, but there, anyway.
Everything else . . . would be false." This revelation takes Riobaldo beyond God and the Devil, to an existential statement: "I
made my own misery." There is no Devil, there is only man, he
concludes. He stands alone in a shapeless world, impressing his
will and imprint on it. In building his personal code of ethics he
assumes his fate.

Grande Sertão, like the Talmud, is an intricate and somewhat
unwieldy colossus. Not all is perfection. The wasteful convention
of the listener, which is bothersome at first, and sometimes
retardatory later, seems unnecessary and unreal. Riobaldo is a
great raconteur. He needs no specific audience. But here is
another pitfall. Riobaldo has a breath-taking tall tale to tell.

Little wonder he gets carried away with himself. He talks circles around us. Because the hectic pace of word and imagery he sets at the beginning has to be maintained throughout, the verbiage sometimes tends to short-circuit the narrative. The circular structure helps clog the pipes. In spite of constant action and movement, many pages seem static. The very wealth of detail, one of the beauties of the book, is numbing in the long run as it begins to cancel itself out. Then there is the matter of Diadorim, who, unlike the other characters, all—except perhaps for the women, who are less individualized than the men: they tend on the whole to be fairly conventional figures—vivid portraits, rounded out at their fullest point, never quite materializes. Perhaps she was not meant to. She is an airy character out of legend and romance, and perfectly acceptable as such, but the illusion strains and shatters whenever it comes into contact with the hard realities of the psychological novel. The result of imperfect fusion is a certain amount of leakage. The fact, for instance, that Riobaldo could remain ignorant of Diadorim's sex through years of communal living seems impossible at face value and not entirely convincing as parable. The incongruity remains unresolved. Finally, there is an element of fatigue toward the end of the book, which leaves us at loose ends. The last lap is the longest, and dwindles by attrition. There is a drop, and a gap. From the moment Riobaldo gave up his career as a jagunço to the present day when he is telling his story years have gone by. We are carried across them in a couple of perfunctory paragraphs.

But these are trickles that only slightly weaken the main flow. The substance of the book remains intact. Even when still, somehow it continues to move underneath. Nothing can undermine its deeper resonance and humanity. Its surface glows because it is lit from within, and lives because it always carries beyond. There is a constant sense of spiritual evolution, because there is significance in every gesture. If the eye sometimes tires, the mind rushes on. And that is what matters. In Riobaldo not only a man but a metaphysic is at stake. In a trial held in the open plain by the jagunços, in which each opinion is a verdict,

the pitched battle of human voices is amplified to become the
roar of the ages. In a soulful herd of sleepy zebus roaming in a
meadow under the weight of some ancestral sorrow is all the pain
and sadness of anguished man torn between his suicidal impulses
and a helpless longing for some forgotten immortality.

The "metaphysical germ" in Guimarães Rosa is perhaps that
point of tension in every man where the death wish meets its
opposite, the instinct for survival. It is the seed that contains
both, in precarious balance, side by side. They grow together, the
two legs a man stands on—a foot in this world, the other in the
next—joined at the crotch of pain.

Such, in bare outline, might be the general sense of *Primeiras
Estórias,* a particularly intriguing book, full of forked tongues of
fire, brief flares that split into cold flames. In them burns the
sertão, but not so much its physical being now as its phantom
form. *Primeiras Estórias* is made of essences. The "metaphysical
germ" is in something like its pure state. It inhabits very short
stories that just barely envelop it. Each is an open socket
bristling with live wires. Only one or two of the stories have been
translated, and they are of difficult access to the foreign reader.
They are written entirely on the subliminal level of language, in
lower octaves, pitched almost below earshot. Yet one thing is
clear. The vision is closer, more inward, more intimate than
before, to the point of vertigo. There is no rim, only a threshold,
where we stand for a moment, in extrasensory perception, on the
point of taking off for somewhere else. Guimarães Rosa has
preceded us there, and back. *Primeiras Estórias,* he tells us, followed a near scrape with death he had in 1958. He speaks of a
circulatory disease, "blood metabolism"—a sudden blowout. A
change occurred in him, he says, a new attitude was born. "What
exactly happened, I can't say myself. It was just something I felt.
A new way of feeling." He was a man who had been to the other
side, and lived to tell of it.

"The Third Bank of the River" is the title of one of the
stories. And that is where they all seem to take place. Some are
like fables, turned inside out to become reveries. There is a child
of unknown parents on an impressionistic voyage through mem-

ory that becomes a mythical search for identity. There is the story
of Sorôco, cut loose not only from his ancestry but also from his
descendants. It is based on an incident the author remembers
from his childhood. An old man, a butcher, bearded, in rags, was
seeing his mad daughter off at the station. She was about to be
shipped off to an asylum. In the story, Sorôco's plight is made
twice as grim. Both his mother and daughter are being sent away.
In their derangement they wear festive clothes for the funereal
occasion. As the train rolls out of the station, bearing them off in
a barred coach, they raise their voices in an eerie song that seems
to set every tongue to tolling, so that soon the village air is ringing
like a huge bell. Each man, a victim of his own separate heart attack, joins in where he can, in a discord and cacophony under
which there is a strange harmony. For the third bank of the river
is the land every soul craves for. There the drowned come out to
shore, the tired rest, the wounded are healed, the lost are found,
the living reconciled with the dead. All that is needed to get there
is a slight shift in sights, as the bottom falls out of the barrel. So it
happens that an honest family man one day cuts himself adrift
on a boat, abandoning kith and kin, to become a river bum. The
urge comes on him like an access, a sudden frenzy, and nothing
can hold him back. Perhaps it is easier to be forever severed from
those you love than to be eternally joined to them. For years,
oblivious to the world, he sails up and down in frugal splendor,
without so much as a fire to warm him at night, living from
handouts. In time his wife dies, his daughter marries and moves,
his son is left alone to mourn for him. The boy grows, ages. His
father is still at large. And now the son is, too. He inherits the
old yen and yearning. He would replace his father on the boat if
he could. Not that he jumps at the first chance offered him. When
the old man, or his ghost, appears around a bend in the river,
raising his arm in greeting, as he beckons him from the other
side, he is so petrified that his hair stands on end and he runs for
his life. But later he regrets having missed the boat, instead of
rocking it, and asks to be sent down the river in it when he
dies.

Since he pulled out the last stops in *Primeiras Estórias*, Guimarães Rosa seems to have been cutting more corners all the time. Nowadays he is working on a series of sketches—he writes two a month—for publication in a medical journal that has a wide circulation in the back country, even in areas not reached by other magazines or newspapers. The arrangement suits him nicely. It is good for both his pocket and his reputation, he says. It also imposes an excellent discipline. The stories must be short, a maximum of two pages, so that every word counts. "Control is always good. It keeps you on your toes, forces you to find new means." It also requires "a lot of vitamins," he says heartily. For the man who has been through the eye of the needle can put a story on the head of a pin.

V

Juan Carlos Onetti,

or the Shadows

on the Wall

MONTEVIDEO, the capital of a welfare state fallen on hard times, has become a drab gray city. When we were there in July—the middle of winter in the Southern Hemisphere—the weather was unseasonably muggy. Heavy clouds hung overhead, the depressing remnants of a long heat wave. A strike of public employees, utility workers, etc., had added paralysis to bureaucratic blight; drought had brought power rationing; the streets were dark. Garbage strewn on doorsteps blew about in a listless wind. There was a general feeling of glumness and apathy. As usual in times of economic crisis, the accompanying devaluation was not only monetary but human as well. Life goes on, but in an atmosphere of unreality. The wear and tear shows in the worried glances of people hurrying into offices lost in the interiors of old buildings with stalled elevators.

In the slow drizzle, trudging down the street in a bulky coat, stooped under the weight of the city, is a sleepwalker on a sleepless night. Like the city, he looks tired and middle-aged. He

[173]

is tall, gaunt, with splotches of white in his gray hair, insomniac
eyes straining behind horn-rimmed glasses, painfully grimacing
lips, a high professorial forehead, and the slouch of an aging
clerk. His grandfather was a stockbroker, his father a customs
official, and he, the protagonist of an unfinished book he has
been writing for years and publishing in installments, under
different titles, is "a lonely man smoking somewhere in the
city . . . turning toward the shadow on the wall at night to
dwell on nonsensical fantasies." He seems friendless, idle, and
absent, and has always been that way, because of some flaw of
nature, some inner lack dating at least as far back as adolescence,
when he already "had nothing to do with anyone." He lives in
solitary confinement, withdrawn and practically unattached. It
was this physical and emotional isolation, he has said, that
turned him into a writer in the first place, in spite of himself, for
unknown reasons, out of a habit that became his "vice, passion,
and misfortune." He bears his cross as if atoning for some
nameless guilt that can never be expiated or forgiven. Such is the
picture we have of Onetti, the lone wolf of Uruguayan letters,
whose habitat, according to the critic Mario Benedetti, is the
disaster area of those fated to suffer "the basic failure of all
bonds, the general misunderstanding and miscasting of lots in
life."

Onetti, an ardent Arltian, belongs to a "lost" generation that
came of age around 1940, when the intellectual life of the
country was being reassessed against a background of demagoguery and political disenchantment, of totalitarianism in Europe, and nationalism—with pro-Axis sympathies—in Argentina.
In Uruguay a reactionary government ruled the country from
1933 to 1942, eroding faith in democracy as the corruption lurking
under the monotonous surface of bureaucratic stability became
daily more obvious. There were many broken lives in those days.
Onetti speaks of the nihilism of his generation—portrayed in
massive detail in his second novel, *Tierra de Nadie* (No Man's
Land, 1941)—as a delayed echo of the epidemic malaise of the
twenties. But, of course, Onetti lived it as an endemic phenomenon. For him, it was the disillusionment and resulting indi-

vidualism of an era in which he was one of those who fell by the wayside.

In Uruguay, as in its next-door neighbor Argentina, the thirties and forties marked a period of great literary ferment. Until then Uruguayan culture had flourished in circles that followed European fashions and had been eclectic and cosmopolitan. By some curious but significant quirk of fate, Uruguay contributed Jules Laforgue and Lautréamont, and later Jules Supervielle, to French literature. At home in the nineteenth and early twentieth centuries it had nourished the usual schools of academicians and traditionalists. Toward 1915 or 1920, disquieting underground movements had begun to be felt in the work of Quiroga, where an era's neurasthenia had suddenly turned introspective and touched somber depths. But Quiroga was something of an anomaly in his day—when no one wanted to fish in troubled waters—and his work remained exceptional. At the turn of the century—the heyday of Modernism in all of Latin America—the general mood, in spite of literary agonies imported from Europe, was hopeful and optimistic. The first decade of the century, balancing the stresses created by the vast wave of immigrants that reached the shores of the River Plate between 1880 and 1910, saw the rise of a middle class that found its truculent but whimsical spokesman in the person of Florencio Sánchez, our singlehanded inventor of the theater of social realism. It was a period of economic development for the River Plate, which prospered through the First World War. Symptoms of the age were political commitment and social reform, literary experimentation and radicalism in government. The euphoria, as we know, lasted until about 1930. The climate of the period was put in a few words by the Argentine poet Carlos Mastronardi, who, looking back on it wistfully across the years some time ago, said: "We were the last happy men."

The thirties, with the coming to power of nationalist groups, changed all that. There was the beginning of panic and collapse in intellectual circles. Isolated figures at first—an Arlt, who discovered unsuspectedly disruptive behavioral patterns in the humdrum and the commonplace—started to draw a bleakly pessimistic picture of their society. With the usual lag in time, the River Plate, reflecting worldwide insecurity, was caving in under the dislocations of the twentieth century. The atmospheric distress contaminated regional literature—for instance, the works of Uruguay's grim soul-searcher, Francisco Espínola. But it was essentially an urban phenomenon. Toward 1940 it was widespread. It throbbed with poetic splendor in the essays of our great "agonist," Ezequiel Martínez Estrada, who bared a continent's inherited ills mercilessly in his belligerent sociological mural, *Radiografía de la Pampa* (1939). His *La Cabeza de Goliat* (The Head of Goliat) was to give an incisive diagnosis of the ravages of urbanization. Suddenly, it seemed, the battle call of the thirties, "Here and now," had issued in the age of debunking, of violent indictments and denunciations of a system already in crumbling decline. Our novel, still suffering from upper-class nostalgia—therefore threatened with becoming an extinct species —had to catch up with the times to survive. Which was easier said than done. Adapting, for it, meant not only getting reorganized but shifting its foundations. It was a slow process, a timid growth, but far-reaching in its effects. As literary "schools," once active but never very cohesive, broke up, for the first time our writers, living in exacerbated isolation in anonymous big cities, turned their eyes inward, to build subjective worlds. In this they were part of a pattern that reflected not only the fall of established values but the facts of daily life. A new type of human being, a creature of twilight, rootless, rancorous, frustrated, displaced, populated our big cities. He was not so much the Marxist underdog as the spiritual outlaw, the moral discard. Arlt had aleady drawn his prophetic portrait. Now Onetti followed suit, with the dour shrug of a man shouldering the burden of a sad responsibility. In a prefatory note to *Tierra de Nadie,* whose action takes place in the Buenos Aires of 1940, Onetti has said: "I paint a group of people who may seem exotic in Buenos Aires but are nevertheless representative of a generation. . . . The fact is that the most important country of the young South American continent has started to produce a type of morally indifferent individual who has lost his faith and all interest in his own fate." He adds, defining a bankrupt attitude conditioned by the surrounding indigence: "Let no one reproach the novelist for having undertaken the portrait of this human type in the same spirit of indifference."

In his first published work, *El Pozo* (The Pit, 1939), the gloomy protagonist, Eladio, a thinly veiled projection of the author, had already recorded his skepticism in regard to personal commitment, his phlegmatic unconcern for anything resembling direct action or involvement. With sad irony Eladio confesses his total lack of social consciousness, of "popular spirit." The tone, as in most of Onetti, is confessional. Why even bother to put pen to paper? wonders Eladio, thinking out loud for the author. The willful answer is in a kind of militant argument for self-expression. "It's true I don't know how to write," he admits. "But I write about myself." Eladio, with his apoplectic inhibitions, is the classic Outsider. He lives disconnected from the world, stranded within himself, adrift in his tiny corner on the borderline of humanity, without any possibility of joining the mainstream. He begins and ends in himself. Which is why his single ambition is "to write the story of a soul, all by itself, without any of the events it had to mix in whether it wanted to or not." Though, of course, whether he "wants to or not," he forms part of the unconscious community of the lonely, the diaspora of the estranged. Even in his alienation, or because of it, he is the representative of a time and place, a frame of mind, an epoch. It is this fact that gives his experiences relevance and validity. To have realized this is Onetti's merit. In a literary scene still too often made up of inflated social canvases, painters of the soul like Onetti are a rarity. But, if only because in the last years they have been producing much of our best work, they have begun to seem inevitable. That our literature is gradually shifting its focus from object to subject, in appearance, perhaps, narrowing its perspectives, is actually a clear sign of our growing self-awareness and, of course, the price in pain and distress that we are paying for it. The price may be high, but, then, who can deny that the stakes are, too? Meditating on the world of solitary inner lives he has created out of what might pass for superfluous materials in the age of industrial waste, Onetti, a man who has never bar-gained, said in an interview in 1961, without immodesty: "All I want to express is the adventure of man."

For Onetti, who seems to suffer from permanent pangs of conscience over his life, the adventure has been a dismal one. We are trying to piece it together with him, up in a small hotel room in the shabbiness of downtown Montevideo, overlooking an expanse of limp rooftops and cluttered back yards. Perhaps the rain, which is sprinkling hot splinters outside, makes him take a particularly dim view of things. With its drone in the back-ground, the conversation, like a worn record, progresses in fits and starts. Onetti is a man of few words, most of them mumbled or swallowed entirely. He sits slumped, chain-smoking, hunching his shoulders every now and then, looking miserably uncom-fortable.

"To think someone has come all the way out here just to talk to me," he says in his usual slightly bored and vaguely deprecat-ing tone, but perhaps with a little inward smile, in which it seems to us we can detect a trace of coquetry.

We met the night before at a party, where we listened to a needle in a tired groove churning out tangos by the immortal Gardelito, who, though dead many years, was, as the saying goes among his devotees, sounding better than ever; and after a sentimental drink or two Onetti, an old fan, became harsh, ponderous, mournful, and finally sullen.

Now he has come in with a heavy shuffle, a sign of chronic exhaustion. In periods of insomnia he does not eat or sleep for a week. He smokes, drinks, and fidgets; then he collapses for days. He has left his post at a branch of the municipal library to come speak to us, and he has been with us for no more than a few minutes when the phone rings. His wife is worried about him. He has wandered out of work without warning her. Soon she arrives, startling us: a tall blonde of Anglo-Austrian descent, brisk, witty, pink-cheeked, with charmingly puckered lips and a fretful look. At the sight of her he hangs his head guiltily over some imaginary or remembered offense he has committed. But on the whole he seems more relaxed with her around. She jollies

him along, occasionally prompts him. And he takes heart, and
opens up a bit. But it is difficult for him to talk about his work.
He does not believe in the possibility of true communication.
"The deeper experiences are intransmittable," he says. He is
obsessed with the notion that the things he says are misinterpreted, the jokes he cracks turned around and held against him.
"The misunderstanding is so frequent." He hates to look back.
He never rereads his books. They would upset him. "The
sensation of the past is painful to me," he says. His immersion in
his work is so extreme that it acquires terrifying proportions in
his mind. He is afraid to "abandon" himself to his writing.
Remembering his books afterwards seems to affect him in the
same way. He has left them behind, forgetting them as he has
forgotten his own life—they are so much a part of it. "I am not a
writer except when I write," he says. Like Proust or Faulkner—
especially the latter, with whom he identifies in more ways than
one; we think of Faulkner's legendary shyness—he inhabits a
world of his own, outside literary currents. When he is done with
his books, they tend to get scattered or lost, he never knows
exactly how or why. The case of *Tiempo de Abrazar* (Time for
Embracing), an unpublished novel—his first, begun around 1933,
when he was twenty-four years old—was typical. Shortly before
the war, four copies of the book were submitted to a contest in
Buenos Aires. Eventually—in 1943—some loose fragments appeared in the Uruguayan magazine *Marcha,* but the rest of the
manuscript seems to have been mislaid and he has never taken
the trouble to recover it. Perhaps out of his own carelessness and
neglect, it was years before his work began to be published. He
forgets how long *El Pozo* gathered dust on his desk before it saw
the light of day. Then it was ignored. In his time Onetti knew all
the difficulties of a literary career without "connections" in an
inhospitable environment with an unreceptive public: the lack
of incentive, the impossibility of financial independence. The
first of his books to attract attention was *Tierra de Nadie,* which
won a prize in a contest organized by Losada, a publishing house
then newly founded by a Spanish exile who, like so many of his
countrymen, had set sail to seek fortune across the ocean, far

from the Civil War. But that was of little help to Onetti. His
books have always lost money; which is why almost every single
one of them has been put out by a different publisher. The idea
was "to spread the damage," he says. He almost gave up on *Los
Adioses* (Good-bys, 1954). It was all set up for printing—even the
type was cast—when the house that had bought it went broke
and shut down. The loss might have gone unnoticed but for a
friend who fortunately rescued the manuscript and passed it on
to a guardian angel of the arts, Victoria Ocampo—her famous
little magazine *Sur* had by then given its name to a publishing
house—who generously published it at her own expense. But it
was something of a flop, and Onetti soon lost track of it. Whether
there have been any more editions after the original one he does
not know, though he heard somewhere—probably one of those
false rumors that keep plaguing him—that the book had been
reprinted in Havana. He wonders—perfunctorily—whether they
will split the losses with him. At least now he is beginning to
receive his share of critical recognition at home and abroad.
Which seems only fair. Though of uneven quality, his work has
provided our postwar literature with some of its finest moments.
Perhaps because he has never had the money for the classic Latin-
American pilgrimage to Europe—the farthest he has ever been
from the River Plate, until a recent visit to the United States, is
Bolivia—there is something genuinely home-grown about him
that goes a lot deeper than the strident feelings or protestations
of self-conscious literary nationalism that characterize so many of
his countrymen. He is perhaps the closest thing we have to a
truly autochthonous writer. Years of commuting between Buenos
Aires and Montevideo have made him one with the soul and
character of the area. He did not invent the urban novel in
Uruguay; the genre already existed, in a somewhat high-minded
form, in the days of Reyles. But at a time when Europeanized
circles did not consider local settings grand enough to be of
universal concern he set himself the job of going beyond the
purely picturesque or physiognomic to explore the city's hidden
face. Uruguay's lack of epic or heroic themes or burning issues—
exploited Indians, hardship zones such as mines or oilfields,

military dictatorships—has not bothered him. He has devoted himself to a more intimate task: the imaginative re-creation of a spiritual landscape. Santa María—his Yoknapatawpha County— is a mythical town; but its feel, its mental features, the psychological traits of its inhabitants, are distinctly Uruguayan. In Onetti accuracy of observation combines happily with insight and intuition. In the apparently incidental or anecdotal he finds the key to what is authentic and important. In this he is in the direct line of descent from Robert Arlt, the first to discover the metaphysical in the microscopic. Onetti's emphasis is on minute states of mind, "intensities of being," as he calls them, in the gray continuum that surrounds him.

It all began in Montevideo, in 1909, where Onetti spent his youth through secondary school. He speaks of it in a dwindling voice, as if he were trying to remember a lost version of some forgotten story. An attitude which is of the essence of the man and the writer. "I was born with it," he says of his writing. He was a child who told tales about people—"lies," he calls them harshly. And he means it. Perhaps the word indicates a qualm inherent in those who inhabit a fantasy world subject to slanderous and freakish twists of the imagination. If anything can be said about his work, it is that it is hypothetical in outlook, more shading than substance. It is made of half-thoughts, interrupted gestures, statements stealthily proposed, examined, denied, contradicted. He is less interested in arriving at the truth of a situation than in isolating its components—its alternatives— which are likely to yield as many falsehoods as facts. The variants are inexhaustible. The reader looking for a final authoritative version is disappointed. Nothing ever quite works out or adds up in Onetti. We have a hard time finding out who he is. His family seems to have little or nothing to do with him. The name is of British, probably Irish, descent; originally it was spelled O'Nety. In the mid-nineteenth century his great-grandfather was the private secretary of General Rivera, the leader of the insurgent forces that fought against Argentina's bloody dictator, Rosas, who was trying to extend his influence to Uruguay.

"He became Rivera's secretary under very curious circum-

stances," says Onetti with the shadow of a smile. Great-grandfather O'Nety ran a general store in a small town in the interior
of the country. "And one day Rivera went by on his way to one
of the ten thousand revolutions there were in those days, and
spent the evening with the old man. They played cards—General
Rivera's great passion. And the idiot was so overcome with
admiration for the personality of General Rivera that he picked
up right then and there, loaded all his possessions into a horse-
cart, and since he knew how to read and write, unusual talents in
the back country, he was named Rivera's secretary. According to
some very old letters preserved by an aunt of mine, I've seen that
the name was O'Nety. I've dug up some information, and it
seems that my great-great-grandfather, the first to come here, was
an Englishman born in Gibraltar. My grandfather was the one to
Italianize the name, probably for political reasons, environmental reasons—I don't know." By then the family lived in
Montevideo. Onetti touches on the subject, but immediately
glosses over it. As for his mother, she was Brazilian, the offspring
of landed gentry—"slaveowners," says Onetti gloatingly—in Rio
Grande do Sul.

We find out little about Onetti's early years. After high school,
when he was about twenty years old, he moved to Buenos Aires,
the promised land, where he took random courses in the university and held innumerable odd jobs—which he refuses to name,
bored or ashamed of them—before eventually making a career of
journalism. He was with Reuter's News Service, became their
Buenos Aires bureau chief in the early forties. At the same time
he was associated with and helped edit *Marcha* in Montevideo.
After Reuter's, he was editor in chief—up to about 1950—of an
Argentine magazine, *Vea y Lea*. Then he was in charge of a
publicity magazine called *Ímpetu*. It was a very small magazine—subsidized, or owned, by the Walter Thompson advertising
agency—that came out once a month and paid him enough to
scrape by on.

He says, not particularly gleeful: "It was restful work, because
all I had to do was make up an editorial, a lot of blah, blah,

public relations, and all that sort of stuff. The rest was translations stolen from *Printer's Ink* and *Bertelsmann*."

He was in Buenos Aires until about 1954, when vaguely political aspirations brought him back home. It was the time of the electoral triumph of Luis Batlle Berres in Uruguay. Friends in the ruling party had him drop everything to come and join them. He took over the party paper, counting on an optimistic promise that he might be given a consulate somewhere (a promise that never materialized). He remained with *Acción*—to which he still contributes occasionally—for two or three years. After which he moved to his present library job at the Institute of Arts and Letters.

Better than his external career, his inner course can be traced in his books, which contain no direct references to personal—or worldly—matters but are, more than with most authors', an almost complete spiritual autobiography of their creator. It took him some time to find his way into his fictional world. But he was busy mapping himself out from the beginning. He tells us about his first attempt, *Tiempo de Abrazar*. It was an adolescent love story involving a virginal vamp—a Lolita-type compound of seductiveness and false innocence—whose perishable youthful bloom the protagonist struggles to rescue from the devastation of time and age. The girl is the first of a long series of pseudo-virginal female adolescents that populate Onetti's books, high priestesses of erotic love usually endowed with a combination of morbid sensuality and bitter misanthropy that makes them at once devastating and inaccessible. The physical contacts they grudgingly submit to are a sorrowful and desultory affair symptomatic, in Onetti's scheme, of the forces of disintegration at work in all human relations. In Onetti's ordinarily middle-aged protagonists—his other selves—there is a desperate yearning for vanished youth, innocence and purity, corroded images to which they cling, rusted by time and undermined by memory. They live in the nonexistent past, in the shambles of approaching death and decay, as life passes them by. They have grown old without ever growing up, barely surviving or subsisting through the years, after some distant—and more or less nebulous—fall from grace into the sordid facts of life. Thus, we have Ana María in *El Pozo,* a joyless little sexpot who inspires a sad lust in the protagonist. His absurd love for her, which exists entirely in the sublimated realm of reverie, is a cynical front behind which he disguises feelings of guilt and remorse. It is nothing but an exorcism—an alibi. The fact is that he has once raped or in some way humiliated her—an impulse that in Onetti functions as a form of wish fulfillment—after which, for understandable reasons, their relations were discontinued. But in his vagaries the climactic act of violence repeats itself indefinitely with a high poetic charge, as if it had been an act of love. The switch is an attempt on Eladio's part to trick himself out of the trap he has set for himself. But it is too late. In Onetti a single moment of bad faith— or bad luck—derails a life forever. Perhaps because "love is marvelous and absurd, and incomprehensibly visits all kinds of souls. But absurd and marvelous people do not abound; and even those gifted with those qualities retain them only for a short time, in their early youth. Then they start accepting things and that's the end of them."

For Onetti, growing out of adolescence into adult life means compromising with impotence and despair. Hidden somewhere in the process is a loss that can never be made up. Says Onetti: "I think that happens to everybody." The sense of having strayed, of things left undone, opportunities missed, chances overlooked, is universal, says Onetti. He has always been haunted by it. The feeling is vague—a sort of chronic uneasiness. "Each person, out of convenience, even intellectual convenience, tries to pinpoint the cause of the trouble, to find something concrete and say: 'This is it.' Even if it isn't." The effect is numbing. But numbness is the human lot. Onetti defines his characters in terms of their omissions. "Because that's the way I am." In fact, in his early work—*El Pozo, Tierra de Nadie, Para Esta Noche* (For Tonight, 1943)—the characters are little more than episodes in his own mental processes. They are passing fancies that flicker in and out of existence like dream figures. Their sole reality is their subjective charge. And that defines their function. They are dreams dreamed by an author who in turn is dreamed by them.

They have only a shadowy secondary—subsidiary—existence and
no dramatic substance.

Passing himself off as his narrator is a favorite Onetti device. "I
feel freer, more like myself, working this way," he says. Thus
Eladio, an inchoate writer, is doubling for the author when he
sits down to compose a page of his journal reflecting, as he puts it
with heavy irony, that "a man ought to write the story of his life
when he reaches the age of forty, especially if interesting things
have happened to him." The point is, of course, that nothing has
ever happened to him worth mentioning. And what little has
happened is a lot less real or interesting than what he has
imagined. Reality is tedious and destructive, never up to the
high standards of fantasy. Perhaps in this notion lies the source
of the narrator's sense of inferiority which his dreams compensate
for, providing him with a means of working off his obscure
grudge against the world. Because "facts are always empty." It is
out of this sense of inadequacy that the author invents surrogate
characters who in turn perpetuate themselves in an endless
succession of other invented characters that are all his mirror
images. "For the writer," says Onetti, "his world is the world.
Otherwise he is cheating." What this amounts to in practice is
that reading an Onetti book is a schizophrenic experience. The
reader is in constant flux between the mind or perceptions of the
narrator-protagonist and those of the author, the two being
practically indistinguishable. Onetti's figments would cease to
exist the moment no one looked at them. They are in the mind's
eye and gain access to their borrowed reality only in so far as
there is an onlooker to bear witness to them. That is why Onetti
says he writes "for his characters." They are his inner inventory.
Exposing and outlining himself in them is his way of offering
himself through them. Even in their spuriousness, the subjective
load they carry is a sign of his abiding affection for them. He has
been accused of emotional poverty. The charge is not unfounded.
He is not versatile with his emotions. But he says: "The characters don't function unless you love them. Writing a novel is an
act of love."

Nowhere is this more visible—or more relevant—than in what

may well be his masterpiece, *La Vida Breve* (A Short Life, 1950), a book that is all chaos and ferment, a monument to evasion through literature. "An open book," he calls it fondly. An appropriate term. It is a plotless series of imaginings that unfold in the mind of a viewer—one of the author's delegates into the shadow world—in the form of gestures and situations. The title, deliberately ambiguous in its allusiveness, was taken from the words of a French song quoted in the book. Says Onetti: "I wanted to speak about several short lives, to show different persons leading these short lives." Sharing them, transferring them to each other, might be more exact. As he says: "The end of one would be the beginning of another, and so on indefinitely." Of course, the "several" lives are really one life, multiplied, relayed many times. It appears in the form of certain types of scenes that repeat themselves at odd intervals, like cyclic rites, in which certain shapes of persons recur, are transformed into others that resemble them, and die to be born again. Every chapter provides a choice or option within the limited possibilities available. Seen from another angle, *La Vida Breve*, which contains the germ of everything that followed in Onetti's subsequent work, is a long pregnancy that ends in the birth of a subject and a fictional world. Onetti seems to have caught a sudden—incomplete but ultimately lucid—glimpse of the whole road that lay ahead of him. Here, for the first time, we encounter Santa María, "a small town extending between a river and a settlement of Swiss laborers." Here, in the narrator's overactive imagination, we witness the birth of Díaz Grey, himself the narrator and central intelligence in later works. *La Vida Breve* is a dreamworld that later becomes the real world. Dreams used symbolically, says Onetti, are a cheap device. For him they are not transparent Freudian metaphors subject to pat clinical interpretation but an added dimension of reality.

The protagonist, or figurehead, of *La Vida Breve*, Bransen, is a colorless minor employee in a publicity firm who, attempting to find a way out of the dreariness of his life, dreams himself into the person of Díaz Grey, a doctor he conjures up out of some vaporous literary reminiscence, presumably for a film script he has been commissioned to write for his friend Julio Stein. A chance meeting in the hallway of the rooming house where he lives supplies him with a third identity. A fourth—the author, multiplied, occasionally dissolved, in the roles he shares—complicates the strange cast of characters. Bransen's various split personalities are in constant tension, nourishing and starving each other as they compete for supremacy. There is doubt up to the end as to which will impose itself at the expense of the others. The center of the whirlpool—the eye of the storm—is a static tableau, a set piece of décor in which Bransen, in suspended animation, stages the drama: his room. The immutable setting, says Onetti, was "stolen" from a still life by Ivan Albright that depicts objects on a table, among them a pair of empty gloves that retain the shape of the hands that have been in them. Bransen inhabits this unchanging picture. From there he spins out his fantasies, which branch off in all directions in an intricate pattern of criscrossing lines in which each intersection is a new starting point. The author, hovering over his shoulder, is an active participant in every story. In each, there is a woman who is all women and enacts the standard parts in the female repertory, appearing under the different guises of sister, wife, mistress, prostitute. The protagonist, in vicarious raptures, escapes from one life into another, improvising as he goes. But every apparent escape leads to a dead end.

Of all Bransen's surrogate creations, it is the doctor Díaz Grey (Dorian Gray?) who acquires the most depth and substance and gradually gains the upper hand over the others, finally supplanting the author himself. Bransen simply—and arbitrarily—places him in the nondescript Santa María "because I had once been happy there, years before, for twenty-four hours and for no particular reason." Bransen is referring to the usual Onettian moment of truth and beauty in his life, now gone forever. He searches for it everywhere, particularly in an old blurred picture of his wife, Gertrudis, with whom he has broken up. He finds a semblance or duplicate of her as she was in the days of her bloom in the image of her younger sister, who occasionally replaces her in his fantasies. Gertrudis suffers from his same aging pangs, and the consequent desire to impersonate herself in her previous roles. Her symptoms are physically portrayed in a typical Onetti sequence: she is seen in the shifting postures that mark the steps of her mental retreat, reviving old gestures and attitudes in a regressive order that leads back through time to what we assume will end in fetal position. Like Bransen, she is in search of "the only faintly glimpsed and as yet incomprehensible origin of everything that was happening to me, of what I had become and what cornered me." To break the irreversible pattern of his life is the compulsive need of every Onetti character. The solution—if one can call it a solution—that Bransen finds is to lead a phantasmal existence outside time. He is a sort of calamitous Walter Mitty. At times he thinks he can assume his condition. He tells himself that perhaps "if I cherished and deserved my daily sadness, if I coveted it, longed for it, steeped myself in it until my eyes and every last syllable I uttered were full of it"—in other words, if he accepts and installs himself in it—then "I would be safe from revolt and despair." But that is just another false comfort, a final snare.

The single nightmare theme is orchestrated in every pitch and key. There is no real chronological sequence; all actions and events are simultaneous. They take place in a sort of eternal present which is the time of the mind that is breeding them. There is a minimum of plot. Or, rather, there are many bits and strands of different plots forming an aimless patchwork that would be completely incoherent were it not sustained by a single even tone as hypnotic and inexorable as the senselessness of reverie. Bransen is a case beyond repair. He lives in "the unforgettable certitude that there is no woman, no friend, no house, no book, even no vice anywhere that can make me happy." Little keeps him alive: "the awareness I have of myself, misunderstandings. Nothing else. . . . Meantime, I remain what I am, an unalterable, timid little man married to the only woman he seduced or who seduced him, incapable at this point, not only of being anyone else, but even of wanting to be someone else." He is resigned to the slow torture of "a short life" that has declined into living death. So is everyone else; for instance, his friend,

Lagos, whose whole life is a sham that no longer fools anybody
but which he maintains "because he is afraid, because he is old,
because every Lagos he invents is a possibility—ultimately, a
possibility of oblivion."

What is left, under such desolate circumstances, are small
deaths and resurrections, such as the act of love, an "imposed
exercise" in the performance of which Bransen becomes a
"manipulator of immortality." At least passion is "personal," a
situation in which he can "be myself once and for all and then
immediately forget myself." But of course this is no real release
from the surfeit of self. Because the partner remains elusively out
of reach. Besides, each new woman is a reincarnation of the
women who preceded her and a premonition of the ones who will
follow, ad infinitum. Instead of being annulled, Bransen is
reproduced in her. His predicament is not a matter of the
weariness of age, or decadence, Bransen stresses, but simply of the
way life is. His last and only hope is that even the damned are
not condemned to a particular life or course of action, but only
to "a soul, a certain disposition." Therefore, he reasons, "one can
live many times, many different, longer or shorter, lives." However devoid of faith a man may be, he can still "enter into many
games," pretend to others in order to convince himself, to keep
the farce going. Because "any passion or faith contributes to
happiness in so far as it keeps us entertained or helps us forget."
The lines already drawn cannot be effaced, but perhaps the
original terms could be modified or restated, the beginning
forced "to occur again, differently this time." And if "the memory of the first beginning" could be altered, then perhaps the
new beginning would be strong enough "to alter the memory of
what followed." Except that, however hard Bransen tries,
"neither my hands nor my memory could hit on the right clue"
to get the wheel turning. Nevertheless, the search, which is like
"a quiet madness, a melancholy rage," as if he were being called
somewhere for no purpose and yet could not refuse to answer the
call, goes on. He continues to "suppress words and situations," in
hopes one day of coming upon "that single moment that will
express everything: Díaz Grey, myself, and therefore the whole

world." It will be a moment of plenitude, containing all things, among them the key to life's lost paradise, "the days cut to the size of our true self."

Behind the search—for order, serenity, impossible perfection—one suspects is a nostalgia for an experience of the divinity in a godless world. There is a Kafkaesque bishop who expounds at one point, as a spokesman for an unseen and paradoxical God, that man must understand that "eternity is now" and that he—man—is "the only end." Therefore, the bishop recommends—curiously arguing, not for Hedonism but stoicism—man must put all his enterprise into being himself, if only for the sake of argument, at all times and against all obstacles. Since he was not consulted on the rules of the game or invited to give his opinion on whether or not he wanted to play it, the only way for him to beat it is to enter into connivance with it. Says Bransen, echoing these words of wisdom: "The whole science of living . . . consists in the simple expedient of being flexible enough to fit into the gaps between the events we have not provoked, not forcing things, always, simply, being." The road to salvation, if there is one, is to "keep the consciousness of death alive in every cell of our bones." The dismal alternative, into which most of Onetti's people fall, is the habit of accepting "what one sees of oneself in the eyes of others," adopting the fraud as the genuine article, and acting accordingly. Better to "despise whatever must be obtained through effort, whatever does not fall into our hands by miracle." Then we will be "free of the past and the responsibility of the future, reduced to an event, strong in proportion to our ability to dispense with things." The prescription is not merely utilitarian but ultimately mystical. It proposes an aesthetic method as well as a form of mental accommodation. Communing with his fictions is the author's way of resolving his conflicts. The hypostatic existences born out of him in the act of writing are his temporary liberation from his inner stalemate. Their adventures take him through a mirror to the far side—the outer edge—of ordinary experience, where answers precede questions and he can, as he says, relax and drag his feet for a while, having found inner leeway. The author lives through the lives of his characters.

The trouble is that their lives are short. Prolonging and sustaining them requires a huge imaginative effort. The creation, via Bransen, of Díaz Grey and his world committed Onetti to a task of years and heroic feats of concentration. It has always been a tenuous and unstable fiction that a moment's absentmindedness could obliterate. Already in *La Vida Breve,* says Onetti, "there are several attempts on the part of the narrator to keep Díaz Grey alive." The ubiquitous but incurably ephemeral doctor keeps slipping away from Bransen, who "sets him back up again, shelters him, damns him, puts him by the window to look out at the river. At a certain moment he says: 'So many days have gone by since I was last able to see Díaz Grey.' He has to bring him back to put him on his fated course again." A lot is at stake. Like God and His creatures in some eminently symbiotic scheme, Onetti and Díaz Grey depend on each other.

Evidence of this is *Un Sueño Realizado y Otros Cuentos* (A Dream Fulfilled and Other Stories, 1951), written between 1941 and 1949—or more or less simultaneously with *La Vida Breve*—and first published in the course of the years in the Buenos Aires newspaper *La Nación*. Here, amid a lot of peripheral stage machinery, we can see Onetti assembling and dismounting the props that support his framework. *Un Sueño Realizado* is setting and background for *La Vida Breve*. Onetti is projecting antecedents, plotting case histories, feeling his way into attitudes, customs, and habitats. People and faces are in uncertain suspense, shadows flashing on the screen and flickering off in the blink of an eyelash. We have no clear concept, no over-all view, of the situation yet; but Onetti's main themes are all present. The hypocritical idealism of adolescence is exposed in "Bienvenido, Bob" (Welcome, Bob). The shabbiness of false hope—in this case a man who swindles his boss to fulfill his Danish wife's ruinous yearning to return to the land of her childhood—is portrayed in "Esbjerg, en la Costa" (Esbjerg, on the Coast). Again, there is the death of illusion on contact with reality, in the title story, "Un Sueño Realizado." And, most notably, there is our friend Díaz Grey—grown independent of his progenitor, Bransen—in a familiar dilemma: the recollection, from the unfathomable depths of age, of the one moment of possible redemption in his life, which he threw away when he betrayed the trust of the woman who had offered him her help and love ("La Casa en la Arena"—The House on the Sand). The retrospective view of Díaz Grey ties up some loose ends in his story, but actually raises more questions than it solves. The past, in Onetti, is mythologized. Remembrance is a distant vantage point in which old scenes recur full of problematic variations. In "La Casa en la Arena" we are told what actually happened, what the protagonist imagined had happened, what he wished had happened, and what may, for all we know, still be happening, all of these different phases of the experience superimposed as time holds still around them. Onetti does not want to crystallize his world; he wants it to remain fluid. Therefore his various accounts of events, even when they cover the same grounds, may not coincide. Facts in one book may contradict those given in another, or even elsewhere in the same book. Inconsistencies need not be accounted for. What remains unchanged is the atmosphere of loss and drift, resentment and cynicism, that absorbs his creatures with their vague urges, their flashes of hate toward others, their perverse fantasies and obscure qualms and regrets. They are fixtures in a closed circuit that seals off all escape routes and makes all conclusions foregone. The town is little more than an extension of their boredom, staleness, and misery. Everywhere there are "fat and badly dressed people." The settings are grubby bedrooms, sweaty bars, fetid back streets, or "any smelly office." The detailed description—sometimes ad nauseam—of the gestures and movements of minor characters thickens the paste, adding to the cumulative agony. Every twitch and contortion has its place in the system. Even as the protagonists reflect the author, the secondary characters enact the moods of the protagonists. They form overlapping images that act as objective correlatives of a single state of mind. "That's the way I am. The small detail in persons or situations is enormously important to me," says Onetti. The traits scattered among the surrounding human specters belong less to individual persons than they do to the ensemble, to the repertory of the book as a whole. Personifying the décor is a way of rendering it dynamic, humanizing it. Onetti's figments are never rounded persons; they are choreographic figures. He says he could never create the complete psychology of a Babbitt. Nor would he want to. He deals with a single emotional—almost abstract—type: the stranger. Often his characters are actually out-of-towners of vaguely foreign genealogy; there is a predominance of Nordic or Germanic names that enhance this effect. They lead an erratic existence, "a grotesque life," married to flabby women, too big for their small lives, too small for their fantasies, straitjacketed by their past, eroded by "the quiet underhanded work of time."

A somewhat painful subject must be brought up in relation to Onetti: his style. Over the years it has gone through subtle but steady changes that throw considerable light on Onetti's intentions. In *El Pozo* the language was careless, straightforward, almost journalistic, in the Arltian manner—decidedly antiliterary. In *La Vida Breve* it had become more elliptical, but without taking on any added syntactical complications, retaining its aura of artlessness. In *Un Sueño Realizado*—as in *Tierra de Nadie* and, increasingly, in *Para Esta Noche*—there is more artifice. Onetti is echoing a master who has had an enormous influence on him: Faulkner. The influence is conscious and deliberate, and Onetti sees no reason to apologize for it. But it is sometimes embarrassing to the reader. *Un Sueño Realizado* is made of tortuously long and graceful Faulknerian sentences that contribute to the cloistered atmosphere of the book but, because of an excess of imitated mannerisms—intricate modifiers, pleonastic subclauses, redundant adjectival expanses—sometimes seem affected. Onetti loves the circular and static, perfectly suitable devices in a world of fates settled in advance, where every life is a sentence served backward, predestined and therefore in some sense tautological. The reiterative style is an integral part of the manic-depressive atmosphere. But in strong doses it can begin to seem like a noisy contrivance, more hysterical than inherent. In Faulkner accumulations of words add force and momentum to the story; in Onetti they too often merely distract and diffuse. Onetti admits and does not attempt to justify, his Faulknerian variations. He merely points out the obvious difference between his and Faulkner's conceptions of the world. Faulkner is a tragedian; Onetti, if one can coin a term, is a pathetician. He shares with Faulkner the use of a fictional site as his setting, a preoccupation for inner architectures with metaphysical overtones. Otherwise—above all, temperamentally—they have little in common. Their respective frames of reference are entirely different. And perhaps that is where the trouble lies. Faulkner's characters live outside him, in time and history; they are endowed with independent means of action and individual consciences. Onetti's characters are at once more intimate and more abstract. Living at such close quarters with their creator, they have become disembodied. The more said about them, the less real they seem. They are floating essences. Words bury them. Whether or not Onetti has overcome this danger is a matter we leave unresolved. The Faulknerian trance has had such a lasting hold over him that even today he claims that the best thing he ever wrote was a translation he did years ago of a story from *These 13*.

One of his works most damaged by contact with the Faulknerian mode was *Los Adioses,* an involuted chronicle of futility that ends in suicide. A moribund athlete—one of Onetti's melancholy maniacs—retires to die in Santa María. He rents a house on a knoll outside town, where he secludes himself, alternately receiving two apparently rival women who have an agreement to visit him separately. Letters, in the possession of the narrator (in this case not one of the protagonists but the owner of the general store, who keeps the refugees in supplies), subsequently reveal the women to be his wife—and a daughter by a previous marriage. The loneliness and essential selfishness of the suicidal impulse are the subject of the story. The protagonist, reduced to the last imaginable extreme, clings to the forlorn hope of privacy in death, because "he had only that, and did not want to share it." The language overloads a thin plot which, typically, unfolds at second hand, progressing through gossip, rumor, and indirection. The effect is somewhat hazy. The surprise ending—based on withheld information—does not seem implicit. Yet in a sense *Los Adioses* represents an advance over *La Vida Breve,* or at least a new phase in Onetti's work. The narrator, though not dispensed with, has been relegated to a secondary plane. The protagonists—whose impenetrable mystery ultimately remains intact—have at least a semblance of an objective existence outside him.

A considerable improvement in this vein, and one of Onetti's most readable books, because of a skillfully handled element of suspense in it, is *Una Tumba sin Nombre* (A Nameless Tomb, 1959), an enigma without a complete solution that generates some of the excitement of a good detective story (a genre the author is much addicted to; he says he wishes he could plot as well as Raymond Chandler). The setting, as usual, is Santa María. The subject is the moral corruption and consequent compunctions of an errant adolescent, Jorge Malabia, who pours out his guilt to a sympathetic listener, and chronicler: Díaz Grey. As Díaz Grey records it with bloodthirsty relish—picking up odds and ends to complete the picture from Tito Perotti, Jorge's roommate at the university, and spicing the racy mixture with his own acid speculations—it is a gory tale. It involves an amoral young woman, Rita, an ex-maid in the Malabia household, once the mistress of Marcos Bergner, the brother of Jorge's sister-in-law, Julita. Exploited, then abandoned, by Marcos, Rita has taken to whoring for a living in Buenos Aires, where Jorge meets her while studying at the university and sets up house with her. *Una Tumba sin Nombre,* with all due allowances for its Onettian vagaries, is a Bildungsroman. The occasion for Jorge's growth is his enslaving passion, which is at least partly self-imposed. As a child, the commentator reveals, Jorge used to spy on Marcos and Rita through the keyhole, fascinated by their love-making. It is his tormenting memories of Rita in intimate postures, become obsessive with time, that somehow make him feel entitled to possess her now, as if she had been destined for him. He picks her up, installs her among his belongings, and although he has a generous allowance of his own and he knows she is dying of tuberculosis, lives off her for months, completely abandoning his studies. A curious twist is the motivation Onetti

provides for the melodrama. Rita, bound from the beginning to
occupy the unmarked tomb of the title, attracts disaster and
thrives on humiliation; she is one of the insulted and injured of
the world. Jorge turns out to be a sort of minor Raskolnikov. He
acts out of gratuitous malice, pleased to imagine himself in the
shoes of Rita's ex-pimp, Ambrosio, whose identity he borrows on
the theory, as he tells Tito Perotti, that "I can never regret
anything because whatever I do will have to be within the limits
of human possibility." Of course—as we gather from the distor-
tions and refractions out of which the story gradually takes
shape—he learns better. His intellectual arrogance, his middle-
class smugness, have led him into some of the cardinal sins on
Onetti's list: hypocrisy, cynicism, and above all, the false pride
that tempts the gods. His righteousness is a disguise for coward-
ice, his rebelliousness for conformity. Onetti—or Díaz Grey—
does not blame him. He merely exposes him. Jorge has tried to
find a way out; he has failed. His crime—the crime of phoni-
ness—was in pretending he could win in the first place. Covering
up his failure compounded it. The author's—or narrator's—
verdict is dispassionate. Such is life. Jorge's defeat is everyone's
defeat. As they filter through to us, the facts of the case remain
somewhat enigmatic. We have to sift shifting points of view.
Here Onetti has hit on a compromise formula he uses with
varying success in his later books. Díaz Grey, the seeing eye, is
only a partial witness. Sometimes there is none. Certain passages
are told straight. Others are once, twice, or even three times
removed behind layers of lenses. Díaz Grey, not quite emancipated from his creator, has become a sort of universal conscience,
a father confessor and faceless guilt-bearer for others. His independence is strictly putative, conditional—a convenient assumption for narrative purposes, pending the author's suspension of
belief in him, whereupon his fickle autonomy will instantly
vanish. Which is what happens once he has provided the necessary angles and insights. Suddenly slight differentiations are
abandoned. The author becomes the actor. He is directly involved when he qualifies his—or Díaz Grey's; here the two
fuse—account of Jorge's adventures as a liberating experience for

him, who, in living it down or, more precisely, writing it out, has
gained the upper hand over at least one of life's "daily setbacks."

In *La Cara de la Desgracia* (The Face of Misfortune, 1960) we
find Onetti making a clean breast of the things he will obviously
never be entirely rid of. Written in an unusually polite and slick
style for him, told directly in the first person, with its share of
ambivalences and blackouts, it is another story of guilt and
noncommunication. The setting is a resort somewhere in the
coastal area of Santa María, where the protagonist, in retreat,
searches his conscience over the recent death of his brother,
declines responsibility for the brother's widow, and on the side
conducts an intermittent love affair on the beach with a deaf
girl—another nymphomaniac virgin—who pays for their love (a
scandal against the order of things: the rules of mourning,
human solidarity in suffering) with her life. The germ of *La Cara
de la Desgracia* was a story called "La Larga Historia" (The
Long Affair) that Onetti had written many years before (in
1944). The lighter accent, the more flippant tone, cannot hide
the fact that his standard themes appear in a more muddled form
than usual. There are too many blind spots. But we strike a new
note here. The narrator-protagonist is another of Onetti's
dreamers; but, though as usual mortally wounded by life, he is
no longer entirely the helpless victim of circumstance. He has
begun to develop a strategy with which to fight back. He is an
embryonic ancestor of the saintly sinner that appears in Onetti's
later work, for whom criminal intent miraculously becomes a
twisted form of faith and inner harmony.

The novel that comes closest to fulfilling this paradoxical
scheme is *El Astillero* (The Shipyard, 1961). The hero, or central
figure, of *El Astillero* is Larsen—who took his first bow, in a
minor role, in *La Vida Breve*—one of Onetti's Scandinavian-
sounding outsiders. The name is not misleading. Larsen is a man
with a shady background; he was expelled from Santa María five
years before for running a house of prostitution. Now he is back
in town to take a job in a dilapidated shipyard owned by a
bankrupt tycoon, old Petrus. The shipyard is a carcass, and has
been for ages; it functions only on paper, with a shadow board

and a couple of superannuated administrative employees who while their time away in empty offices, busying themselves to keep up a pretense of work as they sell the useless machinery out from under Petrus' nose. In spite of which Larsen makes a grand entry. He has himself named general manager, spends his time going over old inventories and moth-eaten documents of forgotten shipwrecks, blatant in his imposture, drawing an imaginary salary while old Petrus is presumably maneuvering in the summits of bureaucracy to get his business back on its feet. For Larsen the musty shipyard is a last chance of doing something significant with his life; a chance in which he does not believe, of course. It is all an act and show—a flagrant hoax. He preys with predatory aplomb on the situation. He courts the pregnant wife of one of his employees while at the same time fanning a flame in Petrus' idiot daughter, whom he hopes, or purports to hope, to marry in order to inherit the nonexistent business. The whole action is made up of meaningless ritual motions leading nowhere. The shipyard will never be rehabilitated. Eventually documents come to light revealing an ancient fraud Petrus had perpetrated in better days. The old man is denounced to the police and arrested. All plans collapse. Everyone disowns everyone else. The whole scheme is discredited. But not before Onetti has made his point. Better to gnaw at an old bone than to have none at all.

Speaking of the atmosphere that prevails in *El Astillero,* Onetti, shivering, says: "It's like wearing a wet coat on a rainy day." He speaks of "the closed world in which unfortunately I live nowadays when I write. Also in general. I have many periods of absolute depression, of a sense of death, of nonlife. Maybe if I changed my habits, if I went on a diet—a good doctor might be able to cure me," he adds wryly. But perhaps, he reflects with a wisp of a smile, the doctor would turn out to be as impotent and ineffectual as Díaz Grey. In any case, he would arrive too late for Larsen, who has driven himself into a last hermetic solitude that finally leads to suicide.

Larsen, as do all Onetti characters, suffers from advancing age, an obsessive fear of death, a hopeless longing to rescue his wasted life, and a compulsive need to retreat through time to recuperate that moment of truth presumably buried somewhere in the lost blitheness of childhood. But there is a new element—the one just barely hinted at in *La Cara de la Desgracia*—that distinguishes him from his predecessors. The seed was planted in that passage of *La Vida Breve* where Bransen thinks of assuming his condition, installing himself in it, hopeful that perhaps in sitting it out he will be relieved of it. So it is that we find Larsen accepting the inevitable, taking it for granted, actually entering into partnership with it, becoming its accomplice. Since there is no chance of breaking the rules of the game, he must master them. "If they're mad," he says to himself, "then I must be, too." Alone in his game, he had distrusted it. But since others seem to accompany him in it, "it must be the real thing." The decrepit shipyard is a reduced model of an absurd and godless world made of senseless routines, where living is a gamble with deadly risks: a "concerted lie." Old Petrus knows it. "Years back he had stopped believing there were any profits to be derived from the game; he would continue to believe, with violence and joy, unto death, in the game itself." Larsen, an old hand at deception, decides to follow suit. He knows the odds are stacked against him. Outwitting the intelligence behind the game, if there is one, is impossible. What counts is to go through the motions. His management of the shipyard is an act of defiance, a challenge— and a prayer—thrown in the face of the deity. It glows with the splendor of a Faulknerian grand design. There are also distinct Dostoevskian undertones in it. Larsen is a sort of diabolic, and at the same time strangely phlegmatic, weaver of absolutes—a Stavrogin. His gesture is symbolic. It is an open provocation. The shipyard is an antichurch with its reigning apostle, Larsen, the high priest of despair, officiating daily at its uninhabited altar. Starting out as a pimp to the prostitution of life, he has ended up as a theologian building his pointless architecture in the face of the incriminating evidence of his condition, out of the stuff of his defeat.

After *El Astillero*, which can be said to culminate the second phase of Onetti's work, we have a pause which he fills with a mortuary exercise in Faulknerian craftsmanship, a collection of stories called *El Infierno tan Temido* (The Hell We Dread, 1962). We are back in a Santa María now so intensely felt that it is almost lost in the glare. Somehow it seems less credible than before. The verbal flood has become more convoluted as the author's backstage maneuverings become more devious and remote. Díaz Grey, Petrus, and other staples reappear, but in residual form. The foreground is occupied by marginal characters, sometimes outlandish visitors on their way through town, who flare into existence for a second, then recede into the surrounding vacuum. The language is of no help. The compliment of imitation Onetti pays his master sometimes verges on parody. Nevertheless, the characteristic Onettian mode is present. The best of the stories deals with the sad predicament of an aging lecher infatuated with a frivolous actress who succumbs to extracurricular temptations, elopes with one of them, then tortures her admirer for the rest of his life mailing him obscene photographs she has posed for in compromising postures, as if to get back at him for saddling her with his charity and forgiveness, intent on blaming him for her inability to atone for her own weakness and treachery.

Shifting the blame is also the topic of the rather careless and superficial *Tan Triste Como Ella* (As Sad as She Is, 1963), "a sketch that didn't quite come off," as Onetti says himself, recognizing its poverty, which gives it the distinction of being probably the worst thing he ever wrote. He committed the mistake, he says, of describing something—a marriage on the rocks—that had actually happened (to him? He has been married three or four times) and that therefore enslaved him to the facts, dampening his inventiveness. The story reads like a self-conscious love letter that soon dwindles into radio drama. A curious slip for a writer at such a late stage in his work. But Onetti has too little distance from his work to take an objective view of the results. He lacks judgment and perspective. His latest work, *Juntacadáveres* (The Corpse Collector, 1964) has also been disappointing. It seems like a rehash of *El Astillero,* made of leftover materials that amount to little more than a poor duplicate of the original. Says Onetti,

more or less subscribing to the verdict: "The trouble is that I'd
already started to write *Juntacadáveres* when one day, going
down a corridor, I had a vision of the end of Larsen. That's in *El
Astillero*. So all of a sudden I left off writing *Juntacadáveres*.
Perhaps when I returned to it I couldn't get into it properly any
more." Or perhaps *El Astillero* spilled over into it, contaminated
it. In a sense, they are both the same book.

Yet *Juntacadáveres* is an interesting and important addition to
Onetti's theologic architecture: another cathedral built in the
ruins. We are no longer in the shipyard; we have been flashed
back to the days when Larsen ran a whorehouse. But the
whorehouse is also a sort of visionary construction raised against
the absurdity of life. The book chronicles the town's reaction to
the whorehouse: the political interests involved, the opposition
from the church, civic circles, and ladies' action groups. Larsen,
the great sinner, the saintly cripple, presides at his Black Mass
amid sacrilege and anathema. Born a diehard, handicapped from
the start, he will dip into his depleted stocks until he reaches the
bottom of the barrel. Founding the house has been an old
ambition. And that is his advantage. He has waited so long for
his chance that when it finally comes it is like a posthumous
favor, "like marrying on one's deathbed, believing in ghosts,
acting for God." Therefore, in a sense, he is invulnerable. In any
case, his utopian construction is no worse than any other: a house
of worship comparable to the church inhabited by the local
priest or the ragged remnants of the phalanstery founded on the
rim of town by one of his most bitter enemies, Marcos Bergner
(righteous in his condemnation of Larsen though he is a veteran
of communal orgies and squalid love affairs). In fact, the various
forces that line up against him under the guise of high moral
purpose all derive from the same premise: the simple human
need on the part of each person to impose his individual order
on the surrounding chaos. The opposing points of view, by any
measurable standards, are all equivalent, and cancel each other
out. It is a conflict not so much of personalities as of inner
priorities. The language, calculated to hold tensions in delicate
balance, quotes itself to the point of plagiary, falling into a sort

of rhetoric of numbness that has an almost parasitical effect on the action. But perhaps that is fitting and proper. It sets the tone. The town is deep in the doldrums. Dead faces roam the streets. Even the physical world seems to languish. The days are bleak and windless. Time drifts by like a whisper. Travestied intentions dissolve into vacant pantomimes. We have Díaz Grey, whittled down by time; and Jorge Malabia, here aged sixteen, a sensitive boy who secretly writes poetry and is on the verge of straying into the abysmal perversities of manhood. Jorge's respectable family, invoking its traditions of civic decency, inveighs against the whorehouse, while actually conspiring with it: Jorge's father, making the best of a bad deal, is the man who has rented out the land for the house. Jorge himself ripens and blooms in the throes of a sickly lust for his brother's deranged widow, Julita. But he is no more at fault than anyone else. In Onetti's scheme, those who stand for law and order—to save face—are at bottom the most hollow and corrupt. By contrast, those who struggle against the order of things, however crookedly, are at least worthy of a pitying respect. Such is the case of the abominable Larsen. In an aberrant world where raising a glass, getting out of a chair, going through a door are gestures that require almost superhuman effort, he is a man with a vocation, touched by a divine madness—an unheroic rebel fired by weakness, anguish, his fear of solitude and death. Little matter if he draws a blank at every turn. He has leverage. The contest of wills that takes place between him, on the one hand, and the priest or Marcos Bergner, on the other, may be nothing, says the author, but a form of artistic rivalry. The author is one of the rivals. So is his double, Jorge. And so is Díaz Grey, who again, as in *Una Tumba sin Nombre*, has been cast in the role of the informed witness and scapegoat, perhaps one of the elect destined to carry the burden of human sorrow. There is a moment when Jorge confronts him—as he might confront the author—and blames him for everything that has happened in town, for seeing it, understanding it, permitting it. It is, says Onetti, as if the boy were blaspheming against God. We remember that the ageless Díaz Grey was born as a god in *La Vida Breve*, fully grown, to live and be lived by others. Now, going down a staircase one day, he suddenly feels, as he has many times before, that he may kill himself. It is as if the supreme Master of Ceremonies, summoned out of nothingness for a moment, had leaned out and breathed His blessing on him.

Juntacadáveres, the ultimate in Onettian scope and structure, seems like a last stop on a long road leading back where it started from. One wonders where Onetti can possibly go from here.

Putting the question to him is like asking for a weather forecast. He has an image he is brooding over. What will become of it depends on meteorological conditions. Meantime he is taking notes, sketching situations. He grabs his ideas where he finds them. He has been remembering the time of Eva Perón's death in Argentina, when crowds of worshipful admirers lined up for days outside the Ministry of Labor to snatch a glimpse of her embalmed body, which had been put on display in a glass case. It was a time of national mourning, of mass necrophilia, says Onetti. There was talk of having the venerable corpse canonized. The collective cult of the dead, one of life's most sacred rituals, is a subject that appeals to Onetti. He knew Eva Perón well because he had frequent access to her when he was working for Reuter's.

He says: "We were in contact with a Catalonian embalmer who was installed in the Presidential Palace in Olivos. We called him every night to find out whether or not the moment had come yet. 'No, unfortunately not,' he'd say. 'Nothing yet.' He used to distribute a pamphlet on the method he'd developed in his specialty. He didn't reveal the method—it was secret. But he gave examples of people he'd treated. There was an incredible photograph of a five- or six-year-old child in a sailor's suit. He'd been dead for years. The family kept the corpse in the closet and for every birthday and every anniversary of the child's death they took it out, put it on a chair, and had a family reunion around it." One can imagine the scene—or a similar one based on it—laid in Santa María. We are already familiar with the cast of characters. "The narrator will be Jorge Malabia, twenty years later. There will be the line of mourners. Of course the whole

thing will be turned around to bring out its absurdity." Onetti
recalls the historical events involved. "When Eva Perón died, the
line for the wake lasted a week or ten days, or more." Eva had
been pickled and preserved by the Catalonian expert. But the
treatment had to be constantly renewed."They kept locking up
all the time to take her out. Because the doctors at Eva Perón's
bedside had been Catholics. They knew of the plans to embalm
her, and the Catalonian doctor wasn't notified in time. She'd
died in the morning, I think, and the news wasn't released until
eight-thirty in the evening, when all the clocks in town were
stopped. By then the corpse had started to rot. To keep it in
shape, it would have had to receive its first injection at the
moment of death. So the work failed. . . . Now, what I want to
do is this: The way the line was organized . . . In reality, at
first, it was spontaneous. The people were devoted to Eva Perón.
For the working classes she was a saint. She gave away thousand-,
ten thousand-peso bills, houses, automobiles; all photographed,
of course, for propaganda. There was the Eva Perón Foundation,
her Cities for the Young, which functioned exclusively when
there were important visitors from abroad. . . . But then the
wake was put in the hands of a publicity firm. The line was
organized so five persons could go in at a time. Then the doors
were closed, or blocked by soldiers. The idea was to have the line
move at the rate, let's say, of half a meter every fifteen minutes.
So it would be there permanently. . . . So the trick I have in
mind is simple: to slow the rate down even further. To have the
line advance, say, a tile a day. Then take someone standing in
the line and have him live it: fall in love with a woman, marry
her, all while standing there. I'm exaggerating; but that was
what happened up to a certain point. People had to knock on the
doors of houses to use the toilet. They ate in the street, slept and
made love there. The Ministry of Labor was full of floral crowns.
In the early mornings there were orgies, while the soldiers stood
by, watching. That's an important factor in my book: the
sensation of death, its connection with erotic behavior."

What will all this lead to? Onetti is sure to erect another of his
temples of despair out of it. If anything, he regards the prospect

with detachment. His pessimism seems to have become almost generic. He is resigned, as Jorge in *Juntacadáveres,* to furnish his empty world with the shapes of his fictions, to create faces and gestures, needs and ambitions, and appropriate roles to which they can be appointed, the better to be sacrificed. The fate assigned each man is impersonal, he wrote in *La Vida Breve.* It can be fulfilled only in so far as it is the fate of all men. It does not allude to his true self, which is elsewhere, out of sight and circulation, a humble offering waiting to be put before the gods, who may choose to regard it as a small masterpiece or a penny dreadful.

VI

Julio Cortázar,

or the Slap in the Face

THE years have shown, in our part of the world as elsewhere, that those who live at odds with their land are often the ones that understand it best. Perhaps only they are in a position to hit the nail hard enough to drive it home. If in our novel feelings of brotherhood are giving way to open provocations that occasionally end in assault and battery, it is because it needed a bit of effrontery to make it live more vibrantly. World War II was something of a dividing line for us. It brought a drastic century to our doorstep at a time when we had already begun to part company with ourselves. This was particularly true of Argentina, a land of fallen idols. There the morning after dawned early. And with it were born the kiss of death and the slap in the face.

For our literature, they were blessings. There is something healthy, in a communal art, about the novel that establishes its own premises. When our writers were accomplices of reality, they ended up being swindled by it. But now they are astute enough to tread warily where once they would have rushed in blindfold. There is a distrust of reality that has blunted its extortionary edge. Once upon a time the novelist was desperate to establish a peaceful coexistence with his surroundings. Today he can do without it. It never existed anyway. Because under the appearance of friendly agreement lurked that old enmity which, from the beginning of time, whether it took the form of intolerable love or bitter antagonism, has nourished man's long-standing quarrel with the world.

That we have begun to accept this quarrel, instead of glossing it over, is a hopeful sign for us. Discontent and maladjustment have brought excitement to our literature, which now dares to challenge not only the immediate but the irremediable. The Latin-American novelist today fights an unequal battle and stands a good chance to go down in it. But that is just the point. By laying himself open all the way in his work, for the first time he leaves something in it that can survive him. He is not merely a disgruntled misfit but the eternal rebel. If he seems to have come to a parting of the ways with his society, it is because his relations with it are too passionate not to be forever ambivalent. If there is harshness in his words and violence in his gestures, it is because honesty is brutal. Our old writer, even in his moments of diatribe, was never really outspoken on fundamental matters. There were always unmentionable or untouchable areas that stayed out of range. But now the novelist, working in the depths of a new solitude, is beginning to find the words for a truer dialogue.

The fact is that since Arlt, our novel which used to barely skim surfaces has gone under to the root of things. It took a plunge in Marechal's revolutionary *Adanbuenosayres* and another in Onetti's *La Vida Breve*.

In the fifties and early sixties it delved into the shadows of Argentine society in the work of Ernesto Sabato. Lately, after a penitential silence of many years—he was snubbed in 1948 by the literary establishment because of his Peronist sympathies—there has been the return of a somewhat depleted Marechal, in a recent arcane medley, *El Banquete de Severo Arcángelo* (1966). Marechal, continuing his old fight against Ordinary Life in the technological robot age, invites us to an infernal feast that, like Trimalchio's Agape, Plato's banquet, or the Last Supper, may turn out to be a prelude to beatific vision. He is a man with an "Arcadian obsession," a "messianic madness." Embodied in his Cyclopean hero, a metallurgist turned alchemist, he has come to the end of his rope, exhausting human possibilities, and entered a "frontier zone" of rotating tables and spinning chairs designed to reproduce the cosmic whirl. We are in the realm of pure symbol, a giant existential foundry, a power plant exploded by nuclear fission, to return us to a distant idyllic Watershed. There is much of the sleight of hand in *El Banquete de Severo Arcángel*. Yet in its mystic embroidery we recognize the touch of a Magister Ludi willing to bet his life and fate on mysterious games of fortune. But in this area, since *Rayuela* (Hopscotch), Cortázar rules supreme. He is our greatest prestidigitator.

Cortázar is the evidence we needed that there is a powerful mutant strain in our literature. It leads toward a mystic borderline. "Where frontiers end, roads vanish," says Octavio Paz. And so it is with Cortázar. He works toward the outer limits of experience, thumbing his nose at the world. He is a brilliant wit, and a tireless innovator, who has given us a lot to ponder. The tendency in certain circles has been to accuse him of a lack of seriousness, probably with some justification, at least to the extent that he insists on pulling chairs out from under us all. Certainly there is an element of the practical joker in him. But it lives in close quarters with the visionary. How Cortázar became what he is is a disconcertingly difficult question to answer. In his early days he was a sort of Borgian aesthete, a qualifier to which he is not entirely invulnerable even today. But there was a change in mid-road. For a while he leaned on the traditional props of the psychological novel. But that was a transitory stage. Whatever genre he touched, he seemed immune—or soon inured —to its conventions. He is a man of strong antibodies. Nowadays he has no use for what he considers easy effects: pedestrian dramatic situations, platitude or pathos. He travels along his own circuits. His importance is hard to assess. He wonders himself what it all amounts to. "I don't flatter myself that I'll be able to achieve anything transcendental," he says, skeptically. But there is little doubt that he already has. He is perhaps the first man in our literature to have built a complete fictional metaphysic. If, as all originals, he would seem to be a bit of an aside for the moment, the shock waves his work has spread may well be echoes of the future.

Cortázar, a true Argentine, is a many-sided man, culturally eclectic, elusive in person, mercurial in his ways. He is not a man who gives himself easily. There is something adamantly neat and precise about him that verges on punctiliousness. He received us two or three times and was always affable and straightforward with us, but perhaps a bit impersonal. There were areas that remained out of bounds. And those were the ones that counted. It was in his whimsical moments that we caught some hints of the true Cortázar, the man who imagines old aunts falling flat on their backs, families building gallows in their front gardens, governments collapsing on Leap Year, and mirrors clocking time on Easter Island. Behind these figments is a mind with as many facets as a diamond, as intricate as a spiderweb. Physically Cortázar is something of an anomaly for a Latin American. He cuts a considerable figure, well over six feet tall, lanky, long-legged, and freckled as a Scotsman. There is a child in his eyes. He looks much too young for his age. In fact, his generally boyish air is almost unsettling. An eternal child prodigy keeps winking at us from his work.

Cortázar has an intriguing background that makes him heir to an old dilemma. He was born in 1914, of Argentine parents—in Brussels. His ancestors were Basques, Frenchmen, and Germans. He has spent a lot of his time welding opposites. From the age of four he was brought up in the outskirts of Buenos Aires, a city whose instincts and attitudes run deep in his work. No one has stronger emotional ties with his land than Cortázar. But intellectually he has lived beyond it, in a broader context. There has been agony in his constant inward migration between physical roots and spiritual affinities. The displaced persons in his books testify to the length and depth of a conflict that has never been satisfactorily settled. Yet in some way it has been put to fruitful use. Cortázar has always managed to rise comfortably above the narrowness of our cultural outlook. Like Borges, he has always been something of an expatriate at heart. "My generation," he says, "was considerably at fault in its youth in that it lived, to a large degree, with its back turned to Argentina. We were great snobs, although many of us only realized that later. We read very few Argentine writers and were almost exclusively interested in English and French literature, with a bit of Italian and American literature thrown in, and some German literature, which we read in translation. It wasn't until we were about thirty years old that suddenly many of my friends and I discovered our own tradition. People dreamed of Paris and London. Buenos Aires was a sort of punishment. Living there was being in jail." So unbearable was it, in fact, that at the age of eighteen he and a group of friends made an abortive attempt to set sail to Europe in a cargo boat. Yet when he finally made it there—he moved permanently to Paris in 1951—instead of breaking his attachments with his land he took it with him, and has been wrestling with its phantom shapes ever since.

Compared to that of some of our more prolific writers, Cortázar's production has been slim: three novels—one unpublished—a bit of poetry, a few dozen short stories. But almost every bit of it counts. Creative fatigue, that common ill of our authors toward middle age, when an early bloom is ruined by faulty plumbing, is unknown to him. An unflagging inventiveness and imagination, combined with sure marksmanship, have kept him steadily growing in stature through the years. Today, at the height of his powers, his restless and inquiring mind tells him his work is more unfinished than ever.

He was first heard from around 1941—the exact date is vague in his mind—with a small book of sonnets, published under the pseudonym of Julio Dénis, that he no longer cares to talk about. The sonnets were "very Mallarméan," he says succinctly. He had lofty aims at the time. There was a long silence, and then in 1949 he published *Los Reyes* (The Kings), a series of dialogues on the subject of the Cretan Minotaur, rather stately in style, abstract, intellectual, overrefined, reflecting his bookish addiction to classical mythology. There was nothing of particular note in those early works. But already in 1951, only two years after *Los Reyes*, he made what seems a complete about-face and came out with a stunning little volume called *Bestiario*. It was lean and luminous, and struck a keynote: the fantastic, suddenly revealing a master sorcerer. Cortázar had read his Poe, Hawthorne, and Ambrose Bierce, as well as his Saki, Jacobs, H. G. Wells, Kipling, Lord Dunsany, E. M. Forster, and, closer to home, Lugones, the old master Quiroga, and, of course—Borges. He was a skillful storyteller—too skillful, perhaps. Five years later, in *Final Del Juego* (End of the Game, 1956), he was still hard at work conjuring up his spells, a bit too scrupulously. Repeated exercises in an unchanging vein had given him an unfair advantage over himself, he says; he had begun to doubt his progress. There were already clear signs of a transition into new territory in his next collection of stories, *Las Armas Secretas* (Secret Weapons, 1959). Among them was "El Perseguidor" (The Pursuer), which marked a break in his work. It issued in what we might call his Arltian phase. Without sacrificing the imaginary, he had begun to draw live characters taken from real life, with their feet on the ground. His style had also become more muscular, less "aesthetically" pleasing. Perhaps until then playing with literature had been his way of creating a fantasy world around himself to shield him against certain unpleasant realities. But now, more at home with himself, he took a closer look at the world. What he saw he described in 1960 in his first novel, *Los Premios* (The Winners). It was the somewhat defective and shapeless book of an author fumbling toward a subject and new forms to go with it. It was followed, in 1962, by *Historias de Cronopios y de Famas*, an assortment of loose notes, sketches, brief insights into hidden dimensions that demonstrate the author's fondness for fruitful improvisation. The Cronopios and Famas, playful poltergeists with coined names and strange habits, were blobs in a bubble world in some ways not unlike the real one. With this book Cortázar seemed to pause and take a deep breath. What followed was a hurricane. It was called *Rayuela* (1963)—an "antinovel" that shows every sign of having represented a major breakthrough for him. *Rayuela* is a therapeutic book, intended as a complete course of treatment against the empty dialectics of

Western civilization and the rationalist tradition. It is an ambitious work, at once a philosophical manifesto, a revolt against literary language, and the account of an extraordinary spiritual pilgrimage. The Cortázar of *Rayuela* is a deep-sea diver who comes up with a full net. He is a man of many means, contorted, contradictory, exuberant, paradoxical, polemic: not only a great wit and humorist, outshining all others in our literature, but also—as he shows in a pithy appendix somewhat detached from the main body of the narrative—a brilliantly aggressive, if slightly pedantic, literary theorist.

Cortázar is a married man. He and his wife, Aurora, who value their independence above all things, earn a living as free-lance translators for UNESCO, where their job, as he says somewhat wryly, is to help "maintain the purity of the Spanish language." They take it in stride for about six months a year, including an annual trip to Vienna for a meeting of the Atomic Energy Commission, then spend their holidays in retirement in their summer house in southern France or in Venice. They like to go gallivanting together, and their taste tends to the unusual. They frequent provincial museums, marginal literatures, lonely side streets. They resent intrusions on their privacy, avoid literary circles, and rarely grant interviews; they would just as well never meet anybody, Cortázar says. They admire the ready-made objects of Marcel Duchamp, cool jazz, and the scrap-metal sculptures of César. Cortázar once spent two years of his life translating the complete works of Poe; Aurora is an excellent translator of Sartre, Durrell and Italo Calvino. Cortázar visited the United States in 1960, principally Washington—and New York, where he spent most of his time in the Village, window-shopping in back alleyways. Something of what struck him there he pulled out of his bag of tricks later in portraying the American characters in *Rayuela*. He has always been a sort of intellectual pickpocket. To pick and choose—making an intelligent use of chance and coincidence—is also to create, he says. As proof of this he offers the long delirious insert in the appendix of *Rayuela* called "La Luz de la Paz del Mundo" (The Light of the Peace of the World), for the text of which he is indebted to one Ceferino

Piriz, a "mad genius" residing somewhere in Uruguay, who submitted it to a contest at UNESCO as his contribution to solving the problems of the world. It provides a Master Plan for dividing our globe into color zones and distributing armaments according to surface and population. Cortázar liked it because he saw it as a perfect example of the kind of raving madness that pure reason can lead to—the last thing the mad lose is their reasoning power, Chesterton said—so he lifted it, without changing a word. And the truth is that it seems very much in place in a fictional landscape where farce and metaphysics join hands to beat a path across ultimate lines, among elements of apocalyptic scenery that seem to have come out of some monstrous clearance sale in a flea market or a Turkish bazaar.

By contrast, the Cortázar home, a three-floor pavilion overlooking a quiet, shady courtyard, is a world of light and order. Our visit takes place on a dark autumn night. A gust of wind sweeps us in the door. We shake a bony hand, and a narrow spiral staircase leads us up into a spacious drawing room with austere furnishings: a low central table, flat modern sofas, Venetian blinds, abstract paintings on the walls. The Cortázars took over what must have been an old barn or stable some years ago in a state of decrepitude and completely remodeled it. Their thin years are over. A black crossbeam supports the ceiling. A tribal sculpture—a souvenir from a trip to Africa—looks down on us with a beneficent smile. In *Rayuela* there is a circus tent with a hole in the top, through which the protagonists catch a glimpse of Sirius. Here, too, on clear nights, you can see the stars through the skylight. A bookcase which spans a whole wall reflects Cortázar's somewhat unconscionable preferences: 60 percent of the books are in French, 30 percent in English, only a splenetic 10 percent in Spanish.

Cortázar sits with his long legs crossed, his hands clasped on his knees, prim and prudent. He is a man of intellectual passions, reticent about himself. Yet where his work is concerned—he is unassuming, but without false modesty—he speaks freely, and always to the point.

Although he made what one might call his official literary

debut—with *Los Reyes*—when he was thirty-five, he has been
writing practically all his life, he tells us. "Like all children who
like to read, I soon tried to write. I finished my first novel when I
was nine years old. . . . And so on. And poetry inspired by Poe,
of course. When I was twelve, fourteen, I wrote love poems to a
girl in my class. . . . But after that it wasn't until I was thirty or
thirty-two—apart from a lot of poems that are lying about here
and there, lost or burned—that I started to write stories." But he
did not publish them. There was caution, and perhaps some
arrogance, in his delay. "I knew instinctively that my first stories
shouldn't be published," he says. "I'd set myself a high literary
standard and was determined to reach it before publishing
anything. The stories were the best I could do at the time, but I
didn't think they were good enough though there were some
good ideas in them." He reworked some of the ideas later. But "I
never took anything to a publisher. For a long time I lived far
from Buenos Aires. . . . I'm a schoolteacher. I graduated from a
normal school in Buenos Aires, completed the studies for a
teacher's degree, and then entered the Liberal Arts School of the
university. I passed my first-year exams, but then I was offered a
job teaching some courses in a town in the province of Buenos
Aires, and since there was very little money at home and I
wanted to help my mother, who'd educated me at great cost and
sacrifice—my father had left home when I was a very small child
and had never done anything for the family—I gave up my
university studies at the first chance I had to work, when I was
twenty years old and moved to the country. There I spent five
years as a high school teacher. And that was where I started to
write stories, though I never dreamed of publishing them. A bit
later I moved to Mendoza, to the University of Cuyo, where I was
offered some courses, this time at the university level. In 1945–46,
at the time of all the Peronista troubles, since I knew I was going
to lose my job because I'd been in the fight against Perón, when
Perón won the presidential election, I resigned before I was
backed against the wall as so many colleagues were who held
onto their jobs, and found work in Buenos Aires. And there I
went on writing stories. But I was very doubtful about having a
book published. In that sense I think I was always very clear-

sighted. I watched myself develop, and didn't force things. I knew that at a certain moment what I was writing was worth quite a bit more than what was being written by other people of my age in Argentina. But, because of the high idea I have of literature, I thought it was a stupid habit to publish just anything as people used to do in Argentina in those days when a twenty-year-old youngster who'd written a handful of sonnets used to run around trying to have them put in print. If he couldn't find a publisher, he'd pay for a personal edition himself. . . . So I held my fire."

The confidence and equanimity with which Cortázar confronted his literary prospects might suggest a particularly favorable atmosphere at home, but there was no such thing. He had to make it more or less on his own. His family, on both sides, were all white-collar workers. They belonged to that category of half-educated people "who, as Chesterton said, are the worst kind. Which has nothing to do with affection. These are strictly intellectual matters. . . . But I was lucky in one sense. In the normal school where I studied, an abysmally bad school, one of the worst schools imaginable, I nevertheless managed to make a few friends, four or five. Many of them have become brilliant poets, painters, or musicians. So, of course, we formed a sort of hard core of resistance against the horrible mediocrity of the teachers and the rest of our schoolmates. It's the only way to survive in Argentina. When I finished my studies I kept in close contact with those friends, but later, when I left for the country, I was completely isolated and cut off. I solved that problem, if you can call it solving it, thanks to a matter of temperament. I was always very ingrown. I lived in small towns where there were very few interesting people, almost none. I used to spend the day in my room in my hotel or boardinghouse, reading and studying. That was very useful to me, and at the same time it was dangerous. It was useful in the sense that I consumed thousands of books. I certainly picked up a lot of book knowledge in those days. It was dangerous," he adds, looking back with indulgence on those years of encyclopedic erudition, "in that it probably deprived me of a good share of vital experience."

An illustration of this problem is *Los Reyes*—now out of print:

a series of dialogues ("a dramatic poem," he calls it) on the subject of Theseus and the Minotaur. "There are dialogues between Theseus and the Minotaur, between Ariadne and Theseus, and between Theseus and King Minos. It's a curious approach to the subject, because it's a defense of the Minotaur. Theseus is portrayed as the standard hero, a typical unimaginative conventional individual rushing head on, sword in hand, to kill all the exceptional or unconventional monsters in sight. The Minotaur is the poet—the being who is different from others, a free spirit, who therefore has been locked up, because he's a threat to the established order. In the opening scene King Minos and Ariadne discuss the Minotaur, and you learn that Ariadne is deeply in love with the Minotaur—her half brother, since they're both children of Pasiphaë. Then Theseus arrives from Athens to kill the Minotaur, and that's when Ariadne gives him the famous thread so he won't get lost when he winds his way into the labyrinth. But in my version the reason why she gives him the thread is that she hopes the Minotaur will kill him and then follow the thread out of the labyrinth to join her. In other words, my version is the exact opposite of the classical one."

Not that the switch made much of an impression on the Argentine literary public. *Los Reyes* was not exactly received by acclamation, says Cortázar. It was hardly noticed. Though Borges had liked it enough to preview it in a magazine he was in charge of at the time, when it appeared in book form there was "an absolute and total silence."

But he was not discouraged. By then he was looking well ahead. "I was completely sure that from about, say, 1947, all the things I'd been putting away were good, some even very good. I'm referring, for example, to some of the stories of *Bestiario*. I knew nobody had written stories like that before in Spanish, at least in my country." He was in no hurry. A short novel that he had finished at the time, which some friends had tried to get published for him, had been turned down for "its nasty words," a rejection that did not bother him in the least. Again, on the eve of his trip to Europe, in 1951, a few close friends who knew the stories of *Bestiario* in manuscript form

snatched them from his hands to show to the Editorial Sud-
americana, which published them immediately, but without any
success. In the meantime, even when he was in Buenos Aires, he
had been leading a very solitary life. He was satisfied to have a
small but distinguished audience, which, aside from Borges, a
staunch supporter to whom he acknowledges a special debt of
gratitude, included his friends and the few readers of the little
magazine (*Los Anales de Buenos Aires*) that had printed *Los
Reyes.*

Los Reyes was originally published in a limited edition by a
friend, Daniel Devoto. It was never sold commercially or reissued
in any form. Which is something less than a tragedy, according to
Cortázar, because "the truth is, I'm still very fond of *Los Reyes,*
but it really has little or nothing to do with anything I've written
since. It's done in a very lofty style, very polished and high-flown,
fine in its own way, but basically very traditional. Something like
a cross between Valéry and St. John Perse."

Nevertheless, the book introduces an image that makes a
recurrent appearance in his work: the labyrinth. Here it is mere
frontispiece and curlicue, but there is a Cortázar who attaches a
deeper significance to this archetypal symbol. He says he is the
last to know what obscure biographical sources—or literary reminiscences—may lie behind it. But in its web he discovers remnants of a childhood pattern. He remembers that "as a child,
anything connected with a labyrinth was fascinating to me. I
think this shows in a lot of my work. I used to construct
labyrinths in my garden. I set them up everywhere. For instance,
from my house in Banfield"—a suburb of Buenos Aires—"to the
station there were about five blocks. When I was alone, I used to
hop all the way. My labyrinth was a fixed road I'd laid out for
myself. It consisted in going from sidewalk to sidewalk and
jumping to land on certain stones I liked. If I miscalculated for
any reason, or didn't land on the right spot, I had a feeling
something was wrong, that I'd failed somewhere. For several
years I was obsessed by that ceremony. Because that's what it was:
a ceremony."

Ceremonial children's games are omnipresent in Cortázar's work, often with labyrinthian implications. The whole of *Bestiario* is like the title story, where the emotional problems of a sensitive little girl take on nightmarish proportions in the form of a ferocious tiger she imagines inhabiting the back room of a mansion full of interconnecting doors and criscrossing corridors. In "Casa Tomada" (House Taken Over), a brother and sister are gradually crowded out of house and home by the encroachment of unknown occupants (their ancestors?) who keep appropriating rooms and slamming doors in their faces. In "Los Venenos" (Poisons) in *Final del Juego,* the labyrinth is an anthole with mazes of underground passageways. Then, of course, there is the labyrinthian street game that gives its name to *Rayuela.*

Cortázar throws light on his intentions, remarking that *Rayuela* was originally to be entitled *Mandala.* "When I first got the idea for the book, I was very much taken with the notion of Mandala, because I'd been reading a lot of books of anthropology and above all of Tibetan religion. Besides, I'd been in India and I'd seen many reproductions of Japanese and Indian mandalas." A mandala, he recalls, is a sort of mystic labyrinth—"a design, like a hopscotch chart, divided into sections of compartments, on which the Buddhists concentrate their attention and in the course of which they perform a series of spiritual exercises. It's the graphic projection of a spiritual process. Hopscotch, as almost all children's games, is a ceremony with a mystic and religious origin. Its sacred value has been lost. But not entirely. Unconsciously some of it remains. For instance, the hopscotch played in Argentina—and France—has compartments for Heaven and Earth at opposite ends of the chart. Now, I suppose as children we all kept ourselves amused with these games. But I had a real passion for them."

There are also labyrinthian overtones in *Los Premios,* where passengers on a mysterious boat attempt to gain access to the stern following a staircase down into the hold, into darkness and confusion. It is not easy to come out on the other side. The road is a long obstacle course—another sort of mandala that evolves as the plot unfolds. In an existential sense, says Cortázar, one might interpret the need the characters feel to reach the stern, to run a fore-set course, as a desire "to become realized as persons, as human beings. That's why some make it and others don't. It's a simpler notion, more rudimentary than in *Rayuela*."

In *Rayuela* the mandala is a course that leads to a "beyond," to a "fall toward the center," into what Cortázar, who dreams of an Iggdrasil that will bind heaven and earth, describes as "a state of immanence" where opposites meet and one simply "is." *Rayuela* is an invitation to plunge through time in order to gain the far shore of eternity. It suggests a jump into the waters of selflessness, as well, says Cortázar, as what Musil called "the search for the millennium: that sort of final island where man would at last find himself, reconciling his inner differences and contradictions."

Oriental philosophy, in particular Zen Buddhism and Vedanta, offers "metaphysical positions" that have always appealed to Cortázar. Vedanta, for instance, is predicated on "denying reality as we understand it, in our partial view of it; for instance, mortality, even plurality. We are all illusions in each other's minds; the world is always a way of looking at things. Each of us, from his standpoint, is total reality. Everything else is an external, phenomenological manifestation that can be wiped out in a flash because it has no real existence; its reality exists only, one might say, at the expense of our unreality. It's all a question of inverting the formula, shifting the weights on the scale. For instance, the notions of time and space, as they were conceived by the Greeks and after them by the whole of the West, are flatly rejected by Vedanta. In a sense, man made a mistake when he invented time. That's why it would actually be enough for us to renounce mortality—I've spoken about that somewhere in *Rayuela*—to take a jump out of time, on a plane other than that of daily life, of course. I'm thinking of the phenomenon of death, which for Western thought has been a great scandal, as Kierkegaard and Unamuno realized so well; a phenomenon that is not in the least scandalous in the East where it is regarded not as an end but as a metamorphosis. The difference in the two outlooks is partly a difference of method: what we pursue discursively, philosophically, the Oriental resolves by leaping into it. The illumination of the Buddhist monk or the Master of Vedanta (not to speak, of course, of any number of Western mystics) is a bolt of lightning that releases him from himself and raises him to a higher plane where total freedom begins. The rationalist philosopher would say he is sick or hallucinated. But he has reached a state of total reconciliation that proves that by other than rational ways he has touched bottom."

In his own way, in *Rayuela*—via his protagonist, Oliveira, a man between two worlds, like his author—Cortázar has, too. Or at least he has tried to. "The attempt to find a center was, and still is, a personal problem of mine," he says. All his life he has been injecting it into his work without finding a concrete solution for it. Even the inexhaustible *Rayuela*, which provides a sort of unending catalogue of avaliable alternatives, in the end can offer only partial subterfuges. "*Rayuela*," says Cortázar, "shows to what extent the attempt is doomed to failure, in the sense that it isn't that easy for one to unburden oneself of the whole Judaeo-Christian tradition one has inherited and been shaped by."

Yet the search for alternatives started early in Cortázar. Perhaps the search, in ersatz form, is implicit in all fantastic literature. This would be the Quirogan, the Borgean, lesson. In this sense, Cortázar's fantastic stories, with their mysteriously disjunctive patterns, seem premonitory. Their language, a kind of shorthand, full of whispered hints and coded signals, performs an almost ritual function. The stories are like incantations, psychic equivalents of magic formulas. One might compare them to charms that open doors, allowing the author a way out of himself. There is also what we might call a more practical side to them. Cortázar describes them as a sort of occupational therapy. "They're charms, they're a way out," he says, "but above all, they're exorcisms. Many of these stories, I can even single out a concrete example, are purgative, a sort of self-analysis." The case in point is "Circe," where a woman makes repulsive sweets with cockroaches inside, which she offers to her boyfriends. "When I wrote that story I was going through a time of exhaustion in

Buenos Aires because I'd been studying to become a public translator and was taking a whole battery of exams, one on top of
another. I wanted to have a profession, to be financially independent, already with the idea of eventually moving to France. So
I packed all the work for my degree into eight or nine months. It
was backbreaking. I was tired and I started to develop neurotic
symptoms; nothing serious—I didn't have to see a doctor. But it
was very unpleasant because I acquired a number of phobias
which became more preposterous all the time. I noticed that when
I ate I was constantly afraid of finding flies or bugs in my food,
food prepared at home and which I trusted completely. But time
and again I'd catch myself scratching with my fork before each
mouthful. That gave me the idea for the story—the idea of something loathsome and inedible. And when I wrote the story, it
really acted as an exorcism, because after I'd written it I was
immediately cured. . . . I suppose other stories are in the same
vein."

The stories leave a varied impression on the reader. Some are
subtle word games—crossword puzzles. Others, like "Omnibus"
(Bus Ride), one of the most speculative—and therefore most
suggestive; which is why it has been interpreted as everything
from a parable on death to a political allegory—seem to go
crashing through barriers into unknown realms, to dip into
orders of experience that are normally closed to us.

"The truth," says Cortázar, "is that though these stories, seen,
let's say, from the angle of *Rayuela,* may seem like games, while I
was writing them and when I wrote them I didn't think of them
that way at all. They were glimpses, dimensions, or hints of
possibilities that terrified or fascinated me and that I had to
exhaust by working them off in the story."

Some were written at a sitting, spun out with almost supernatural force and intensity, says Cortázar—and the reader senses
this. They were produced in a state of grace, which the author
invites us to share with him. He is "on to" something, and points
the way. Dramatic congruity or psychological verisimilitude is
not important to him. The experience imposes its own terms.
What counts is that we be able to relive it—not as a vicarious

experience, comfortably identifying with characters and situations, but in the flesh, as it were. We are in a closed circuit, armed with verbal formulas that, when invoked, will unleash the same sequence of events inside us as they did inside the author.

The source of a story's power, says Cortázar, is inner tension. The higher the tension the better it transmits the author's pulsations. "What the exact method for transmitting these pulsations is, I can't say, but in any case it depends on the ruthless execution of the story. The tense wiring permits a maximum freedom of action. In other words, I've watched myself writing at top speed—all in one breath, literally beside myself, without having to correct much afterwards; but that speed had nothing to do with the preparation of the story. I'd been concentrating my forces, bending backward to tighten my bow, and that increased my impetus when I sat down to write the story. The tension isn't in the execution of the story, though of course it remains trapped in the tissue from where it is later transmitted to the reader. The tension as such precedes the story. Sometimes it takes six months of tension to produce a long story that comes out in a single night. I think that shows in some of my stories. The best are packed full of a sort of explosive charge."

"Structures," he calls them. Words are mere touchstones in these stories; one finds oneself reading between the lines. The language is disarmingly simple and straightforward. There are no verbal flourishes, no tortured effects. The tone is conversational. The surface is crystal clear. But intangible forces are building up underneath. The clarity is made of shadowy undercurrents that gradually fuse in a climax with cathartic after-effects. The reader, swept along, spills over the brim, delivered of himself.

An experience of this sort, no longer projected through fantasy but seen in the context of real life, becomes the actual theme and subject of a story somewhat later in the highly speculative "El Perseguidor," which in a sense makes Cortázar's previous work obsolete by rendering its preoccupations explicit. The setting of the story—flagrant throughout—is Paris. When Cortázar wrote "El Perseguidor," he had long liquidated his affairs in Buenos

Aires. He seems to be making this point in every line. But
Cortázar points are turnstiles, and tend to roll over on themselves.
And so in "El Perseguidor" we find ourselves in the numinous
areas of Arltian lowlife. We are introduced to an underworld
character, Johnny Carter—alias Charlie Parker—a Negro saxo-
phonist, a man gifted by nature with metaphysical senses but of
few intellectual resources, for whom music is not only a form of
expression—a release into being—but an instrument in his search
for an exit into godliness. Johnny, who walks the cemeteries of the
earth, trying to revive the dead, hears echoes of divine voices in
broken urns. He is a kind of blind seer—a starchaser, a man with a
thirst for the absolute. He feels his true self mortgaged in space
and time, a hostage waiting to be ransomed from the bondage of
individuality. His talent is his strength, but also his undoing. Because basically he is a poor lost soul, ignorant of his powers, who
lives in anguish and torment without ever knowing why. He has
intimations of eternity, but cannot shape or grasp them. He
thrashes about in hopeless confusion. The road leads downhill,
through drug addiction into final madness. Like Oliveira—a
man asphyxiated by intellectuality—and also Maga—a sort of
embodiment of the poetic instinct in its pure form—in *Rayuela,*
he has sudden intuitions, moments of inspiration, almost of
mystic communion with the universe, but is too inept or, in his
case, simple-minded, to form any sort of coherent strategy out of
them. They remain unfulfilled, mere flashes in the dark.

Cortázar says of "El Perseguidor": "In everything I'd written
until that moment I'd been satisfied with inventing pure fantasies. In *Bestiario,* in *Final del Juego,* the mere fact of imagin-
ing a fantastic situation that resolved itself in a way that was
aesthetically satisfactory to me—I've always been demanding in
that area—was enough for me. *Bestiario* is the book of a man
whose inquiries don't carry beyond literature. The stories of
Final del Juego belong in the same cycle. But when I wrote 'El
Perseguidor,' I had reached a point where I felt I had to deal
with something that was a lot closer to me. I wasn't sure of myself
any more in that story. I took up an existential problem, a
human problem which was later amplified in *Los Premios,* and

above all in *Rayuela*. Fantasy for its own sake had stopped interesting me. By then I was fully aware of the dangerous perfection of the storyteller who reaches a certain level of achievement and stays on that same level forever, without moving on. I was a bit sick and tired of seeing how well my stories turned out. In 'El Perseguidor' I wanted to stop inventing and stand on my own ground, to look at myself a bit. And looking at myself meant looking at my neighbor, at man. I hadn't looked too closely at the human species until I wrote 'El Perseguidor.' "

When he wrote *Los Premios*—and the unpublished *El Examen* (The Exam)—a bit later, he had already gone a long way toward remedying that deficiency. In *Los Premios,* the search for a "way out"—playful at times, in spite of its underlying seriousness—has taken on an added dimension: now it is not only part of the subject matter but a procedural element. The characteristic Cortázar light touch is present, here put to work to make things happen—in the Nerudan phrase—"without obstinate form." Cortázar is a freer man than he was before, more conversant with social and psychological reality. The aesthete is never far away, but his workings take more devious forms. They might appear, for instance—as they do in *Rayuela*—in a lengthily erudite, and usually archly humorous, conversation on art, music, or literature, but casually, mixed with other components, sometimes almost irrelevantly, and never as anything more than means to an end. Cortázar says he started the book during a long boat trip—out of boredom, "to keep myself entertained"—letting it develop randomly, plotless. "I saw the situation as a whole, but in a very undefined and general way." He never knew for sure, from one chapter to the next, what to expect of himself. The result is rambling: a slow sprawl. It seems to be going nowhere. But it has pull. There are shrewd characterizations, some of them based on real people. Cortázar says: "I started to enjoy myself with the characterizations in the first chapters, which are too long, but I didn't have the faintest idea what was going to happen afterwards, though I'd already written quite a few pages. It was fascinating to me for a while to pretend I was also one of the characters of the book. It meant that I didn't have any advantage over them, I wasn't a demiurge deciding fates on a whim. I faithfully respected the rules of the game." They were complicated rules that sometimes remained on the drawing board. But toward the middle of the book the plot and themes suddenly coalesced and finally condensed in an adroitly handled resolution.

The subject, on the surface, is a holiday cruise—a tour offered to a number of otherwise generally unrelated people who have been thrown together on board by sheer coincidence, simply because they all happened to draw winning numbers in a lottery. On a primary symbolic level, it is an inner trip each passenger takes toward self-confrontation. But it is also the author's own inner trip toward himself. The obstacles are many. The end remains equivocal and unattainable. Its physical representation is the stern of the boat, which for some unknown reason has been closed to the passengers. No one has access to it. Not even the author. "I was in the same position as Lopez or Medrano or Raúl," he says. "I didn't know what was happening astern either. It's a mystery to me to this day."

Mystery is ever present in the book; the stern is shrouded in it. We do not know what to make of the situation. Certainly it must be very grave. But who knows? It may all be a funereal joke. In any case, there are many disturbing signs on board. The crew behaves strangely. There are inexplicable absences—for instance, that of the boat doctor. The atmosphere becomes sinister, then mutinous. We suspect an illegal traffic of some sort. But nothing is revealed. We are probably in the hands of some mischievous underworld cartel ruled by an infernal overlord who may turn out to be our other self.

A seductive aspect of *Los Premois*—and proof that Cortázar was looking at the world when he wrote it—is the psychopathological portrait it gives of the Porteño character. Cortázar is the furthest thing from a sociological-minded novelist, but, though he has a tendency—as he admits—to overlap instead of differentiating his characters, he draws their essential traits well. A touch of satire adds spice to the narrative, particularly since it has the poignant edge of self-satire. The satirical intent is secondary. "Whenever the plot brought me face to face with ridiculous or disagreeable aspects of social relations," says Cortázar, anxious to establish this fact, "I drew them as I saw them. I had no reason not to. But the novel wasn't made for that purpose by any means. The critics tended to see *Los Premios* as an allegorical or satirical novel. It's neither one nor the other.' Nevertheless, these diverse ingredients enrich the texture. We are shown a sort of cross section of Porteño types: two circumspect and whimsical schoolteachers; a sedentary, fatuous old Galician millionaire; a high-minded homosexual; a promiscuous woman of the world with catholic tastes; an unbeautiful adolescent stranded in his doubtful sexuality; a representative from the Boca, the Genoese quarter in Buenos Aires, which produces outstanding specimens of what is known as the "reo porteño"—well-meaning, bighearted roughnecks, fanatic football fans, "completely guileless, terribly dumb, but made of good stuff, basically genuine and worthy"; a young honeymooning couple distinguished mainly for their smug self-satisfaction and rudeness. A large supporting cast—made up mostly of colorful "popular" characters, among them the cantankerous personnel—provides an occasionally loudmouthed backdrop to the drama.

A mystifying character in *Los Premios,* apparently something of a holdover from Cortázar's Minotauran days, is Persio, a stationary, more or less abstract, figure, a philosopher, a bit of an astrologer, who meditates the length of the work, commenting on the action in oracular asides that appear in the form of interior monologues. He has little stage presence; he gives a sort of synthetic view of things, but in such abstruse language and so rarefied a tone that he often obscures what he is meant to illuminate. There is a whole literary clutter in Persio—the author's personal memorabilia—that suggests the bookworm and sometimes the wastebasket. Persio, in the course of his mediations, gives a symbol of the whole adventure on board the *Malcolm* equating the image of the boat with the shape of a guitar in a Picasso painting. Cortázar says that here again he was playing by ear. "After the first two chapters, one that takes place in the café on shore, the other showing the arrival on board the ship, you have the first monologue of Persio. When I'd written those first two chapters I suddenly felt—and when I say 'felt,' I mean it literally—that the next thing had to be a different vision. And then Persio automatically became the spokesman for that vision. That's why I numbered his chapters differently and put them in italics. Besides the language there is completely different." The intention, the reader might think, may have been to create a sort of alter ego of the author. But there is more to it than that. "Persio," says Cortázar, "is not a spokesman for my ideas, even if he is in some sense, just as some of the other characters are, too. . . . Persio is the metaphysical vision of that everyday reality. Persio sees things from above, like a sea gull. He gives a kind of total and unifying vision of events. There, for the first time, I had an inkling of something that has been inhabiting me ever since, which I mention in *Rayuela* and which I'd now like to be able to develop fully in another book. It's the notion of what I call 'figures.' It's a feeling I have—which many of us have, but which is particularly intense in me—that apart from our individual lots we all inadvertently form part of larger figures. I think we all compose figures. For instance, we at this moment may be part of a structure that prolongs itself at a distance of perhaps two hundred meters from here, where there might be another corresponding group of people like us who are no more aware of us than we are of them. I'm constantly sensing the possibility of certain links, of circuits that close around us, interconnecting us in a way that defies all rational explanation and has nothing to do with the ordinary human bonds that join people." He recalls a phrase of Cocteau, to the effect that the individual stars that form a constellation have no idea that they are forming a constellation. "We see Ursa Major, but the stars that form Ursa Major don't know that they do. In the same way, we also may be forming Ursa Majors and Ursa Minors, without knowing it, because we're restricted within our individualities. Persio has some of that structural view of events. He always sees things as a whole, as figures, in compound forms, trying to take an over-all view of problems."

If Persio's abstract viewpoint seems a bit of an interference, it may be because we suspect it of being less metaphysical than aesthetic: a formal superstructure introduced artificially to satisfy the author's—and the reader's—instinct for order. But here we are on uncertain ground. The reproach has been held up to him more than once, says Cortázar. "But I have to say I've never held it up to myself. Because, in fact, Persio's monologues, though perhaps mainly aesthetic in effect, were born of an almost automatic writing, at great speed and without the control I deliberately kept over the rest of the novel. Instead of being conscious readjustments, they're like escape valves for a subconscious process. Besides they were written in the exact place where they stand. They weren't added afterwards as they might seem to have been. I'm sorry if they seem tacked on, but each fitted in exactly where it seemed to belong in the book. Something kept telling me there was a need to interrupt the sequence, to allow that other vision of things to take over for a while. Of course, the reproach may still hold, because what counts is the result, not the needs of the moment." Perhaps the real justification for Persio's synthesizing vision can be found in Cortázar's later work, where the aesthetic and the metaphysical chase each other tirelessly until at last they meet in *Rayuela*. Persio in *Los Premios* is the author's hand, still hesitant, for the first time attempting to make the two terms compatible.

More successful is the existential level of *Los Premios*. There, vividly real to us, always fundamentally true in word and gesture, half a dozen human fates play themselves out under high pressure, as the author, in accordance with a secret scheme that gradually emerges from the shadows, realizes himself through them. Among them is Medrano, a dentist who has behaved like a heel, abandoning his mistress on shore, and finds the trip an occasion to do some soul-searching. A dramatic turn of events, masterfully travestied by the author, precipitates him into having "what the Zen Buddhists call Satori: a sort of explosive fall-in toward himself." Medrano is a man who never watched too closely where he stepped. Perhaps there is a parable here about an author who graced many pages before stopping to take stock of himself. The time had come for remedial action. Medrano realizes what a thin line he has been walking. So off he goes—and the author, figuratively speaking, with him—down the hatch, "on a headlong plunge which in the end he pays for dearly: with his skin."

Which is only as it should be. Because Medrano, like Johnny Carter, is a member of Cortázar's family of starstruck searchers, who know that the true road is a difficult one, often to be purchased at a high price, with life—or sanity. The latter—and perhaps the former—is the case with Oliveira in *Rayuela*. Oliveira, a triumphantly backboneless character, pursues a devious path down a blind alley to destruction. At the end of the book, past the point of no return, we are uncertain as to whether he has committed suicide or simply fallen into complete madness. But the question is immaterial. What we know is that he has made a concerted effort, the length of his unwholesome but edifying adventure, to undermine himself at every step, to subvert rational barriers and collapse logical categories, and that finally he has lost his footing and gone off the deep end into bottomless waters. There is something heroically Quixotic about his career. Within his abjectness, the uncompromising—and sometimes perverse—doggedness and dignity with which he pursues his search give him a kind of pseudo-tragic stature. Oliveira lives in extremities, a ruinous shadow of himself, going from stranglehold to deadlock. A chronic dreamer, his predicament is that of the man who, by means of sterile sophistries, empty paradoxes, synthetic rationalizations, has pushed himself to the point where he is incapable of finding a reason to live or to do anything. Everything is the same to him: love, abstract thought, art, causes. He can find irrefutable pretexts to justify—or negate—all of them. He has chosen "a course of inaction, instead of action"; his energies go to waste in "a purely dialectical movement." It is easier for him "to think than to be." In his battle to "be," his weapons are mockery, outlandish farce, absurdity, outrageous clownishness.

"I detest solemn searches," says Cortázar. Which is one reason why he admires Zen. "What I like above all about the masters of Zen is their complete lack of solemnity. The deepest insights sometimes emerge from a joke, a gag, or a slap in the face. In

Rayuela there's a great influence of that attitude, I might even say of that technique."

As an example, he mentions the chapter about the wooden board toward the end of the book. Oliveira has returned to Buenos Aires after all his Parisian mishaps: his estrangement from Maga, the death of Maga's child, Rocamadour, his desperate and fruitless posturing. He runs into an old friend, Traveler, in whom he eventually begins to recognize a sort of double of himself—an avatar of one his own previous, more enlightened, phases; and at a given moment in his confusion—which is compounded by acute bachelor pains—he starts to identify Traveler's wife, Talita, with his lost Maga. He has hotheaded dreams about her. Tensions mount and the problem comes to a head in an excruciatingly funny scene that has every external appearance of being completely insignificant. Oliveira and Traveler occupy rooms on opposite sides of the same street; their windows face each other. Oliveira, who has been setting up living quarters, asks Traveler for some necessary implements; Talita is charged with delivering them. To shorten her road, Oliveira spans the distance between the two windows with a long wooden board, inviting her to cross over it. She accepts, taking her life in her hands. As she confronts Oliveira, halfway between him and her husband, hovering in mid-air, forty feet above the street, masks drop, baring faces in separate solitary agony.

"The chapter of the wooden board," says Cortázar, "I think, is one of the deepest moments in the book. Because lives are in the balance. Yet, from beginning to end, it's treated as a wild joke."

In *Rayuela*, jokes, gags, are not only dramatic elements but stitches in the narrative fabric. Whole scenes are built on them. Cortázar is a great improviser. His humor can be harsh, hectic, grotesque, ironic, jeering. The episodic construction he uses favors his ends. He is a master of parody, jabberwocky, wordplay, non sequitur, obscenity, and even cliché, which he exploits with predatory relish. Farce alternates with fantasy, slang with erudition. Puns, hyperbole, innuendo, sudden shifts and dislocations, all the resources of comic art, including virtuoso nonsense passages, are put to work with inexhaustible versatility.

Cortázar explains that certain forms of Surrealism may throw light on his methods. Modern French literature in general has left a deep mark on his work. Though as a young man he had so little sense of values, he says, that he could hardly distinguish between Montaigne and Pierre Loti, "I changed radically as a result of reading certain French writers—for instance, Cocteau. One day when I was about eighteen I read Cocteau's *Opium*. It was a flash of lightning that opened a new world to me." He threw out half his library and "plunged headfirst into the world Cocteau was showing me. Cocteau put me on to Picasso, Radiguet, the music of the Group of the Six, Diaghilev, all that world between 1915 and 1925, and Surrealism: Breton, Eluard, Crevel. The Surrealist movement has always fascinated me." He is one of those who think Surrealism was one of the great movements of the century, until it was ruined by the Surrealists themselves, among others, when it became a mere literary movement instead of an attitude toward life. Cortázar has also been a great reader of some of Surrealism's direct ancestors: Apollinaire, Lautréamont, Alfred Jarry. "Jarry," he says, "was a man who realized perfectly that the gravest matters can be explored through humor. That was just what he tried to do with his 'pataphysique'— to touch bottom via black humor. I think that notion had a great influence on my way of looking at the world. I've always thought humor is one of the most serious things there are." The respect for humor as a valid means of investigation is the sign of a high civilization, he believes. It indicates an ability to go prospecting for buried treasure without reaching for big phrases. "The English know that better than anybody. Much of great English literature is based on humor."

Humor, suggests Cortázar, can also be a useful defense mechanism in the more "surrealistic" circumstances of daily life. He remembers it served him well in Argentina in the forties when reality had become "a sort of waking nightmare" to him. Twenty years of social and political unrest came to a head with the advent of the Second World War, a difficult time in Argentina for anybody with a conscience. The country had bought neutrality—and an unprecedented surface prosperity—at the cost of self-respect. It was a period of hypocritical pacifism, of sham positions, false alliances, petty interests, and shabby betrayals. Then came the added foolishness of Peronism. Cortázar, like so many of his disillusioned contemporaries, after a brief brush with politics when he was on the staff of the Liberal Arts School in Mendoza—he was actually imprisoned during a student mutiny—withdrew to the sidelines, into what he says frankly "may well have been nothing but escapism." The intellectual found himself in a somewhat ludicrous quandary in those days. Because resistance to the dictatorship had polarized public opinion at opposite ends of the spectrum, his problem was where and how to take a stand in a situation that allowed for no middle way. For those who, like Cortázar, believed there were underlying elements of genuine value in Peronism as a social movement but could not accept the leadership of Perón and his wife or, on the other hand, find any effective way to channel their opposition to the regime without playing into the hands of other political speculators and opportunists, a possible solution was to disconnect themselves rather guiltily from the scene, laughing it off as best they could.

Laughter, in all its dimensions, is the key to *Rayuela*. Its aim is to catch the reader off guard, penetrate his defenses, and set off uncontrollable reflexes. Cortázar tiptoes among weighty matters like a housebreaker. Part of the effect he achieves in his best scenes is a result of the enormous distance that exists between the narrative surface and the underlying reality it encloses and encompasses. At moments a meeting occurs: parallel lines intersect. There is a burst of light. The multiple contrasting levels of a scene and the disproportions and incongruities existing between them often create a sense of high pathos.

"I think one of the moments in *Rayuela* where that works best is in the breakup scene between Oliveira and Maga. The scene is a long dialogue where a number of things come under discussion, none of which appear to have anything to do with the matter at hand. At one point they even burst out laughing and roll on the floor. There I really think I managed to get an effect that would have been impossible if I'd simply exploited the pathos in the situation. It would have been just one more breakup scene, like so many others in literature."

Another similar scene is the death of Rocamadour. The author plays it for laughs. It occurs in a dingy hotel room, during a smoky bull session, with jazz records in the background. Maga and Oliveira have gone on the rocks. The climate is one of despair. But all sorts of grotesque incidents distract from the scene: knocks on the ceiling, an irrelevant quarrel in the corridor. Rocamadour is agonizing. But nobody wants to rock the boat. Everybody, including, notably, the author, looks the other way.

Throughout all this—battered, bankrupt, demoralized—Oliveira continues his search for ultimates. In *Rayuela* the motif of the search is orchestrated at every possible level, including the level of language. Words are a process of elimination. We beat a path toward a distant shore, a sort of ulterior calm in the eye of the storm, a final turn in the thread leading to the center of the labyrinth. Language has a specific function in *Rayuela:* to talk the problem out until it has been exhausted or annulled—or exorcised.

"The whole of *Rayuela* is done through language," says Cortázar. "There's a direct attack on language to the extent, as it says explicitly in many parts of the book, that it deceives us practically at every word we say. The characters in *Rayuela* keep insisting on the fact that language is an obstacle between man and his own deeper being. We know the reason: we use a language that's entirely outside certain kinds of deeper realities we might gain access to if we didn't let ourselves be misled by the ease with which language explains, or purports to explain, everything." As for the "center" Oliveira touches at the end, "an end that remains undefined—I don't know myself whether Oliveira really jumped out the window and killed himself or simply went completely mad, which wouldn't have been too great an inconvenience since he was already installed in an asylum; he kept switching roles, from nurse to patient, and back, like someone changing clothes—I think that was an attempt on my part to demonstrate from an Occidental viewpoint, with all the

limitations and shortcomings this implies, a jump into the absolute like that of the Zen Buddhist monk or the Master of
Vedanta."

For Oliveira common sense has led nowhere. Therefore, to
break his mental block, abandoning words, he resorts to acts. But
where does this leave the author? Oliveira's acts must be described in words.

"There we touch the heart of the matter," says Cortázar.
"There's a terrible paradox in being a writer, a man of words,
and fighting against words. It's a kind of suicide. But I want to
stress that at bottom I don't fight against words as a whole or in
essence. I fight against a certain usage, a language that I think
has been falsified, debased, made to serve ignoble ends. It's a bit
like the accusation—a mistaken accusation, it turned out to be
finally—that was brought against the Sophists in their day. Of
course, I have to fight by means of words themselves. That's why
Rayuela, from a stylistic point of view, is very badly written.
There's even a part (chapter 75) where the language starts to
become very elegant. Oliveira remembers his past life in Buenos
Aires, and does so in a polished and highly chiseled language. It's
an episode that's written fussing over every word, until, after
about half a page, suddenly Oliveira breaks out laughing. He's
really been watching himself all the time in the mirror. So then
he takes his shaving cream and starts to draw lines and shapes on
the mirror, making fun of himself. I think this scene fairly well
sums up what the book is trying to do."

Language must be of paramount concern to the writer, says
Cortázar, in a literature which still demonstrates such glaring
lacks in this area as ours does. Our difficulties he attributes in
part to the bad influence of foreign translations. The apprentice
writer is at their mercy. The language of translations is a landless
abstraction, a sort of bloodless jargon that reduces every style to a
common denominator. "In a country where there's a real literary
tradition, where literature reflects the evolution of language, as
might be the case in Spain, France, Germany or the United
States, there evidently writers work with a sense of inherited
responsibility. They have an acute sense of style, a well-trained
ear, and high formal standards. In Argentina we have none of

this." If pompous, labored styles still abound among us it is because writing, regarded as a performance, imposes a posture. The writer clears his throat, fans out his tail feathers, and "reproduces on the cultural plane the typical attitude of the ignorant, semiliterate man who, when he sits down to write a letter, finds it necessary to use a completely different language from the one he speaks with, as if he were struggling against some physical impediment, overcoming a series of taboos."

Cortázar's work denounces this false language. He works "against the grain," as he says. Just as he is anti- or parapsychological in his approach to character—that chip in the cosmic kaleidoscope—he is antiliterary in utterance. Morelli, a waggish professor he creates in the appendix of *Rayuela* to give voice to some of his ideas, is speaking for him when he proposes a novel that would not be "written" in the ordinary sense of the word, but "unwritten." We can take this bit of Morelliana as a point of departure for Cortázar, who for some time now has been struggling to devise a "counterlanguage" that will establish new circuits, dispensing with the conceptual baggage and other mental obstacles that hamper true communication.

"The book I want to write now," he tells us, "which I hope I can write, because it's going to be much more difficult than *Rayuela*, will carry this to its final consequences. It will be a book that will probably have very few readers, because the ordinary bridges of language that the reader logically expects will have been reduced to a minimum. In *Rayuela* there are many bridges left. In that sense *Rayuela* is a hybrid product, a first attack. If I manage to write this other book, it will be a positive contribution in the sense that, having concluded the attack I mounted against conventional language in *Rayuela*, I'm going to try to create my own language. I've already started to work at it, and it's no easy task. The ideal would be to arrive at a language that would reject all the crutches (not only the obvious ones but the others, the ones under cover) and other trappings of what is so cheerfully referred to as a literary style. I know it will be an antiliterary language, but it will be a language. The point is, I've always found it absurd to talk about transforming man if man doesn't simultaneously, or previously, transform his instru-

ments of knowledge. How to transform oneself if one continues
to use the same language Plato used? The essence of the problem
hasn't changed; I mean the type of problems that were pondered
in Athens in the fifth century before Christ are still basically the
same today because our logical categories haven't changed. The
question is: can one do something different, set out in another
direction? Beyond logic, beyond Kantian categories, beyond the
whole apparatus of Western thought—for instance, looking at
the world as if it weren't an expression of Euclidean geometry—
is it possible to push across a new border, to take a leap into
something more authentic? Of course I don't know. But I think
it is." The problem is not only to replace a whole set of images of
the world but, as Morelli says, to go beyond imagery itself, to
discover a new stellar geometry that will open new mental
galaxies. Here is where the "figures" come in.

Says Cortázar: "The concept of 'figures' will be of use to me
instrumentally, because it provides me with a focus very different
from the usual one in a novel or narrative that tends to indi-
vidualize the characters and equip them with personal traits and
psychologies. I'd like to write in such a way that my writing
would be full of life in the deepest sense, full of action and
meaning, but a life, action, and meaning that would no longer
rely exclusively on the interaction of individuals, but rather on a
sort of superaction involving the 'figures' formed by a constellation of characters. I realize it isn't at all easy to explain this. . . .
But as time goes by, I feel this notion of 'figures' more strongly
every day. In other words, I feel daily more connected with other
elements in the universe, I am less of an ego-ist and I'm more
aware of the constant interactions taking place between other
things or beings and myself. I have an impression that all that
moves on a plane responding to other laws, other structures that
lie outside the world of individuality. I would like to write a
book that would show how these figures constitute a sort of break
with, or denial of, individual reality, sometimes completely unknown to the characters themselves. One of the many problems
that arise in this scheme, a problem already hinted at in *Rayuela,* is to know up to what point a character can serve a purpose
that is fulfilling itself outside him, without his being in the least

aware of it, without his realizing that he is one of the links in that superaction or superstructure?"

In attempting to answer this question, Cortázar will have to bear arms against conventional notions of time and space. Having already denied us ordinary identification with characters and situations, Morelli, in *Rayuela,* goes a step further. He points to the "error of postulating an absolute historical time" and suggests that the author should not "lean on circumstance." A principle Cortázar has already begun to put into practice in a new collection of stories called *Todos los Fuegos el Fuego* (The Fire of All Fires). He can point to a story in this collection that ignores stereotyped time. "A single character lives in Buenos Aires today and in Paris in 1870. One day he's strolling in downtown Buenos Aires and at a certain moment, without any break in the continuity, suddenly he's in Paris. The only person who may be surprised is the reader. A covered gallery—a sort of out-of-the-way territory I've always found very mysterious—symbolizes his passage from one place to the other. In France it's winter, in Argentina it's summer, but there's no clash in his mind. He finds it perfectly natural to live in two different worlds (but are they really two different worlds for him?)."

In a sense, this is the crucial point Cortázar has been trying to settle in all his work. No small part of Oliveira's problem in *Rayuela* is the fact that he is a rootless soul, inwardly divided between "two different worlds"—a "Frenchified Argentine," as he calls himself. And "nothing kills a man faster than being obliged to represent a country," the author quotes Jacques Vaché in the epigraph that introduces the first part of the book. Says Cortázar, a man who has learned that the problem is not to adapt to a country but to become acclimated in the universe: "I use the phrase ironically, because I think it's obvious from everything I've written that I've never considered myself an autochthonous writer. Like Borges and a few others, I seem to have understood that the best way to be an Argentine is not to run around broadcasting the fact all the time, especially not in the stentorian tones used by the so-called autochthonous writers. I remember when I moved to Paris, a young poet who is a very well-known critic and essayist in Argentina today bitterly reproached me for leaving and accused me of an act that sounded a lot like treason. I believe that all the books I've written from Paris have resoundingly disproved him, because my readers consider me an Argentine writer, even a very Argentine writer. So the quote is ironic in regard to that sort of flag-waving Argentinism. I think there's a deeper way of being an Argentine, which might make itself felt, for instance, in a book where Argentina is never mentioned. I don't see why an Argentine writer has to have Argentina as his subject. I think being an Argentine means to share in a set of spiritual and intellectual values, and non-values of all sorts, to assume or reject these values, to join in the game or blow the stop whistle; just as if one were Norwegian or Japanese. It has nothing to do with sophomoric notions of patriotism. In Argentina there continues to be a grave confusion between national literature and literary nationalism, which are not exactly the same thing. In any case, the Argentina that appears in my later books is largely imaginary, at least where concrete references are concerned. In *Rayuela*, for example, the Porteño episodes, excluding the few topical references to streets and neighborhoods, are set against a completely invented background. In other words, I don't require the physical presence of Argentina to be able to write."

We might speak of the "metaphysical" presence of Buenos Aires in *Rayuela*. Perhaps that is the key to the whole thing. Buenos Aires in Cortázar—its gestures, its humor—is not a city but a skyline, a rooftop, a springboard into that longed-for "kibbutz" or nirvana, where differences vanish. Morelli, always useful in a tight spot, agitates for a race of writers who are "outside the superficial time of their era, and from that timeless point where everything is raised to the condition of a 'figure,' where it acts as a sign, not a subject for description, try to create works that may be alien or inimical to their age and their surrounding historical context, but which nevertheless include this age and context, explain them, and ultimately point them on a transcendent course that finally leads to an encounter with man."

"One must travel far while loving one's home," said Apol-

linaire in a phrase that supplies the epigraph for the second part
of *Rayuela*. It gives the essence of the Cortázar adventure. It is
one of the forms—perhaps the most personal—of this adventure
that Oliveira lives in *Rayuela*. Oliveira is a split personality in
pursuit of a multiple mirror-self that forever eludes him. Which
is why his plight becomes acute as he wistfully confronts his
double, Traveler. He touches parts of a lost self—a vanished
unity—in others. The theme of the double, with its infinite
variations, is a constant in Cortázar's work. It can take an oneiric
form as in the story "La Noche Boca Arriba" (On His Back
under the Night) where a man in his sleep retreads ancestral
paths, or again in "Lejana" (Faraway Image), where a woman on
a honeymoon trip in Hungary meets herself coming the other
way on a misty bridge, just as she had previously dreamed she
would; or serve as the basis for a meditation on immortality, as it
does in the intellectually more stringent and exacting "Una Flor
Amarilla" (A Yellow Flower). Doubles, says Cortázar, are like his
"figures"—or, rather, reversing the equation, "the figures are a
sort of apex of the theme of the double, to the extent that they
would tend to illustrate connections, concatenations existing
between different elements that, from a logical standpoint,
would seem to be entirely unrelated."

Cortázar's illustrations, always bifocal at least, sometimes take
us to odd places, not only mentally but also geographically. The
mental fringes his characters inhabit are faithfully reflected in
the marginal settings they frequent. In *Rayuela* we quickly lose
our bearings as the scene shifts from a dark corner under a bridge
to a mental hospital—in Cortázar a conference hall can suddenly
become a urinal—to a circus with a shamanic hole in the tent.

"I like marginal situations of all kinds," he says. "I prefer back
alleyways to main thoroughfares. I detest classic itineraries—at
every level." An example of this attitude is his hobgoblinish
Historias de Cronopios y de Famas, which is full of those serious
jokes he is so fond of: instructions for mounting a staircase, for
winding a clock; a sketch about a man who loses his head and
learns to detect sounds, smells, and colors with his sense of touch;
a section called "Ocupaciones Raras" (Strange Occupations),

which works its effects under the skin, on raw nerve ends. In
Cronopios corpses grow nails, the bald drop their wigs. There is a
warning against the dangers of zippers. The author is constantly
emptying his pockets under the table. When the book appeared
in Argentina, it was received with clacking dentures. Poets
treated it with respect, says Cortázar, but the few critics who
mentioned it were shocked. They deplored the fact that such a
"serious writer" could stoop to such unimportance. "There," he
says, "we touch on one of the worst things about Argentina: the
stupid notion of importance. The idea of doing something just
for the fun of it is practically nonexistent in our literature."
Cortázar provides a cure for this ill. *Cronopios* came to him like
a sudden twinge, a shot in the dark. "In 1951, the year I came to
Paris," he tells us, "there was a concert one night in the Théâtre
des Champs Elysées. Suddenly, sitting there, I thought of some
characters that were going to be called Cronopios. They were
somewhat extravagant creatures that I didn't see very clearly yet,
a kind of microbes floating in the air, shapeless greenish blobs
that gradually started to take on human traits. After that, in
cafés, in the streets, in the subway, I started writing stories about
the Cronopios and the Famas, and the Esperanzas, which came
later. It was a pure game. . . . Another part of the book, 'The
Manual of Instructions,' I wrote after I got married, when
Aurora and I went to live in Italy for a while. You have Aurora
to blame for these texts. One day, mounting an endless staircase
in a museum, out of breath, she said suddenly: 'The trouble is
that this is a staircase for going down.' I loved that phrase. So I
said to Aurora: 'One ought to write some instructions about how
to go up and down a staircase.' " He did. Similarly, in *Rayuela,*
he composed a certain circus scene because it served "as a chance
to include some elements of humor, of pure inventiveness: for
instance, the mathematical cat, which I had a good laugh over."

Oliveira also has a good laugh over it—but it is a hollow
laugh, the laugh of a man being led to the gallows. It has the
ring of crisis.

Hilarity, in Cortázar, often becomes a sort of seizure. His
comic pangs are like death throes. His comic scenes are really
brink situations in an almost Dostoevskian sense. *Rayuela* is

made up almost entirely of brink situations. Apart from their dramatic effectiveness, they provide the author with strong motor impulses. "For one thing, they heighten reader interest, which I always keep very much in mind. They're another form of inner tension in the book. Besides, I think these brink situations are a kind of displacement for the reader, a way of estranging him. They shake him up a bit, shift the ground under him. But, above all, they are the situations where the ordinary categories of understanding have either collapsed or are on the point of collapsing. Logical principles are in crisis; the principle of identity wavers. Brink situations are the best method I know for the author first, then the reader, to be able to dissociate, to take a leap out of himself. In other words, if the characters are stretched tight as bows, at the point of highest tension, then there's the possibility of something like an illumination. I think the chapter about the wooden board in *Rayuela* is the one that best illustrates that. There I'm violating all the laws of common sense. But precisely because I'm violating those laws by placing my characters and therefore also the reader in an almost unbearable position—it's as if I were receiving a friend sitting in a bathtub in tails and a top hat—at that moment I can really get across what I want to say. What I was trying to say in the chapter of the wooden board is that at that moment Traveler and Oliveira have a sudden complete meeting of minds. Perhaps this is where the notion of the double takes concrete form. Besides, they're gambling for the possession of Talita. What Oliveira sees in Talita is a kind of image of Maga." It recalls the first image in the book: Maga on a bridge—over a sacred element: water—in Paris. Bridges and boards are symbols of passage "from one dimension into another."

There are other means of passage in *Rayuela*, among them one that turns out to be a descent into Hell. There was already a staircase leading down into nether regions—the hold of the boat—in *Los Premios.* Here the image is more chilling—and specific. Oliveira and Talita ride a dumbwaiter down into the madhouse morgue. Instead of hot coals we have a deep freeze. Oliveira stands clearly revealed in this scene. Toward the end of it he suddenly kisses Talita. Talita, who is no fool, rushes back up to tell Traveler what has happened, complaining: "I don't want to be somebody else's zombie." She has caught on, and "I think the descent into Hell was perhaps the way to create the necessary tension to permit that almost inconceivable moment. Under the circumstances, there could be no misunderstanding. Talita is terrified by what she has just seen in the morgue. She and Oliveira are in a situation of extreme tension, so extreme that right afterwards—the whole scene takes place literally on the borderline for Oliveira—he returns to his room and starts to set up his system of defenses, convinced that Traveler is going to come and kill him."

Extravagant as ever, Oliveira surrounds himself with a sort of huge spiderweb, made of networks of threads he extends all over the room, hoping Traveler will trip and tangle in them. Pans of water irregularly, but strategically, scattered on the floor fortify the stronghold with a moat. Thus buttressed, Oliveira props himself up to wait on the windowsill. And fate closes in. When Traveler opens the door, he finds Oliveira on the point of throwing himself out the window. Oliveira has just caught sight of Talita-Maga down below, in the courtyard, tromping on a hopscotch chart. He comes full circle. He has been an inveterate dabbler in deep waters, an "enlightened bum" for whom the first principle of self-respect was never to beg a question, to do it to death worthily instead. We see him for a moment congratulating himself over his downfall. Who knows what may happen? Breaking down may mean breaking through. His dead end may turn out to be the reverse side of a new beginning. On the other hand, his final loss may be in finding himself.

Oliveira is the creation of an author for whom literature—an act revolutionary by nature—has a high missionary purpose as an instrument for reform and renewal. Which is why, whereas "as a young man literature for me was the great classics—and also the best of the avant-garde, let's say the most established names: Valéry, St. John Perse, Eliot, Ezra Pound—the Goethian tradition, we might call it, now that literature interests me a lot less, because I find myself more or less at odds with it. Nobody can deny its remarkable achievements; but at the same time it's entirely circumscribed within the mainstream of the Western tradition. What interests me more and more nowadays is what I would call the literature of exception. A good page of Jarry stimulates me much more than the complete works of La Bruyère. This isn't an absolute judgment. I think classical literature continues to be what it is. But I agree with Jarry's great 'pataphysical' principle: 'The most interesting things are not laws but exceptions.' The poet must devote himself to hunting for the exceptions and leave the laws to the scientists and the serious writers." Exceptions, says Cortázar, "offer what I call an opening or a fracture, and also, in a sense, a hope. I'll go into my grave without having lost the hope that one morning the sun will rise in the west. It exasperates me with its obedience and obstinacy, things that wouldn't bother a classical writer all that much."

A problem Cortázar might have to wrestle with—if the sun did suddenly rise in the west for him one day—would be the communicability of this vision. How to transmit it? Would it be something that was "in the air"—that others also would see? One might perhaps assume that if he found the words to express it he would be telling us something we were already—though wordlessly, incoherently—telling ourselves. He would precede us, but only to make our realization, as it were, simultaneous with his. In *Rayuela* he speaks of an experience that would be latent in every page, waiting to be relived by the reader who would come prepared to discover it as his own.

In this sense, from the point of view of our literature, *Rayuela* is a confirmation. We could say it is our *Ulysses*. Like Joyce, Cortázar, by a sort of inner triangulation, measuring a personal magnitude, has fathomed our world in exile. From his solstice he has found our equator. It was partly a matter of pinpointing things, he says. A book like *Rayuela,* on the one hand, gives the reader a lot he was already prepared for. "Generally the books that a generation recognizes as its own," says Cortázar, "are those that haven't been written by the author alone but, in a sense, by the whole generation." *Rayuela* is one of those books. It raised blisters when it came out in Argentina. It sold out its first edition of 5,000 copies—editions of 10,000 being considered runaway best sellers—in a year. Since then the mailman has often been at the doorbell, usually with gratifying news. "The mail I've received on *Rayuela*," says Cortázar, "proves that this book was 'in the air' in Latin America. Many bittersweet letters say: 'You've stolen my novel,' or: 'Why go on writing when my book should have been like *Rayuela?*' Which goes to show the book was latent somehow, and imminent. I happened to be the one to write it, that's all. But that is only one side of the problem. The other side is that, obviously, a significant book also has to contribute something new. There must be a step forward."

And here is where *Rayuela* shines. The "step forward" it offers is a new concept of the literary experience that may come to live a long life in our literature. *Rayuela* is the first Latin-American novel which takes itself as its own central topic or, in other words, is essentially about the writing of itself. It lives in constant metamorphosis, as an unfinished process that invents itself as it goes, involving the reader in such a way as to make him a part of the creative impulse.

If there is any objection one can raise to *Rayuela*, it is that too much of it functions on the kind of intellectual premises the ordinary reader would be likely to break his teeth on. Its erudition, pursued at times to unnecessary lengths, is intimidating. Oliveira—we gather somewhere in the text—is a frustrated writer. His problems are formulated in what we might call a writer's terms, with a somewhat undigestible wealth of literary allusions. Effects depend heavily on the cultural backlog the reader can call on. None of this seems very intrinsic to the purpose of the book, unless we assume the premise implicit throughout that the writer's or the artist's problems, and even the terms in which they are expressed, can be equated with those of man in general. Cortázar argues that in Oliveira he created "a man of the street," as he says, "an intelligent and cultured man, but at the same time perfectly commonplace and even mediocre, so the reader could identify with him without any trouble, and even outdistance him in his own personal experience." Yet Oliveira may well seem out of reach to the ordinary reader. And here is the flaw. But is it that? Cortázar admits that *"Rayuela, like so much of my work, suffers from hyperintellectuality. But,"* he adds, "I'm not willing or able to renounce that intellectuality, in so far as I can breathe life into it, make it pulse in every thought and word. I use it quite a bit as a freeshooter, firing always from the most unusual and unexpected angles. I can't and I shouldn't renounce what I know, out of a sort of prejudice in favor of what I merely live. The problem is to give it new intentions, new targets and points of departure."

In this labyrinthian enterprise he has succeeded beautifully. It has been his way of following the thousand different threads of self that lead toward the center of being. "I think no road is entirely closed to any man," he says. And certainly he has found more than one opening into the further reaches of experience. An achievement of no small moment for a man who confesses in *Rayuela* to "the somewhat belated discovery" that "aesthetic orders are more a mirror than a passageway for metaphysical longing."

Anything, even to fall back, rather than remain static has been his motto throughout his career. He allows himself no false reconciliation with himself or the world. "The world is full of people living in false bliss," he says. He will continue to trip himself up as he goes along. The important thing for him is to keep his inner dialogue going. Learning to speak to himself has been his way of trying to talk to others. He has just begun to find his voice. "When all is said and done," he says, "I feel very much alone, and I think that's as it should be. In other words, I don't rely on Western tradition alone as a valid passport, and culturally I'm also totally disconnected from Eastern tradition, which I don't see any particular compensatory reason to lean on either. The truth is, each day I lose more confidence in myself, and I'm happy. I write worse and worse, from an aesthetic point of view. I'm glad, because I think I'm approaching the point where perhaps I'll be able to start writing as I think one ought to write in our time. It may seem a kind of suicide, in a sense, but it's better to be a suicide than a zombie. It may be absurd for a writer to insist on discarding his work instruments. But I think those instruments are false. I want to wipe my slate clean, start from scratch."

VII

Juan Rulfo,
or the Souls of the Departed

OLD-LINE regionalism, though much diminished from the days when it was a tidal flow in our literature, is still a current to be reckoned with. Unfortunately, a lot of what it hauls along is old-fashioned stuff of little more than pictoric interest. The old regionalists who started producing the bulk of our literature around the twenties were mediators between man and nature. Their function was less literary than agricultural. There was a wilderness to be tamed, an unmarked land to be given man's image and imprint. There were remnants of tribal cultures to be explored, catastrophes to be recorded. It was in the nature of things that literature, when it made itself heard at all, appeared as part of a collective effort.

Social conflicts—in feudal fiefs, mines, tropical plantations—gave this literature urgency and momentum. A branch of it, perhaps the sturdiest, taking its cue from the venerable Alcides Arguedas, who denounced the exploitation of the Indian in the Bolivian highlands in his epochal *Raza de Bronce* (Race of Bronze, 1919), found its cause in protest. Another, well represented today in the work of Peru's José María Arguedas, a fine sociologist, subordinated the epic to the interpretive. A

third, the least fruitful, petered out into folklore. But whatever
the emphasis, the basic characteristics of this literature were always the same. It gave a picture, not a portrait. Its lines were
general and usually at once roughly drawn and overly stylized. At
its best it was colorful and informative. It had poetic moments in
Peru's Ciro Alegría, a pleasant truculence in El Salvador's Salar-
rué, a militant force in Ecuador's Jorge Icaza. It became experimental with Mexico's Agustín Yáñez, highly expressive with José
María Arguedas, and even rose to mythological altitudes with
Guatemala's Miguel Ángel Asturias, who eclipsed all his contemporaries in the genre. Recently, when it was going a bit stale,
it had new life breathed into it by a talented Paraguayan storyteller, Augusto Roa Bastos, an excellent stylist who, without
basically altering the genre, has given it a new literary dignity.

On the whole, regionalists today are literate writers. Their work
has reached an acceptable level of achievement. But, in spite of
subtle refinements in methods and techniques, which rarely tran-
send basic limitations, they are essentially in the old pamphleteering tradition. They still tend toward either the tract or the travel-
ogue. They work from set situations which, needless to say, are
often as real today as they were forty or fifty years ago—at times
even more pressingly so—but from a literary point of view have
long been exhausted. Their faceless characters, sometimes colorful enough but seldom more than silhouettes with a few generic
traits, are soon forgotten. The stress they put on local dialect
helps their work date fast. There are few exceptions to the rule.
Perhaps the only one today is Mexico's Juan Rulfo.

Rulfo, a thin man with a lean look, was born on May 16, 1918,
in the rocky state of Jalisco, some three hundred miles, as a bird
flies, northwest of Mexico City. The northern part of the state,
where mountain goats cling to high ledges, is densely populated,
but his area, extending south of the capital, Guadalajara, is dry,
hot, and desolate. Life in the lowlands has always been austere.
It is a depressed area long gutted by droughts and wildfires.
Revolutions, crop failures, soil erosion have gradually displaced
the population. Much of it has moved to Tijuana in hopes of
finding migrant work across the border. It is a population largely

made up of hardy Creoles—the Indians who occupied the region before the Conquest were soon exterminated—who trace their ancestry back to Castile and Estremadura, the more arid parts of Spain, and are therefore, as Rulfo says, "accustomed to work ten times harder than the farmer of central Mexico to produce the same." They are a dour people reduced to a bare subsistence, who have nevertheless given the country a high percentage of its painters and composers, not to mention its popular music (Jalisco is the cradle of the ranchera and the mariachi).

Says Rulfo in his sorrowful voice: "It's a very poor state. But the people work a lot. They produce a lot. I don't know how they manage to produce so much. They produce too much. Jalisco is the state that produces the most corn in the whole country. It's not a very large state. I think it's the eighth state in size in the country. But it produces enough corn to feed the whole of Mexico. It has more cattle than any other state. But as soon as you leave the capital there's a lot of misery. Corn is a great destroyer of the soil. So there's no good soil left. In some areas it's completely worn out."

He sits hunched in his chair in our hotel room, off Mexico City's clattering Paseo de la Reforma, the lines of his gaunt face drawn tight, his long hands with big surface veins like raw nerves awkwardly folded on his lap. He talks quickly, in nervous haste—he is what is known in his land as a "slow starter," he says, like one of those rifles with delayed action that often backfire—frowning painfully. He is like his land: prematurely aged, deeply furrowed, careworn.

There are blanks in his past. Rugged terrain fades into a hazy background.

"I was born in what is now a small village, an agglomeration that belongs to the district of Sayula. Sayula was an important commercial center some years ago, before and even after the Revolution. But I never lived in Sayula. I don't know Sayula. I couldn't say what it's like. . . . My parents registered me there. Because I was born at the time of the Revolution, or rather, of the revolutions, because there were a series of them. . . . I lived in a village called San Gabriel. I really consider myself to be

from there. That's where I was brought up. San Gabriel was also
a commercial center. In the old days San Gabriel was a prosperous town; the royal road to Colima passed through there." San
Gabriel was on the highway that led inland from Manzanillo,
the port of entry used in colonial times for imports from the
Orient; in its heyday there was such wealth that the stores were
measured by the number of doors they had. "San Gabriel and
Zapotitlán were the most important towns of the region from the
seventeenth century down to the Revolution." They were first
settled under the "encomenderos": usually soldiers who were
granted lands by the Crown in reward for their services, with the
local population thrown into the bargain. These encomenderos
concentrated the population into a few main urban centers that
were relatively easy to administer. That was how San Gabriel
and Zapotitlán were formed, also Tolimán, Tonaya, Chacha-
huatlán, San Pedro, etc. But that was long ago. Since the
Revolution there have been years of sunstroke. Nowadays, "in
that zone, there are five or six villages left. They are hot lands,
between 2,500 and 3,000 feet high." Changing trade routes,
desert winds, have swept them into decay. There is little hope of
improvement. The process is irreversible. Some villages still seem
alive; but on closer inspection nothing is going on there any
more. The few superannuated inhabitants are stolid and tight-
lipped. "They are a hermetic people. Perhaps out of distrust—
not only toward strangers but also among themselves. They don't
want to talk about their things. Nobody knows what they do,
how they make a living. There are villages devoted exclusively to
graft. The people there don't like to be asked any questions.
They settle their affairs in their own private personal way, almost
secretly." The landscape itself—45 percent of Mexico is sheer
desert—is decrepit. The living are surrounded by the dead.

The dead haunt Rulfo. Perhaps because, like so many people
of his antediluvian region, he has been uprooted and has lost
track of himself. He remembers how his childhood village, now
a dust bowl, a lunar crater, was gradually depopulated. "There
was a river. We used to go bathe there in the hot season. Now the
river has run dry." One of the reasons why the water no longer

flows is that the woods in the surrounding mountains—which enclose the area in a monolithic horseshoe—have been cut down. Most people have migrated. Those who have stayed behind are there to keep the dead company. "Their ancestors tie them to the place. They don't want to leave their dead." Sometimes when they move they actually dig up their graves. "They carry their dead on their shoulders." Even when they leave them behind, they continue to bear their weight.

So with Rulfo, whose ancestry seems remote, therefore perhaps doubly cumbersome. He has also dug up old family graves in search of his lost origins. "My first ancestor came to Mexico around 1790, I think, from the north of Spain." "Historical curiosity" has sent him browsing, usually in vain, through libraries, bank vaults, and civil registries. Mexico is a country of missing files and misplaced documents. Particularly his area, which is buried in administrative confusion. "It was an area that didn't belong to Jalisco originally. Jalisco was called Nueva Galicia. It was conquered by Núñez de Guzmán in 1530. But my area was called the province of Ávalos. Because it was conquered by Alonso de Ávalos, the man who pacified Colima and the southern part of Jalisco. The province of Ávalos was part of Nueva España, in other words, of Mexico City, the capital of the viceroyalty. Though it was near Guadalajara, the capital of Nueva Galicia, it had no political or religious connections with Guadalajara. For many years the documentation of the province of Ávalos was lost, because most of those villages were decimated by plagues and fevers, sometimes by the Conquerors themselves. One of my ancestors on my mother's side was called Arias. . . . There's a curious fact here. Most of the Spanish Conquerors were adventurers, jailbirds: monks who weren't monks, priests who weren't priests, people with criminal records. They gave themselves names that don't exist. For example: Vizcaíno. I'm called Vizcaíno on my mother's side. But Vizcaíno is a name that doesn't exist in Spain. There's the province of Vizcaya. Here the name of the province was used to coin a surname. In other words, all the Vizcaínos were outlaws. It was very common among those gentlemen to change their names. They dropped their patro-

nymic and named themselves after their province instead. That's
where genealogy breaks down." The diagnosis holds good for
most families of "high birth" in Mexico today, he says. If you
trace them back far enough, you invariably end up with either a
priest or a criminal. "That's why 'highborn' dynasties are false,
formed entirely on the basis of wealth. It's hard to draw the lines
here. In Ávalos it's impossible. There the villages were razed by
the Revolution; the archives were burned. The only documents
available were copies on file in Mexico City. So it was difficult to
get down to the bottom of things. Now, many facts can be found
in banks in the United States. Because the expeditionary forces
that occupied California set out from Ávalos. So the banks there
have collected the documents of the period for their own information. They have the best files. Because it was a chapter in the
history of California, Texas, New Mexico, and Arizona." Rulfo
has carried his search to all those places.

What he knows about his family is that his paternal grandfather was a lawyer, his maternal grandfather a landowner. His
parents were from the more densely populated northern part of
the state, known as Los Altos (The Heights). "It's an overpopu-
lated, very eroded zone inhabited by people who started moving
south around the turn of the century. How my parents reached
the south I don't know. The highlander, besides being from the
highlands, is tall. Longback, people call him, because of his long
waist." Rulfo inherited this trait. He wears his trousers low on
slim hips. He also has light eyes. They are common in his region,
where the country girls are often blonde and blue-eyed. They are
also poor. They go barefoot. "There were never any big landholdings in that area. There were always small properties. The
country people have always been very poor. The only time they
put on their shoes is when they go into town. . . . The habits in
those villages are still matriarchal. There woman commands. As
a matter of fact, the power of the matriarchy made itself felt
during the revolt of the Cristeros. It was the women who led the
revolt."

The hardships of the time—starting around 1926, under President Calles, a centralizer who tried to impose constitutional

uniformity on the country—are one of Rulfo's childhood memories.

"The revolt of the Cristeros was an internal war that broke out in the states of Colima, Jalisco, Michoacán, Nayarit, Zacatecas, and Guanajuato, against the federal government. There was a decree that enforced an article of the Revolution, according to which priests were forbidden to mix in politics and the churches became the property of the state, as they are today. A set number of priests was assigned to each village, in accordance with its population. Of course, people protested. Those are very reactionary, very conservative villages—fanatics. There was a lot of conflict and agitation. The war, which was born in the highlands, in the state of Guanajuato, lasted three years, until 1928." By then it had extended to Rulfo's area. In the very first days of the war he lost his father. Six years later he lost his mother. He had been sent to Guadalajara to study at the age of eight, and when she died he was taken in by French Josephine nuns, who ran schools in almost all the important towns of Jalisco. He had relatives in Guadalajara: "the Rulfos, a very prolific family, especially on the female side." But somehow no one seems to have claimed him. His grandparents were all dead, except for a maternal grandmother—an old lady descended from "an Arias family that had come to settle in the area in the sixteenth century, probably from Andalucía"—who was almost illiterate.

Rulfo remembers the orphanage as a sort of reform school. He boarded there for several years. He says softly, lowering his eyes: "That's very common in Mexico. Still today many people in remote villages who want to educate their children and have no one to entrust them to, send them to boarding schools."

Perhaps closer to his true feelings is that line in one of his stories where he might well be evoking the loneliness of the orphanage when he says, with typical understatement: "It's difficult to grow up trying to cling to something which is dead at the root."

It was a hard struggle for the melancholy country boy transplanted among the relative splendors of a pseudo-metropolitan Guadalajara, a stiff-necked town with aristocratic pretensions which was actually, as he says, little more than an outpost of provincial snobbery living off the frayed remnants of its colonial pride. After grade school, hoping to become self-supporting, Rulfo went into accountancy. Accountants always managed to make a living, even in the most rundown times. But soon he had to cut corners. "With a cousin of mine, one of the Vizcaínos, I'd just gotten into high school when a general strike was declared. The university closed down for about three years." To continue his interrupted studies Rulfo moved to Mexico City. That was in 1933, when he was fifteen years old.

What the first months or years must have been like in the bustling capital for an impoverished youngster without friends or connections is something Rulfo does not talk about. But they left their mark on him. It was an itinerant life of odd jobs, always hand to mouth. Besides accountancy, Rulfo studied some law—"very irregularly." In his free time he attended literature courses at the university. In 1935 he landed a job with the Immigration Department—an obscure, but therefore, presumably, more or less safe, bureaucratic post that he occupied for ten years. It was no sinecure. When the Second World War broke out, with Mexico keeping to the sidelines, but nevertheless sympathizing with the Allied cause, he helped process the crews of impounded refugee ships—mostly tankers—of Nazi Germany. The ships were docked in Tampico and Veracruz, and the crews, which were treated more or less as war prisoners, were interned in military camps in the interior, often near Guadalajara, which became a great center of foreigners. It was unpleasant work, and in 1947, glad to be done with it, he switched to publicity work with Goodrich rubber. He was in the sales department there until 1954. In 1955 he was with the Papaloapan Commission, formed to implement an irrigation program near Veracruz. It was a pet project of President Miguel Alemán, who aspired to create a sort of Mexican TVA in the region. On a river with a seasonal overflow that swept away local villages, the commission built a power center. It plotted highways. But, because of mismanagement and lack of funds, the ambitious project failed. Back in Mexico City in 1956, Rulfo helped himself along by doing scripts and adaptations for

commercial movies. He had hopes that something of value could
be done in the medium. But that was another chimera. "The
result was not too positive," he says, shrugging. The year 1959
brought another change. He worked in TV in Guadalajara.
With the backing of the new Televicentro, which subsidized his
effort, he began compiling yearbooks of historical illustrations
that were another attempt to piece together the missing evidence
of the past. "The thing is, in Guadalajara the only cultural
activity is a bank, the Industrial Bank of Jalisco, which publishes
a history book every year as a gift to its clients. So I had an idea:
to try to incorporate the whole history of Jalisco from the days of
the early chronicles, and bring it out regularly, once a year, as
before, in book form. To make up for the poison people were
being fed on television, they'd be given a book." Whether the
plan failed or the planner was retired, Rulfo does not say.

Nowadays—on a job he has held since 1962—Rulfo works at
the Instituto Indigenista (Indian Institute), an organization devoted to the task of protecting and integrating primitive Indian
communities bypassed by progress, which has pushed them to the
fringes of Mexican life, where they become fodder for political
agitators. It is tiring and depressing work that keeps him constantly on the move. He disappears for days at a time on some
lonely mission into the misty backlands, and returns looking
haggard, as if back from a lost weekend. Every trip is an added
blow to him. On off days he sits humped over his desk in his
antiseptic office on an upper floor of the Institute, starting every
time the phone rings anywhere in the building and reaching for
the receiver next to him as if the call were always for him. He is
forever under the pressures of waiting. At any moment he might
jump up and vanish. Around him are glass walls that shake and
clatter as workers bang away in the hall. When no one is looking
he slips out of the office like a shadow, rides the elevator down in
silent concentration, and ducks around a street corner. Visitors
who catch him on the way out, suddenly unavoidable, become
honored guests. He makes an endless bustle, opening doors and
pulling out chairs for them, excruciatingly shy, gazing at them
out of frightened eyes. Installed at his desk in his dark suit,

kneading his nervous hands, looking perpetually worried and disoriented, he is like a harried village priest at the end of a long day, sighing in the solitude of his confessional. On those rare evenings when he has time to devote to his writing he floats out into the thin mountain air, full of whispers that drive him to the penitence of nightlong work. Though perhaps a little above medium height, his stoop makes him seem slight: a wisp of a man on a devious course through the shifting colors of nightfall, to a hard labor that may yield a few finished lines or simply become a sleepless cramp. He writes very little—his reputation rests on two books—probably because of some monumental block in him. Perhaps his life is not his own. Somewhere along the line—he was married in 1948, and lives in a house with many children—it fused with the life of his country, beat fast when the pulse was strong, then stopped with it. He says: "Stability in Mexico is deadlock. We've come to a complete standstill."

On a late afternoon in June, after hunting him down for a week, at home and at work, only to keep losing track of him—he has been called away, he is unavailable, he breaks an appointment—we finally meet him in the lobby of our hotel, where he arrives in trepidation, with a long shadowy face and darting eyes. He is late—by several hours—he has been held up, and he is dismally embarrassed. Upstairs he sits in a low chair, staring at the floor. He is ready to make for the door. He has a thousand things to do. Besides his missions for the Institute, he has been working on an experimental film with a theme of social protest. He describes it as a series of sketches interspersed with Vivaldi music, perhaps not unlike Buñuel's famous *Las Hurdes*. Overcoming his shyness, he wanders off on a meek man's compulsive monologue, stringing disconnected thoughts together, touching on everything and nothing, then falling into a tongue-tied silence. Again and again the conversation trails off. We are in a state of suspended animation. "I only know how to express myself in a very rudimentary way," he says with a gentle smile that crinkles the corners of his eyes.

He is a man who does not quite know how he came to literature—a somewhat belated vocation with him—except that one day he simply woke up in it. Perhaps the one to blame for this is the village priest of San Gabriel, back in the days of the wars of the Cristeros. For a time Rulfo stayed on a family farm with his grandmother, a pious lady who could hardly read anything outside her prayer book, which he suspects she recited from memory—she had once tried to go on a pilgrimage to Rome to see the Pope—but whose house contained a small library belonging to the local parish. The priest had left it there in safekeeping when the government troops turned his house into an army barracks. The Rulfo household was under federal protection, because Rulfo's mother was related by marriage to one of the colonels serving against the Cristeros. Rulfo had the books all to himself. "So I read all of them." Most of them, he says, were not biblical texts but adventure stories. They made his thoughts run ahead of him. He has been trying to keep up ever since.

But it was not until many years later, about 1940, in the solitude of the big city, that Rulfo first put pen to paper. He produced a fat novel—which he later destroyed—about life in Mexico City. "It was a conventional sort of book, very high-strung, but at bottom no more than an attempt to express certain solitary feelings. Maybe that's why it came out so highstrung. It wasn't convincing. But that was just it. The fact that I wrote it at all seems to mean I was trying to find a way out of the solitude I'd been living in, not only in Mexico City but for many years, since my days in the orphanage."

He describes the book as having been written in "a somewhat rhetorical language that I was perfectly well aware of myself. That wasn't the way I wanted to say things. So, practicing ways to free myself of all that rhetoric and bombast, I started cutting down, working with simpler characters. Of course I went over to the opposite extreme, into complete simplicity. But that was because I was using characters like the country people of Jalisco, who speak a pure brand of sixteenth-century Spanish. Their vocabulary is very spare. In fact, they practically don't speak at all." The result was his first story, "La Vida no es Muy Seria en sus Cosas" (Life Is Not to Be Taken too Seriously), published in

1942 in a Guadalajaran magazine called *Pan*. Limiting his scope, withdrawing within the starkness of personal memory, he seemed to have found his way. In 1945 he published his now-famous story, "Nos Han Dado la Tierra" (The Land They Gave Us). The stories of the next few years, a meager but vintage crop, were collected in 1953 under the title of one of them, *El Llano en Llamas* (The Plain on Fire). In 1953 and 1954, on a Rockefeller grant—during his work on the Papaloapan project—he wrote *Pedro Páramo*, which appeared in 1955.

Rulfo's brief and bright course has been one of the wonders of our literature. He has not blazed any new trails; to the contrary, he has been content to tread along traditional paths. But his footsteps go deep. He writes about what he knows and feels, with the simple passion of a man of the land come into contact with elemental things: love, death, hope, hunger, violence. With him, regional literature loses its pamphleteering militance, its folklore. Experience is not filtered through the prism of civilized prejudice. It is laid out straight, with cruel candor. Rulfo is a man attuned to the primitive poetry of desert landscapes, dusty sunlit villages, seasonal droughts and floods, the humble joys of the harvest, the hard labor of poor lives lived out always close to plague and famine. His language is as frugal as his world, reduced almost to pure heartbeat. He has no message. He sings the swan song of blighted regions gangrened by age, where misery has opened wounds that burn under an eternal midday sun, where a pestilent fate has turned areas that were once rolling meadows and grasslands into fetid open graves. He is a stoic who does not inveigh against treachery and injustice, but suffers them in silence as part of the epidemic of life. His theme is simply human sorrow in dispossession. He writes with a sharp edge, carving each word out of hard rock, like an inscription on a tombstone. Therefore his work glows with a lapidary purity. It is written in blood.

"So much land, for nothing," says one of the characters in *El Llano en Llamas,* gazing around him at the desolate expanses spreading out of sight in the sweltering haze. And that sets the tone of the book. Its impressionistic sketches—it would be stretching a point in some cases to call them stories—are quick glimpses into the soul of ruin. They are not all related in time or space. But the same spirit inhabits them all. The region, generally, is that of southwestern Jalisco, extending roughly from Lake Chapala west through Zacoalco to Ayutla and Talpa and south through Sayula and Mazamitla toward the border that separates Jalisco from the states of Colima and Michoacán. Armed bands laid the area waste during the Revolution. Then, as the population straggled back, there was the revolt of the Cristeros, during which there was "a sort of resettlement. The army concentrated people in ranch houses and villages. When the fighting got more intense, the people were moved from the villages to larger towns. So the land was abandoned. People looked for work elsewhere. After a few years they didn't return any more." The agrarian reform was no help. It was very disorganized. "The land was distributed among small tradesmen instead of farmers. It was given to the carpenters, bricklayers, barbers, shoemakers. They were the only ones that formed a community. To form a community, you needed twenty-five people. All those twenty-five people had to do was get together and ask for the land. The country people never asked for it. The proof is that until this day they have no land. The farm worker was accustomed to being entirely dependent on the landowner he served. He was a tenant farmer who had his land on loan, cultivated it, and paid for it with half his yearly crop." The confusion favored real estate speculation. There has been no change for the better in recent years. Today the small farmers of Jalisco "have nothing to live from any more. They barely survive. They go down to the coast looking for work, or cross the U.S. border as day laborers. They come back in the rainy season to plow some little plot of land at home. But their children leave as soon as they can." There is no hope for these regions, says Rulfo. They are slated for disaster. Forty or 50 percent of the population of Tijuana comes from there. Families are numerous, with a minimum of ten children. The only industry is mezcal, the plant from which the tequila is taken. Significantly, there is a town called Tequila, northwest of Guadalajara. The mezcal and the maguey—source of an alcoholic beverage called pulque—are classical products of impoverished lands on the road to disintegration.

Rulfo mourns these lands. *El Llano en Llamas* is a quiet funeral oration to an area that is breathing its last. A pall of doom hangs in the air like a heavy storm cloud. The rule is resignation. A rough courage under a habitually apathetic surface flares up in intermittent spurts of violence and brutality: savage banditry, predatory blood feuds. It is an area of hunted men and deserted women, where "the dead carry more weight than the living." "If there's nothing to be done, there's nothing to be done," people say, bowing their heads, awaiting the relief of death. Because that is their only firm faith, their last illusion, that "some day the night will come" and peace along with it, as they are laid to rest among immemorial shadows in the darkness of the grave.

The trials begin with childhood, as in "Es que Somos Muy Pobres" (We Are Very Poor), where a young girl, whose older sisters, determined to wring what pleasure they can out of their destitution, have gone the way of all flesh, is, in turn, fated for perdition as her hopes of marriage vanish when her poor dowry —a cow and a calf—is swept away in a flood. Even bleaker is the lot of the child in "Macario": an orphan boy brought up in an inhospitable foster home, whose sole comfort is being breast-fed by a kind cook turned wet nurse, whose milk tastes of daffodils. Macario lives under the threatening shadow of his foster mother, who wags a chill finger at him, promising him hell for his misconduct. To please her—she is a neurotic insomniac—he spends his time killing frogs in a nearby pond—their croaks keep her awake—and cockroaches in the house. Gnawed by obscure pangs that the author pinpoints in vivid images, he has seizures, hears the drums of fairs pounding in the street, and beats his head against the floor. With a kind of quiet sadistic glee, he mashes bugs underfoot, littering the house with them. He spares only crickets which, according to an old wives' tale, chirp to cover the laments of souls in Purgatory.

The dark urges that propel people to their undoing are portrayed in "Acuérdate" (Remember), a brief sketch of a village type, a young dandy who suddenly, for no known reason, turns bad, to become a criminal and a renegade. He wants to go straight. He tries his luck as a policeman, then thinks of priesthood. But a blind force leads him on to violence, until at last he is hanged from the tree that, in a final act of free will allowed him by an ironic fate, he selects himself.

The Revolution, says Rulfo, unleashed passions that have become habits in some of these villages. Though on the whole crime has moved toward the coast lately, certain towns in Jalisco still live from it. It is a business and a way of life. A case of this is the story "La Cuesta de las Comadres" (Gossips' Slope), told casually, by a lackadaisical narrator, with the nonchalance of a people for whom death is always close and life has little value. A marauding gang of bandits and cattle rustlers—the Torricos— terrorizes the fertile slope of small lots that gives the story its title. It is one of those places where time has taken its toll. Over the years the population, driven by those nameless illusions that haunt all of Rulfo's characters, has disbanded. Partly to blame for the exodus are the Torricos. The narrator knows them well. He once went stealing bales of sugar with them, and nearly left his skin behind. Later, because Remigio Torrico accuses him of having murdered his brother, Odilón, who was actually killed in a brawl in town, in self-defense—he is being threatened with a machete—he kills Remigio by coolly sticking a baling needle in his ribs. All this is told in a matter-of-fact tone that adds a sinister thrill to the story. The setting is the no man's land around Zapotlán. The most grisly things happen in those places, says Rulfo. "A while back, in Tolimán, they were digging up the dead. No one knew exactly why or what for. It happened in stages, cyclically. . . ." A scar on the landscape may turn out to be an open sewer. "Among those villages, there's one called El Chantle, which is full of outlaws. There's no authority there. Even government troops stay away from the place. It's a town of escaped convicts. You see that kind of people elsewhere, too. As a rule, they're the calmest people in the world. They carry no arms, because they've been disarmed. You talk to them and they seem completely harmless. They're very peaceful, usually a bit sly, never quite on the level, but at the same time without any bad intentions. Yet behind each of those men there may be a long list of crimes. So you never know whom you're dealing with, whether with a gunman for a local warlord or an ordinary farmer." Often the forces of order are no more enlightened than the delinquents they track down. In "La Noche que lo Dejaron Solo" (The Night He Was Left Alone), we have a fugitive from justice doggedly stalked day and night by shadowy pursuers, who mop up his whole family. Stumbling home to his hut at night, through the smoke of a bonfire, he sees the corpses of his two uncles dangling from a tree in the corral. Troops are gathered around the corpses, waiting for him. As he blunders off into the brush to splash headlong across a river, he hears a voice say with savage logic: "If he doesn't get here before tomorrow morning, we'll knock off the first man who comes along, that'll settle accounts."

Another man pursued is the protagonist of "El Hombre" (The Man), whose flight sends him over horizon after horizon, carrying the weight of his guilt. He is a killer who has done away with a whole family. Shifting points of view throw light on his agony, foreshadowing techniques used later to fine effect in *Pedro Páramo*. The first part of the story is told objectively, in two times: one corresponding to the perceptions of the pursued, the other to those of the pursuer. Halfway through there is a switch to a first person narrator—the fugitive—then later to the point of view of a witness: a shepherd testifying before local police authorities. All are flimsy figures with fickle gestures, flickers of life that soon fade in the vastness of the plain.

In the land of the damned no one is to blame for his follies, and yet everybody is guilty. For, even stripped of their humanity, men continue to pay for it. The guilt may be nameless, but no less onerous for that, as in "En la Madrugada" (At Dawn), where a farmhand is thrown into prison, accused of having killed his master in a fight, and, though he remembers nothing, he says to himself, almost with exultation: "Since I'm in jail, there must be a reason for it"; or it may be very precise and specific, as in "Talpa," where an adulterous pair—man and sister-in-law—take

the deceived husband, who has been afflicted with the plague, on
a long pilgrimage to the Virgin of Talpa, whom they hope to
reach "before she runs out of miracles." The trip has a double
intent. The sick man is a burden to them; they know that the
bone-wearying trip will make him die faster. And so it happens.
On the way their charge, perhaps not unaware of their designs—
which they are only half aware of themselves—becomes a sort of
martyr and flagellant. In a fit of blind fervor he rips his feet on
boulders, bandages his eyes, then drags himself along on all
fours, wearing a crown of thorns. His pain is also their suffering;
it dramatizes a common predicament. When he dies, his survivors
are not acquitted of their sin. Their love dies with him.

Guilt is again a major theme in "Diles Que No Me Maten"
(Tell Them Not to Kill Me), a story of vengeance. An old crime
which time has not repealed catches up with the protagonist, who
is tied to a stake by the son of a man he murdered years before,
given a few shots of alcohol in a moment of wry compassion to
dull the pain, then summarily executed. But he might just as
well have been spared. A lifelong fear of retribution has already
made him die a thousand deaths before that. There is a streak of
humor in his end. The bullets pumped into him settle accounts
many times over. They are really nothing but so many coups de
grâce on a corpse.

Grief is strife. Physical poverty is moral indigence. It spreads
its mortal fumes into even the most intimate recesses of personal
life, polluting love, undermining trust and friendship. This is
the topic of "No Oyes Ladrar los Perros" (Hear the Dogs Bark-
ing), which traces the footsteps of a beleaguered father who
carries his wounded son into town to see the doctor, heaping
reproaches on him along the way. In Rulfo there is almost always
bitterness and recrimination between parents and children; they
fail each other even in helping each other. What one generation
can transmit to the next is little more than an age-old impotence.
The young, eternally disinherited, are cast defenseless into the
world, to suffer the long agony of life. Those who have nerve and
fiber make good. The others wither away, or become miscreants.
"Your children leave you . . . they thank you for nothing . . .

they drain you even of your memory." Relations between man
and woman are no happier than those between parents and
children. In "Paso del Norte" (Northern Pass) we have the story
of a young man who leaves his family to cross the U.S. border as a
wetback. He is met by a hail of bullets. He returns to his village
in defeat, only to find that his woman has left him. Abandoning
his children, he vanishes after her, destined from then on to roam
the country like a soul in pain.

There are always those who, in their own wretched way, thrive
on the ills of others. A case in point are the roving bandits of "El
Llano en Llamas," who sack ranches and set fields on fire as they
go galloping across the plain, chased by government forces that
never seem to catch up with them, or misfire when they do. They
are the verminous Zamora band who, "although we have no flag
to fight for at the moment," keep fit slitting throats and hoarding
booty. The leader plays "bull" with his prisoners, who are made
to stand unarmed as he charges them with a sword. They derail
trains and steal women. Bad luck has the narrator serve a term in
jail, from where he emerges a somewhat chastened man. Perhaps
a woman who awaits him with open arms—in a somewhat
sentimental ending—outside the prison gate will save him. But
the chances are that he will ride again. Or he might find some
other way to scrape by, as Anacleto Morones, in the story of the
same name, which reveals Rulfo as a biting ironist. Anacleto, a
mere derelict, makes a thriving career for himself as a "santero"
—peddler of religious images—combining high salesmanship
with religious quackery. He builds a fine reputation, and rakes in
the profits. Among his worshiping supporters are a bunch of
hypocritical old hags who have succumbed to his charm in more
ways than one. He has become the "saintly child Anacleto." The
women want him officially canonized, appeal to Lucas Lucatero,
his son-in-law, to testify to his miracles. Ambushed by them,
Lucas Lucatero refuses to cooperate: Anacleto was a fraud. His
greatest miracle, it turns out, was impregnating his own daughter, Lucas' wife. Lucas has killed him and buried him under the
floor boards.

Perhaps, all things considered, Lucas Lucatero and Anacleto, himself, were once no worse than the honest peasants of the moving "Nos Han Dado la Tierra," which still stands as one of Rulfo's best stories. With a sort of impersonal pity that makes the tale doubly poignant, he tells of a group of men allotted lands in a barren desert region under a government distribution program. They are sent far from the fertile fields bordering the river, which have all been commandeered by powerful landlords. The group, now reduced to four men, has trekked for eleven hours, with sinking hearts, across the empty wasteland, out of which "nothing will rise . . . not even vultures."

Yet life goes on. "It is more difficult to revive the dead than to give birth to new life," Rulfo writes somewhere, summing up the general attitude. In this faint hope, scant lives find a driving force. Tapping it at the source has been Rulfo's achievement. His sketches are quick probes. It is the small touches that count. He has weaknesses as a storyteller. Excessive poetization freezes some of his scenes. His characters are sometimes too sketchy to deliver their full human impact. They are creatures of primeval passion, entirely defined by their situation. Because of their lack of inner resource, ultimately they inspire little more than pity. And that is the danger. We are often on the verge of falling into pathos. But the attentive reader will go beyond that. There is a deeper grain running through the stories. To live, in Rulfo, is to bleed to death. The pulse of the days beats hard, carrying off hope, gutting life at the core, spilling forces, emptying illusions. He can evoke the fatigue of a long day's march across barren spaces in a quiet phrase, "It seems to me that we've gone a lot farther than the distance we've covered," or a lifetime's inexpressible distress and longing in the voice of a woman who says of her absent man: "It's still time for him to return." Of the mother who has lost all her children, he writes simply: "It seems she had a little money, but spent it all on burials." It is the ability to close in suddenly and strike home that at moments gives Rulfo the dignity of a tragedian. His style is as stark as his landscapes. Its marks are discipline and economy. Its impact is cumulative. It has the pull of irresistible impulse.

One of the most characteristic stories of *El Llano en Llamas* is

"Luvina," the name of a village on a limestone hill, laboring under its obscure curse, in an area swept by a dusty black wind that seems to carry volcanic ash. It is a "moribund place where even the dogs have died." Like the once fertile slope in "La Cuesta de las Comadres," it is a ghost town on its way to extinction. "I'd say it's the place where sadness nests, where smiles are unknown, as if everyone's face had been boarded up," says the narrator, an ex-resident, warning a traveler away from it. He ought to know: "There I lived. There I left my life." Nowadays Luvina is populated only by "the old and the un- born . . . and lonely women." Those who have stayed, as usual, are retained only by their dead. "They live here and we can't abandon them," they say. They will continue to sweat out their sentence, thinking: "It will last as long as it has to last."

Which is more or less the outlook of the inhabitants of Comala in *Pedro Páramo,* where the living, if there are any, are indistin- guishable from the dead. Comala is a dreary place, hardly more than a dip in the landscape, but for those trapped there, a burning pit set "on the hot coals of the earth, in the very mouth of hell." There flesh and blood have either petrified or evapo- rated. Only a shadow life remains, made of dwindling figures on otherworldly errands who turn out to be the lost souls of the departed.

Pedro Páramo is the story of a local caudillo, a classical specimen of the breed, whose unrequited life is reconstructed in groping retrospect from whispers, hearsay, rumors, and other debris of his passing through this world by his wayfaring son, Juan Preciado. Juan Preciado, full of vague illusions, in search of a lost childhood, returns to Comala after an absence of many years, fulfilling a promise he made to his mother on her death- bed. He is there to collect her memories, perhaps to plumb his own past. We recognize a variant of the Mexican myth of the illegitimate child, born of rape, eternally in quest of his un- known father.

Juan Preciado finds a deserted village—there is a real village that goes by that name just south of the Jaliscan border, near Colima—made of voices and echoes. A dusty road leads down into the village. From a muleteer he meets along the way—Abundio, a natural son fathered by the caudillo, therefore Juan Preciado's stepbrother—he learns that Pedro Páramo is already dead. So, it will soon dawn on him, is everyone else, including himself. It is August, midsummer, a time of blazing heat. He wanders in a kind of sickly bloom. His encounters all turn out to be ghosts or delusions. These villages, says Rulfo, are like grave-yards, dedicated to the cult of death. A Christian respect for the dead has mixed with pagan ancestor worship. There are certain days of the year—for instance, the first days of October—when the dead are said to return to haunt the living. "There's the idea that those who die in sin are doomed to roam upon the face of the earth." They are the souls in pain who find no peace. Soon Juan Preciado feels that his head is "full of sounds and voices." He is actually telling the story from the next world. His pass-ing—or awakening to the fact that he has passed—is recorded halfway through the book. He is found in the street one day, cramped and clammy, as if he had literally been frightened to death. Which was just what happened. "He was killed by mur-murs," a voice says. From his tomb, deep underground, listening to the restless stirrings of the dead, he continues to piece together the story of Pedro Páramo.

The time is around the turn of the century, the eve of revolutionary disruption. The rise and fall of Pedro Páramo has the elements of a case history. The setting, Jaliscan in general contours, is meant, says Rulfo, to be more representative of Mexico as a whole than of any particular province. He is less interested in factual accuracy than in insight. "I've been all over Mexico and I've seen some tremendous personal fiefs in the state of Guerrero and other parts of the country. If I located *Pedro Páramo* in Jalisco, it was simply because that's what I know best. I have the unfortunate tendency to place certain imaginary characters in specific geographic surroundings. I like to give the atmosphere of a place."

Who is Pedro Páramo?

He is not the absentee landlord who ruled northern Mexico, where the Revolution started. This type of landlord had huge properties, resided in the capital, leaving his lands, which he had often never laid eyes on, in the hands of an administrator, and educated his children in Europe. Pedro Páramo, on the other hand, "is the prototype of the medium-sized landowner there used to be in Jalisco, a man who lives on his lands and works them himself. He is not above plowing and planting side by side with his men." But that makes him no less rapacious in his lust for absolute power over the region he commands.

Out of the twilight of collective memory, a sharp figure gradually takes shape. Back in the old days Pedro Páramo inherited the considerable property known as the Media Luna (Half-Moon) from his father, Don Lucas, who was murdered by a farm hand, leaving his son full of hate and rancor for the community, which soon learned to dread him. Pedro Páramo, until then simply a young gay blade, driven by his grudge and ambition, takes the reins firmly in hand. Follows a period of violent reprisals. Consolidating his power, Pedro Páramo buys or chases out his neighbors, forging deeds and bills of sale, moving boundaries and, when the occasion calls for it, resorting to every degree of force and violence. Don Lucas left many debts which he does not intend to settle. A shyster lawyer in his pay helps him finagle things to his advantage. His largest creditors are a group of sisters called Preciado. Pedro Páramo decides to marry one of them, Dolores, who has been pining for him. Dolores never has a chance. Pedro Páramo is in a hurry. Through the good offices of Fulgor Sedano, his overseer and right-hand man, a smooth negotiator, she is persuaded to accept him at once, even though the moon is "unfavorable"—she is having her period—according to the local witch doctor. Pedro Páramo, no man to respect others' feelings, barrels on. All this Juan Preciado, Dolores' son, learns from the dream-figure of Eduviges Dyada, a close childhood friend of his mother, who recalls in the silence of the tomb how she—who also loved Pedro Páramo—substituted in bed for Dolores at the crucial moment to help her through her wedding night. Which did not prevent Dolores, trampled, and soon stranded, by Pedro Páramo, from picking up shortly after that and leaving town forever.

Meantime the Media Luna flourishes. There are emergencies. One day the harbingers of the Revolution arrive. There are rumors that Pancho Villa is in the area. Then come the Cristeros. But, typically, Pedro Páramo finds a winning compromise each time. He "joins" the Revolution to save his own skin. He invites the rebels over, promises them money and supplies, then sends one of his trusted henchmen, Damasio, off with some men to fight in their ranks and keep an eye on them. The plan costs him nothing. He does not even have to support his troops. They plunder neighboring ranches, thus even in destruction ultimately favoring the interests of the boss of the Media Luna.

But not for long. The first blow strikes with the death of the apple of his eye, his troublemaking son, Miguel, a bad sort who has already killed a man at the age of seventeen and sampled half the girls in the neighborhood. Only his father's influence keeps him out of prison. Until finally, on his way home one day at dawn from one of his nightly forages, he meets his fate when he is thrown from his horse. It is somehow the beginning of the end for Pedro Páramo. With clear foresight he realizes at once what he is in for. "I'm starting to pay. Better to start early, in order to finish soon," he says, suddenly, in misfortune, rising to full stature. In the view of Miguel laid out for burial he senses his own approaching downfall. "He seems bigger than he was," he says wistfully.

In the end what undoes Pedro Páramo is the same thing that undoes everyone else in Rulfo: illusion. In his case it is his impossible love for Susana San Juan, "a woman not of this world." Susana was a childhood playmate with whom he bathed naked in country streams and flew kites in the windy season. Susana—an airy image he carries in him forever as an aftertaste of lost innocence, a yearning for impossible fulfillment—is a strange girl, a sort of Ophelia, brittle and sensual, always on the dim edge of sanity. She has visions and nightmares. She lost her mother young, was then traumatized by her father, Bartolomé San Juan, a wishful-thinking miner in search of buried treasure with whom she has an equivocal relation. Once he lowered her dangling at the end of a rope into the nether regions under the floor boards to pick up what he thought was a gold nugget, only to have her find a skeleton. To worsen matters, in her teens she loved Florencio, of whose warm embraces she has been dreaming ever since. He was murdered by orders of Pedro Páramo. Widowed, she has lived with her lonely father, who took her away to a mining town to forget. The incestuous climate he creates around her, says Rulfo, is his way of trying to reach her, to bring her back to reality. We are dangerously close to the psychoanalytic truism of childhood trauma. But nothing definite is said. There are only "threads" of suggestion and allusion. After a lapse of thirty years, thoroughly broken, the old man agrees to be lodged by Pedro Páramo, who in exchange demands the hand of his daughter. He is signing his own death sentence. Susana becomes his wife. But in name only. Her feverish spells worsen. She tosses in bed at night, calling for Florencio. When she dies, tormented by the local priest—a picker of the dead—Pedro Páramo, distraught, has the church bells in Comala ring for three solid days. But nothing can bring her back. To precipitate matters, the bells create a sort of holiday atmosphere in town. Whereupon, in revenge, Pedro Páramo decides: "I'll cross my arms and Comala will starve to death." And so it happens. He burns his possessions, neglects his lands, and spends the rest of his days staring up the road along which Susana was taken to the cemetery. The inner drama—such as it is—has its outer equivalences. Rivers dry up. People leave. It is as if the very existence of Comala depended entirely on the will of a single man. The power of the caudillo had given the area a cohesion and stability of sorts. Now there is a complete breakdown. The spirit has simply gone out of the place. Says Rulfo: "It's really the story of a town that dies out on its own. Not because of anything or anyone." It simply ages and wears out. Pedro Páramo embodies the general sense of inner fatality. Tired, disillusioned, he waits for death. It comes the day Abundio, the muleteer, suddenly become an avenging angel, drunk after the death of his own wife, for which he obscurely blames Pedro Páramo, sticks a knife in him. For Pedro Páramo it is a moment of final plenitude. "This is my death," he says with fruition, greeting it as an old friend.

Such is the general line of the story. But its intentions lie beyond mere chronology. Pedro Páramo is a face in a broken mirror, an image gradually composing on the surface of troubled waters. A whisper here, a hint there, float him up out of the wreckage. The picture is given in shifting panels, bits of speech suddenly overheard, a rumor blown out of a doorway. All around him, in secret confabulation, are babbling voices and vanishing specters. Says Rulfo, never quite sure how he manages to do what he does: "I imagined the character. I saw him. Then, wondering how to handle him, I logically thought of a ghost town. And, of course, the dead live outside space and time. That gave me freedom to do what I wanted with the characters. I could have them come in, then simply fade out." There is a sort of telepathy at work. The reader intuits the hidden course of the narrative. The treatment of characters and events is strictly phenomenological; we are in a world of effects without causes, shadows without substance. Again, as in Rulfo's stories, it is often the small details that fix a scene: a quick impression, a twist of the tongue. There are vivid minor characters: the local priest, Padre Rentería, whose obsequiousness before the powerful, who patronize his church, turns his apostolate into a hollow mockery. Denied absolution by his confessor, he prays in pantomime, invoking a long rosary of saints that ripple through his mind as if they were sheep jumping over a fence. There is the tremulous Eduviges with her cobwebbed memories; an incestuous brother and sister who lodge Juan Preciado one evening; the psychosomatic Dorothea, who suffers from some obscure qualm of conscience over what may have been an imaginary pregnancy or an aborted baby, we are never sure which of the two, though it is clear that she is irretrievably damned in any case in her role as procuress for Miguel Páramo.

Pedro Páramo has its shortcomings. There is a typically Mexican mother figure languishing in the background. Whenever her image is evoked, we hover on the edge of the maudlin. Then—why not say it?—the figure of Pedro Páramo himself is an old standard. The clipped style, the oblique focus, do not alter the fact that basically we are going over familiar ground. The characterization is too slight—and conventional—to add anything new to the theme of the local despot. Pedro Páramo's overpowering instinctual drives, his retrograde mentality, his rule through blackmail and brooding over a lost love that symbolizes vanished innocence, are all literary staples. But here they are merely props for poetic vision. Rulfo does not tell a story. He captures the essence of an experience. *Pedro Páramo* is not epic, but elegy.

A good part of its merit rests on the use Rulfo makes of the simple rhythms of popular speech. The emotional charge they carry is such that he can obtain maximum effects with a minimum of means. "It's a spoken language," he says. But it is not the voice of the author that speaks; it is the voices of the characters. Rulfo simply arranges, orchestrates. But, above all, he listens. The life of his books is in the language. Of course, he says, "it isn't a calculated language. I don't go out with a tape recorder to take down what people say and then try to reproduce it afterwards. There's none of that here. That's simply the way I've heard people speak since I was born. That's the way people speak in those places." For him, the rhythm of speech is that of life itself. It marks a stride. And Rulfo is right in step with it. To keep time he will sacrifice volumes of rhetoric. He has always been against the tendency toward the baroque in Latin-American literature. He says: "I try to defend myself against the baroque, and I'll continue to do so, with all the means at my disposal." The strength of his work is in its restraint. From the proliferous luxuriance of a huge manuscript several hundred pages long he has been known to extract the few precious drops of sap that will go to nourish a perfect story.

In a country of literary cliques and coteries, Rulfo has always pursued a lone star. He seems to have no connection with anyone. Agustín Yáñez, a distinguished colleague who is Minister of Education today, is from his home state. Rulfo hardly seems to have heard of him. It would be hard to imagine two more different temperaments. Rulfo belongs to that race of men for whom writing is a very intimate affair that takes place in the dark of night. He is superstitious and secretive about his work, which he keeps undercover. He will talk about anything but that. A guarded silence on the subject is an old habit with him. As a young man quietly learning his craft by candlelight, he knew none of his literary contemporaries. He read a few literary reviews, he says, but otherwise kept to himself. All he knew was that "it seemed I had to become a writer." Later, between about 1948 and 1952, he admits he was associated with a group called América, publishers of a magazine of the same name. "The group is necessary to launch your career," he says a bit wryly. But this was a particularly scattered group that included the most heterogeneous people. About all they had in common was the urge to get together once in a while in a Chinese café to drink coffee and hold bull sessions. The circle shrank and expanded as people came and went, until finally there was no one left. Fortunately, says Rulfo, the magazine no longer exists.

What is his relation to Mexican literature as a whole?

He seems uncertain about that. Back in his school days, there was not much Mexican literature, he says. The authors read in Mexico in those days were Vasconcelos, the political writers of the Revolution, the chroniclers of the time: Martín Luis Guzmán, Mariano Azuela. "But even they weren't read much. Mexican literature had almost no value. For instance, the novel of the Revolution was considered simple reporting. A lot of books were published—proportionately speaking—but they weren't read. The tendency was to read foreign literature. In schools, Spanish literature. On one's own, Russian literature—imported from Spain, where it was translated and published, but not Spanish literature. United States literature, which was also published in Spain. We knew Dos Passos, Sinclair Lewis, Elmer Rice, and Hemingway. There was a great vogue of translations in Spain just before the Revolution, especially works of social criticism."

From the beginning Rulfo—a traditionalist unhampered by traditionalism—struck out in his own direction. In the few literature courses he took in his free time he was bothered by the habit teachers had of teaching the worst of Spanish literature— "Pereda, the generation of 1898 . . . I knew that was the backwardness of Latin-American literature: the fact that we were absorbing a literature that was foreign to our character and disposition." Besides, Spanish culture was decadent. "They had theologized even with mathematics." Spain had isolated itself for centuries from the world. That was one of the factors that had permitted the Latin-American countries to gain their independence. But culturally they were not yet emancipated. He readily recognizes his Spanish ancestry, Rulfo tells us, seized by a sudden curious scruple as we discuss the subject. He adds, amusingly, that an early ancestor of his was even a member of the royalist forces of Callejas that fought against the Mexican Revolution. Nevertheless, he reproaches Spain with provincialism and linguistic decay. "What pains me about Spain, for instance," he says, "is that it is losing its language." This is something he often discusses with people, invariably getting himself into an argument. The case is exactly the opposite in Latin America. On the one hand, Indian dialects have enriched the language. On the other, there are isolated areas where it has preserved its classic purity. He realized long ago that "Spain had no culture to give America." He was always particularly fond of Russian literature—Andreyev, Korolenko—and, above all, a great admirer of Scandinavian literature: Selma Lagerlöf, Björnson, Knut Hamsun, Sillanpää. "Once upon a time I had the theory that literature had been born in Scandinavia, then gone down to Central Europe and spread from there." He is still an assiduous reader of Halldor Laxness, whom he considers a great renewer of European literature, from a position diametrically opposed, say, to that of French intellectualism. United States literature, he thinks, has also had a salutary influence in latter years. But Rulfo, with his love of the diaphanous, favors the Nordics, because of their "misty atmosphere." The same factor inclines him toward the work of the Swiss novelist, C. F. Ramuz, whose portraits of simple village souls in conflict with a hostile environment have strong connotations for him. Rulfo does not pretend his predilections are based on sound judgment. He has a curious taste for Jean Giono, whom he regards as an unappreciated talent in French letters. Giono, says Rulfo, breaks with the artifices of the Jules Romains and Mauriac tradition, which, he claims, produces works so indistinguishable that "you don't know whom you're reading. They all write the same." In any case, they all sound "written." And that is what he has always tried to avoid. "I don't want to speak as you write, but to write as you speak."

If he has come anywhere near achieving his purpose, he says, it is because he never really developed his style consciously. "It was something that was there already." He detected it, and took it as he found it. In this he may have helped point the way for some of Mexico's younger writers, who have begun to listen more carefully to the language spoken in the streets. Not that he has imitators. He shudders at the thought. But his work may have called attention to the literary potential of popular language. "So the person who writes that way is not influenced by *Pedro Páramo*," he says. "He simply stopped to listen to the language he was talking, and realized of what use it could be to him."

Ten years have gone by since *Pedro Páramo,* and Rulfo, a busy man in a harsh city, has been strangely silent. He is vague about what he has published, when. He seems suddenly anguished when the subject is raised. He mentions "a story in the same line as those of *El Llano en Llamas,* which was supposed to be part of the book. I don't know what happened to it. . . . It was misplaced, and then it was too late to include it in the book." According to rumors, his mildness and modesty are such that he has little control over the editorial work done on his books. The French edition of *Pedro Páramo,* for instance, is fatter than the original. What could have happened? Perhaps some papers got shuffled along the way. . . .

At the moment he has other things in mind. As people wonder whether he will ever be heard from again, he is trying to bring himself to release an eternally forthcoming novel he has finished and torn apart a thousand times, called *La Cordillera.* "I'm sort of working at it," he says. Recently he thought he was done with it, then decided to go over it once more. It had to be completely reconsidered. "I thought it was a bit too dense." He would like to talk about it, but "it's a bit difficult to explain." The setting, again, is provided by the villages of Jalisco. "But taken from their base this time. Starting with the sixteenth century." Rulfo traces the lives and fortunes of a family of "encomenderos" from its origins, through generations of wars and migrations, down to the present day. As usual in his work, the voyage is mental, a memory evoked in bits and strands by the dead's descendants. "It's really the story of a woman who's the last descendant of the family." She is probably another lost soul branded by a forgotten past that she wears as a birthmark. Because the sense of history, in Rulfo, is that it may be forgotten but not left behind. Therefore, what he has tried to do in his work is "to show a reality that I know and that I want others to know. To say: 'This is what has happened and what is happening.' And: 'Let's not fool ourselves. If it's fatal, then let's act accordingly.' But I don't think I'm a fatalist at heart. . . . Above all, what I want to do in *La Cordillera* is to show the simplicity of country people, their candor. The man of the city sees their problems as country problems. But it's the problem of the whole country. It's the problem of the city itself. Because, when the countryman moves to the city, there's a change. But to a certain extent he continues to be what he was. He brings the problem with him." Proof of this is the sad-eyed Rulfo, who will undoubtedly continue to live with the problem for a long time to come.

VIII

Carlos Fuentes,
or the New Heresy

WHILE old problems grow new ones are born. In Mexico, a land of herculean conflicts, they come in multitudes. In the past decade or so there have been the ravages and benefits of metropolitanism and its by-products, which, among other things, have given a new look to its literature.

Modern Mexican literature, as most things in Mexico today, starts with the 1910 Revolution, an explosive force whose liberating influence was felt at every level of the country's life and culture. 1910 was the year of the reopening of the National University, inoperative since it had been shut down by Emperor Maximilian; the year when a famous local poet, González Martínez, noisily twisted the neck of the Modernist swan; the year of the great art exhibition that revealed Orozco, Rivera and Siqueiros; and also the year when a group of young enthusiasts under the fiery leadership of José Vasconcelos, disgusted by Mexico's educational vacuum, got together to found the freewheeling Ateneo de la Juventud (Atheneum of Youth). A few decades earlier the apathetic Emperor Maximilian had been shot by Benito Juárez, whose subsequent land reform program was meant to disfranchise the clergy and the colonial gentry under whose economic stranglehold the country had been stagnating since the days of the Spanish Conquest. But the confiscated properties Juárez put on public auction simply changed hands. Under his ironhanded successor, Porfirio Díaz, a new privileged class, the "Porfirian aristocracy," mercenary and positivistic, came into power. Its standards were commercial, its fashions, not surprisingly, European. It ruled through favoritism, monopoly, and centralization. The Revolution, essentially middle class in impulse, in spite of its peasant heroes, was the birth of national consciousness, "a sudden immersion," says a shrewd commentator, Octavio Paz, "of Mexico in its true self." In the chaos that followed there was no beacon light for the founders of the new state. They worked in the dark, heirs to distant echoes of European liberalism, but—the Russian Revolution was still a thing of the future—without any direct ideological influence from abroad. Mexico had to make itself. For the moment it seemed to have been spontaneously generated. It had simply burst into existence—"dared to be," as Paz says—and was forced to improvise as it went, choosing outlooks and philosophies at random. A natural first step was for it to turn in on itself to tap its own undiscovered resources. Fossilized under feudal structures, waiting to be revived, was a rich Indian past. Overnight, discarding its mask of Europeanism, Mexico became arrogantly "Mexicanista." But "Mexicanism" looked forward as well as backward. There was that ingrained sense, so often described by another intelligent observer, Alfonso Reyes, that the American continent as a whole, and Mexico in particular, had not only been discovered but invented. It had started as a European utopia. Its essence or reality, as Paz says, echoing the theme, had consisted in being always a future plan, a projection. What defined it was not its first, but its final, cause. And so now, with the Revolution as catalyst, when the dust settled on the battlefields, a Mexico at once autistic and utopic, spontaneous and premeditated, drank at the source as it marched toward new horizons.

It was the twilight of Modernism, the declining years of the Rubén Darío era, and literature was coming out of its ivory tower.

Modernism itself, once implacably Parnassian, had contributed indirectly, on the one hand, to the internationalization of art in America and, on the other, in its later stages, to the discovery of local tradition. Toward 1905 the versatile Nicaraguan Rubén Darío, had suddenly turned to celebrating Indian lore, though mostly for the purposes of myth and color. There was much of the daydream in Darío's work. But at the same time poems like his "Canto a la Argentina" were a proud assertion of Latin cultural values against the encroaching ways of the "Colossus of the North." Years in Europe had somehow opened Darío's eyes to realities at home. As usual in our culture, he had first seen the evidence from afar, and sensed his identity when he was in danger of losing it. For him, as for so many Latin Americans of all ages, the shortest way home was around the world. "To come home," says Paz, a man who knows whereof he speaks, "first you must take the risk of leaving. Only the prodigal son returns." One of Mexico's "prodigal sons" was a revolutionary poet called López Velarde, who put his somewhat strident lyricism—a Modernist tic—to work full time for the cause of nationality.

The cause was soon taken up on all sides, by the members of the Ateneo de la Juventud above all, who broadcast it far and wide. It was sometimes misinterpreted. Contemporary with the Revolution was Mexico's "generation of 1915," which included such prime movers as the Colonialistas, who looked back with misguided devotion on the relics of Mexico's colonial past. They were followed by the Contemporáneos and the Estridentistas, who experimented in various ways with combinations of modern form and revolutionary content. Meantime, in 1921, a period of enlightened educational reform was ushered in when Vasconcelos was named rector of the National University. Under his guidance, poets and academicians—Torres Bodet, Carlos Pellicer— joined forces in exploring the depths of the Mexican soul. They bore witness to confusion. Often they drew a desolate picture of spiritual displacement. Among them in the twenties and thirties were the "poets of solitude": José Gorostiza, Xavier Villaurrutia —both born around 1900—and, a bit later, Alí Chamucero and Octavio Paz. There was also the well-known crop of "revolutionary" novelists: Mariano Azuela, the author of such dour docu-

mentaries as *Los de Abajo* (The Underdogs, 1928), and Martín
Luis Guzmán, whose huge canvases—placed under the sign of
the eagle and the serpent, Mexico's emblems, and culminating
with a biography of Guzmán's friend and comrade-in-arms,
Pancho Villa—chronicled the whole revolutionary saga in a vein
halfway between fiction and reportage. Both Azuela and Guzmán were Maderistas, partisans of Mexico's first revolutionary
president, Madero, who was soon disposed of by assassination,
and their work, much of it written in the heat of battle, reflects
their disenchantment with the course of events after the fall of
their leader. But they were too close to events to have any real
perspective on them. Less in the thick of it, from the thirties on,
were the novels of Agustín Yáñez, often made of childhood
reminiscences that evoke the depressing landscapes of Yáñez's
native province, Jalisco. Yáñez, a mythologist, pioneers ambitiously, if not always too successfully, in the use of modern
literary techniques borrowed from such models as *Point Counterpoint* and *Manhattan Transfer*. More incisive, perhaps, since it
started to overcome its gullibility, has been the literature of
protest, characteristically Marxist in outlook, as in the bleak
works of José Revueltas, a skillful psychologist who in the forties
and fifties moved his settings to the city, thus helping to lay the
groundwork for the urban novel.

At mid-century, its past and future in uncertain suspense,
Mexico was still a country in search of a definition. With the
Revolution fading into the background, the early fifties were a
moment of reappraisal. "The history of Mexico," Paz was writing
at about this time, "is that of the man in search of his affiliation,
his origin." Easy labels—Europeanism, nationalism—had become handicaps. The Mexican had begun to outgrow them. He
was a hybrid product. But even that notion now seemed unsatis-
factory. The tendency, says Paz, was for the Mexican to assert
himself as a separate and distinct entity, descended from neither
the Indians nor the Spaniards, autonomous, self-contained, "a
child of the void." The return to the sources and the concomi-
tant mestizo mystique that had nourished the postrevolutionary
years had ended in a sense of spiritual orphanage. Wrote Paz,
summing up: "The Revolution has been unable to relate its

redeeming and explosive force to a world vision, nor has the
Mexican mind resolved the conflict between the insufficiency of
our own tradition and our need for universality." Therefore a
central concern of Mexican thought at this time was to distill the
"essence" of Mexicanism. Suddenly everyone seemed to be devoted to ontological investigation and cultural psychoanalysis.
The theme soon became obsessive and occasionally reached fatuous proportions, as in the work of Uranga—*Análisis del Ser del
Mexicano* (Analysis of Mexican Being)—who declares flatly that
a philosophy that does not take Mexicanism as its cardinal theme
is un-Mexican and doomed to fade as fast as a hothouse flower.
Paz, a poet, is wiser. He constantly evokes the Mexican's feeling
of solitude and isolation. But in that "labyrinth of solitude" he
finds a form of communion. For him Mexicanism is not a
mechanical rallying cry but a sense of shared responsibilities.
Which seems to be the most reasonable attitude open to the
Mexico of the sixties. Perhaps today at last, relatively safe in his
continuity, the Mexican can feel, as Alfonso Reyes long ago
foresaw he would, that he is joined to his people not only by
inherited genetic traits or collective interests but by the deeper
community of spirit that comes from daily contact with common
problems and experiences. His true identity, he has begun to
discover, is in his individuality. Which is another way of saying
that to be a twentieth-century Mexican is to be a contemporary
of all men.

No one could be better fitted for this role, by background,
temperament, and upbringing, than Carlos Fuentes, a handsome
young man-about-town who is one of the most worldly names in
our literature. He was born in Mexico City in 1928, but spent
most of his childhood and early youth on the move between
various American capitals—Santiago de Chile, Rio de Janeiro,
Buenos Aires, Montevideo, Quito, Washington—to which duty
assigned his father, a roving career diplomat with more than
thirty years in the service, most recently as Mexican ambassador
in Rome. Mounting the paternal family tree we find globe-
trotting Germans and Canarians. There was a great-grandfather from Darmstadt, a Lasallian Socialist who exiled him-

self under the Bismarck regime and landed in Mexico to plant coffee in Veracruz. That was around 1875. His son became a banker and was later displaced from Veracruz by the Revolution and ended up in Mexico City. On the maternal side, Fuentes recalls a grandfather who was a merchant in the Pacific port of Mazatlán. His wife was a school inspector. "Typical petit bourgeois stock," Fuentes says cheerfully of his pedigree.

No doubt he has had to live it down. But at the same time he has enjoyed its advantages. He received a polished education in some of the best schools of the continent, including Chile's thoroughbred Grange. He learned English when he was four, in Washington. French, a less fluent language for him, he picked up in 1950 reading Balzac's *Peau de Chagrin* with a dictionary on a boat trip to Europe. He was on his way to study international law in Geneva. By then, like his father, he was in the diplomatic service. The year he spent in Geneva he was a member of the Mexican delegation to the International Labor Organization, as well as cultural attaché to the Embassy. Back in Mexico, he held several bureaucratic posts at the university, was eventually named head of the Foreign Affairs Ministry's Department of Cultural Relations. By the time he was out of law school in 1955 he was already launched on his literary career. He was a founder of the prestigious *Revista Mexicana de Literatura* (Mexican Review of Literature). Its editorial principles reflected his conviction that art was passion and discipline, and that "a culture can be profitably national only when it is generously universal."

In a continent where literary activity closely reflects economic conditions, a sign of modern Mexico's enterprising spirit is the fact that Fuentes, for several years now a successful young executive in the world of letters, lives entirely from his writing. He commands a wide range, from fiction to essays, articles—some written directly in English, for such magazines as *Monthly Review*, *Holiday* and the *Nation*—and movie scripts. A good part of his income comes from his movie work. He has collaborated with Abby Mann on a film version of *The Children of Sánchez*, and worked with Luis Buñuel on a cinematic adaptation of Carpentier's novelette, *El Acoso*. Recently, with a group of restless young artists, among them the versatile illustrator José Luis Cuevas, he has been active in experimental cinema, a new movement in Mexico, backed by a team of imaginative technicians in rebellion against the notorious commercial tyranny of the Producers' Syndicate. He has contributed scripts, a couple of them derived from his own stories. They have helped spread his reputation, both at home and abroad. He is one of the most widely read of our serious novelists. His work has been translated into thirteen languages. Financial independence has helped him maintain his freedom of movement. Like almost all men of conscience in Latin America, he is on the left in politics—a friend of Mailer, a great admirer of C. Wright Mills, the "true voice of the United States"; affiliations that have cost him more than one visa to the United States—but as a freethinker, not a salesman for any particular faith. He is equally unself-conscious about his nationality. He takes a civilized view of his constant hedgehopping trips to near and far places. If his travels eventually all take him back to Mexico, it is, he says with a charming smile that must scandalize some of his flag-waving countrymen, because he finds peace to work there. "After all, it's cheap, the climate is good, and there's privacy. It's easy to isolate yourself in Mexico."

Being as much in demand as he is, he has to. The solution has been a large, rambling house "straight out of an Emily Brontë novel" in a shady residential suburb, San Ángel Inn, where lovers of colonial architecture have set themselves up among iron grills, tiled patios, trap doors, wooden beams, and other discards rescued from surrounding demolition sites. A pleasantly solid, if basically makeshift, style distinguishes the area, which combines modern convenience with a sort of patrician grace. There are winding streets leading to dead ends and fragrant gardens with swimming pools and playgrounds. Cabs, the only reliable means of local transportation, invariably lose their way coming off the freeway from downtown. Indian laborers and their families squat over their open fires at lunchtime, with their backs to the street, where affluence thunders by in flashy sports cars.

The Fuentes home is up a quiet blind alley. He receives us at the cool carriage entrance, in an open blue shirt, jaunty white slacks, and tennis shoes. He has a smooth charm and quick wit that immediately set one at ease. He is also disarmingly candid about himself. He speaks of his work, his achievements and interests in an offhand way that would seem almost glib if it were not so completely straightforward and sincere. He has a sportsman's bounce and vitality that reflect his youthful and dynamic outlook on life. Urbanity comes naturally to him. With his glamorous wife, the actress Rita Macero, a celebrated beauty, he is often in the limelight. There could be no kinder host. "Ask me anything you want. I'm a talking machine," he tells us with a wave of his arm, as he leads us through an ample courtyard from where we catch a glimpse of a big garden with swings and flower beds, into a shadowy sitting room with heavy sofas and high ceilings. We follow him up a precipitous corkscrew staircase, around hairpin bends, into another tall room featuring a huge feudal fireplace surrounded by stratospheric bookshelves and filled with plump cushioned settees, stone carvings, statuettes on stands, and tortured scrap-iron figurines. Patches of wall are studded with Picasso prints and abstract paintings. There is a workdesk in a windowed nook in a corner, its wide surface piled high with papers, and a flat coffee table in the middle of the room, in front of the fireplace, where there are stacks of up-to-date magazines and recent books by American authors, notably Mailer and Flannery O'Connor. Chatting, we settle to a sociable drink. Fuentes, in an outgoing mood, sits on the floor, his legs spread out, then gathered under him, chain-smoking.

He describes himself as a hypochondriac at work. "I write with the nerves of my stomach, and pay for it with a duodenal ulcer and a chronic colic." For the anointed, the road to Paradise leads through Hell. "Because I intuit that, I write novels," he told an audience not long ago, in a conference à la Mailer which, he says, turned into a sort of public striptease. He lives as he writes, he said, "out of excess and insufficiency, will and will-lessness, love and hate." He quoted Mailer, the man with a thousand chips on his shoulder: "One writes with everything that lives for one:

love, violence, sex, drugs, loss, the family, work, defeat. But, above all, with something that concerns nobody but the writer." What that is need not be named. It dates from far back.

"I was already writing as a child. I published things in Chile, for instance, when I was twelve or thirteen; stories that appeared in the Bulletin of the Chilian National Institute, in the Grange magazine, when I was studying there, and so on." His official entry into the public domain was in 1954. That year a Mexican writer, Juan José Arreola, founded a publishing house for young writers called Los Presentes (Writers Today). "So all those of us with an itch," says Fuentes, "started to write like mad for the publishing house."

The result, for him, was his first book of stories, *Los Días Enmascarados* (Masked Days), written in some haste, "with a series of themes I'd been carrying around inside. I sat down and got the book out in a month, to have it in time for the 1954 Book Fair." It is out of print today; but he obligingly outlines it for us. Its elements of mythology, which broke a moratorium on an old debt, were a nod to Mexico's Indian past.

Perhaps the choice of themes was inevitable. The past, in Mexico, says Fuentes, "weighs heavily, because although the Conquerors, the Spaniards, carried the day, Mexico, because of its particular political and historical makeup, has given the final victory to the conquered. That's what the statue of Quauhtemoc means. In Lima you have the statue of Pizarro, in Santiago that of Valdivia. Here the defeated have been glorified. Why? Because Mexico is a country where only the dead are heroes. If Francisco Madero, Emiliano Zapata, or Pancho Villa were alive today, with his finger in profiteering and graft, he wouldn't be a hero any more, would he? Our heroes are heroes because they were sacrificed. In Mexico the only saving fate is sacrifice. . . . The nostalgia for the past in Mexico is a direct result of the original defeat, of the fact that Mexico was a country that lost its tongue, its customs, its power, everything. It became a nation of slaves. The Spanish we speak in Mexico is a Spanish of slaves, made entirely of circumlocutions. But there's another factor to consider. If a typical neocapitalist country, such as France or the United States, can be governed without revolutionary rhetoric, Mexico hasn't reached that level yet. It isn't prosperous enough. When there's an abundance of goods to be distributed, you can forget about rhetoric. In Mexico the government has to justify itself with a series of myths. We all know it was the middle class that led the Revolution to triumph in Mexico. But this middle class presents itself wrapped in myths. In other words, the ruling class, alias the Partido Revolucionario Institucional, alias the President of the Republic, equals: the nation, the Revolution, the glories of the past, the Aztecs, everything. So they have to promote a revolutionary rhetoric that strikes deep chords in Mexico, because it is at the source of political power."

In *Los Días Enmascarados,* which belongs to a germinal stage in his work, Fuentes at once exploits and castigates some of the ancient formulas and primitive modes of life that survive in modern Mexico. "The best story in the book," he says, "can still be obtained, because it was included in the *Antología del Cuento Mexicano* (Anthology of the Mexican Short Story). He is referring to "Chac Mool" named after the god of rain in the Aztec pantheon, whose powers do not seem to have been dimmed by modern civilization. Fuentes says that in 1952, when the god's sculpted image was shipped off on a European tour as part of a Mexican art exhibit, there were storms on the high seas. Rain followed it wherever it went. "It became famous as a rainmaker. For instance, peasants in certain valleys of Spain where it hadn't rained in living memory would mail a few pesetas to the Palais de Chaillot. The money was put on the god's stomach, and after fifty years rain fell in those valleys. When Chac Mool crossed the English Channel there were the worst storms anyone could remember. . . . That was what gave me the idea for the story. It's about a little clerk. In the Lagunilla (Mexico's slummy downtown flea market) he finds a replica of Chac Mool. He puts it in his basement. The basement mysteriously floods. Chac Mool sweats out a coat of slime. He starts to take on a certain fleshiness and flexibility, and suddenly he appears to the protagonist in his bedroom and gains complete control over him, but in an equivocal way, chasing him out of his house to meet his death in

Acapulco. When a friend brings the corpse home, he finds a strange greenish Indian occupying the dead man's place in the house, wearing his dressing gown, all decked out, perfumed, made up. . . . In the end the owner replaces the god in the flea market."

Many of the loose ideas roughly sketched out in *Los Días Enmascarados,* says Fuentes, were incorporated in a more full-bodied form into *La Región Más Transparente.*

La Región Más Transparente (Where the Air is Clear, 1959)—the Spanish title alludes ironically to the phrase uttered by Humboldt when he discovered the high Valley of Mexico—was the book that established Fuentes. It is an all-embracing novel, at once a "biography of a city," as Fuentes calls it, and "a synthesis of present-day Mexico." Fuentes has done some comprehensive research into Mexican life and mores. The product of his efforts is a survey and complete accounting of the state of Mexico in the early fifties, an attempt at a definition and a search for an identity. The social atmosphere of Mexico City is portrayed at all levels, from the upper middle class, the new industrial caste, and the blighted remains of the old feudal aristocracy to the eternally downtrodden proletariat, with special emphasis on the classes in flux, the upstarts and parvenus, social climbers and opportunists. The general impression we have is that of a country born of a revolutionary fervor that soon betrayed its cause as time sedimented and institutionalized it and the rebels of the past installed themselves at the top of the pile as heads of banks and industries. Though some of the old reforms have prevailed, Mexico is shown as living through a period of restoration. The main action of the novel takes place in 1951, but branches back into the revolutionary era to trace the ascending or descending course of its protagonists. It is a bitter chronicle of corruption and egoism. The technique is cinematic: quick scenes reel by, hard to focus on, blurred especially in opening chapters, which deal with the gaudy club and cocktail party act, but later falling into a clear pattern as the spotlight centers on the human prototypes that embody modern Mexico.

In a society of displaced persons, each man hangs on where he

can. The lack of a common philosophy, a national purpose, a
sense of unity and solidarity, allows for the sacrifice of the weak
to the strong, the principled to the pragmatic. Such is the picture
Fuentes draws. He sees a world in turmoil, with constantly
shifting values, racked by struggles for supremacy, balanced on
the edge of destruction. The underdogs of today become the
precariously privileged of tomorrow. Every life is at once boom
and bust. In Mexico, says Fuentes, things happen quickly; a lot
of mileage can be burned in a very short time. Progress is a
bright comet that drags a long dusty tail after it. Just beneath
the modern habit is the old tribal gesture. With heavy irony,
Fuentes conterpoints the atavistic strain in Mexican life with the
modern cult of the efficient and the effective. Each attitude has
its representative in the scheme. There are throwbacks, like Ixca
Cienfuegos, made of residual elements, and bandwagon riders
like Librado Ibarra, a dowdy turncoat become a crooked labor
lawyer, or Roberto Régules, also a high-powered shyster lawyer,
both mouthpieces for a class sprung out of nowhere that claims to
have created its own values, and therefore considers itself entitled to exercise its rights and prerogatives at will in the
surrounding vacuum. There are also victims of the system: the
old syndicalist in decline, who is shot in the back; the prostitute
and wetback cast to the fringes of society by exploitation and
unemployment; and the rich man's plaything: the blind mistress-
concubine, sensual and pathetic in her role as an object of her
master's greedy passion for luxury items. Towering above considerations of humanity, or even common decency, are the universal symbols of power: social acceptance, political influence,
and material possessions that include mansions, yachts, automobiles, and people.

Spokesman par excellence for the dubious forces of evolution is
the self-made banker, Federico Robles, whose spectacular rise, via
ruthless expediency, from a humble sharecropper background to
the heights of unscrupulous wheeler-dealerism in some sense
typifies modern functional and utilitarian Mexico. Robles is a
builder, and is proud of it. His standards are those of the status
seeker. To complement his financial empire he has purchased a

beautiful mundane wife, Norma Larragoiti, who shares his ambition, with a special knack for turning frivolity into a form of
high protocol. She lives feverishly, with a contemptuous laugh at
critics who accuse her of being snobbish and nouveau riche. Her
position is the product of her talent, she says. Name and money,
and the benefits derived from them support her claim that she, a
child of shopkeepers, has, through sheer guts, become the best the
country has to offer. And, in a way, she is right. Her thirst for
power and prestige has a primordial force. Success, for those who
wield it with a flourish, has its dangers, but also its splendors. Thus
Robles, who uses her as she uses him, willingly admits that he
belongs to "those who have dirtied their hands." And why not?
"Without me, without the handful of Robles who have built the
country in the last thirty years, there would be nothing. Without
us, without our minimum circle of power, I suspect everything
would have been lost in our people's traditional apathy." He is
not ashamed to represent the voice of vested interest. The best
arguments in his favor are his achievements. They are clear
evidence of the fact that "here there is only one truth that
counts: either we build a prosperous country or we starve. The
only choice offered us is between wealth and indigence. And to
attain to wealth, our main concern, to which all others should be
subordinated, must be to hasten the march toward capitalism." If
the prescription seems a bit simple, the fact, in hard practice, is
that it works—for him.

Not everyone shares his point of view. But those who contest it,
wondering about the rightness of the country's course, all too
often have nothing better to offer in exchange. They are
doodlers, not doers. Such is the case of the perpetually hesitant,
ineffectual, and puritanical journalist and poet, Zamacona, a
moral crusader who wastes his time in soul-searching speculations
on the subject of Mexican "eccentricity." Mexico is "eccentric,"
according to Zamacona—who uses the word in its etymological
sense—because it is an accident in the order of things, a subcultural backwater that has lost its identity in its pathological aping
of foreign cultures and customs. It has become a sort of dust bin
for whatever the tide brings in from other parts of the world.

Though radically alien to Europe, it has accepted "the fatality of total European penetration." At the same time it has remained outside all logical patterns: "a cloister, with its back to the world." It has been raped, not enriched. Therefore, in search of its lost purity, it has confused origins with originality. There is no pure element in a mestizo country like Mexico, where the basic mixture is not only ethnic but spiritual. Mexico ought to define itself, not backward but forward. "Rather than being born original, we become it. . . . We have to create both our origin and originality." The solution is for Mexico to strike a balance between what it is and always will be and what, without travestying itself, it can become. Meantime Zamacona sees grim prospects ahead. The hardships of Mexican reality, he says, perhaps with a touch of poetic license, are sterner even than life in the European concentration camps, because "the most terrible experience, Dachau or Buchenwald, only underlined the principles at stake: liberty, human dignity," whereas in Mexico nothing can justify "the destruction of the Indian world, our defeat in the war with the U.S. . . . our hunger, our barren fields, our plagues, our murders, our violence." What positive results have come out of it all? In the end, with a fervent belief in Mexico's saving mission, which he conceives of in messianic, almost Dostoevskian, terms, he argues for a sort of Christian humanitarianism in social affairs, in which each man, as Christ, would assume the pain and blame of his fellow men and offer himself in personal atonement for them. He compares Mexico to the figure of Lazarus, dead only to be reborn, shouldering his fate. Thus he represents the somewhat narcissistic claim of passive individualism in a depersonalized society.

At the opposite end of the spectrum is the belligerent, half-mythical figure of Ixca Cienfuegos, a personification of the lingering presence of Mexico's aboriginal past with its pre-Columbian rites and ancient blood feuds. Ixca, a ubiquitous shadow of retribution threaded into almost every scene, functions as a sort of seeing eye in the book, at once a symbol and a gadfly. He is the voice in the back of everyone's conscience. He has access into every social milieu: "official circles, the parlors of high life," the business world, at one moment passing for "some banker's magic brain," the next for a gigolo or a simple street peddler. We never know for sure who he is, but his role is clear. He is the witness, the man who knows the truth about everyone, reads their secret desires, sees through them, urging them to plunge into the depths of themselves, where they will find their ultimate reality. "Be yourself," is his battle cry. He is the devil whispering backstage, a god of ancestral sacrifice prompting the characters of the drama to their downfall. For him Mexico signed its death sentence when it severed the umbilical cord that joined it to its primitive rites and rhythms. "The first decision is the last." The primeval impulse gone astray, the country's pulse stopped. Zamacona's notions of personal responsibility make no sense to him, because the whole thesis leans on a concept of personality "capable of receiving, and generating, sin, redemption, etc." But there is no such personality in the "nameless tumult," the "twisted mass of bone, stone, and rancor" that is Mexico—"a country where there are no people." Ixca's world is that of depersonalization—traditionalist, collectivist. The "be yourself" he slips into the ears of his victims, says Fuentes, is nothing but a "moral snare." He echoes their own thoughts, to delude, mislead, and finally sink them. Because Mexico, preset in its course from the beginning, is "incapable of evolution," it will inevitably be claimed by its past, its dead heroes, its lost memories. The rest is mask and appearance, a sheer optical illusion, disguising the decay of a land that has lost its soul and spirit of solidarity. As his companion in witchcraft, the widow Teódula, says: "We are approaching the parting of the waters." The currents have begun to flow upstream, and the present will vanish in the backwash. And so it happens in the book, that in a drastic series of natural and man-made disasters, everyone meets his fate, in ruin or death. As Ixca, their Nemesis, in a last metamorphosis, fades into thin air down a nameless street, dissolved in the "vast and anonymous" city, there is a final holocaust in which masks fall away to reveal the "true" face behind them.

The desperate search for the "true face" of Mexico is the subject of the book. The various points of view propounded by the different characters are its dialectical poles. The action swings back and forth between them, never quite becoming drama. Usurping the center of the stage is a "symbolic play" that the author, with hindsight, frankly calls "too obvious." *La Región Más Transparente* is a talky book. Its compulsive preoccupation with "Mexicanism" has dated it.

Fuentes says as much. But it must be seen in its context: that special moment that was felt to be a crossroads in Mexican history. In prerevolutionary days, under Porfirio Díaz, says Fuentes, there had been "a sort of extralogical imitation" of foreign forms in Mexican culture that "had kept the Mexican past completely suffocated." With the Revolution the pendulum swung in the opposite direction. It was a triumph of the popular spirit.

"The Revolution discovered colors, flavors, forms, sounds that perhaps reached their maximum expression in pictorial art, in the muralist movement, though also in the music of Carlos Chávez, of Revueltas, in the novels of Azuela, of Guzmán, etc. But after the first stage of discovery was over there was the need for a second stage: a recapitulation. A balance had to be made. The dead weight had to be canceled out. Symbols had to be sifted and condensed. Representative of this more discriminating attitude was the movement born in 1950 under Octavio Paz and the Hyperion group—Zen, Portilla, Villoro, etc.—around the problem of 'Mexicanism.' But 'Mexicanism' in itself is an abstraction. There is no Mexicanism. There are only Mexicans. That was the next step. So, on the one hand, revolutionary art, officially canonized, wore itself out in repetitions, till it became sheer caricature. The imitators of Siqueiros and Rivera in the end produced nothing but a sort of revolutionary pop art. On the other hand, the whole movement formed around the discussion of 'Mexicanism' also fell into a series of abstractions that it tried to install as general laws, at the expense of the individual differences of live Mexicans." The lines of battle had been overdrawn. "I think at the time there was a widespread theoretical absolutism in Mexico that seems antiquated when seen from the perspective of 1965, but was nevertheless real enough in 1955–1957 when the book was written. The ideological alternatives were clear-cut. One of them was the possibility represented by the government of Lázaro Cárdenas (1934–1940): that of a popular regime, a type of Mexican socialism built from the bottom up with popular participation and the full weight of Marxist thought present in every act of government. The other was the political thesis of Miguel Alemán, which came as a counterrevolutionary reaction in 1946, armed with the precepts of Hamiltonism: wealth accumulates on top, then gradually filters downward. Politically and economically, those were the alternatives available."

La Región Más Transparente in some sense was designed to provide a forum for the conflicting opinions of the day. All seem equally tentative. None is decisive. A typical character is Zamacona, with his anguished doubts and messianic complex, which afford opportunities for gleeful satire.

"Zamacona," says Fuentes, "is a composite portrait of many Mexican intellectuals. Many recognized themselves in him. Because, in the whole 'Mexicanist' movement there was that redemptionist attitude. So I think *La Región Más Transparente* reflected—intentionally, of course, though without any attempt to expound personal theories—the excessive and somewhat mythical preoccupation over nationality, ancestry, and patrimony rampant at the time in Mexico. At the same time it aspired to give a critical report on the Revolution, at a moment when it could be seen in perspective, as it couldn't have been by the documentary novelists who wrote in the saddle, riding to battle with Pancho Villa." Which is why *La Región Más Transparente*—a book that inaugurates a new mood in Mexican literature—has been called "the other novel of the Revolution." It takes stock, reaches a summation. It had to be written long after the facts, says Fuentes, "just as the novel of the French Revolution wasn't written on the spot by Chateaubriand, but by Balzac and Stendhal, forty or fifty years later."

At times more like a memorandum than a mural, the book has its glaring defects. It is random and disjointed: a montage made of loose slides, occasionally as gaudy as poster art. It squanders its resources. It is transparent in its methods, overexplicit, often dazzled by its own virtuosity. The characterizations tend to be flat, the dialectics tendentious. There is almost no discernible plot line, only a semblance of dramatic progression. Too much is articulated in long speeches, frequently monologues that fall into the unhappy category of "deep" talk, with people wondering solemnly who they are, where they are going, what is Mexico, etc. The satirical intent of many episodes is undermined by ponderous mannerisms—such as endless cigarette smoking—that turn people into postures. Exchanges and confrontations, instead of being acted out, tend to remain verbal. There are intriguing but basically unconvincing figures like Ixca Cienfuegos and catastrophic events not inevitable enough to seem more than gratuitous. But in the end something fundamentally solid remains. The lushness and beauty of the prose, that often make a virtue out of apparent carelessness, carry many fine pages. There are memorable scenes in the life of Federico Robles, probably the best-realized, or least idealized, character, and that of his proud and willful wife, Norma, whose insolence gives her an almost tragic stature as she flouts conventions with reckless abandon and goes down fighting her way through a torrid love affair. Then there is the passionate death and transfiguration of Ixca Cienfuegos. Fuentes is not only an excellent wordsmith. He also has a fine ear for the rhythms of street talk. Some of his best touches are in humorous or pathetic popular scenes. Nor does he shy away from bravura passages of glowing rhetoric, among which is one of the high points of the book: a succulent descriptive enumeration of the sexual organs of prostitutes, as rabid and rapturous as Melville's song to the whiteness of the whale.

The wonder is that Fuentes, who borrows freely, with uncanny facility, from some of the most elaborate techniques of the U.S. novel, got away with as much as he did. The obvious influences, especially of Dos Passos, in his use of seeing eyes, flashbacks, headlines, time breaks, forced contrasts, and other devices, might well seem stale to a U.S. reader long familiar with such filigreed refinements of the narrative idiom. Fuentes recognizes that *La Región Más Transparente* is technically derivative, but feels that is inevitable, and not at all embarrassing to the Latin-American novelist, who, as he says, perhaps out of a sense of cultural inferiority, has always felt free to shop abroad for his forms of expression. The reason, paradoxically, may be isolation. Mainstream literatures do not directly imitate one another; an attribute of universality is the awareness that what has been done in one language has been done for all time in all languages. Distance, on the other hand, "eccentricity," fosters mimicry. It is only recently that our works have been translated into other languages; therefore our writer feels very little responsibility toward culture as a whole. He thinks in terms of contributing something, not to the world but only to his own local tradition. This has been an important limiting factor in our arts. We take without giving, less in an attempt to do something new than to prove we can do what others have done.

There are clear remnants of this attitude in Fuentes. "The dark angel of le temps perdu hovers over everything in Latin America," he wrote in a recent article. The result, in our art, as in other areas of our life, is "an unnatural and exciting process of growth, an impatient telescoping of stages that were leisurely arrived at in Europe and the United States." The scramble to catch up will sometimes mean slapping the most unlikely bedfellows together. Thus, in *La Región Más Transparente,* we will find some of the disciples of Joyce presiding over the children of Sánchez. It would not be unfair to say that the book reflects—and sometimes parrots—most of the literary habits prevalent in the United States between 1920 and 1940. It could almost be called a pastiche.

Dos Passos, Faulkner, and D. H. Lawrence are the authors Fuentes singles out for special mention. He says: "I was interested in time play, and their different ways of looking at time were helpful to me. Apart from whatever tendency a first novel may have to be a showcase of literary parentage, I was reading Dos Passos a lot, looking for a way to build dead time into a novel. In Dos Passos everything is in the past tense. Even when he places his action in the present, we know it is past. In Faulkner everything is in the chronic present. Even the remotest past is present. And in D. H. Lawrence what you find is a tone of prophetic imminence. He is always on the brink of the future; it is always there, latent. So I very consciously drew on those three influences, three aspects of time I wanted to counterpoint and overlap in *La Región Más Transparente.*"

The particular influence, often remarked, of Dos Passos and other "experimental" writers of his generation on Latin-American literature as a whole, Fuentes ascribes to "obvious reasons. Because Latin America is caught in a perpetual cultural lag of at least forty or fifty years, forms reach it with delay. The substance of Latin-American experience itself is in perpetual delay. Now the moment has arrived when it finds a very adequate form of expression in the kind of literature John Dos Passos was producing forty years ago."

It is a tribute to Fuentes' talent that imitation does not stifle *La Región Más Transparente.* There are errors in the book, "some of them serious," he admits, but on the whole it is well paced and consistent within itself. The diversity of styles, says Fuentes, was dictated by the subject matter, that of a heterogeneous city spreading amorphously amid violent contrasts and dislocations. The language, a product as much of instinct as of reflection, had to be broad enough to embrace the whole spectrum without atomizing it.

Very different in tone and procedure is Fuentes' second novel, *Las Buenas Conciencias* (Clear Consciences, 1959), the first of a cycle (which has recently been abandoned), therefore intended as a firm base for the future edifice. By contrast with *La Región Más Transparente, Las Buenas Conciencias* is an orderly, measured, and sober little book, austerely structured and, if anything, too efficiently engineered. The setting is no longer Mexico City, but Guanajuato, a colonial town that Fuentes describes as the epitome of provincial conservatism. The Independence movement was born there, and its aristocratic inhabitants—proud traditionalists, haughty guardians of the quintessence of the old Spanish style, founders of Mexico's most venerable Jesuit university—regard themselves as representing "the summit of the spirit of Central Mexico." In fact, they personify obscurantism and hypocrisy.

A favorite son of theirs is young Jaime Ceballos, the protagonist, of a family of shopkeepers who made good, now leaders of the community, who awakens to social realities via sexuality in a moment of adolescent crisis. We recognize the traditional Spanish theme, consecrated by García Lorca, of religious fervor as a precipitate of sensual stirring. Family pharisaism and social injustice are felt as passionate physical torments by Jaime, for whom revolt becomes a high calling. It leads inevitably to a crisis of faith. He seeks the true Christian path, not in the false piety of church ceremony but within himself. Like Zamacona in *La Región Más Transparente*, he feels fated for martyrdom, destined to assume the blame for the ills of humanity. Coming out of the throes of puberty, he has found not only a vocation for social action but also his separateness, his individual worth.

Jaime catches his first glimpse of the road to salvation in a childhood memory. He had once—in a scene reminiscent of the opening pages of *Great Expectations*—hidden a refugee from justice in his barn. In the man's tortured face—he was being persecuted for trying to organize a cooperative—he had seen an image of heroism and dedication. The fact that he had not been able to prevent the man's final arrest and imprisonment had been a source of shame and guilt to him ever since. His scruples are sharpened in conversations with his mestizo friend, Lorenzo, a young firebrand touchingly devoted to becoming a labor lawyer in the capital. Then there is Jaime's poor mother, Adelina, long snubbed by the family because of her low birth, now reduced to misery and prostitution. Adelina, unprotected by Jaime's weak father, Rodolfo, was kicked out of the house shortly after giving birth to Jaime, who was brought up in an atmosphere of rigorous puritanism by Rodolfo's sister, Aunt Asunción, and her husband, the bastion of conservatism, Jorge Balcárcel. It is in his reaction to the sanctimonious respectability of his elders that Jaime finds the strength to rebel.

But the true road is difficult. In the background, wrapped in his immutable false dignity, is the stiff graying figure of Balcárcel, reigning inexorably over the family, hand across his chest, with his sententious moral pronouncements; the frustrated Asunción, childless because of her husband's sterility—she is an embodiment of the loneliness of people who spend a lifetime suffering in silence, constitutionally unable to raise their voices to mention unpleasant truths—finding her only fulfillment in the possession and domination of her adopted child. Then there is the saddest nonentity of them all, Rodolfo, reduced to the status of a poor relation in the household, spinelessly selling clothes behind the counter in the old family store. Rodolfo, Balcárcel, Asunción, are all lives swept under the carpet. Each, in his own way, has paid his price for a spurious peace of mind.

Against these odds there is little Jaime can do. Opening his eyes is not enough. When the time comes for him to meet the crucial test he fails. The climax of the novel is reached in the scene where Rodolfo, in a moment of redeeming courage, rising out of the ruins of his broken life, suddenly speaks his mind. "How different we are . . . from what we could be," he announces to the family over the dinner table. A shocked silence follows these unutterable words. For once, an issue has not been evaporated. At that moment Rodolfo wins Jaime's heart. A gesture is expected from Jaime. He has his cue. But Jaime is silent. He lets the moment blow over, and everything returns to normal. Shortly after that Rodolfo dies, abandoned by the son from whom he had hoped to hear a word of forgiveness. As the family confessor tells Jaime: "He expected nothing out of life but your love. . . . But you sentenced him to die in pain and despair. You're a coward." Jaime bows his head. He realizes he is too weak to fight. Having come to a parting of the ways with his true believer friend Lorenzo, he runs up into the seclusion of the attic to beg God to make him be like everybody else, to spare him the extremities of "love and pride, crime and sacrifice." As he has confessed to Lorenzo: "I couldn't be what I wanted to be. I couldn't be a Christian. I can't face my failure alone; I couldn't stand it; I have to lean on something. The only thing I can lean on is my aunt and uncle, the life they've prepared for me, the life I inherited from my ancestors." He falls into line. He capitulates. Recognizing his failure, Fuentes tells us, is "an act of honesty, paradoxically the one act of honesty he has in the novel. The only one. The only time he is absolutely sincere with himself. The one time he admits the truth."

Las Buenas Conciencias has some striking qualities. The lines of the drama are clear and strong; the horrors of hypocritical moral righteousness are eloquently described. In spite of the starchy prose, there is a leisurely elegance about the book that is one of its most engaging features. The measured pace, says Fuentes, is conscious and deliberate. It was meant as "a stylistic and thematic base" for the tetralogy the book was supposed to introduce. "The idea was later to leave the world of Guanajuato, with its nineteenth-centuryish, Balzacian, Pérez Galdosian forms, to take the protagonist"—who has already appeared in a minor role in *La Región Más Transparente*—"to Mexico City. With the change of setting, there would be a change of style and rhythm. In other words, the style of *Las Buenas Conciencias* was going to be destroyed by the novels that would follow it. Its function within the whole picture was to provide a sort of ironic comment.' A Jamesian omniscient author enhances this effect. At the same time the muted display limits the tonal range. As usual in Fuentes, the central problem dealt with is that of "individual responsibility in an evolving community." The search for a personal base, outside caste and family, is a classic theme perhaps best served by distance and objectivity.

But it is precisely in these requirements that *Las Buenas Conciencias* seems to fall short of the mark. The author is not entirely free of the moral righteousness he criticizes. There is an implicit judgment of Jaime on every page, which acts as a constant interference in the mind of the reader. To prove a point, Fuentes in fact gives it away. At moments he weighs in so heavily that he verges on didacticism. The characterizations are too conventional, the issues too obvious, the progress of the story too predictable. Again, as in *La Región Más Transparente*, though the chattiness is gone, too much is resolved verbally. In reality, *Las Buenas Conciencias* reads as a sort of exemplar, contrived to teach a lesson and deliver a message. Which may well be an unsurmountable obstacle for any book. It is weakest at its most crucial point: the ending, which seems pat. Jaime, a purely figurative convert to prejudice, reasons out his change of heart without living it. The author hovers at his shoulder, rationalizing it. "Bad writing," says Fuentes with a smile. He intends to remedy that in the next edition.

Meantime we are left with some powerful images: the barren Asunción, fresh out of bed in the morning after a sleepless night, inspecting her unused breasts and wilted belly in the mirror, then, with a proud toss of her head, clasping her robe tight at the throat, as she stalks out of the room to start the day; the paragon of virtue, Balcárcel, caught with his pants down, half drunk in a whorehouse; Jaime on his knees, devoutly raising the skirt of Christ in church to inspect His anatomy, then, as he awaits the divine sign that will single him out forever, fervently kissing His "crucified feet"; again, Jaime, a hermit in sackcloth and ashes, whipping himself raw with thorns, and later, prostrate under the weight of his bloodied conscience, with a sudden streak of sadism, stoning a cat to death in the street.

In a more expansive vein is *La Muerte de Artemio Cruz* (The Death of Artemio Cruz, 1962), started during a stay in Cuba in 1960, therefore presumably written from the perspective of the Cuban Revolution, for which Fuentes' sympathies are well known. Not that it grinds any political axes. It is not artificially topical. But it reflects Fuentes' strong commitment to the cause of social reform. Like *La Región Más Transparente*, its view is panoramic. But the panorama this time is mental. The camera has been turned inward, to focus on the mind of the protagonist, who relives his life and, by extension, that of modern Mexico, on his deathbed.

Artemio's story, which ranges far and wide in space and time, is that of the Mexican Revolution. He grew up with it, flourished and declined with it. He fought as a rebel leader in its early heady days, saw it spread its titanic promise, only to dwindle and finally come to a complete standstill. Like Robles in *La Región Más Transparente*, he has known love, loyalty, and courage, but he compromised, treacherously trading them in for the cynicism and disillusionment of empty material success. His loss is Mexico's. Thus, in his tortured memory, a youthful love affair that returns to haunt him coincides with the euphoria of his revolutionary days; his loveless marriage of comfort and convenience, with the Revolution's hollow aftermath, when it became institutionalized. In his middle age, an adoring mistress offers him the possibility of a spiritual rehabilitation. But he is already beyond return. Once more the revolutionary ideal momentarily flares up in him when his son goes off with flaming eyes to fight in the Spanish Civil War. This coincides with the period of the leftist government of Cárdenas in Mexico. But the fitful hope soon vanishes. Lorenzo is killed in Spain; Artemio, brokenhearted, loses his last ray of light. He is what he has made of himself. All he can do now is continue to live off the fat of the land, accumulating riches, tormenting himself and those around him, and counting his days, which are numbered. His death closes a chapter in Mexican history.

As a portrait of moral disintegration, *La Muerte de Artemio Cruz* has some remarkable moments. Its strength is in its concentration. It is a drama of conscience. To a considerable extent Fuentes has achieved the complexity of characterization needed to give Artemio specific weight and gravity. He has avoided the dangers of caricature. Artemio Cruz, the prototype of the Mexican caudillo, is a type of personality, he says, that "given our tendency in Mexico to see things in black and white, is easily classifiable as black. My intention, which became increasingly evident to me as the character developed, was to show there's no such thing as black and white. Artemio Cruz is at once the book's hero and antihero."

A measure of Fuentes' maturing skill as a novelist, in *Artemio Cruz,* is his ability to shift his focus to show the different sides of things and draw rounded portraits. Artemio grows in the course of his adventures. True, his life circumscribes him. but in the end, though deteriorated, in a sense he is a bigger man than when he started out. He has learned. He knows. Filling his pockets and buttering palms are not the whole of him. He can be, in turn, humorous, shrewd, hardheaded, cruel, endearing, taciturn, admirable, pitiable. He can barrel on stage, slapping backs, like a politician on the stump, but he is also capable of reflection. He cheats, but catches himself at it. He sees himself as he is. Which is not an unmixed blessing. But it gives his experiences meaning and reasonance. Besides, like the feather-headed Norma in *La Región Más Transparente*, he is life-size because he loves life. This is at once his redeeming feature and his cross. For once, in a type of literature usually made of paper dolls and pasteboard cutouts, we are above slogan and panacea. There is a depth of penetration that humanizes. Tragedy, Fuentes realizes, is consciousness.

Dramatically, with its memorable scenes of revolutionary campaigns drawn in a vigorous and colorful prose, *Artemio Cruz* represents a notable advance over Fuentes' previous work. There is a prodigality without diffuseness. Less impressive are some of the techniques resorted to, often mere cosmetics. As in *La Región Más Transparente*, Fuentes is concerned with time play. To overlap different periods in time, he uses interior monologues, flashbacks, and a curiously incongruous device consisting in a kind of voice of conscience that addresses the protagonist in the second person and the future tense, a disembodied accusative that tortures the syntax and disrupts the action. Methods that seemed fresh and spontaneous in *La Región Más Transparente* have become automatic reflexes. Fuentes is at his best in "straight" narration. The most effective passages in *Artemio Cruz* are linear. Elsewhere he tends to get lost in fireworks. His great enemy is facility. In *Artemio Cruz* many otherwise dense and subtle pages are loaded down with a mechanical dead weight that seems expert but superficial.

A different reproach can be leveled against *Aura* (1962), an unconvincing little mystery novelette that raises the problem of personal identity. The setting, inevitably, is an ancient cob-webbed mansion inhabited by an eccentric old lady—who seems to have read *The Aspern Papers*—and her double, a fantasy-embodiment of her childhood self whom she conjures up by an act of the will in the person of a young girl called Aura. A scholarly lodger employed in the house falls in love with Aura, the enchanted maiden who awaits her gallant rescuer, and is absorbed into the prevailing trance. When he emerges from bondage, older and wiser, he has discovered Woman as Sorceress.

Aura takes its cue from a quote attributed to Jules Michelet:

"Man hunts and battles. Woman plots and dreams; she is the mother of fantasy." It never overcomes this bit of literary inanity. The elusive Aura seems only mildly spellbound. The trouble is structural. For a meaning to be revealed, it must first be withheld. Yet here it is handed to us almost from the beginning. In a story that proceeds on two levels, the second depends on the first. To be a parable, *Aura* must first hold up as a ghost story. But this is where it collapses, to become a mere fairy tale without suspense or illusion. Even the writing seems lax and tenuous. Everything works out too easily. Yet, curiously, Fuentes has a high opinion of *Aura*. The reason may be its frontal attack on the theme of personal identity, a constant—and characteristically Mexican—preoccupation in all his work. It is carefully programed into *Artemio Cruz* and raised to the national level in *La Región Más Transparente*. In *Aura* it appears in its most distilled form. It even becomes a part of the psychology of the story, which threatens the reader's identity by slyly attempting to enmesh his perceptions with those of the central character. In fact, *Aura* is addressed to a second person, whose identity—he is at once actor and spectator, protagonist and reader—remains ambiguous throughout. Though remote from "social" reality, it reflects, or refracts, a vision of human nature. After all, says Fuentes, "every story is written with a ghost at your shoulder." The ghost, in *Aura,* is Woman, "the keeper of secret knowledge, which is true knowledge, general knowledge, universal knowledge." Carnal contact with her is one of the archetypal forms of initiation into the mysteries of the world.

A more successful venture into the realm of "secret knowledge" is *Cantar de Ciegos* (Tales of the Blind, 1964), a collection of stories that contains some of Fuentes' best work. Fuentes is one of the very few Latin-American writers who have mastered the disciplines of the short-story form. Perhaps because of his close acquaintance with U.S. literature? He says readily: "I love the form. I like the neat, rounded structure of the short story." Here the temptation toward slickness seems to work to his advantage. He can pull a fast switch or wrap up a tidy plot as well as anyone writing today.

The title of his collection is an allusion to the ancient belief that the blind are seers, authorized to read the hidden truths in men's hearts and reveal their secret crimes. There were the blind bards of antiquity, and the blind oracles. There is also a tradition of blind street performers in Spain, who recite woeful tales during the fairs, usually with the aid of a child with a pointer, who marks off the gory episodes on a series of illustrative panels propped in chronological order on a scaffolding. The result is something like a cross between gospel singing and Grand Guignol. The emphasis is on the abysmal and the bizarre.

So, in *Cantar de Ciegos,* which satirizes regressiveness, posturing, faddism, and banality in Mexico, Fuentes rolls out family skeletons for one of the great peep shows of Mexican literature. There is the arty Elena in "Las Dos Elenas" (The Two Helens), who after seeing the film *Jules et Jim,* proclaims herself an emancipated believer in the ménage à trois, in which she imagines she will be fully "complemented," unaware of the fact that her triangular plans are being outdone by her husband, who is having an affair with her mother. There is a mysterious moral assassination in the "compounded fable" called "Un Alma Pura" (A Pure Soul), a story of brother-sister incest that exposes the morbidities of "machismo" (maleness) and leads its heroes through pregnancy, abortion, and suicide. "A la Víbora de la Mar" (Into the Serpent of the Sea) revisits—and revises—the Daisy Miller theme. A humpy middle-aged spinster who runs a gift shop in Mexico City has saved up for a vacation cruise on board an English boat, where she falls in love with a man with an Oxford accent who passes himself off as the scion of a wealthy Philadelphia family, but turns out to be a homosexual gigolo. In "La Muñeca Reina" (The Queen Doll) a nostalgic narrator on a poignant search for a childhood playmate finds a recluse whose crippled deformity has been kept out of sight in a shuttered house by her parents, a necrolatrous couple enshrined in memories of better days, who worship her image in the shape of a wax doll. "Vieja Moralidad" (Old Morality) deals with the corruption of a dubious innocence. A child lives with an obscene grandfather who sleeps with his housekeeper and hurls insults at the priests that go by in the street. Old aunts obtain a court order to remove the child to safer surroundings. But it is a change from bad to worse. The lecherous grandfather is a saint compared to the frustrated dowager who adopts the child only to seduce him. "El Costo de la Vida" (The Cost of Life) is about a knifing in an alley, and "Fortuna Lo Que Ha Querido" (Fortune Was What He Wanted) shows us a fashionable pop painter whose prowesses with the fast crowd and fame among the cultists do not prevent him from discovering his incapacity, or unwillingness, to love. An epigraph quoted from Raymond Radiguet clinches Fuentes' point. Mexico is young and old. There is already a strain of decadence in its sophistication. But the old way of life is still present. The new Mexico thrives on intricacies. It has begun to live dangerously.

Times have changed since the days of *La Región Más Transparente,* says Fuentes. Options and alternatives are no longer as clear-cut as they used to be.

"What has happened? That the world itself has moved at a different pace, erasing many of the ideological differences. We've had the whole phenomenon of neocapitalism and the increasing similarity between Eastern statism and the capitalist structures of the West. And Mexico has a very intelligent, very shrewd governing elite that has caught on to the way neocapitalism is going and started to apply its principles in Mexico. In a country that has reached the stage of what Walt Whitman Rostow would call the take-off, the Mexican government, especially the government of Díaz Ordaz, the present government, has started to introduce the theories and practices of neocapitalism into Mexican life. So the whole picture has changed. Culturally what has happened is that there has been a great reaction against chauvinism, against obsessive 'Mexicanism.' The elite above all, the intelligentsia, the young people, the students no longer stand in front of a mirror wondering what it means to be Mexican. All the new movement in art headed, let's say, by José Luis Cuevas, the new writers, the new film makers—they all take their Mexicanism for granted. The problem is to be a man, isn't it? So their art reflects this new personalization and ambiguity."

Also reflected in Mexican art today is the growing isolation of
the Mexican artist, which, says Fuentes, "is due to something
quite clear, I think. Traditionally in Latin America, starting
with Independence, there was a sharp division that Sarmiento
pinpointed, even used as the title of one of his works: *Civilization versus Barbarism [Facundo]*. Obviously the intellectual elite
of the semifeudal Latin-American world was invariably on the
side of civilization against barbarism. The choice was easy then.
You were with the cultivated elements in your society, who all
supported civilization's great saving project, inspired in the
French Revolution and the constitution of the United States,
against the feudal remnants of the Spanish inheritance. . . . I
think today if there are writers like Vargas Llosa, like Cortázar,
like myself, it is largely because that choice is no longer so simple.
In other words, the modern world has come to Latin America.
Through a series of developments: the arrival of U.S. capitalism,
the rise of a purchasing class, new goods and services, consumer
industries, television, mass entertainment, all this has contributed to modernizing life in the big Latin-American cities. So the
choice is no longer between civilization and barbarism. Civilization is here to stay. So the writer who was part of a small elite
that extended from the left wing to the right wing of the ruling
oligarchy, ignored by that same oligarchy, which regarded it with
supreme indifference, but nevertheless with more chance of effective action and a greater influence over events, has suddenly
found himself submerged in the petite bourgeoisie. The epic
choice that produced an epic literature—*Doña Bárbara, La
Vorágine, Don Segundo Sombra*—has therefore given way to a
literature by nature more equivocal, more critical, with a certain
strain of anguish and ambiguity, produced by people displaced
from their traditional positions, faced with the need to create
forms that are more personal, more highly elaborated, and much
more solitary. Where this first happened, I think, was in Mexico,
because of the Revolution. One of the aspects of the Porfirio Díaz
dictatorship it fought against was the notion of the intelligentsia
as an elite. The birth of popular art in Mexico, demagogic as this
art was at times, nevertheless, among other achievements, con-

tributed to this trend in that it destroyed the possibility for the artist or writer to act as the member of an elite. He was relegated to the level of the rising middle class. And we all know what the artist's problems are within the middle class. Especially the Latin-American artist, who has a sort of nostalgia for the elite days, who always yearns a little for that golden age."

This yearning is no doubt at least partly due to the fact that, cast to the sidelines by the march of events, the artist has begun to feel extraneous and irrelevant. The elite writer, in a sense, was an axis of the social wheel. In countries chronically swinging between dictatorship and anarchy, "bereft of democratic channels of communication, lacking a free press, a responsible Congress, independent labor unions," Fuentes has written, "the individual novelist was compelled to be, at once, legislator and reporter, revolutionist and thinker." He was the nation's conscience, in charge of evaluating and assessing, as well as maintaining "a continuity of relationship between social manifestation and literary imagination." He was a sort of minister without portfolio, who, Fuentes says to us now, expanding on the subject, "played the role of a redeemer, extended a helping hand to the oppressed Indian, the exploited peasant. That's the attitude at the root of all Latin-American literature. It was a literature of protest in which the writer supplied all the means of communication that were missing in Latin America."

By contrast, nowadays the writer is trapped within a class whose values he is constantly forced to reject. His work is an outlet for nonconformity and rebellion. A problematic situation which, nevertheless, has its advantages.

"Because it's evident," says Fuentes, "that the novel as such was born as a form of opposition, of rebellion on the part of the writer, on the part of life itself, as expressed by the writer, against the rigidity of social patterns. In other words, without alienation there would be no novelist. Alienation is at the source of the novel. So it seems quite natural to me to be within the middle class and at the same time fighting it. I may even go so far as to say—perhaps a bit cynically—that it's the only way to write good novels. . . . And I don't in the least," he adds genially, "share the illusion that we're on the way to a better society where alienation will disappear. We can see that clearly in Soviet society: the new structures of the Socialist state create their own alienations—alienations from the new system. And once again the novelist is channeling the forces of life against paralysis and stratification. That's the ambiguity of the novel: in the face of a custom-tailored art made of fixed patterns, the novel arose as a revolt against established order. But when the order the novel was advocating became a fact, the novel found itself in the paradoxical position of having to criticize what it had defended. I think this is equally valid in relation to Socialist order. That's why it's so important for us today to have novels like those of Cortázar and Vargas Llosa, which show that the novelist of the left in Latin America has lost his original innocence. For instance, in a novel like *La Ciudad y Los Perros,* obviously there's a tragic vision of the world, which contradicts, but at the same time includes, the author's sense of justice. In other words, justice, in Vargas Llosa, is no longer the naïve concept that it was in a Gallegos. It is part of a more complex vision that envelops and dramatizes it: the tragic vision. In Vargas Llosa the tragic vision has been completely assimilated. Vargas Llosa does not flatter himself that the battles of the pen, or even those of the battlefield, are going to bring about a utopic change. Not in the least. In the perfect society, children will still die."

As for our fluorescent society, Fuentes regards its increasing dehumanization and spiritual bankruptcy with somber pessimism. For the intellectual, he says, there is always the possibility of forming his own moral code and cultivating the sensibility that leisure and education have granted him. But that is "a false possibility. It's of no interest to anybody." The modern Candide, locked out of his back yard, roams the streets, become a face in the crowd.

"Islands of echoless monologues," Gorostiza has called his countrymen. His contemporary Villaurrutia, in quiet anguish, evokes the "endless silence" around him, in which voices are "a mute appeal that remains unanswered."

Mexico's urban novelists particularly—José Revueltas, the

popular Luis Spota, Fuentes himself—reiterate this theme. It shadows the fantasies of Fernando Benítez, and colors the work of younger authors, whether poets—Marco Antonio Montes de Oca—or novelists—Sergio Galindo, Tomás Mojarro, Fernando del Paso.

Fuentes has finished a new novel, *Cambio de Piel* (Change of Skin)—it will be published simultaneously this year in Mexico, Italy, and the United States—in which he weaves a delicate counterpoint between modern life in the historic village of central Mexico called Cholnla and life in that same village in the days of Cortes. Once again, he says, it is "the story of a conflict between an individual and the world," more specifically,"between those old, cherished private notions with which we try to justify our lives and the passion of a world that contradicts them." There are chasms on every page.

But even deeper, perhaps, will be the chasms in what was to be the second novel of the *Buenas Conciencias* cycle, a work now in progress: *Galatea*. Faithful to its namesake, it portrays a girl who is the victim of a series of Pygmalions or, rather, Svengalis, who instead of shaping her destroy her. "It's a totally personal novel," Fuentes tells us. "It's about a girl in Mexico City, about the difficulties of growing up in the city, but completely unrelated in theme to *Las Buenas Conciencias*. It's an isolated, inner life, where corruption becomes something of a synonym of innocence. You can only live by sticking your neck out, dirtying your fingers, exposing yourself."

Fuentes is not alone in his new subjective emphasis. The young Mexican novelist, influenced less by his predecessors in the genre than by such introspective poets as Pellicer, Gorostiza, Octavio Paz, is bound, he says, for "personalization: the novel of inner life. Above all, I believe that, in contrast to the old tendency writers had to form schools and movements, to overstate their position, today, precisely because of the ambiguities of Mexican life, the trend is in the direction of a series of very individual manifestations on the part of each writer. There are no common labels any more." The general tone is one of intimacy. In this there has been a clean break with the past.

Fuentes himself has never subscribed to any literary movement that would merit the name. The *Revista Mexicana de Literatura,* with which he is still associated, is an independent venture. Literarily speaking, he says, since its founding in 1956, it has always stood for "a rejection of localism, of the picturesque, of chauvinism, and the parochialism of Mexican literature." Politically it stands for "a rejection of every ideological a priori, an interest in the tiers monde, freedom of judgment with regard to the United States as well as the Soviet Union."

Openmindedness, however, is no synonym of disengagement. Fuentes, who refuses "the newly minted cliché of the crisis or decadence of the novel," feels close to such postwar U.S. novelists as Styron, Mailer, and Bellow. With Mailer, he says, he shares a predicament: entrapment in the middle class; and a reaction, in the form of "many existential, even nihilistic, attitudes. If I have anything in common with Mailer, it's the conviction that a new anarchic left is forming within the neocapitalist countries, and that this current offers us new literary modes and characters." Proof of this is *Cambio de Piel,* which is "narrated by an aging Nihilist, a middle-aged beatnik, a rebel without a cause who is pushing forty." If Mailer speaks of "infinitely broadening human possibilities," Fuentes, taking an equally long view of his art, says: "Whatever the society he lives in, the writer must always come up with a new heresy to renew that aspiration to liberty which is, perhaps, the closest we can come to liberty itself."

The possibility of falling into marginalism does not bother Fuentes. "One wonders," he says, "whether the novelist is not doomed to become increasingly marginal as the neocapitalist phenomenon of social and economic pluralization develops in our countries. But always with a transcendent and messianic purpose." Because, as he firmly believes, "in a perpetually unfinished world, there is always something that can be said and added only through the art of fiction."

IX

Gabriel García Márquez,
or the Lost Chord

HE is stocky, but light on his feet, with a bristling mustache, a cauliflower nose, and many fillings in his teeth. He wears an open sport shirt, faded blue jeans, and a bulky jacket flung over his shoulders. Pátzcuaro is a moody mountain lake about two hundred miles west of Mexico City, on the road to Guadalajara. A quick nightfall after a hard rainy day on location—he is filming with an experimental group in the muddy streets of a nearby village—brings a faraway look to his eyes. His name is Gabriel García Márquez.

"A casualty list," he calls Colombian literature. The fact is that practically since the days of José Eustacio Rivera's traumatic *La Vorágine* (The Vortex, 1928), not much of literary note has been coming out of Colombia. The reason seems to be a kind of national smugness that extends to every area of Colombian life. Colombia is a stronghold of Catholic conservatism, instinctively traditionalist in politics, purist in language. Its writers have been academicians and grammarians. There were exceptions, of course. Every schoolchild in Latin America has read Jorge Isaacs' idyllic nature poem *Maria* (1867), one of the high points of our Romantic novel. There were some noted Modernist poets like

José Asunción Silva. But, in the field of the novel, Colombia has had the distinction of producing some of the worst works on the continent. Enough to think of the sickly tropicalist, Vargas Vila, immensely popular at the turn of the century for a series of sweaty potboilers that made a cult of pornography and a fetish of exoticism. More presentable was the work of Tomás Carrasquilla, a regionalist in the realist vein, the first to expand the scenic sketch to novel length. Today Colombia has an accomplished biographical essayist in Germán Arciniegas. But only García Márquez has succeeded in giving Colombia imaginative existence in fiction.

A strenuous life that might have wrecked another man has provided García Márquez with the rich hoard of personal experiences that form the hard core of his work. For years he has been living in Mexico. He would go home if he could—he says he would drop everything if he were needed there—but at the moment he and Colombia have nothing to offer each other. For one thing, his politics are unwelcome there, and he has strong feelings on the subject. Meantime—if life abroad can be an ordeal, it also has its compensations—he is like a jeweler polishing his gems. With a handful of books behind him, each born of the labor of love, like a pearl in an oyster, he has begun to make a solid reputation for himself. There was *La Hojarasca* (Windfall, 1955), then, in quick succession, *El Coronel No Tiene Quien le Escriba* (No Letter for the Colonel, 1961), *Los Funerales de la Mamá Grande* (Big Mama's Funeral, 1962), and *La Mala Hora* (Hard Times, 1962). He is a founding member of that somewhat loosely knit group of young internationalists, all under forty— Fuentes, Vargas Llosa—whose work is changing the face of our literature. They are not a clique or a clan but a circuit: a sort of informal club that seldom meets but keeps in touch across national boundaries, joined by the sense of achievement common to those who are breaking new ground. García Márquez, as independent as any of them, speaks of their "team spirit." One thinks of a sort of literary New Frontier. Wherever talent turns up, as it is likely to do almost anywhere nowadays, the word spreads fast along the grapevine. Like the other members of the Group, García

Márquez is aware of the fact that he is bearing the banner of progress—he says the ebullience of the Latin-American novel is the only answer today to the sterility of the French nouveau roman—and he is fiercely proud of it. At the same time, eternally self-questioning, he worries and wonders about himself. He is an intense, elusive, somewhat absentminded man who will do anything to reach people, to be loved, as he says, even write books. He has made a virtue of what may have started as an emergency. He works on a small scale, at high pressure, looking inward, with all the passion of the exile who carries house and home around with him.

Thanks to García Márquez, the most interesting spot in Colombia today is a tiny tropical village called Macondo, which is not on any map. Macondo, set between dunes and marshlands on one side and an impenetrable sierra on another, is a decadent, dusty little coastal town, like thousands of others in the heart of the hemisphere, but also very special, at once strange and familiar, specific and general, immediate as an insight, remote as an image of a forgotten landscape. Its visible lines chart a secret course. It is one of those places a voyager reaches without ever leaving home, sure to arrive before he sets out. Macondo is everywhere, and nowhere. Those who travel there take an inner trip to a port of call that is part of the hidden face of a country.

García Márquez was born there, in 1928—in Aracataca, a dot of a village in the torrid Atlantic zone of Santa Marta, probably not unlike Macondo, which is named for a banana plantation he knew as a child. He grew up there and, in a sense, he still lives there.

Macondo has a troubled history. It was first settled in the late nineteenth century by refugees from the civil wars that were devastating the Colombian countryside. The wars—"a long and painful reality in Colombia," he says, however mythical they may seem in his work—ended about 1903, but their consequences continue to be felt down to the present day. Macondo had its period of boom between 1915 and 1918, the time of the "banana fever," a sort of minor gold rush that populated the area with fortune hunters: that human "windfall" that hope brought in and soon blew off again. When the Banana Company left town, prosperity went with it, never to return. Those who could, scattered. Those who remained struggled on. There was little to encourage them. Macondo was left with its old feuds and betrayals, its vanished heroes, its festering delusions of grandeur. It drifted into apathy and despair. There was a period of banditry, when the town was sacked, then there were plagues and epidemics that turned it into an open sewer. It was racked by droughts, washed away by diluvial rains. A "pacification" program only helped it stagnate. The blight was upon it. Fiscal ruin? In part. But the real problem in Macondo is moral gangrene. It is a town of guilty consciences, with a grudge against the world. The past was buried without being exorcised, and is back, a dark ferment that has become a collective nightmare. No one sleeps well in Macondo. There is an atmosphere of distrust and suspicion, repressed violence and hostility. With bad drainage, time brings dreads and presages. True, the sultry days go by in undistinguishable succession, with little to ruffle their calm other than the visit of an occasional circus, the arrival of the weekly mailboat. But, for those who can read the signs, every minute is weighted with the threat of imminent disaster. The heat is on. Macondo has developed a sixth sense to detect trouble. And, as everybody knows, these are apocalyptic times. There are guerrillas in the back country. The village doctor distributes clandestine leaflets, the barber has a sign up saying, "Forbidden to talk politics," the priest is blind and deaf, the tailor's shop is a nest of sedition. History is about to catch up with Macondo. The bad omens are multiplying. Not long ago birds fell from the sky. Macondo—Colombia's Jefferson, Mississippi, with a touch of the small-town tedium of Winesburg, Ohio—is on the eve of a final holocaust. García Márquez captures and fixes the moment. Nothing has happened yet. But in a sense everything has. The night before—a long wake—is a clear premonition of the morning after.

Distance has evaporated Macondo. Its contours are hazy, its statistics uncertain, its geographical—and demographic—features somewhat vague. It may well be more than one place. Sometimes, the way García Márquez paints it, it seems hardly more than a hamlet, at others—a "solution of convenience," he says—a town big enough to merit daily train service from the capital. It has only one movie house, but at least two priests whose tenures overlap, and half a dozen retired colonels, all with claustrophobic memories. There are many small factual inconsistencies. But they hardly matter. If Macondo is manifold in detail, it is one in mood. What counts is not what it is but what it suggests. It lives only for the inner eye, which sees more than it is shown. Like all mythical places, it is a part that evokes the whole: an image rippling off the edge of vision, into peripheral shadows that linger just out of sight, throbbing to make their presence felt.

If there is something a bit miraculous about Macondo, it may well be the fact that a man who left it as far behind him as García Márquez did, ever found his way back there. It was already a memory in 1940, when he moved to Bogotá to study with the Jesuits. He was twelve, a child with glowing eyes, suddenly forced to outgrow himself. The idea never much appealed to him, he says, and he probably did a bad job of it. The marvels of city life made little impression on him. He was a desultory student. His studies—high school, then an inglorious bout with law at the University of Bogotá—were an interruption of a private fable he continued to live. He got them over with as fast as he could.

Earning a living was another long obstacle course. He did some newspaper work with his left hand. Meantime, to keep the currents flowing, he began to write stories. In their shifting hues he hoped to catch his reflection. He was reading a lot of Joyce and Kafka, "juggling" possibilities, and the result was negative: "sheer trickery." He was on the wrong track. He would destroy those early stories if he could get his hands on them, he says, but they have been filed away for posterity in the stacks of *El Espectador* of Bogotá, the liberal daily whose literary supplement was the first to publish his work. In fact, it was on the basis of one of these stories that—in 1946—he got into journalism. For several years he was on the staff of *El Espectador,* as reporter and

editor. His assignments kept him on the move, traveling the
length and breadth of the country. Then came a stroke of good
luck: in 1954 the paper sent him as its correspondent to Europe.
Headquartered for nine months in Rome, he discovered the
Experimental Movie Center, which immediately caught his
fancy. The movies had always fascinated him. He took a director's course and sent film reviews home relaying his impressions.
Then came Paris, the hub of the wheel, from where he branched
out into Eastern Europe. In the midst of all this hopping about
something had started to snap into focus. With a new sense of
urgency, he was hard at work on an undiscovered book made of
many secret chapters, one of which eventually settled to become
El Coronel No Tiene Quien le Escriba.

It was smooth sailing for a while, until the end of 1955, when
the Rojas Pinilla dictatorship, bearing down on opposition at
home, closed *El Espectador.* The paper had never failed him
with its monthly remittances, but now he was left out in the
street, waiting for a check that never came. He spent a year not
knowing how he was going to pay for his next meal. He remembers a shabby existence in a dreary hotel room in the Latin
Quarter, Rue Cujas. He owed his rent for the whole year, a total
of 123,000 old francs, an astronomic amount in those days. Somehow, he notes with a kind of morbid relish, there seemed to be
nothing much he could do about it. In fact, he may have rather
enjoyed himself. It was one of those ambiguous situations that
seem fantastic enough to have a gruesomely appealing side to
them. In any case, he was too busy to pull himself out of it. And,
strangely enough, the hotel, sensing distress, was kind to him and
never tried to collect. He says the management trusted him
because they saw him working in his room the whole time, and
even lost clients, because of his overnight typing. Eventually, still
on a shoestring, he smuggled himself into a maid's room on Rue
d'Assas—with the maid.

The spell broke in 1958 when—with a stop along the way in
Colombia to marry his bride, Mercedes, who had been waiting
for him those four endless years—he transferred himself to Caracas. There, at the editorial desks of *Momentos* and *Elite,* he

finished another chapter of his secret book, *Los Funerales de la Mamá Grande.* In 1959, when Castro entered Havana, he was appointed to open an office for the Cuban news agency, Prensa Latina, in Bogotá. The next year—the year of Khrushchev's shoe —he represented Prensa Latina at the United Nations' Fifteenth General Assembly. It was an honest living for a while. But his relations with Prensa Latina soon went stale. He resigned when the militant element in the party began to breathe down his neck.

In 1961 he came to Mexico with a hundred dollars in his pocket. When he was down to his last ten dollars, "the Group went to work." They found him a place to live in the handsome residential suburb of San Ángel Inn, where he may have taken up permanent residence for all he knows. In Mexico he finished *La Mala Hora,* which was somewhat mysteriously—and messily— published in Spain. Nowadays he has won his share of literary prizes, but they bring no money—he makes a living doing scripts in odd places for "new wave" movies. One of his stories, "En Este Pueblo No Hay Ladrones" (There Are No Thieves in This Town), was filmed by an experimental group for presentation at the 1965 Locarno Film Festival. Meantime, restless and fidgety in these secondary tasks, which absorb vital energies, he finds time where he can to dip into his reserves, a bottomless barrel that deepens as he goes.

The evening we spend in the thin mountain air of Lake Pátz-cuaro with our host and guardian angel Gabriel—who insists on writing our hotel bill off on his expense account; the lean years have given him a lavish sense of hospitality—is strangely ex-hilarating. The setting: a quiet colonial wayside inn with ram-bling archways, rows of small dark rooms peeping out on to inner patios with potted plants and tidy flower beds. On an announce-ment board outside the sedate dining room are rosters and film-ing schedules. The day starts at 6 A.M., and ends early. There is a dank lounge—empty—and a smoky entertainment hall with unused ping-pong tables. Occasionally hectic footsteps go patter-ing down the tiles, a heavy key jangles in a lock. But there is little movement after dark. We sit in our room feeling silly with our note pads: we are not allowed to use a tape recorder. Angel Gabriel, tightening his belt, comes out of a dark bend in the corridor with lights in his eyes. He lets himself into the room stealthily, a bit on edge, wondering what is going to happen to him, but at the same time, it seems, rubbing his hands in anticipation. He likes the idea of having guests from afar; he is happy to have someone to talk to. That the subject of conversation is himself makes things a bit dangerous, but therefore all the more intriguing. "A pity you can't stay longer," he says, hearing we plan to leave the next day at noon. Who knows what he might come up with if we did stay on. He has a way of startling himself with his own thoughts. Now—the night is fragrant and full of surprises—he lies back on a bed, like a psychoanalytic patient, stubbing out cigarettes.

He talks fast, snatching thoughts as they cross his mind, winding and unwinding them like paper streamers, following them in one end and out the other, only to lose them before he can pin them down. A casual tone with a deep undertow suggests he is making a strategy of negligence. He has a way of eavesdropping on himself, as if he were trying to overhear bits of a conversation in the next room. What matters is what is left unsaid.

He writes in the same way, without a set plan, in a sort of total alert, registering imponderables. He has no cut-and-dried recipe by which to perform. "I have firm political ideas," he says. "But my literary ideas change according to my digestion." If he tells a story, it is less to develop a subject than to discover it. Theme is less important than wavelength. His facts are provisional, valid not as statements but as assumptions, what he feels today he may discard tomorrow. If in the end not everything adds up to a net result, it is perhaps because we must subtract, not add, to reach a final balance. His world has no beginning or end, no outer rim. It is centripetal. What holds it together is inner tension. It is always on the verge of taking concrete shape, but remains intangible. He wants it that way. Its relation to objective reality is that of an eternally fluctuating mental portrait where resemblances at any given moment are striking but tenuous. Because García Márquez never fully defines his terms, their possibilities

remain inexhaustible. A single source has fed all his books, which
grew side by side in him like different aspects of a single basic
image. In fact, *El Coronel No Tiene Quien le Escriba, Los
Funerales de la Mamá Grande,* and *La Mala Hora* were all more
or less written together, each an echo of the others, a hint containing its sequel or, inversely, deriving from it. Thus in the
beginning there was meant to be only one book, *La Mala Hora,*
which would be all-encompassing. "I wanted to put everything I
knew into it," says García Márquez. He worked on it for five or
six years, without ever seeing the end of it. There was too much
of it. As he tried to structure it—from an obese opening on—he
kept excluding fatty tissue. Passages broadened, then were
dropped, only to grow separate roots and take on a life of their
own. That was how *Coronel*—and most of the stories in *Funerales,* where the same characters and situations recur—was born.
Originally, *Coronel* was an episode in *La Mala Hora.* But as the
protagonist took on weight and girth, it bulged, and was finally
disgorged. He had to take time out to unravel the strand before
returning to the main spool. Other strands led in many directions, fusing, splitting, ramifying, but always, ultimately, winding back on themselves.

Having struck a rich vein, García Márquez has been tapping
it ever since. He realizes the dangers of such a procedure, but the
compulsive need to tell and retell the same stories, to go over the
same material again and again, wringing new shadings out of it
each time, is something of an umbilical force with him. He constantly rereads his books. He can quote at length from them. He
knows them almost by heart. To keep them alive and burning,
he has to review them every day, ceaselessly retreating along
familiar landmarks, in hopes of finding a way around them. But
he always circles back to the starting point. There seems to be no
way out. He says: "I don't know what book I'm writing any
more." All he can do is pick up the pieces. Each is a precious
fragment of the larger work, another touchstone in the dark. He
clutches at every hint and sign. The reason is an acute case of
homesickness: for a place, and a time. He has been away too
long. "I'm losing contact with my myths." He will do anything to

kindle them, because they light the way back to his lost childhood.

"I had a fabulous childhood," he says. He hardly knew his
parents. His absent mother he imagined as a huge shadowy lap
on which he had never sat. He met her for the first time when he
was seven or eight years old. She had left him to be brought up
by his grandparents. They ran a strange and prodigious household. "They had an enormous house, full of ghosts. They were
very superstitious and impressionable people. In every corner
there were skeletons and memories, and after six in the evening
you didn't dare leave your room. It was a world of fantastic
terrors. There were coded conversations." He remembers himself
as a frightened and dazzled child perched on the edge of a chair
in a corner, or barricaded behind the furniture. At the foot of
his bed loomed the ominous shape of a huge gilded altar
decorated with plaster saints whose eyes shone in the dark. His
grandmother, an eerie presence always hovering nearby, used to
tiptoe in at night to tell him bedtime stories. She was a nervous,
jumpy, unpredictable person, constantly in a frazzle, given to
seizures and visions. His grandfather, on the other hand—he
occupied a minor political post in the village bureaucracy—was
his dear friend and companion, "the most important figure in my
life," says García Márquez, who has modeled more than one
character on him. Together they took long walks and went to the
circus. The old man had fought in the civil wars, which had left
deep scars on him. He had once had to kill a man. The act
haunted him ever after. "You don't know how much a dead man
can weigh," his grandson remembers him saying with a sigh. He
died when the child was eight years old. It was the end of an era
for García Márquez. After that, he says, he felt rather jaded.
Growing up, studying, traveling, "none of that particularly
attracted me. Nothing interesting has happened to me since."

Everything he has written to date, he says, he already knew or
had heard before he was eight. It takes him years to be able to
draw on the residues of his experiences. They have to settle first.
And he lets them take their time. To transpose he must first
restore. It is delicate work, for which there is no sure method. He

plays by ear. Things seem to come to him from nowhere, out of the haze of a past at moments withheld, at others full of missing places and people. If he invents anything, it is almost by mistake. "I only write about things I know. People I've seen. I don't analyze." His job is to be receptive. "I'm not too sure where people fit in, or what they mean." They come to life in a sudden gesture, a remembered account, a forgotten voice, twitch and flicker out. He treads lightly among his figments, grabbing them as they go by. The wary man sleeps with an eye open, ready to jump up each time his heart beats fast. Half the time he finds himself groping in the dark.

But the intermittent vigil may also be rewarded. It was in *La Hojarasca,* which he began when he was nineteen, though it was published only eight years later. *La Hojarasca* is an embryonic book, only a crude promise of what followed, but full of fire and brimstone that provide a colorful historical backdrop for the rest of his work. In *La Hojarasca* García Márquez was turning the dead over in their graves. They were at the helm. The period covered—1903 to 1928—in the history of Macondo antedates the author. It ends the year he was born.

Tortuous monologues around a corpse in a coffin tell the story of Macondo's boom and decline as reflected in a family's fortunes through three generations, each of which supplies the drama with a narrator and—purportedly—a point of view. There is that characteristic García Márquez figure, the old Colonel, wrapped in martial splendor, honorably retired from the battlefield, after years of somewhat vague association with the forces of the civil war. He lost his first wife in childbirth, remarried, and fathered a daughter, Isabel, who lives with him in the ancestral home—a replica, says the author, of his grandparents' dwelling—after having been abandoned by her flighty husband. The old Colonel, Isabel, and her son, a young boy who is a projection of the author, are the three spectators who bear witness to a tragedy that involves them all.

The book opens on a wake. An old friend of the family has hanged himself. The members of the family pass mental review, reconstructing his stormy career. He was a mysterious doctor of obscure background and doubtful extraction—perhaps a foreigner: he used to read French newspapers—who moved in with them years before bearing letters of recommendation from some common acquaintance whose identity is never revealed. There is the suggestion of a hidden kinship: he keeps reminding Adelaida, the Colonel's second wife, of "someone." For years he was the only doctor in town. He was a strange man who practiced in monastic silence under the Colonel's protection, solitary, taciturn, and uncommunicative. During the "banana fever," when other doctors came to town with the growing population, he gradually withdrew from the world, shunning all company, finally locking himself in his room. There, a prey to the frenzies of celibacy, he spent hot sleepless nights, writhing on his empty mattress. Rumors were that he used to sneak out now and then to court the barber's daughter, a poor addled soul who saw spirits and eventually, it seems, gave birth to one. Then one day he eloped with the household maid, Meme, who had already survived an abortion at his hands and was pregnant again. He set her up in great style, dressed her as a society lady and sent her to church to shock the town. He even bought her a business with the money he had been saving over the years. When she disappeared, he was accused of murdering her to prevent her from poisoning him.

At this point, feeling in town was running strong against him, and he was less than conciliatory. During the period when the town was being attacked by bandits and the other doctors had their hands full beating off the vultures, he refused, for reasons known to him alone, to help out with the wounded, thus finally earning everybody's undying enmity. Adelaida is convinced he is the devil incarnate. Certainly, another undeveloped hypothesis suggests, he is either a God-seeker gone astray along crooked paths or an evil spirit. Frictions grow to the point where it seems the populace is about to lynch him. The local priest, with whom he has subterranean connections of a nature that remain undisclosed, steps in to save him.

Now, in death, the doctor still manages to bring out the worst in people. There is the danger of rioting in town. He seems to touch a raw nerve in people, to release pent-up fears and hates. In fact, he is something like Macondo's conscience, which cannot be put to rest. Bowing to popular pressure, the town's new priest, Padre Ángel, has refused to authorize his burial in hallowed ground. Only the old Colonel—who owes him his life from a time when Macondo had been flattened by the flu—stands up for him. Over vigorous ecclesiastical objections, he keeps an old promise to see his doomed friend decently buried. But the doctor's spirit may still rise from the grave to haunt the town. An epigraph quoted from Sophocles' *Antigone* comments wryly on the scene. Like Polynices, whose corpse was cast as carrion to the birds of prey, the doctor dies unmourned. But the passions unleashed against him foreshadow the scourges that will be visited on his tormentors.

La Hojarasca—a great success in Colombia: it sold thirty thousand copies when it first came out, thanks, says García Márquez, to his friends in the newspaper world—is a somewhat makeshift book, written in starts and spurts that never quite fuse to become a single impulse and often fade out before reaching fulfillment. The author seems to be turning his subject upside down and inside out, without ever finding its cardinal points. The reason, he says, is that he got carried away. He was a man possessed during *La Hojarasca,* as he never has been to the same extent again. It was a spontaneous book, completely innocent of all "literary" intent—the only one of his books, he thinks, that has true "inspiration." He remembers that when he was working on it he was swept along by a single great rush of ideas that poured out of him at all times. Those were his Faulknerian days.

In Faulkner—there was also, he insists, the Virginia Woolf of *Mrs. Dalloway*—he had found a medium and a manner to go with it. Like so many of our writers before him, he came on Faulkner as a thirsty man comes on a fountain of fresh water. He was carried away. "When I first read Faulkner," he recalls, "I thought: 'I must become a writer.' " The chaotic materials that went into Faulknerian art, he says, were much like the raw stuff of life in Colombia. Faulkner showed him how this elementary turbulence could be manipulated and transformed. He was enlightened—but overwhelmed.

If *La Hojarasca* is a failure, it is largely because it is written in a borrowed idiom that never becomes a personal language. Its interwoven plots and subplots, overlappings and backtrackings, its involuted time play, are all more or less perfunctory devices that defeat the purpose they might be expected to serve. The separate monologues of the three narrators are not complementary because they do not reflect separate points of view or characterize the viewers. Whoever is speaking, the voice is always the same. Man, woman, and child, in thought patterns and vocabulary, are indistinguishable. Each contributes a slab of straight narrative to a single block of events that need not have been broken up in the first place. The result is not density but monotony. Related faults are certain episodes in the life of the child—episodes marginal to the main action—that seem irrelevant and unconvincing. They were meant to give the child—whose characterization is particularly deficient—more body, says García Márquez, a parallel existence outside the immediate scene of the wake. But they merely distract. On the whole, one can say that a lot of energy goes to waste in *La Hojarasca,* which for all its genuine emotional charge remains shapeless and diffuse.

But not all is loss. Certain distinct elements of the García Márquez style are already visible. There are prototypes: the grandfatherly Colonel, the soul-searching doctor, the stalwart figure of woman, always, in García Márquez, a bastion in adversity. There are those mysterious affinities between people related to one another by some hidden trait they share, perhaps born under the same star, therefore doomed to labor under a common curse. There is the case of the doctor and the local priest, who resemble each other as brothers and both arrived in town on the same day. They seldom meet, but when they do they seem to see eye to eye for a minute, as if each recognized himself in the other. Many hints are never fully explained. There is an element of deliberate mystification in *La Hojarasca.* There are cryptic references, suppressions, blanks, blind spots. We often seem to be on the verge of a revelation that never comes. García

Márquez avoids revelations, which he considers "a bad literary
device." Yet he often builds up to them. He admits he promises
more than he can deliver. After the build-up, any resolution
would seem pedestrian or melodramatic. Therefore he avoids it.
He likes to take the reader to the edge of the obvious, then drop
him, leaving him in suspense. The method is not always successful. Indeed it can be irritating. But it adds to the ominous
atmosphere. And, after the book is shut and put away, that is
what remains. Macondo is an anguished town in the throes of
dark portent: senseless wars, general pestilence, and decay. The
mood is epidemic.

Among its victims is the doddering old Colonel of *El Coronel
No Tiene Quien le Escriba*, a cantankerous, meteorological
creature, the best realized of all García Márquez' characters in
what is probably his most finished work. The distance between
La Hojarasca and *Coronel* is that between profligacy and absolute economy. Midway stands a thorough reading of Hemingway's stories, great favorites of García Márquez. Not that there is
any direct influence. The relation to Hemingway is platonic; a
matter of general stylistic tendency. The Faulknerian glare has
been neutralized. It is not replaced by any other. From now on
García Márquez is his own master. He has pared himself down to
the bone. There are no spare parts in *Coronel*. Everything is
done with "a minimum of words." Clarity, precision, understatement, a deceptive simplicity, seduce where rhetoric never could.
There is an air of unspoken things, sudden inklings, heavy
silences, all wrapped in an apparent negligence that defines by
omission, always calling attention to what would seem to have
been overlooked. A single breath of mystery blows through the
book, which is barely a hundred pages long, but shrouded in
luminous shadows.

The old Colonel, a humorous and pathetic figure headed for
complete breakdown, lives in pauperism in a mortgaged house
with his long-suffering wife, waiting for his government pension—
like the author's grandfather, he was treasurer for the aborted
revolutionary forces of Aureliano Buendía, and, because of the
general amnesty declared after the Revolution, is entitled to

compensation—which never comes. Months and years have gone by. The situation has become chronic. A lawyer presumably handling the case only bungles it. The Colonel's petitions get lost in the vast bureaucratic maze of remote government offices, where his enemies probably lurk at every turn. He waits eternally. His heart beats fast each time the mailboat arrives, but in vain. Meantime his son, Agustín, whose name is used as a password by the guerrillas in the brush, has been killed for his revolutionary activities. The Colonel receives daily visits from the kindly Dr. Giraldo, a contact man for the guerrilla forces, who arrives full of jokes and witticisms to cheer him up. The Colonel, who enjoys banter, holds out as best he can. He likes to be spoiled and is not above complaining of his wife's asthmatic coughing and choking, which keeps him awake at night. He has his own minor ailments that change with the season. In the rainy month of October he feels "as if I had animals in my guts." But there is a lot of fight left in him. In fact, one day he has a brainstorm. He has inherited a fighting cock from his son. He will fatten it, then pit it in singular battle against a cock from a neighboring town, and rake in the proceeds. So the monster of illusion is born.

The Colonel can barely support himself, let alone the rooster. But nothing can stop him now. He will sell house and home if need be to keep his spark of hope burning. So the furniture starts going out the door, and before he knows it his wife is reduced to pawning her wedding ring. He meets this new trial with a mixture of stoic composure and reckless good humor. As it happens, the whole town has a stake in the rooster, because everyone has bet on it, sure of making a killing. So contributions start coming in to support the symbol of local pride. Soon the Colonel is living on birdfood. When things get bad enough, he is sorely tempted to sell the animal to Don Sabas, a local bigwig who has been trying to swindle him out of it. But he does not have the heart to do it. He would be letting everyone down. Besides, he has to save face. Nothing can be done now but to sit tight. Winter will pass, he hopes, as he lies in bed, shivering under the covers, the rain will stop leaking through the thatched roof, and then, God willing, "everything will be different." He can stand it. If his wife takes a somewhat jaundiced view of the whole affair, she will just have to bear up. As for himself, he can always manage. If things don't work out, so much the worse. He is accustomed, not to say addicted, to misfortune. Above all, he has his dignity to think of. He is a man who wears no hat "so as not to have to take it off to anybody." Comes a sunny day and, fickle as a weathervane, reflecting every climatic change, he is full of optimism. He rises avidly on creaking joints to proclaim: "On a morning like this you want to go out and have a picture taken." Spring is back. He wants to plant roses. The pigs will eat them, says his wife, the voice of common sense. But he has an answer for that, too: "Think how good it must be to eat a pig fattened with roses."

Few characters in Latin-American fiction are as endearing as the decrepit old Colonel, who lives long after his story is finished. He is a sort of aged baby, a withered wonder child, wise and silly, touching and human, enchanted and misguided by life. He has not only a personality but a soul.

Only a slight anecdote supports the book. But it is enough for the character to evolve. García Márquez says his purpose was not so much to tell a story as to complete a characterization. His method is not exhaustive—the Colonel is not a rounded character, nor is he meant to be—but intuitive. The man is wholly present, with his full "human weight," as the author calls it, in every act. Latent areas support those in view. García Márquez knows the value of silence. He can be eloquent without saying a word.

Much of the effect of *Coronel* is in its quiet, wry humor. The most moving passages are often those written with a smile. The tongue in cheek is always the other side of a painful grimace. García Márquez does not think of himself as a humorist, if the term means anything. He says the humor in his books, which always seems to strike people, is incidental. He distrusts humor, especially the commonplace joke thrown in simply to fill a vacancy. Besides, he says with a twinkle, he always thought he was humorless. The smiles sprinkled through his books were dropped there in passing, when they happened to fit the occasion.

Nevertheless, he admits under duress, the Colonel was originally conceived as a comic character. Obviously the author had a lot of fun with him for a while. But then something went wrong. He was working on the book in Paris when his newspaper closed down and his monthly checks stopped coming. His situation was very much like that of the old Colonel, and there was nothing the least bit funny about it. If he laughed while he was writing, it was a laugh edged with painful insight. The Colonel knows each laugh may be his last. Laughter helps him weather his wife's logic. It disguises sorrow and bitterness. In reality, as the charitable Dr. Giraldo realizes, every joke he cracks is another turn of the screw. So it is in a brief exchange he has with the predatory Don Sabas, a diabetic who has to sweeten his coffee with saccharine and complains: "It's sugar, but without any sugar in it." To which the Colonel, "with a sad sweetness on his tongue," answers: "It's a bit like tolling without bells." He imposes such respect on the people around him that when he is caught in the billiard hall, during a curfew, playing roulette with a clandestine note in his pocket, benevolent police officers let him walk out the door without searching him. But, at home, a wave of unbearable suffering suddenly invades him as he remembers with melancholy gloom that he and his wife have been "orphaned" by their son.

The Colonel and his wife, temperamentally poles apart, are a study in contrasts. In García Márquez men are flighty creatures, governed by whim, fanciful dreamers given to impossible delusions, capable of moments of haughty grandeur, but basically weak and unstable. Women, on the other hand, are solid, sensible, unvarying and down to earth, paragons of order and stability. They seem to be more at home in the world, more deeply rooted in their nature, closer to the center of gravity, therefore better equipped to face up to circumstances. García Márquez puts it another way: "My women are masculine." That may be only a slight overstatement. He sees women in profile, immutable as effigies, purposeful and resolute. They are less complex than his men, usually mere abstractions: a moving force in the background. Typical was the sexless Isabel in *La Hojarasca.* "There isn't much of the erotic in my books," he says. There are no love scenes, few moments of passion, or even—except for occasional loose vagaries—of sensuality. For one thing, his women as a rule are well past the age of anxiety. The Colonel's wife is cut of the same cloth as Isabel, worn and warped by life but still equal to all situations, a Rock of Gibraltar against winds and tides. She has backbone. Perhaps García Márquez projects a personal nostalgia into his female characters. Men, in his world, drift rudderless or flit like powdery moths into the light, only to burn their wings. In woman they find refuge and comfort. Woman is not a person but a principle.

Clear proof of this is "La Siesta del Martes" (Tuesday Nap), the earliest—it dates back to about 1948—and the author's favorite of the stories of *Los Funerales de la Mamá Grande*. It tells of the arrival in Macondo on a sleepy afternoon of a widow and her daughter, who have come to lay flowers on a grave in the cemetery. In the grave is the widow's son. The boy has been killed for housebreaking, and his mother is unwelcome in town. The scene centers on the priest's house, where the visitors have gone to ask for the key to the cemetery. Typically, "Siesta" is based on an incident García Márquez remembers from when he was a child. One day, he says, a woman and a girl came to town, bearing a bouquet of flowers, and the rumor soon spread: "There goes the mother of the thief." What struck him was the woman's unflagging dignity, her strength of character and moral fiber, in the midst of general hostility. In the story the widow cuts a forceful figure, proud and erect, a dramatic silhouette, a bit like a spirit out of a Greek tragedy. The portrait García Márquez draws of the violence of popular feeling in a small town recalls pages in a similar vein in *La Hojarasca*. The hidden threats that lie dormant in the drudgery of daily life are a recurrent theme in his work. But here they have a special force. As the widow, keys in hand, prepares to march out the priest's door to the cemetery, the whole town pours into the streets to glower at her. Like the doctor in *La Hojarasca*, who often braved the stony glare of public disapproval, not without flinching, she will have to walk the gamut. But at this point—the walk itself is not described—the story ends. We are left with a picture of something that has not yet happened. It is in this detail that the story lives. What he first imagined in the story, says García Márquez, was the part he left out. Though not entirely. Somehow what has been omitted is implicit, therefore all the more vivid and powerful.

It is the art of allusion and ellipsis, finely developed in García Márquez, that gives Macondo and its inhabitants their evocative force. *Funerales*—except for the rather specious title story, which satirizes a local matriarchy, while parodying the "official rhetoric" of Colombian newspaper writing—is well served by it. Macondo, as every mirage, leads a chimeric existence. It is less a place than a state of mind. In García Márquez environment reflects inner stress. Setting is character. If the moods of his people are closely tuned to the cycles of nature, it is because seasons are mental phases and outer temperature is a correlative of the climate of the soul. Thus, for the old Colonel, for instance, autumn is restlessness and malaise, winter is depression, spring is euphoria. It would seem at first sight that external factors determine vital attitudes, but actually what happens is the opposite. If in the traditional tropical novel—*La Vorágine,* Gallegos' *Canaima*—man, hardly more than a generic concept, was submerged and dispersed in nature, in García Márquez he has reconcentrated his psychic energies, reabsorbed his shadow. An optical change has taken place. The image is in the eye. Without sacrificing precise sociological observation, at which he excels, García Márquez individualizes, thereby humanizing, his characters. They are valid as types, but also distinct as people. If he tends occasionally to duplicate certain traits—his widows, doctors, and colonels are not always sufficiently differentiated from other stock members of their respective categories—it is not out of documentary concern but because his emotional and imaginative range is limited. A common subjective vision animates all his creations. The roles they play—whether as stars, stuntmen, or understudies—all derive from a single mental repertory.

An unknown grief camouflaged in clouds of hopeless wishful thinking is the common disease in Macondo, where fitful illusion alternates with abysmal pessimism. There is the prodigious carpenter, Baltazar, who, dreaming of fame and fortune, makes a fabulous bird cage for the child of the rich Montiels, only to have his work coldly rejected, whereupon, undeterred, he makes a gift of it and goes around town afterwards spending the imaginary money he has made on the sale.

The Montiels live in a mansion inherited from the local matriarch, Mamá Grande (a sort of latter-day version of Gallegos' Doña Bárbara) who collected vast properties in her lifetime and ruled over them by will and wile for ninety-two years. She had a finger in everything from mining to politics, rigged elections by inscribing dead souls on her voting rolls, dictated public opinion and Christian morals in her domains, and even controlled a stretch of territorial waters outside them. When she died, a virgin, "in a scent of holiness," surrounded by a huge intermarrying family with many illegitimate children, she left trunkloads of false documents and an empire consisting of a total of five municipalities and three hundred and fifty-two families of sharecroppers. The Pope and the President of the Republic attended her funeral, a national event conducted with great pomp and fanfare. She has proved as indomitable in death as she was in life. Her presence continues to inhabit her house long after it has been taken over by the Montiels. They are also an odd lot. Of José Montiel, the paterfamilias, we know that he was rich, tight, and taciturn, and that he died of the "fury." He has been survived by his shrewish widow, who wanders in the empty house calling for her overseer, Carmichael, a crass character who keeps opening his umbrella indoors, bringing down bad luck on everybody. When not scolding Carmichael, the widow sits staring vapidly out the window, thinking of her children, who live in Europe and refuse to return to this "land of savages." Also high on the temperature chart is the cranky Rebeca Buendía, the widow of José Arcadio Buendía, an adventurer who ran off with gypsies as a young man and traveled around the world sixty three times before meeting his mysterious death. Rebeca came to Macondo as an orphan child in the days of *La Hojarasca* carrying her parents' bones in a cloth sack. Now, disabled by age, she has become an embittered old crone who lives in "an enormous house with two corridors and nine bedrooms." She has hot sweats and raving fits. No better off, when you come to think of it, is Nora Jacob, an abandoned wife who suffers the advances of a stiff and prudish suitor, Benjamín, while bedding next door with one of the Asís brothers; or, for that matter, Mina, the town spinster, who earns a precarious living in pathetic isolation with her mother and blind grandmother making artificial flowers that wilt in her hands.

An equally dismal crowd are the representatives of officialdom in Macondo. There is the desultory priest, Padre Ángel, rankled by the general disregard for his investiture, which in fact he abdicated long ago. A qualm tortures him. He once refused an adulterous wife absolution, bringing about a family tragedy. Since then he has more or less given up. He sits in state in his empty confessional. The most colorful thing about him is his housekeeper, Trinidad, a vaguely androgynous adolescent with a throaty voice who sets mousetraps in the church every night and collects the dead mice in a shoebox. Punctually at sunset Padre Ángel, prolonging a habit of years, tolls the church bell twelve times—his sole activity—to ban the town's nightly film, which comes under such titles as *Midnight Virgin*. He might be sounding his own knell.

Macondo is a sinful town. Dr. Giraldo, cheery but ineffectual —a "raisonneur," the author calls him—receives forbidden newspapers and subversive notes in the mail. Guardiola, the barber, plots in silence while thriving on insidious gossip. Aurelio Escobar, the dentist, who sat out the revolution in his back room, gleefully tortures his political opponents while administering to them in the chair. Then there is the spiteful and vindictive Don Sabas, who also has a sadistic streak in him. He is a turncoat: an ex-partisan of the Revolution who bought his freedom denouncing his coreligionists. He also once purchased a woman for two hundred pesos, and got his money's worth out of her before dumping her. Rumor is—there must be a Snopes in the family— he made his money cheating in the mule trade. He is aided and abetted in one of his projects by Judge Arcadio, whose professional polish is the result of ten years of malpractice. In a similar position is the local telegraph operator, who spends his time tapping out love poems to an unknown female operator in another town. The only people doing business in town are the mountebanks, snake charmers, fortunetellers, and herbists. And, of course, the sweaty Syrian shopkeeper, Moisés, who must sell his length of cloth each morning to be able to praise God before midday. And, last but not least, Don Roque, the crooked and stingy bartender, who knows how to make a fast buck when the chance presents itself. In "En Este Pueblo No Hay Ladrones," he makes it off a good-for-nothing called Damasio, who breaks into the bar one night to steal some billiard balls. Unable to unload the loot, after loafing around with it for a while, meantime living off his wife, Damasio decides to return it. Don Roque catches him, calls in the police, and accuses him of having invaded the cash register.

A figure that grows to some prominence and seems to epito-mize the general mentality is the hard-boiled Mayor of Macondo, a shiftless and cynical character who runs the village through his henchmen, but suffers for it. Like everyone else, he has secret pangs of conscience. In his case they take the form of a horrible, incurable moral toothache. It gives the dentist a chance to work on him, with predictable results. There is no help for the Mayor. He pays his price, resigned. After all, his is the common plight. In fact, the Mayor is the soul of Macondo. He embodies its predicament. The author's attitude toward him is ambiguous. Certainly he is seen as a ruinous and despicable figure. But he is no simple caricature of a two-bit local strong man. Evidently, while disapproving of him, García Mârquez felt a deep sympathy for his creation. He was working at a level beyond moral judg-ment, toward understanding. There is a constant effort to grasp what is essential in the character. If the Mayor is as much a victim of the situation as anyone else, he nevertheless provides his own special comment on it. He is what García Márquez calls "a pure person, in the conventional sense of the word," in other words, an ascetic. He drinks only soda water, he is "chaste," constitutionally a stranger to love, therefore lives in terrible soli-tude. There is something unnatural about his austerity, which is obviously self-imposed, to counteract a basic turbulence. The

Mayor is one of those violent and hectic men who have to keep themselves in constant check in order not to stampede. There is panic in his restraint. He lives on the edge of chaos, in the daily hell of the excommunicated. When a circus comes to town and he blackmails the manager out of a female fortuneteller, in exchange for whose private services he will grant the circus a permit to operate on his premises, the ruse backfires. The woman expects to be taken to bed, but he never touches her. He is impotent. He agonizes in front of her. He is the stillborn child of desires that wither on the vine. Struck by his resentful apathy in sexual matters, some readers have wondered whether he is a homosexual. A moot point. In a sketch the author discarded, this accusation is actually brought against him. To allay the doubt, in another draft that was never used the author tried making him the secret lover of a local vamp, the succulent Rebeca de Asís. But that seemed farfetched. So he left the matter undecided.

In reality the Mayor represents a preliminary approach to a subject García Márquez wants to develop more fully one day: the tragic loneliness of despotism. He says he has always wanted to write a book about a Latin-American dictator sitting in his palace, disconnected from the world, an absolute power held in deadly awe by his superstitious, mythologizing people. He would be less concerned with social effects than with the pathology of character. He actually once wrote four hundred pages on the subject, then tore them up because he felt he was not yet ripe for the job. He could not get close enough to the man. He wanted to do an "inside" portrait. He has kept postponing the project—but not, he hopes, indefinitely. What he needs is an angle—an arm to twist. His strength is not in the full portrait of character, but in the quick sketch of conscience. As he stands now, the Mayor is not so much the miniature of a larger model as the essence of a general attitude. His toothache is Macondo's.

Whatever the causes of the toothache, its effects are widespread. They contaminate even the casual visitor to the town. Typical is what happens to the young protagonist of "Un Día Después del Sábado" (The Day after Saturday), an impoverished country boy on his way to the city to obtain a pension for his mother, a retired schoolteacher who wants the money to raise pigs. He stops off in Macondo for a bite at the station hotel, a moth-eaten hovel, misses his train, which carries off his money and documents, and finds himself stranded in Purgatory. It is the time, a few years back, when Rebeca Buendía woke up one morning to find her wire fence demolished by a flock of birds fallen out of the sky. The catastrophe coincides with the arrival of the young man, who seems to bring it with him. He is the Wandering Jew, in whose path, according to lore, all living beings are swept to destruction. At least this is the opinion of Padre Ángel's predecessor, Padre Antonio Isabel del Santísimo Sacramento del Altar, "the meek minister of God who at the age of ninety-four claimed to have seen the Devil three separate times." Padre Antonio Isabel, in his superannuated senility, says Mass in an empty church nowadays, when he is not playing games with the children in the park. He is in a particularly impressionable mood that morning because he had given extreme unction to a dying woman just the night before. He sees the Wandering Jew with flaming nostrils and burning emerald eyes. For Macondo, the young visitor, who brings no more than he finds there, is at once the Infidel and the Messiah. People flock to church for the first time in years, and Padre Antonio Isabel delivers the sermon of his life. Just in the nick of time, too. He was about to be relieved of his duties on the prompting of his long-standing enemy, the widow Rebeca—she has been writing the bishop, her uncle—who has good reason to wish him ill. As he knows, she has the death of her husband on her conscience, though she claims it was a suicide. And perhaps it was. The two are hard to tell apart in Macondo. Both are symptoms of the same affliction.

The history of Macondo, as recorded by García Márquez, reads like a journal of the plague years. There was blight, bust, and banditry in *La Hojarasca,* malice and moral cataclysm in *Coronel.* The mischief continues in *Funerales.* If the birds that fall on the widow Rebeca's fence recall the rats in Camus's *La Peste,* it is, says García Márquez, because "that is the book I would have liked to write." The plague as a symbol of the complete disruption of established values in a country chronically on the verge of anarchy appears in full force in *La Mala Hora*.

Here the misbegotten Macondo, clearly on the eve of a new revolution, breaks out in a rash of slanderous posters that are found plastered all over town one morning. They reveal family secrets, defame characters, demolish reputations. The result is complete pandemonium. The first sign of trouble is when César Montero, a rich lumberman, lets loose and murders his wife's lover, Pastor. The ghosts of the past suddenly revive: old feuds, incests, infidelities. To precipitate matters, a torrential rain floods the town, sweeping houses off their foundations. The crisis —a veritable Old Testament deluge—becomes paroxysmal. The only safe place is a plot of high land near the cemetery belonging to the Mayor, who makes the best of the godsend, selling the land at a handsome profit to the municipality. Macondo is in an orgy of despair. For García Márquez, an evangelist at heart, the picture—which has the atmosphere of one of those wild medieval saturnalias where men chased their women down the street, mothers abandoned their children, and people danced among the graves—resembles the political situation in Colombia today. Politics, in *La Mala Hora*, as elsewhere in his work, are unobtrusive but implicit. As things begin to get out of hand in Macondo, the Mayor, who has been content to stand idly by, finally decides that something has to be done. He declares a state of siege and a curfew.

The specters of repression are back. No one knows who is responsible for the slanderous posters. Neighbors denounce each other. The culprit is never discovered. In the end a scapegoat is found: a boy called Pepe Amador, who is caught circulating leaflets for the guerrilla forces always hanging around nearby. He is tortured and killed. The Mayor, afraid of the repercussions, tries to hide the boy's death by burying the corpse in the prison yard. But the whole town knows the truth. Under the festering shadow of collective blame, each man, alone as Oedipus with his conscience, discovers his own personal guilt. The posters had no single author. They speak for all. Each man has read his fate in them. The floodwaters gradually recede and life returns to normal. But Macondo will never be quite the same again. A murderer lurks in every heart, awaiting the moment of reckoning.

As a parable—if it was intended as such, which is doubtful— *La Mala Hora* is not entirely successful. It leaves too much to chance. It is a random book, by any standard. The construction is episodic, based on a series of short impulses that tend to trail off, or lead nowhere. Characters appear and disappear, scenes bloom and fade without a trace. For instance, the crime of passion that opens the book is soon forgotten; its protagonists are never heard from again. The author often improvises when he comes to a dead end. Characteristic is the solution proposed for the problem of the slanderous posters. It is symbolic, not real; a deus ex machina. Nevertheless, there are moments of emotional landslide in *La Mala Hora* that carry a strong hidden impact. As strings of anecdotes unwind, feeding each other, relaying seismic shivers, we have a sense of a carefully modulated chain reaction that perpetuates itself without ever reaching a climax. Macondo is in a constant state of becoming, a turbid flow that never flushes. If the book ends disappointingly, in mid-motion, as it were, it is, says García Márquez, that it was not really completed. Political and personal problems kept interfering while he was at work on it, until one day on a sudden urge—pressured by friends who wanted him to submit it to a contest organized by the Colombian Academy of Letters—he wound it up as best he could, leaving many loose ends.

What he did not neglect, however, was his language, always one of his strong points. He knows that "the problem of literature is words." He likes his work "clean" and clear-cut. *Coronel*, the ultimate in this vein, was written nine times. "I had the impression I was writing it in French," says García Márquez, referring to its sculptured slenderness. *Funerales* is equally spare and elegant. His sense of direction may not always be reliable, but once he finds his target his aim is sharp enough to split an atom.

How he came by his meticulous purity of style is something of a mystery. Perhaps, one may think, he found a precedent in Colombian purism, which may have a positive side, after all. He denies it. His language is not Colombia, he says simply, but his grandmother. She was a great storyteller. "She spoke this way." Her voice can often be heard like a whisper in the background, reminding García Márquez of the magic childhood world he grew up in, which infests so many of his best pages. There are scenes, gestures, phrases, situations that recur with obsessive regularity in his work. There are sudden beams of blinding light that create a sort of magnetic field around them, charged with unfathomable implications. Their meaning remains deliberately enigmatic. "What gives literary value is mystery," says García Márquez, who always tries to tap "the magic in commonplace events." In everything he writes there is this "lost chord," as he calls it. It may be a cryptic hint, a glimpse of something caught in flight, undecipherable as a dream lost on waking. Whatever its origin or appearance, it alludes to a private mythology that inhabits him like a message from the deep. He takes it as he finds it. He does not want to figure things out too much, he says, for fear of having them slip through his fingers. Therefore, he lets them take their course. For instance, there are frequent references in all his work to a mysterious Duke of Marlborough who seems to have some obscure connection with Macondo's civil wars. García Márquez says his grandfather used to sing a Spanish version of "Marlborough s'en va-t-en guerre." The only "guerre" he knew about as a child was the revolutionary wars the old man had fought in. Putting two and two together, he assumed the Duke had been in those wars. There is another bit of coded information in "La Viuda de Montiel" (Montiel's Widow), where an ancestral voice tells the widow she will die in her sleep "when your arm starts to go limp." His grandmother, he says, once appeared to his mother in a dream with that message, which became a family joke. Another phrase duly recorded in a story he borrowed from his wife, who woke up from a nap one afternoon and said: "I dreamed I was making buttered dolls." García Márquez does not tamper with these phrases; he keeps them in their pure state, with all their mystery intact. He depends on them. They give his work a lyrical quality that he values highly. But, above all, they keep the sources open. He would be lost without them.

To an extent—as he faces the increasingly difficult task of evoking a world that grows dimmer with time, perhaps eventually to vanish entirely—that is his problem today. "I go over my books a lot with a critical eye. I don't change my mind about them. I think they are good," he told us in Pátzcuaro. But his capacity for renewal, he added, is limited. He was being hard on himself. He said, with some rue, that he could only write about the things that fell within the immediate scope of his sensibility. What he could not assimilate directly—for instance, the experiences of a Latin-American dictator or, for that matter, those of his distant revolutionary hero, Colonel Aureliano Buendía, the subject of a fictional biography he once started and also had to throw out—seemed false to him. In a sense, he felt, he had backed himself into a corner with his manic concern for style and technique. He no longer seemed to have the feeling that he knew where he was going, as he had in *La Hojarasca* and, above all, in *Coronel*. "You reach a point," he told us, "where you can write a book on the basis of sheer technique." Cheating a little, he suggested, he could publish every year. It was this "empty virtuosity" that he dreaded more than anything else. The reading public might not notice it. But his friends would. And it is their opinion he respects.

He was going through one of those periods of doubt when he hardly puts pen to paper. At such times, he feels stale and depleted, develops a block, and decides he is finished. Perhaps, on this occasion, the lake had something to do with it. Its brooding presence was like an unhappy phase of his own mind. When he was not on the set, he told us, he worked hard, with dogged persistence, rising at six in the morning "to keep the motor warm." But a whole day's work might yield no more than eight or ten lines of a paragraph that was as likely as not to end up in the wastebasket.

Yet, since then, Angel Gabriel has made a comeback. He has rediscovered his secret book, which is growing faster than ever. The next installment, due to appear in March or April, 1967,

will be called *Cien Años de Soledad* (A Hundred Years of So
tude). It will be the long-awaited biography of the elusi
Colonel Aureliano Bunedía. All of a sudden his creator seems to
have him at his fingertips. "I'm on top of the world," he wrote us
happily in November, 1965. "After five years of absolute sterility,
the book is literally gushing from me, without any problems of
words." He says it promises to run to four or five hundred pages,
a veritable marathon for him. It has visited him like an old
friend. "In a sense, it's the first novel I started to write when I
was seventeen, but much broader now. It's not only the story of
Colonel Buendía, but that of his whole family, from the founding of Macondo to the day the last Buendía commits suicide a
hundred years later, putting an end to the line." There are complications along the way. Names, for instance, in accordance with
Macondo's laws of recurrence, tend to appear in duplicate or
triplicate. A chronology of events and a genealogical table might
have to accompany the book, "because the Buendías were in the
habit of naming their children after their parents, and occasionally havoc reigns. In the hundred years of history there are four
José Arcadio Buendías and three Aurelianos."

Of the José Arcadios, the most notable was the first of the line,
the founder of Macondo, a young patriarch in his day who
arrived in town through the sierra with his plucky wife Ursula,
another of García Márquez' female bastions, and a man's life on
his conscience. He was a bird lover who built traps and cages to
fill the town with his feathered friends. He was also something of
a mad scientist and inventor, and a great friend of an itinerant
gypsy band led by the visionary Melquíades, a globe-trotting
magician who in his various transformations had suffered the
plagues of the world—scurvy, beri-beri, pellagra—and survived
them all. Melquíades and his people, and their descendants, heirs
to alchemic secrets, bring wonders to town: a magnet that rips
nails from the walls, a magnifying glass that concentrates solar
rays, a telescope, a block of ice, flying carpets. With an early
daguerreotype machine of theirs José Arcadio tries to photograph
God, and with their sextants, astrolabes, and compasses he discovers, to the general consternation, that the world is round. His

wife lives to be a hundred and fifteen, and he in his old age goes completely mad and dies tied to a chestnut tree in the yard, chattering away deliriously in Latin and discussing theology with the priest.

But perhaps it is Colonel Aureliano, his son, who casts the longest shadow. He is "the most outstanding member of the second generation, which fought thirty-two civil wars and lost them all." Aureliano, in the course of his adventurous life, fathered seventeen natural children, who were all massacred in a political purge, at least once miraculously escaped the firing squad and died proudly urinating in his yard.

There is, says García Márquez, a kind of finality in it all. *Cien Años de Soledad* will provide "a sort of base for the puzzle I've been piecing together in my previous work. Here almost all the clues are given. You learn of the beginning and the end of the characters, and get the complete story, without gaps, of Macondo." We hear of the first plague—insomnia and amnesia—brought to town by Rebeca Buendía and spread far and wide—until Macondo has to be quarantined—by Ursula's homemade candies; of the arrival of the first Mayor, known as the Corregidor (Corrector), and that of the first priest, Padre Nicanor Reyna, who is levitated each time he drinks a cup of hot chocolate; of the first death, which inaugurates the cemetery with the body of Melquíades; and of the tragic fate of the last suicidal Aureliano, who is born to solitude with an old family stigma: a pig's tail. In *Cien Años,* more than ever, the dead come back to life and flowers rain down from the sky. In spite of which, says García Márquez, "it's probably the least mysterious of all my books, because the author tries to take the reader by the hand so he won't ever get lost or be left in the dark. With this book, I conclude my cycle on Macondo, and turn to something completely different in the future."

What that will be, we have on good authority, is another revivalist effort, this one, according to our source, the promised magnum opus on despotism. It will be called *El Otoño del Patriarca* (Autumn of the Patriarch). "It won't, as I thought," says García Márquez, a man who has finally found the right strings to set his genes to dancing, "be a very long book, only just a bit longer than *Coronel.* I don't know why it hadn't occurred to me before: it has to be the dictator's long monologue as he stands trial in a popular court. I'm working on the notes."

The chances are, we gather, there will be no garbage disposal this time. It was never much of a solution anyway. The worst part about throwing things out, as García Márquez knows, is that one may well live to regret it. A sketch of his entitled "Monólogo de Isabel Viendo Llover en Macondo" (Monologue of Isabel Watching the Rain Fall in Macondo), which he deleted from *La Hojarasca,* has since—friends persuaded him to let it be published in a magazine—become his most anthologized piece, has even been included as a reading in a textbook. Which goes to show once again that one of the perils and pleasures of writing is that one may well be best remembered for the things one has tried to forget.

X

Mario Vargas Llosa,
or the Revolving Door

WE are still on the way to our "complete" novel. The road
has been uphill, but our traction seems to be increasing.
A sign of this is Vargas Llosa. Just four years ago, at the ripe age
of twenty-six, with only two published works to his name
—a collection of short stories and a novel—he already stood
out among our young writers. It was obvious from the beginning
that he was a man with a big natural talent and the dedication
to go with it. Here was someone who knew what he was doing
and had the means to do it. He seemed to have been born with a
golden touch. He had ease, power, self-assurance. Recognition
had come to him quickly, but he had earned it honestly and
could live up to its demands. There is a second novel now, bigger
and better than the first. It is a fiery tone poem in chromatic scale
that scores on almost every level, raising the Latin-American
novel to a new peak.

It took Peruvian literature several centuries to get moving.
The old indigenous traditions recollected by Peru's first man of
letters, the "Inca" Garcilaso de la Vega, author of a set of *Royal
Commentaries,* were already decadent by the time they were
finally ruptured by the Spanish Conquest. Centuries of Spanish

rule practically obliterated them, and interest in them only revived with Independence. Then Ricardo Palma, a lone figure in a bleak cultural landscape, made a polite effort to breathe new life into them with his series of *Tradiciones Peruanas*. His verve as a storyteller earned him a permanent place in the pantheon of Peruvian letters. But when he died no one followed suit. For decades Peru, with its troubled history, remained a cultural backwater. As usual, it was the poets who picked up first. There was César Vallejo (1892–1938), a great bard with a Nerudan sweep, who was a lone eminence in his lifetime. Since then Indian life and outlook have been recorded from the "inside" by the knowledgeable José María Arguedas. There has been the pointillist regionalism of Ciro Alegría. But somehow none of these authors seem quite contemporary any more. Vargas Llosa clearly overshadows them all. He represents a coming of age, a widening of perspectives. He writes about Peru, but his work has a satisfying complexity that gives it a more universal relevance.

Like so much of note in our culture, Vargas Llosa, a quiet man who keeps his thoughts to himself, seems to have come out of nowhere. In a country where economic factors, among others, have reduced literature to the status of a marginal activity, a sideline desultorily practiced by honorable but frustrated Sunday writers, he has distinguished himself for the sort of uncompromising single-mindedness that is a sure sign of authentic vocation. He manages to combine an unusual talent and sensibility with a rare seriousness and professionalism. So far he has shown less depth than temperament. But he is a solid builder. His characterizations, though sketchy, are skillfully patterned and have a kind of germinal force that can only come from healthy roots in rich soil. He is something of a brooder, who can torture a scene without, perhaps, sufficiently complicating its protagonists. But he can always sustain a dramatic moment. If he tends to reduce human nature to a few basic emotions, none of them particularly exalted, he is adroit in handling these emotions, often with tumultuous results. He has a special, Hemingway-like knack for crisp dialogue. A sharp eye for detail and expert timing help give his prose drive and density. He is at home in the world of the modern novel; he ranges freely through a large variety of literary techniques, exploiting them all to good advantage, without falling into mannerism. He is an expert structurer who balances the tensions of plot and character with an unfailing instinct for order and cohesion.

Vargas Llosa was born in 1936, in Arequipa. He has memories of a somewhat traumatic childhood. His parents were divorced before he was born. Soon after, he was transplanted to Cochabamba (Bolivia), where he was brought up by his mother and his maternal grandparents. He remembers he was a spoiled and pampered child, whose whims were law. But not for long. His years of grammar school innocence came to an abrupt end just before he was ten years old. His family moved back to Peru, first to the town of Piura (1945), then, as his parents reunited, to Lima (1946). Piura, which in his mind has become the apotheosis of the shabbiness of small-town middle-class life, was a shattering experience. He recalls a slummy highland outpost in the middle of a sandy wasteland. Lima was an improvement. Three or four years in clerics' hands—in a religious school—delayed the final blow. But the ax fell (in 1950) when, partly because of his dubious literary learnings, he was sent as a boarder to the Leoncio Prado, a peculiar educational institution in an unclassifiable category somewhere between a reformatory and a military school.

The two years he weathered at the Leoncio Prado, he says, probably marked him forever. Certainly they helped shape his outlook on life, which could be described as Darwinian. The Leoncio Prado is the subject of his first novel, *La Ciudad y Los Perros* (Time of the Hero, 1962). The title is revealing. We are in a world where dog eats dog. The key element in this world is raw violence. The weak founder, only the fittest survive. Vargas Llosa draws a painful picture of moral and physical squalor. He is often brutal, he spares no one. He has even retained the name of his school. The portrayal has been considered accurate—or slanderous—enough to warrant an official reaction. When *La Ciudad y los Perros* appeared in Peru in a paperbound edition, a thousand copies of the book were put to the torch at the Leoncio Prado in an official ceremony. Two generals made public declarations to the effect that it was the nauseating product of a sick mind. The author was called an enemy of Peru and a Communist.

Scandal and publicity are the last things one would associate with the person of Vargas Llosa. He is a gentle soul, smiling, shy, introspective. His sudden fame is still a constant surprise to him. *La Ciudad y los Perros* has obtained a far wider audience than he ever expected. It had grown to such gigantic proportions at one point—1,500 pages—that is had never occurred to him that any publisher would be willing to take it on. "I'd thought that as usually happens in Peru I'd have to pay for it out of my own pocket," he says. "It had taken me three years to write. I calculated it would take me at least five years of hard work to publish." Someone suggested Spain. He had his doubts because of the censorship. "Besides, I thought at the time the novel was a complete failure. I was going to let several years go by and then rewrite it." Nevertheless, he mailed it to Seix-Barral in Barcelona. Eight months went by before there was any news. But then one day he received an enthusiastic telegram. And since then fortune has been smiling on him. The book has certainly been overpraised. Critics have gone wild over it; it was a runner-up for the Prix Formentor in 1963. It has won important prizes in Spain, where a jury member for the Premio Biblioteca Breve was moved to acclaim it as the best novel written in the Spanish language in the past thirty years. Publishers have also fallen all over themselves to get their hands on it. It is already in the process of being translated into just about every major language.

Vargas Llosa is a liberal arts graduate—from the University of San Marcos in Lima and the University of Madrid, where he got his doctorate on a scholarship in 1959. His first appearance in the literary world was during his second visit to Piura, in 1952—with a play, *La Huida* (The Escape). He was in the last year of high school at the time, just out of the Leoncio Prado, to some extent self-supporting—he worked part time as a newspaperman—and therefore relatively independent. Piura no longer seemed quite as much of a hellhole as it had before. In fact, he remembers this period as one of the happiest in his life. Lima had, however modestly (mostly in the form of second-rate Argentine touring companies), initiated him into the theater. The medium had appealed to him and during the summer holidays he saw his chance to try his hand at it. *La Huida,* with its elements of legend and mythology, which recommended it to local taste, was given a full performance. It was a community event—and a big success. Whatever its merits, the play was helped along, he says, by his prestige as a big-city visitor. Today he tends to disown it.

In 1958 Vargas Llosa published a volume of short stories entitled *Los Jefes* (The Leaders). Most of these stories center around backstreet life in Lima and Piura, where the struggle for survival is just as tough as it ever was in military school. The protagonists are hard-boiled adolescents—or postadolescents—who live by a system of rugged priorities established in hand-to-hand battle. The prevailing climate is that of gang warfare where grudges lead to deadly feuds that take their toll in blood. Every act is a test of fire. Wits and will, and the force or ability to impose them, are the sole measures of a man's virility. Conflicts are worked out by challenge and contest. What emerges is a sort of cutthroat male ethic, brutal, but in its own way dignified. The author has not yet found his depth. The texture is light. What mainly recommends the stories, apart from their straightforward simplicity, is the sense they give of constituting a microcosmic version of the author's view of the world. But he justly considers them a very preliminary stage in his work.

Vargas Llosa has been deeply marked—"poisoned," he says—by French literature. Back home, in secondary school, he discovered the great nineteenth-century French novelists. He was an assiduous, almost "maniacal," reader of Dumas and Victor Hugo, figures he still considers venerable. But his particular admiration is Flaubert. He did a stint in the Alliance Française in Lima. By the time he was in the university he could read French fluently. The world—to use the words of his countryman Ciro Alegría—must have seemed "wide and foreign." His horizons were enormously broadened by a close reading of Sartre, whose essays (*Situations*) he rates very highly. There are what might be called glandular affinities between his fictional characterizations and those of Sartre's stories (in *Le Mur*—"L'Enfance d'un Chef," for instance). For years he yearned to travel to France. A tour won as a prize in a short-story contest held in Lima (in 1958) by the *Revue Française* brought him to Paris under very favorable conditions. He was shown the town and lodged in a fancy hotel, next door to a beauty queen. In 1959 he returned on his own—under somewhat different circumstances—and, except for an occasional visit to Lima, and in 1965 a two-week stay in Cuba, where he did literary jury duty for the Casa de las Américas, he lived there until early 1966 when he packed up and moved back home.

The first months in Paris were no holiday. He had a wife to support, he was jobless and broke. Home was a garret; the days were spent ringing doorbells to ask for work. Finally he landed a grisly job as a teacher at Berlitz. Salaries were extortionary, working hours practically round the clock. Eventually he graduated to copywork in the Spanish department of Agence France Presse. From there he moved on to the French Radio-TV Network where for a time he held a comfortable evening job of short hours and good pay helping organize short-wave broadcasts to Latin America.

As the charm of Paris gradually wore off for him, he set his mind on returning to Peru. But how to make a living there? He dreaded the thought of newspaper or radio work. In Peru they require demeaning compromises. Vargas Llosa, though of what would seem to be a generally Marxist cast of thought, is not politically militant ("After injustice," he says, "what I most detest is dogmatism"; besides, in his country, where six million people—50 percent of the population—do not vote, politics is a "caricature"), but he realizes that in Peru the press, in one way or another, is a more or less direct instrument of minority interests with which his conscience will not allow him to make peace. What matters to him is to be able to write. That he could do in Paris. The problem of language obsessed him. Like all expatriates commuting between two cultures, he had nightmares about losing contact with his mother tongue. But in his case the danger was not imminent. He made a point of reading and working in Spanish. In a sense, he says, living abroad as a foreigner in a linguistically hermetic society even enriched—"impassioned"— his relationship with his mother tongue. Keeping him company in his voluntary exile was his second wife, Patricia, a Peruvian girl whom he married in 1965 and took to live in a suburb overlooking a windy freeway. Perhaps she gave him the moral support he needed finally to face Peru again.

When we first met him, in early 1965, he was alone in a two-room bachelor apartment with an unmade bed near the Luxembourg Palace. We went in through an old carriage entrance, and up a tortuous, dim staircase to a third-floor landing where the shadows suddenly parted as he opened the door with a smile, welcoming the inevitable trespassers. Guests were on their way out: well-wishers who had dropped by, making him fidgety. In spite of all his efforts to erase his traces, he told us, people always managed to hunt him down somehow. He had his doubts about us, we gathered, and would have avoided us had he been able to. But we already had a foot in the door. And, though he dislikes talking about himself, we sat and chatted for a long while. Around us were overloaded bookshelves, family snapshots, disorderly furnishings—a littered worktable by the window—Peruvian souvenirs: a somewhat discolored but still delicately textured strip of ancient Indian tapestry in a frame on the wall; ritual masks of somber cast, in copper and gold. There were many asides in the conversation, when he lowered his voice, as if there were someone sleeping in the next room. The mortuary splendors of the late afternoon soon dwindled into twilight.

He is a perfectionist who agonizes over the problem children he brings into the world and tries to control every aspect of his work, from conception to publication. *La Ciudad y los Perros* was held up for nearly fifteen months as he haggled over seven or eight lines the editor wanted to suppress. Proofs and manuscripts piled up on his desk as he cut and spliced and picked out last-minute printing errors. His second novel, *La Casa Verde* (The Green House), also needed an interminable amount of minor readjustments. At one point its shadings and involutions expanded it to almost a thousand typewritten pages. In *La Ciudad y los Perros* even the title gave him birth pangs. For a while it was *Los Impostores* (The Impostors)—an allusion to a dominant trait of the characters involved. In *La Ciudad y los Perros* the allusion is more oblique, but no less pertinent. The perros (dogs) are the first-year students in military school. They are so named by the upperclassmen—a significant detail, says Vargas Llosa, because it shows that "the students themselves conceive of the school as a sort of ascesis, an apprenticeship of virility. To earn this virility they have to go through certain tests and trials. They must undergo sacrifice, mortification, and violence to earn their right to be cadets, in other words, to rise from the status of dogs to that of men."

The school, at once a place and a time—adolescence—is a vast proving ground. *La Ciudad y los Perros* is fundamentally a novel of growing up. Its central theme is the initiation into manhood, "arbitrarily, even monstrously conceived," says Vargas Llosa, "by the students as well as by the teachers." The military setting provided by the Leoncio Prado—which is run by professional soldiers—creates a crisis situation that is further exacerbated by the fact that the school is a melting pot open to boys of all social classes: the children of workers, who can gain entry through scholarships; the wellborn, who are interned for their delinquent tendencies. Frictions arise. Everyone is quickly reduced to the minimum common denominator. The hothouse atmosphere favors the development of microbe cultures. Against this background the characters go through unexpected metabolic changes. We have Alberto, born to wealth and affluence, an endearing character, jaunty, well-meaning, but superficial and a bit hypocritical. There is Jaguar, a working-class product, a terrible troublemaker, rabidly instinctual, savagely entrenched in his personal code of ethics, which amounts to a sort of heroic hoodlumism. In opposition to and at the same time in complicity with the students stand the school authorities: Captain Garrido, rigid and dour, an embodiment of the system; Lieutenant Huariña, a spineless bureaucrat; Lieutenant Gamboa, a man of personal integrity, but also a more or less willing, if unwitting, cog in the predatory machinery. The focal point of the drama is

Cadet Arana, a meek soul known to his schoolmates as the Slave. Arana, says Vargas Llosa, is "an intimidated, inhibited, pacifist nature." Organically unable to cope with his surroundings, therefore to fight infection, he is particularly susceptible to the strictures of the regime, which "will accent—or deform—that nature. Because what at bottom is normal—it's normal, isn't it, for a person to be more or less allergic to violence?—will become a warp in him. I think that in the case of the Slave all that violence, that coercion exerted on him by his schoolmates is really nothing but a defense reflex on their part. In that world the best way to show your virility is to impose it at the expense of somebody else. You find someone to pick on. In that sense the Slave is what we might call everybody's scapegoat."

The plot that unfolds in this highly combustible atmosphere has the unsentimental intensity of a true childhood saga. Cava, one of the more sober and dutiful cadets—unlike most of his companions, he seriously envisages a military career—measures up to the principles of his sect—known as the Circle—by stealing some exam papers. His act, promptly discovered, sets off a series of catastrophic events. The whole school is punished: restricted to the school grounds. The one who suffers most from the curfew is the Slave, who has a girl friend downtown. Everyone knows the school's discipline is too much for the Slave, who is constantly on the point of cracking up. As the story goes, Cava is quickly identified as the culprit who stole the exams, and expelled. Someone must have ratted on him. Suspicion falls on the Slave. Jaguar, ruthless leader of the Circle, wreaks retribution on him during a military drill, putting a bullet through his head. A scandal is expected. There is an investigation. The school's reputation is at stake. Nobody has actually seen Jaguar with his finger on the trigger, but everyone, particularly Alberto, who knows to what lengths Jaguar's twisted mind can lead him, realizes he is responsible for the murder. Alberto accuses him before the school authorities. But to no avail. The death has been declared an accident and the case is closed. Rumors must be quashed. Alberto is the only one capable of demanding justice. He seems determined to rise to the occasion. But his moral fortitude is too frail to resist the threats of blackmail that are brought to bear against him by the authorities, who have uncovered some dirty texts of toilet humor he has written. He gives in. So does Lieutenant Gamboa, who has endangered his own career backing him in his accusations. Lieutenant Gamboa is a particularly pathetic case. He is a career soldier, a man of firm principles, decent, honest. He finds himself in a terrible predicament. On the one hand, he is expecting a promotion for honorable—and unquestioning—service. On the other, he has personally received Jaguar's cynical confession. What must he do? Go out on a limb and turn in the culprit? Keep the information to himself? In his moment of truth, he capitulates. As Alberto, he fails the big test.

"Lieutenant Gamboa," says Vargas Llosa, "is a man who up until that moment has never had occasion to question the system in which he is submerged. Everything has seemed very clear to him. He is going to discover a whole new unsuspected dimension of the system. It so happens that the system in which he believed blindly—without stopping to think about it, accepting it as the natural order of things—might turn out to be not quite so congenitally just as he'd assumed. It might be founded on nothing but lies. He is then confronted with the possibility of a choice. He tries to be consistent, coherent, and that creates a terrible contradiction for him. Because, precisely, in order to be coherent, consistent in regard to that system, he needs to disrupt it, in the process damaging himself. He doesn't rebel. He submits."

The author does not judge him—he secretes the context, puts its constituent elements to work, then records the events that follow, hovering overhead like an omniscient presence in perpetual flow through characters and situations. He plunges us into an ocean of willful terrorism. The reader absorbs the environment by a sort of osmosis. The law of the land is lawlessness. The hardships the students impose on themselves are immeasurably more rigorous—and intricate—than those inherent in the official structure. Every man is a prisoner of his own baser instincts: sadism, various forms of deviate or anomalous sexuality: bestiality, homosexuality, onanism. We have an almost gratuitously masochistic character, Boa, one of the members of Jaguar's gang, who has sexual relations with a little bitch called Malpapeada. He tortures the poor dog with relish (at one point he breaks her leg). His cruelty is not only disinterested but even an affirmation of affection. "Boa is the most instinctive of all the characters," the author tells us. "His means of expression are entirely on the instinctual level. Instinct is what prevails in him; it's the strongest bond joining him to the world and to others."

Violence, says Vargas Llosa, "is a sort of fatality in this world." At any rate, it appears in its pure form here. But, in the author's vision, it is a dominant characteristic not only of adolescent environment but of all human society, and in particular his own, where class stratification has become so thoroughly petrified that there is little room left for any sort of peaceful progress. Outside the school the struggle takes more devious forms, becomes more a matter of wile and guile than tooth and claw. But it continues unabated.

"Speaking generally, I think life in society by its very nature commits man to a series of constant tests, of permanent conflicts which, in accordance with a community's culture, its stage of development, will be more or less forthright or circuitous. In an underdeveloped country these manifestions are epidermic, external. There is no possibility of dialogue, discussion, debate—no channeling. . . . I think in a country like mine violence is at the root of all human relations. It's ever present at all moments of an individual's life. The individual asserts himself, consolidates himself socially, overcoming all sorts of resistances. His personality is formed in opposition to that of others. There's a sort of jungle from which there's no possible escape. Basically it's due to the fact that Peru is a country where the social structures are based entirely on a sort of total injustice that extends to all aspects of life. The resulting violence, depending on where it occurs on the social scale, may take a primitive, outward form as, for instance, in a militarized institution, where that is not only regimented but actually vindicated—the mere fact of considering virility, maleness, and physical prowess as the main human qualities goes to show that—or else a very indirect, very insidious, very underhanded form, as might be the case in upper middle-class families, which aren't aware of being the beneficiaries of the surrounding violence but are nevertheless conditioned by it."

For Vargas Llosa this violence is not only a conditioning but a determining factor in human life. He knows this from long personal acquaintance with it. He says: "I think one can only write from personal experience.Now, my life has been a bit out of the ordinary, and besides, marked by a series of violent events. I was a very spoiled child, very conceited, brought up, I suppose, almost like a girl. So much so that I must have been extraordinarily difficult when my mother put me in school early, at the age of five [in Cochabamba]. That created quite a problem for me. My schoolmates were always older than I was. I felt a gap between us. That cropped up later when I arrived in Peru for my fifth year of grade school. I was ten years old; my classmates were thirteen or fourteen, little men already. It was a horrible year. It was my first glimpse of the adult world." Then came the Leoncio Prado. "My father sent me there." Vargas Llosa's father, a newspaperman who worked for the International News Service, was something of an absent figure in his life. "I met him very late. I'd been convinced he was dead. When I discovered him, there was no longer any possibility of communication between us. We got along very badly the years we lived together. Our characters were poles apart. There was a sort of mutual distrust between us. We were almost strangers. He disapproved of the way I'd been brought up, pampered and coddled, and found me willful and soft. He thought the Leoncio Prado would make a man of me. For me it was like discovering Hell—an unknown reality, the opposite side of life. It marked me to the core. At home nobody had ever raised a finger to me. In school we were kicked around. What counted was craft and brute force. I suppose in a sense that left a certain image of man engraved in my mind that I'm not easily going to get rid of. . . . *La Ciudad y los Perros* bears witness to that time, that atmosphere, and that state of mind. Ever since I was in the Leoncio Prado I wanted to write something about it. Although the idea of writing was something I had before. It was one of the reasons why there were always disagreements between my father and myself. I used to write in Piura, I remember, and my grandparents, my uncles, applauded me for it. They thought it was cute. When my father discovered that inclination in me he was frightened. He thought something was seriously wrong. The Lima bourgeoisie thinks that being a writer or an artist is only a pretext for being either a pansy or a good-for-nothing. The saddest part about it is that in many cases they're right. So my vocation grew and solidified a bit secretly. It was an outlet for my revolt against the Leoncio Prado. At that time literature became something very important for me. Also something hidden. Because in school one didn't dare show any signs of that."

In some ways secrecy was a boon to Vargas Llosa. It forced him from an early date to turn inward, though it also had its inconveniences. It isolated him. "It cut me off completely from what had been my world," he says. "A world for which I have no sympathy, but quite the contrary, nothing but contempt and revulsion; the Peruvian bourgeoisie is the worst thing under the sun: an absolutely noxious class, infected with prejudices, ignorant, and hypocritical. Nevertheless, for a child to feel cut off from his class and not incorporated into any other means solitude and neurosis." In his destitution, "literature was an escape, a way of justifying my life, compensating for everything in it that saddened and disgusted me." It was also a means of recovering a lost reality, bridging a gap to the outer world. He used it, he says, to "vindicate" his situation, "to gain a foothold in the world. I think literature has always been that. The road to it has always led through that type of experience—of alienation. Writing is a way of fighting back, of coming up for air, rejoining a society from which one has—or thinks one has—been excluded, or a family world from which one feels one has been expelled."

The paradox, he points out, is that trying to rejoin the world through literature—through irreality—is really to isolate oneself even more. "As one writes, the gap grows larger, bringing on a proportional increase in the need to write. The literary vocation is like a tapeworm in the pit of your stomach, growing, feeding on itself, constantly demanding more. It really never saves you. It's the exercise of literature itself that keeps the writer going."

Seen from that point of view, *La Ciudad y los Perros* is a

desperate search for wholeness. A sort of vicarious return to the
womb of a lost reality. Vargas Llosa fights hard to minimize and
eliminate the distance that separates him from it. The techniques
he uses all serve this main purpose. They are means of seduction.
Flashbacks, interior monologues, shifting points of view, all tend
almost compulsively to sink us up to our ears in that festering
hotbed in which the characters breed and incubate. The seduc-
tions are not always equally effective. At least one of them is a bit
too coy. Vargas Llosa has the bad habit of withholding vital
information. For instance, there is a whole series of episodes—
often spaced far apart, but tonally and thematically related—
where we are inside the thoughts of a character—the Jaguar, it
turns out—whose identity is revealed only at the very end of the
book. The holdingback is meant to make the ultimate disclosure
doubly forceful, but instead it seems merely obfuscating. The
reason is that we are denied all clues that might put us on the
right scent, which is not only disconcerting but a little unfair. In
the end we feel cheated. Then there is a problem of intensity.
Certain scenes necessarily set outside the school—to place the
characters socially—seem pale in contrast to those set inside.
There were more of them originally, Vargas Llosa says. Cutting
too many out probably contributed to the imbalance. And then
there is the epilogue, which tries to wrap everything up neatly
and ends up a ragbag. Here Vargas Llosa relaxed his hold. There
is a break in the natural sequence of events, then, out of
nowhere, a surprise ending. All these contrivances—born of what
would seem a lack of deeper motivation in the characters—let us
down. But they have a purpose. *La Ciudad y los Perros* is
intravenous. Its success hinges entirely on the author's ability to
maintain in the reader the illusion of an almost physical, visceral
involvement in the flux and flow of reality. The function determines the form. Thus there is a character—Boa—who was created largely to give us direct access, on the sensory level, to this
reality. Boa is a sort of all-seeing eye, a delicate apparatus that
records the visual and tactile aspect of experience—unedited. He
thinks in images and quick perceptions. He never tells a story.
The story tells itself through him.

The author says: "To reveal certain facets of the school it was necessary to relate a series of episodes, of scenes of great crudeness which would have been very difficult to justify literarily without falling into truculence, exhibitionism, or pornography—in other words, into mere artifice, into irreality. Straightforward narration didn't seem the right way to handle those scenes. I tried it in the first version of the novel—through dialogues or purely descriptive passages. For instance, the scenes of collective masturbation; the episode involving the rape of a chicken; the episode dealing with the attempt to violate one of the boys. They were unreal, because of their exorbitance, their gratuitous violence. Reality cannot be bodily transplanted into fiction. The scenes weren't alive. So then it occurred to me that the only way to make them valid would be to present them through intermediaries, third persons—an approach in which violence itself would be cushioned and mitigated. After a series of trial runs I discovered that the best way to cushion those scenes without at the same time diminishing what we might call their definitiveness was to see them through the eyes and consciousness of a roving spectator. But it had to be a very unintellectual spectator, so the violence wouldn't be congealed, rationalized, explained. That was how Boa was born. Boa is always used as an instrument to reveal the most abysmal, most innocently horrible, side of the school. To some extent he's the embodiment, the personification of that horror. Because the fact that he has sexual relations with a dog is rather monstrous, and also perfectly forthright. But it was necessary to convey all that more or less chaotically. Which accounts for his chaotic monologues. He's never seen from the outside. He's a flow, a protoplasmatic existence."

The scenes viewed through Boa have that same protoplasmatic quality. We are enveloped in a sort of miasma. The language performs an important function here. It not only evokes violence but exudes it. It assimilates reality to its own rhythm. It becomes lyrical. Its effects operate on the level of poetic idiom, asserting a hypnotic hold over the reader, who is swept along in the tide, which often carries a heavy load of obscenity and abuse.

"That's one of the problems of realism. I don't think realism in literature can ever be a direct enunciation of reality. Litera-

ture is always a transposition of reality. The segment of life
chosen by the author must be transformed, manipulated, compiled in a very special way to prevent it from being frozen, bled
on its way into literature." The author tells us that once upon a
time he was a great reader—and admirer—of pornographic
literature. But "much less nowadays. Because the great short-
coming of that literature is just that: it's unreal. Not because the
incidents or events it records don't correspond to reality but
because, literarily speaking, they haven't been sufficiently transposed. All those subjects or incidents or events or areas of experience on which society imposes a kind of collective censorship
immediately create resistances in the reader, who tends to reject
them, to refuse to believe in them. The great danger then is to
fall into exhibitionism, which I think automatically invalidates
the experience. That's why in *La Ciudad y los Perros* the crudest
scenes are the ones I worked and reworked the most. They're
much more highly transposed than the others. Since it was impossible to make the students speak without using bad words, under
certain given circumstances that I felt justified those words, I
tried to give them a purely phonetic value. All that more or less
scatological language that might awaken a resistance in the
reader, I went to great pains to impose it on him by virtues of
another sort. I wanted the movement of the prose to be such that
the 'offensive' word would always acquire a character of such
overwhelming necessity that it couldn't be rejected, that it would
be anxiously awaited almost, impatiently anticipated by the
reader. For instance, in the episode of the chickens."

Here we have an episode that echoes and shadows many others.
It is treated as representative, rather than specific. To reinforce
it, instead of isolating it, Vargas Llosa weaves it in with the
chronologically and spatially unrelated scene of the rape of the
boy. The fusion—or transfusion—heightens both experiences.
They percolate into each other. Vargas Llosa compares them to
the two halves of an hourglass. His object, he says, is "to create
an ambiguity, in other words, to associate within a single narrative unit two or more episodes that occur at very different times
and places. So that the currents, flowing back and forth, will

enrich each other." Violence tends to freeze over. He thaws it. The surrounding language becomes "a sort of vertiginous rhythm that progressively captures the reader, so thoroughly submerging him in the scene that in the end he will have to suspend judgment, accept everything, fully integrate himself into it. I think that's the obligation of the writer who wants to be a realist: to use all the means at his disposal to keep reality from dying on the operating table."

Certainly in *La Ciudad y los Perros* the distance between reality and the reader is minimal. Vargas Llosa insists on total participation. "That's why I think the novel is the supreme genre," he says, "because it's the genre that installs the reader at the very heart of the reality evoked in the book. The author's obligation is to keep him there. The authors I admire and reread are never those that demand to be admired at a distance. They're those that snatch me up, sweep me off my feet, and install me in 'their' new world, which will ultimately permit me to discover my own world. Reality is chaotic. It has no order. But when translated into fictional terms it acquires one. The stricter the construction of a novel the better will be the understanding of the world it evokes."

Vargas Llosa works toward the complete grasp of a situation. He will write around a scene until he feels he has wholly encompassed it. There is, of course, the danger that too many devices will draw attention to themselves and defeat his whole purpose by running interference. They do sometimes. But he is skillful enough not to get stuck in the quagmire. A more serious drawback in his method is that it is antieconomical—circular, repetitious: a series of superpositions, backsteps, reconsiderations.

He defends it, saying: "I think every method, every procedure must be conditioned by the fictional material at hand. The best novels are always those that exhaust their material, that don't throw a single light on reality, but many. The points of view that can be brought to bear on reality are infinite. It's impossible, of course, for any novel to exhaust all of them. But a novel will be greater and vaster in proportion to the number of levels of reality it presents. I think that's the reason for the greatness of

War and Peace, for instance. Or that of certain romances of chivalry—the ones produced during the golden era of the genre. The great romances of chivalry give superb representations of their time. They embrace reality on its mythical level, its religious level, its historical level, its social level, its instinctive level. In more recent times there has been a sort of decadence, a shriveling of the novel. Modern ventures into the novel form attempt to give only a single vision, to portray a single aspect of reality. I'm in favor of the opposite: the all-encompassing novel that aspires to embrace reality in all its facets, in all its manifestations. It can never fulfill itself at all levels. But the greater its diversity, the broader the vision of reality, the more complete the novel will be."

Multiple points of view help him out here. There is a Faulknerian trait in Vargas Llosa, who readily acknowledges the influence of the master of retrospection. But in matters of technique only, as he is quick to point out. There is an emotional Faulkner who is completely foreign to him. Emotions in Vargas Llosa are of the cloak-and-dagger kind. He distrusts psychological subtlety and subjectivity. "In Faulkner," he says, "the main interest centers never on external but always on internal reality. The problems he deals with are always fundamentally located in the conscience or the soul. They may be guilt feelings or the sense of responsibility in the face of the deity or the other world. They belong in the realm of inner life. Whereas what interests me primarily is external reality. That's why I have such an admiration for the first modern writer, the one who created the best instruments for describing that external reality: I mean Flaubert. In *L'Education Sentimentale* we are given that living, independent, sovereign fictional reality that will allow us to discover the 'other' reality: external reality. What I also find admirable in Flaubert is the complete authority he assumes over the material he uses, which is what distinguishes him from the novelists that preceded him."

But perhaps more than Flaubert it is the old environmental Naturalist that we sense in Vargas Llosa. In his somewhat obsessive "realism" an old danger is reborn. External reality, if there

is such a thing, is a quicksand. The man who abandons himself
to it ends up being detached from himself. And so it is in the
work of Vargas Llosa, where individualities get lost in the density
of their surroundings. There are no people, only states of mind
that materialize in particular situations. Their reactions are
generic. The person, when he is implied at all, remains diffuse.
He casts no shadow beyond his immediate presence, which is a
shadow itself. His absence suggests a failure of vision on the
author's part. Though, in fact, the omission is intentional. "I'm
convinced," says Vargas Llosa, "that the novel is basically a description of acts. The successful novel is the one that manages to
portray or describe individual characters, social problems, even
purely physical realities through a sequence of acts, of actions.
Everything else must, as it were, transpire from these actions.
Ideas, problems, moral considerations, the author's philosophy,
must radiate from a story, in other words, an action, as heat from
the skin. They must emanate from a substance that is essentially
made up of acts." The problem is to make these acts function in
as many dimensions as possible. Here the naturalistic viewpoint,
essentially diagnostic and behavioral, might be a real handicap.
And, in fact, Vargas Llosa records the movements of his characters—mere aspects of being, momentary slides, in perpetual
shift—in sensual detail, at the most elementary level of interpretation, with no attempt to go beyond appearances. The "metaphysical" or invisible dimension, for instance, is completely missing.
For Vargas Llosa this dimension does not exist for all practical
purposes, as he says, or, if it does, "there's no need to look for it."
His reality is the immediately perceptible reality of the senses.
For him "ultimately literature has never been anything but a
reflection, a reconstruction of this reality through another purely
verbal reality whose final purpose, if we can call it that, is none
other than to allow man to become acquainted with reality itself,
which would otherwise forever remain inaccessible to him."
The highest mission of literature, says Vargas Llosa, is to offer
man the possibility of knowing himself through a full grasp
of all the circumstances that surround him. "I think literature is
an extraordinary instrument of knowledge. An instrument—and

that is where it differs from science and technology—which has an independent reality of its own."

If the invisible areas of individuality are absent from Vargas Llosa's work, it is because "that's one of the characteristics of the reality the novel pretends ot evoke. In *La Casa Verde* I've even tried to find a technical procedure that will make this more obvious. What I've done is almost totally suppress individual personalities, and tried to present collective personalities, that is to say, groups of people who belong to, and embody, various different realities. The point is, I don't believe in the existence of absolutely sovereign individualities. What I think is that in every man there is a more or less standard range of possibilities which gain expression in accordance with the different situations he comes in contact with. What interests me primarily is to set those possibilities into motion. Most men's possibilities of action and reaction are more or less similar. The variants come mostly from the outside, a product of all sorts of conditioning factors: geography, history, childhood and adolescent experiences. That's why I'm interested in human action: man's response to a given situation. I think whatever is exceptional in an individual is never immanent in origin, but always a blend of external—and also internal—elements and conditions that are common to the species."

Vargas Llosa seems to fluctuate between old-fashioned determinism—which leaves us room for free choice—and Sartrean situationalism, a difficult concept to embody dramatically. When, within a given situation, people appear to share more or less interchangeable alternatives, how to give their actions depth and significance? For Vargas Llosa, "the mere fact that they become narrative matter must endow them with an exceptional nature. Otherwise they wouldn't be literature. The greatness of literature is precisely that," he says, "that the most everyday, most commonplace act becomes exceptional. That's why I say literature is the only thing that allows us fully, livingly to apprehend the world."

In this, he says, he learned a lot from those early prenovels— or, according to some, subnovels—the romances of chivalry, which he defends heroically. He recalls how he first came upon the

genre, one always slighted and maligned. "It was during my first
year in the university. I remember a class in the Spanish literature course. The professor devoted only a few phrases to the
romances of chivalry, then quickly dismissed them as coarse,
vulgar, and outlandish. So, out of contrariness, and curiosity, I
started to read the romances of chivalry that were available at
the National Library. And I had the good luck that the first one
I happened to read was the best of all: a book by a Valencian
who wrote in Catalan in the fifteenth century, called Juan
Martorell. Martorell wrote a single book throughout his whole
life, called *Tirante el Blanco* (Tirante the White). It's a marvelous novel, a great cathedral. Very long, very vast, with a series of
ramifications in time, in space. As distinct from the other romances of chivalry, it is more or less tightly structured within its
vastness. And it's not a surface novel as in the case, for instance,
of *Amadis de Gaula* or *Lancelot du Lac*—or even the novels of
Chrétien de Troyes, which I'm very fond of. But they're schematic, like Romanic painting—pure externality. In *Tirante el
Blanco* we already have an omniscient creator. And I think the
novel at its best has always tended toward that. Which is why I
don't agree with the Marxist interpretation of the novel, according to which the novel is a product that was born with the
industrial middle class. Because when Martorell wrote *Tirante el
Blanco,* the middle class had no social significance. And yet here
we already have all the essential features of the genre, which are
still valid today. *Tirante el Blanco* gives us the purely mythical
dimension of the era: the griffins, Morgana, the fairy, the Knights
of the Round Table, the medieval phantoms. It also gives us the
historical reality: the whole expedition to Greece described in
that novel corresponds to a real event, the Catalonian and
Aragonian expedition to Greece conducted by Roger de la Flor.
Besides, the details of battles, the garments worn, the weapons
used, the procedures followed for duels, are all perfectly realistic.
The narration is very skillful. The book records a series of rather
curious psychological phenomena. For instance, Tirante el
Blanco, at a certain moment, discovers Princess Carmenciña with
her duenna, Amor de Mi Vida, who is dressed as a man, playing

games that were probably commonplace at the time but which prejudice had prevented literature from registering until then. They engage in some very curious sexual games. Tirante el Blanco watches them through a slit, and what he sees produces a kind of jealousy in him and a need to go vent it on someone, so he lets off steam cutting off a black gardener's head. All this is presented without any critical attitude on the part of the narrator, as an ordinary everyday event. Martorell wasn't scandalized by it. But his testimony remains. The critical attitude was born with Cervantes. In Cervantes we have mockery, satire, an ironic attitude in the face of his material which, I think, is what ultimately brought about the downfall of the genre."

Mockery, satire, irony, anything approaching humor in any way is taboo for Vargas Llosa. "I've always been completely immune to humor in literature," he says. For him, humor is a creator of distances. "It freezes things, glosses them over. Humor is interesting when it's an expression of revolt; for instance, the insolent, corrosive humor of a Céline. It can be a way of cushioning. But in general humor is unreal. Reality contradicts humor. Humoristic authors have never convinced me or appealed to me. And the professional humorist is a type of author who has always irritated me. I think humor can be an ingredient of fiction, as it is of reality, but that it must always be justified by the context. It mustn't be premeditated." Humor is euphemistic; it veils and mystifies—lets us off, in a way. Which is why, for Vargas Llosa, it is always "conformist in nature."

But here, again, perhaps there are other factors to weigh. If so much of our literature is humorless, it may be because humor is antithetical to the epic tendency. For a man who works from a set of fixed coordinates, there is no room for such disruptive variants. And so it is with Vargas Llosa. He builds on the assumption that man is a calculable quantity whose relations with his immediate surroundings can be defined in accordance with a few primary rules of behavior that are universally applicable. There are never any unfathomables in Vargas Llosa. His blind creatures rush on a headlong course to a common fate that remains impersonal. Vargas Llosa is not a discoverer, he is a recorder. His surface turbulence emanates from wounds that may run deep but are tapped only at skin level, where they become palpable. His floating consciousnesses are physical effluvia. There is no inner man to support the outer gesture.

The virtues and limitations of a stubbornly objectivist narrative method are dramatically visible in the radiant but frustrating *La Casa Verde*. Technically—with Cortázar's *Rayuela* and Guimarães Rosa's *Grande Sertão: Veredas*—*La Casa Verde* is probably the most accomplished work of fiction ever to come out of Latin America. It has sweep, beauty, imaginative scope, and a sustained eruptive power that carries the reader from first page to last like a fish in a bloodstream. A huge circulatory system seems to be at work, irrigating every corner of the book with its countless veins and capillaries. Acts and events are mere shimmers, dots of dye tracing a tinted course as they wash along in the flow. Their pull is irresistible. After a few pages of mesmeric intensity, the reader goes down in a whirlpool. Were it not for its vastness, the book ought to be read at a single sitting: it has to be kept at fingertips, because, powerful as the verbal tow is, the sense evolving from it constantly hangs on a thread. Scenes overlap, different times and places overrun each other—the "hourglass" effect, here pushed to the limit—echoes precede voices, and disembodid consciences dissolve almost before they can be identified. There are few guidelines and a titanic effort, a lot of it spent on guesswork, is required to keep track of all the tenuous strands in the tapestry. The question arises in the course of the four or five interlocking stories that blaze and brim over in a never-ending stream of un-pushed to the limit—echoes precede voices, and disembodied con-be convincingly motivated. When a man has no personal image of himself, how will others recognize him? If his traits are generic, of what specific importance can his acts be? In *La Casa Verde*, where everyone is defined according to a common set of terms, there are conflicts of impulses, not of people. The episodes that portray mental processes play with a kind of abstract fire that often goes up in smoke. Whether populating real or semimythological scenes, the characters seem equally anonymous.

Yet *La Casa Verde*, with its elemental passions, is enrapturing to the senses. It was made for them.

"I've always hoarded the things that have most impressed me in my life," says Vargas Llosa, who describes the book as "a fusion of very different experiences," all of which seem to have sent shivers through him. The oldest of the stories that compose the book dates back to Piura, he tells us, in the tone of someone breaking a long reserve. He tends to dourness, but when he becomes expansive his voice hoarsens with suppressed emotion, lowers at moments to a stealthy whisper.

"It's a story of a brothel in Piura, which I remember vividly from when I was in fifth grade of grammar school. It was a green house—or cabin—in the middle of the dunes, on the outskirts of the city, right in the desert, across the river. For us children there was something fascinating about it. Of course I never dared go anywhere near it. Still it left quite an impression on me. When I returned to Piura in the fifth year of high school, six years later in other words, it still existed. I was a young man who went to brothels in those days. So I went there. And it had a very strange atmosphere, because it was a very special brothel, an under-developed-city brothel. It was nothing but a single huge room, where the women were, and where there was a three-man combo made up of an old blind man, who played the harp, a guitarist known as 'el Joven' (the Young One), and a lumbering giant who looked like a catch-wrestler or a truck driver, who played the drums and cymbals and was known as Bolas (Balls). Because they're almost mythical characters to me, I've kept their names intact in the book. So the clients used to come in there and take the women out to make love in the dunes, under the stars. It's something I've never been able to forget.

"Another thing I remember very vividly from Piura is a neighborhood called the Mangachería: a poor quarter, a slum that was a bit isolated from the city because of the peculiar character of the people who lived there. It was a kind of court of miracles. I always associate it with the courts of miracles in the novels of Dumas. The Mangaches took great pride in those days in the fact that a police patrol had never been in there. The marketwomen would come out and stone them and set the dogs on them. We used to go to the local taverns at night to dance with the 'cholas' [Indian or mestizo women]. Besides, that world

of the Mangaches had very curious political connotations. They
were all Urristas—that is, supporters of the Unión Revolucion-
aria, a Fascist party. A Peruvian dictator, Sánchez Cerro, had
been born there; that was a matter of great pride to them. They
were diehard Urristas. That's another theme I had in mind
connected with Piura."

A third element for the book was provided by a jungle
trip the author took in 1958, between his two trips to Europe. It was a chance occurrence, and a stroke of luck for
him. "I'd never been in the jungle. A Mexican ethnologist
had arrived, so the Instituto Lingüístico de Verano (Summer Language Institute), which operated in the jungle, organized a trip to the tribal haunts of the Aguarunas in the Upper
Marañón River. I was invited to go along. And a new world
opened for me. I discovered the Stone Age right there in Peru.
Primitive tribes and white adventurers living a life apart in that
completely independent region with its own laws, its own separate rhythm—a world of an extraordinary violence that was
established and recognized by all, and where I picked up several
stories, among them that of a personage who immediately fascinated me: a Japanese called Tushía, who's one of the main
characters in the novel. I changed his name to Fushía—without
realizing it; I wanted to keep his name. . . . He was an incredible man. He'd been seen going by years before, thirty years, at
least, from the direction of Iquitos, on his way up the Marañón
toward the tribal grounds of the Aguarunas. It seemed he was
escaping from something. On a raft. And as he went along—we
picked this up in the villages on our way to the Aguarunas,
because he was an almost legendary figure by then—he was
warned: 'Stay out of there. Do you want to be eaten alive?'
Because, of course, in those days the tribes were hostile to white
men and strangers in general. But he paddled up the Santiago
River, where the Huambisas live, and became a sort of feudal
lord. Not only was he not killed, he actually set up house on an
island right in the heart of the Huambisa world and formed a
small army in which apparently there were some white men,
nobody knows who or where from. But the main body of his

personal army was made up of Aguarunas or Huambisas. Where-upon he set himself up in business, periodically raiding all the Aguaruna, Huambisa, Murato, or Capanagua villages—which are the ones that are in the region—at the time when the rubber men arrived to haul off the rubber the Indians had been charged with collecting for them. He'd arrive with his men, armed with rifles and pistols, the Indians with bows and arrows; he'd plunder the village; when there was any rubber, he'd have it carted off to the island; and then later, through middlemen, he'd sell the stuff to the Banco Agropecuario (Agricultural Bank). But, along with the rubber, he also carted off girls. He had a harem. I got to meet a girl who'd been one of his concubines. Unfortunately the young girl didn't speak any Spanish; she spoke only Aguaruna. But through an interpreter she told me how they lived on the island. So then we learned about this man's bru-tality. When he and his men arrived in a village, he'd dress up as an Indian and get drunk as one; he came to speak their language as one of them; and besides he danced, he had celebrations organized, in order to take part in them. He was a man of indescribable cruelty with women.

"But the story of Tushía was connected with the story of Jum. Because the supposedly civilized inhabitants of the area were just as barbaric as the Indians: miserable small-time capitalists, at bottom wretched and half-starved themselves. The inhuman violence that prevails is practiced on the lowest human scale, for ridiculous, insignificant gains. In Santa María de Nieva they'd just strung an Indian (Jum) from a tree. He'd been hanging there for two or three days. They'd shaved his head, burned his armpits with hot eggs. Previous to that, local rubber men had gone to his village, Urakusa, with a group of officers from the military detachment at Borja, and burned it to the ground. The women had been raped in front of him. And all that because the Indian had tried to form a cooperative to sell that rubber—which the rubber men extorted from his people for trifling sums of money—at normal prices in nearby townships. The rubber wasn't even sold to the rubber men. On top of having to give it to them, the Indians had to pay them something extra, according to the system the rubber men had imposed. So this Indian had had the idea of collecting all the Indian rubber and taking a trip once a year to a sizable populated center to sell it there directly. Of course he was severely endangering the rubber men's business. That was why he was tortured—as a public example. In Santa María de Nieva, a missionary center! The missionaries attended the torture. The missionaries are Spanish priests and nuns who are individually very dedicated. They bury themselves in that lost region; twenty years go by; they're eaten up by flies, they fall ill; and finally they become savages. Isolated from the rest of the world, pressured by the surrounding savagery, it infects them without their even realizing it. . . .

"Another thing that made a deep impression on me during that trip to Santa María de Nieva was to see the region's missionary schools at work. The nuns had founded a school there to educate the savages. But the savages wouldn't send their children to school. So the nuns had worked out a very effective strategy. Once a year, before the opening of school, policemen arrived at the mission. They sailed up the rivers on barges with a couple of nuns in search of girls for the school. They broke into the villages and kidnaped the girls. It's incredible. But that isn't the whole story. These girls were put up at the mission; they were taught to read, to speak Spanish, to write, to dress. After two or three years of this treatment, the nuns were in a terrible quandary when the girls had to be disposed of in some way. What to do with them? Send them back to their tribes? That was out. Because in those years, together with the alphabet, they'd learned to abominate the previous conditions under which they'd lived. Because, of course, they were taught that worshiping snakes was monstrous and pagan. Therefore their parents were monsters and savages. The girls had been completely uprooted from their environment. But the nuns had nothing to offer them as a replacement for it. They couldn't keep them indefinitely at the mission. So they gave them away to the local officers and soldiers, to the troops stationed at frontier outposts, or to the rubber men, or to engineers who happened by, as servants. These officers used to go off with one or two or three for their friends in

Lima. So the whole civilizing labor pursued with such good intentions, with such heroism and abnegation, in the end turned out to be something completely unexpected: an involuntary contribution to the skin trade. . . .

"All those things combined shook me up. I brought it all to Europe with me. And when I finished *La Ciudad y los Perros*, I started to let it all out at once. Then, little by little, it began to fuse into a single story. The action is divided between those two places: Santa María de Nieva and Piura. Those are the two poles of the story."

Actually, the story stands on three legs: Piura, the jungle outpost of Santa María de Nieva, and the township of Iquitos. The effect is that of an unsteady tripod that almost imperceptibly keeps shifting weight from one leg to another. Time, in this scheme, is a form of rotation, a sudden vortical descent. At the tip of the maelstrom are the semimythological days of the founding of the Casa Verde.

One day a mysterious stranger, a weather-beaten young man called Don Anselmo, of obscure jungle origin, comes riding his donkey across the dunes into Piura. No one knows who he is or what he wants. But he obviously has hidden designs. He is a sort of wandering minstrel, a harpist by profession with a bit of a magic touch. For a while he stays in the boardinghouse of Melchor Espinosa and frequents the local taverns, where his amiable ways quickly win him many friends. He is an inquisitive young man who soon knows everybody's family background and secret desires. Acting on his information, he starts building his fancy bordello out in the dunes. He has a hunch it might just go over, and he is not mistaken. Scandal and general commotion follow. The local priest, Padre García, thunders against him from the pulpit. But the Casa Verde, a sort of phallic monument to collective jungle memories, survives invective and anathema. All this is told straightforwardly, in a measured, somewhat distant, almost colorless prose that contrasts violently with the strain and stress of the book's more tortuous passages.

The Casa Verde is in its heyday when the hapless Antonia arrives in town. She is the daughter of travelers who are murdered by bandits one morning in the dunes. She is found sprawled in the sand, more dead than alive, her eyes and tongue plucked out by vultures. She becomes the town waif, a poor maimed child of misfortune that everyone pets and pities. A kindly washerwoman, Juana Baura, takes the girl to live with her. Antonia seems doomed to languish in the perpetual twilight zone of the mute and crippled. But suddenly one day she vanishes. Rumors are rife. Has she been murdered? Is she being abused? The town is shocked to learn in time that she has been abducted by Don Anselmo, an Orpheus who has taken a strange shine to his blighted Eurydice and installed her in a private room in the brothel, where she is loved and victimized by him. At this point the mythical Don Anselmo flashes into sudden mental existence. There is a switch, a refocusing of the lens that seems incongruous. The idea was to bring Don Anselmo down to earth, says Vargas Llosa, who worked over these scenes more than any others in the book. But if he meant to touch a mainspring in Don Anselmo, somehow he failed, mainly because fuses are lit which are then allowed to fizzle out. The tortured atmosphere is rendered in hectic torrents of subliminal prose that seem to call on abysmal forces that are momentarily tapped, then evaporated. Antonia is fearful and acquiescent. Don Anselmo founders in a phantasmiagoic mixture of guilt, truculence, erotic frenzy, and hopeless longing for the shadowy creature whose true feelings he will never know. We are caught in his turmoil, but then quickly left on the fringes again. Tragedy strikes when Antonia becomes pregnant and, in spite of emergency measures taken by Dr. Pedro Zevallos, dies in childbirth. The priest apostrophizes the town, which, somewhat too predictably—the scene lacks inner momentum—rises in indignation, storms the Casa Verde, and burns it to the ground. Now we are on the outside of the situation again as Don Anselmo, a shadow of himself, is left in the street with his combo, which includes the Joven Alejandro, who composes tearful ditties, and Bolas, the drummer. They roam the town, eventually ending up in the Mangachería, where they play the local joints and, as the brothel fades from memory, gradually become a local fixture. The years

go by, and now the only remnant of the Casa Verde is a new
brothel downtown that goes by the same name, in memory of
past glories. Don Anselmo, a broken man, and his combo enter-
tain the clients there, hired by its charitable owner, Chunga, a
mermaid full of reproachful memories. She is Antonia's posthumous daughter.

A lot weightier than this rather spurious Piuran saga, which
claims more than its due, is the tale of the mighty Fushía, a
monster of nature prowling in jungle haunts where the sound of
rushes, a batting of wings, the lapping of dark waters are like
echoes from a nether world halfway between daydream and
nightmare. Fushía is a phenomenological creature, less a man—
there is no inner reservoir—than an entelechy, a confluence of
rootless forces in constant motion, like a fast wind on fire,
burning without ever being consumed. Where he goes, always
aflame, his image precedes him, and when he has gone it lingers,
a wraith in the pyre. Because of the melodramatic overtones of
the Fushía story, says Vargas Llosa, he told it almost entirely on
the visceral level, with no attempt at psychological penetration.
Fushía secretes himself in a stream of impressions and perceptions that remain outside him. He seems always vaguely unmoti-
vated, yet that hardly detracts from his high metabolic rate. He is
an adventurer with a long criminal past in Brazil, who has
crossed into Peru via Manaus and landed down and out in
Iquitos, headquarters of the rubber barons, where he opens a
new chapter in his career. Along the way he has picked up
another outcast, Aquilino, a water carrier in a village who
becomes his loyal friend and confidant. Together they have been
up remote jungle rivers peddling baubles and trinkets to the
Indians. A kind of primitive tenderness joins them in a curious
bondage that remains enigmatic but projects a moving spiritual
glow on the narrative. The childlike Aquilino and the predatory
Fushía are both simple souls adrift in uncharted waters.

In Iquitos, Fushía, a canny bloodhound when it comes to
scenting money, finds a job with Julio Reátegui, a local grandee
who prospers in the rubber trade trafficking with the Axis during
the war, his strategic material disguised as tobacco. The shady

dealings are eventually uncovered, but Reátegui is a powerful man and it is Fushía who is threatened with imprisonment. He sweats it out for a while, then escapes with his girl friend, Lalita, mounting the river into Indian territory where, as Reátegui's agent and Aquilino's partner, he has made many contacts which now stand him in good stead. Soon, with Huambisa support, he has set himself up in his island domain. Aquilino, on an eternal beat up and down the river, faithfully keeps him in supplies. A small band of renegade whites help him rule over his Indian hordes: a halfwit called Pantacha, a deserter from a local garrison called Adrián Nieves. Like Fushía, they are all embodiments of environmental forces, urges that remain unconsummated. The violence and savagery of Fushía, never wholly personified, are processes almost alien to him that develop according to organic laws over which he has no control. When they ripen, like Tirante el Blanco lopping off the black gardener's head, he sheds them with a shrug. With the years his malignant influence spreads as he terrorizes the local countryside, but then suddenly his star is on the wane. Changeable as a chameleon, he perishes as one. What starts as a burst of sickly pigment becomes raw scab and tumor. He has caught a leprous infection, and rots away. His legs are eaten up to the groin. He loses his virility, and with it his charisma. His harem disbands. Lalita, released from thrall—he fondles and caresses her in vain—has taken up with Nieves. One day the lovers elope to Santa María where, hoping to bury the past, Nieves settles down as a guide and river pilot. Fushía's end is near. He is little more than a carcass of a man when the aged Aquilino sails him up the river to die in a leper colony.

At the height of the Fushía reign we have the story of Jum and his struggle—fanned by a couple of schoolteachers turned agitators—against the archenemies of his people, the rubber men. Julio Reátegui is ending a term as governor of Santa María when Jum is caught and tortured. The result of the punishment is that, while pretending to be reformed, Jum secretly joins the forces of Fushía. There, among hostile Huambisas, who regard the massacre of his people with indifference if not outright glee, his seesawing existence slowly peters out until we lose sight of him. Meantime, a child whom we suspect to be his infant daughter—though he denies it—has been taken to the mission school of Santa María, where the nuns bring her up under the Christian name of Bonifacia.

At about the time of Fushía's eclipse, Bonifacia, now a proper young lady trained in Christian virtues, comes of age. She seems to have been thoroughly domesticated but, as the nuns soon learn to their chagrin, there is still a spark of virgin savagery in her. When—in the brilliant subterranean scene that opens the book as the nuns, changelings wrapped in spectral rumors, go hunting for prospects in the brush—they bring in their yearly hoard of pupils for the mission school, she sets them loose one night. In return, she is put out the mission door. Nieves, in uneasy semiretirement, and Lalita, now a faded beauty with pustules on her face, take her in and arrange for her to meet a sergeant of the local garrison, Lituma, who loves and eventually marries her. This coincides with the last armed expedition against Fushía's vanished empire. An addled Pantacha is found agonizing on the empty island and his muddled confession leads to the capture of Nieves, who is thrown in jail. Lalita is left with her considerable brood—she has a child by Fushía and several by Nieves—which another soldier, nicknamed Pesado (Heavy) soon arranges to multiply.

Lituma, one of those mysterious two-headed creatures—another Jaguar—that in the Vargas Llosa world change radically according to their situation, ends his jungle service and takes Bonifacia home with him to Piura. There, it turns out, in a rather unlikely switch, he is known as one of the Inconquistables (Unconquerables): a bunch of toughs that roam the Mangachería. We are, somewhat disappointingly—these are the weakest passages in the book—back in street gang territory. His shiftless cronies—the León brothers, Mono and José, and Josefino Rojas, a pimp—bum around with him, making fun of his Indian wife while trying to seduce her. The image of Lituma in Piura, too thin to cast a shadow, is difficult to reconcile with that of the man who was known simply as the Sergeant in Santa María. To identify them seems perfectly arbitrary. Not that they contradict each other. But they have nothing in common either. The intention, says Vargas Llosa, was to show two contrasting aspects of a single person. But, if there is to be contrast, first there must be contact. The images, at some point, must reflect each other. But this is impossible in a character made entirely of surfaces, with no center of gravity. He has the feel of a place, not a person. In fact, Lituma in Piura is a lot more like the other Inconquistables than he is like his double in Santa María. Here the author shuffles many cards, not all of them well. There is an old enemy of Lituma, a rancher called Seminario, with whom there are endless quarrels that end in a laborious match of Russian roulette. Seminario puts a bullet through his head. Lituma is blamed for the crime and carted off to prison. While he is gone, Bonifacia falls into the hands of Josefino, who promptly installs her in the new Casa Verde. The story comes full circle with the return of Lituma some time later to a Piura long past its golden age. A fitful epilogue—a familiar failing—that fills in a few gaps in the story without adding any vital information shows the Pied Piper Don Anselmo, a complete shambles now, on his deathbed.

La Casa Verde moves like a dragnet, on all fronts at once, flushing out swirls of underwater life, where creatures hatch and thrash, sometimes vanishing with a flick of a dark fin, at others curling up on themselves like snakes biting their own tails. A sinuous prose that keeps splitting at the core to ripple off in every direction mingles the streams of many consciences. A hot breath blows through the jungle scenes. Many are built on shifting time levels. A typical approach is the retrospective conversation—for instance, between Fushía and Aquilino as their boat breasts the river to oblivion—that suddenly, without warning or transition, opens up on to the remembered scene itself. The method is disconcerting at first and tends to become mechanical with habit—as in the episodes involving the Inconquistables, where it introduces complications that seem out of proportion to the rather simple set of events—but can also be brilliantly effective. It creates a constant sense of playback and fallthrough. There are no advancing lines in *La Casa Verde,* only closing circles that spiral into each other. They meet and merge in a moment of

violent interchange, then spin off again on their dizzying course
like particles in an accelerator. In *La Casa Verde* man in his
various psychic phases is little more than a momentary exhala-
tion, a floating spirit on the waters, quickly drained of himself as
his molecular image disintegrates.

If, in spite of its breath-taking sweep, its dazzlingly skillful
patterning, its Joycean roll, *La Casa Verde* does not quite fulfill
its potential, it is because it sometimes invests recklessly in areas
that have no payload to deliver. It often goes into debt, and then
defaults. As it grows, its intensity tends to lessen rather than
increase, because a good part of the tension in early scenes is
built on withheld information. We are kept in suspense over
elementary facts that should be quickly disposed of. The plot is
obscured. Identities are vague, circumstances undefined, consequences clearer than their causes. As things begin to fall into
place toward the middle of the book, the law of diminishing
returns sets in. There are too many surprises. They accumulate
information, but not insight. Our curiosity, so sharply whetted
and tantalized, is never really satisfied. There is a good story, we
begin to realize, but little else. It is an end in itself. And that
is not enough. Because underneath, we may suspect, there is
another story, deeper, better, more significant, that remains
untold, and, ultimately, undiscovered. The wider the author's
embrace the more seems to slip through it. We try to see
things through his eyes, but our gaze insists on going beyond,
where he has nothing to offer. There is something wrong with the
"collective personalities" of Vargas Llosa—probably the fact that
they have no autonomous existence. That is the paradox. Vargas
Llosa deliberately avoids subjectivity to fix his attention on
objective reality. But, in attempting to penetrate the object—
which is impenetrable—he simply infuses it with a subjective
charge. The only way to avoid this would be to create independent psychologies among whom the charge could be distributed.
Instead, because of the phenomenological approach to personality, we have floating appearances that at any given moment are
no more or less than what they seem to be. Vargas Llosa's "hourglass," which ought to be an illuminated area where acts and

gestures become meanings, turns out to be a revolving door that whirls us around and out at the same point where we came in.

Yet it may be in that same revolving door that the hope lies for Vargas Llosa as a novelist. If it leads nowhere definite yet, the force of its spin already establishes an orbit. What will be drawn into that orbit in the future depends on the author's field of vision. He has all the means to his end: style, powerful sources, stamina. The rest is a matter of focus.

The four years spent on *La Casa Verde* seem not to have winded him in the least. He has been mulling over a new novel he started some time ago, which he hopes to have time to finish now, in London. "It's the story of a bodyguard," he says in his intriguing whisper, a kind of second breath, "a muscleman who sells his muscle to various politicians. I once met a bodyguard who'd been hired to protect a little local warlord in Peru. He was quite an impressive character. He'd been a boxer. And he was a completely illogical individual. I wanted to try my hand at a novel that would give some idea of Peruvian political circles. I was looking for a character that would open the way into this very special world for me. I think the bodyguard is just what I need."

A slow start, a mass of unfocused material, a sudden spark, and the furnaces will be going full blast. Somewhere around a far bend, over the horizon, an unwritten book awaits Vargas Llosa. "The impossible novel—the total novel," he calls it. It would be, in his words, at once fantastic and psychological, realistic and mythical. It would embrace all conceivable manifestations of reality. "Great novels," he says, "are those that to some extent approach that impossible novel of novels." And it may well be that in attempting to approach it the great Latin-American novel will be written one day.

Index

hidden

Russell, Bertrand, 127
Rusticatio Mexicana (Landivar), 92

Sábato, Ernesto, 24, 207
Sagarana (Rosa), 146, 147, 155
Saki, 211
Salvaje, El (Quiroga), 15
Sanchez, Florencio, 175, 294
Sanchez, L. A., 37
Sand, George, 3
San Martín, José Zorilla de, 4
Sarmiento, Domingo Faustino, 4, 305
Sartre, Jean-Paul, 24, 212, 346, 347, 361
Schopenhauer, Arthur, 103, 117, 118, 123, 127, 132
Scott, Walter, Sir, 3
Seara Vermelha (Amado), 7
Seis Problemas Para Don Isidro (Domecq), 119
"Semejante" (Carpentier), 50
Señor Presidente, El (Asturias), 77, 78, 79, 80, 82, 84, 93
Shakespeare, William, 48, 103, 127, 134
Shaw, George Bernard, 109
Sien de Alondra (Asturias), 96
"Siesta del Martes, La" (Márquez), 328
Siete Locos, Los (Arlt), 16
Siglo de las Luces, El (Carpentier), 22, 46, 49, 50, 58, 60, 64, 65
Sillanpää, Frans Eemil, 273
Silva, José Asunción, 311
Siqueiros, David Alfaro, 276, 291
Sobre la Misma Terra (Gallegos), 11
Soluna (Asturias), 96
Spota, Luis, 308
Stalin, Joseph, 149
Stein, Gertrude, 30, 77
Stendhal, 292
Stevenson, Robert Louis, 109, 113
Suárez, Isidoro, 113
Sueño Realizado y Otros Cuentos, Un (Onetti), 191, 193
Supervielle, Jules, 175
Swedenborg, Emanuel, 103

Tabaré (San Martin), 4
"Talpa" (Rulfo), 261–62

Tamaño de Mi Esperanza, El (Borges), 112, 114
Tan Triste Como Ella (Onetti), 200
Terrás Do Sem Fin (Amado), 7
"Third Bank of the River, The" (Rosa), 171–72
Tiempo de Abrazar (Onetti), 179, 183
Tiempos Nuevos (newspaper), 76
Tiento y Diferencias (Carpentier), 43
Tierra de Nadie (Onetti), 174, 176, 184, 193
Time of the Hero, The ((Llosa); see *Ciudad y los Perros, La*
Tirano Banderas, El (Inclán), 79
Tirante el Blanco (Martorell), 362
Todos los Fuegos el Firego (Cortázar), 237
Tolstoy, Leo, 5, 27
Tradiciones Peruanas (Palma), 4, 243
Troyes, Chrétien de, 362
Tumbra sin Nombre, Una (Onetti), 195, 202
Twain, Mark, 30, 105

Ubico, Jorge, 80, 93
Ulysses (Joyce), 243
Unamuno, Miguel de, 81, 219
Urupês (Lobato), 6

Vaché, Jacques, 237
Valdiva, 284
Valéry, Paul, 77, 104, 217, 242
Vallejo, César, 3, 47, 77, 343
Varèse, Edgar, 46
Vasconcelos, José, 276, 278
Vea y Lea (magazine), 182
Vega, Garcilaso de la, 40, 342
Vega, Lope de, 2, 115
Velarde, López, 278
"Venenos, Los" (Cortázar), 218
Verissimo, Erico, 141
Verlaine, Paul, 103, 120
"Viaje a la Semilla" (Carpentier), 51
Vida Breve, La (Onetti), 22, 186, 191, 193, 195, 197, 202, 205, 207
"Vida no es Muy Seria en sus Cosas, La" (Rulfo), 256

Format by Mort Perry
Set in Linotype Baskerville
Composed, printed and bound by American Book–Stratford Press, Inc.
HARPER & ROW, PUBLISHERS, INCORPORATED